An Introduction to Object-Oriented Systems Analysis and Design with UML and the Unified Process

Stephen R. Schach
Vanderbilt University

Boston   Burr Ridge, IL   Dubuque, IA   Madison, WI   New York   San Francisco   St. Louis
Bangkok   Bogotá   Caracas   Kuala Lumpur   Lisbon   London   Madrid   Mexico City
Milan   Montreal   New Delhi   Santiago   Seoul   Singapore   Sydney   Taipei   Toronto

INTRODUCTION TO OBJECT-ORIENTED ANALYSIS AND DESIGN
Published by McGraw-Hill/Irwin, a business unit of The McGraw-Hill Companies, Inc., 1221 Avenue
of the Americas, New York, NY, 10020. Copyright © 2004 by The McGraw-Hill Companies, Inc.
All rights reserved. No part of this publication may be reproduced or distributed in any form
or by any means, or stored in a database or retrieval system, without the prior written consent
of The McGraw-Hill Companies, Inc., including, but not limited to, in any network or other
electronic storage or transmission, or broadcast for distance learning.
Some ancillaries, including electronic and print components, may not be available to customers
outside the United States.

This book is printed on acid-free paper.

domestic   1 2 3 4 5 6 7 8 9 0 VNH/VNH 0 9 8 7 6 5 4 3
international 1 2 3 4 5 6 7 8 9 0 VNH/VNH 0 9 8 7 6 5 4 3

ISBN 0-07-282646-0

Publisher: *Stewart Mattson*
Senior sponsoring editor: *Paul Ducham*
Developmental editor: *Kelly L. Delso*
Manager, Marketing and Sales: *Greta Kleinert*
Media producer: *Greg Bates*
Project manager: *Natalie J. Ruffatto*
Production supervisor: *Debra R. Sylvester*
Designer: *Adam Rooke*
Supplement producer: *Vicki Laird*
Senior digital content specialist: *Brian Nacik*
Cover design: *JoAnne Schopler*
Typeface: *10/12 Times Roman*
Compositor: *Interactive Composition Corporation*
Printer: *Von Hoffmann Corporation*

Library of Congress Cataloging-in-Publication Data

Schach, Stephen R.
    An introduction to object-oriented systems analysis and design with UML and the unified
process / Stephen R. Schach.
        p.   cm.
    ISBN 0-07-282646-0 (alk. paper) — ISBN 0-07-121510-7 (international)
    1. Object-oriented methods (Computer science)   2. UML (Computer science)   3. System
analysis.   4. System design.   I. Title.
QA76.9.O35S24   2004
005.1'17—dc21
                                                                2003042144

INTERNATIONAL EDITION ISBN 0-07-121510-7
Copyright © 2004. Exclusive rights by The McGraw-Hill Companies, Inc. for manufacture and
export. This book cannot be re-exported from the country to which it is sold by McGraw-Hill.
The International Edition is not available in North America.

www.mhhe.com

To Sharon, David, and Lauren

The following are registered trademarks:

Access	Internet Explorer	Rational
Ada	Java	Requisite Pro
American Express	JBuilder	Rose
Ant	Linux	SAP
Apache	Lucent Technologies	Software through Pictures
ArgoUML	Mac OS	
Avis	Macintosh	Solaris
Battlemap	MacProject	SourceSafe
C	Mastercard	Standish Group
C#	Microsoft	Sun
C++	Netscape	Sun Fire
COBOL	*New York Times*	Sybase
Coca-Cola	Objectory	System Architect
Communicator	OMT	System/360
Cutter Consortium	OO-COBOL	Teamwork
CVS	Oracle	TurboTax
DB2	OS/360	UNIX
EDS	OS/370	Visa
Excel	Palm Pilot	Visual Basic
FORTRAN	Peachtree	Visual C++
Fortune 500	PeopleSoft	Visual Java
Foundation	PL/I	Windows
General Motors	Post-it note	Word
Hertz	Project	ZIP Code
IBM	Prudential	zSeries
Informix	PVCS	

Preface

This book is a textbook for the first course in object-oriented systems analysis and design. The material conforms to the guidelines of IS'2001 (Course IS'01.7, Analysis and Logical Design); in particular, the student does not need to have any programming knowledge. The book uses the Unified Modeling Language (UML) to model information systems and the Unified Process as the methodology.

The primary objective of this book is to ensure that, by the end of the course, every student is able to perform object-oriented analysis and design. This objective is achieved in three different ways:

- Pedagogics: The steps of object-oriented analysis and design are carefully explained. After each step has been presented, it is illustrated by applying it to the first of the two running case studies. Then, when each step has been explained and illustrated separately, all the steps are applied to the second running case study.

- Organization: The material on object-oriented analysis and design (Part 2 of the book) is presented as early as possible by keeping Part 1 of the book as short as possible. The result is that the student has most of the semester or quarter to master the material on object-oriented analysis and design.

- Practice: The only way to become proficient in object-oriented analysis and design is by doing it repeatedly. Accordingly, there are different types of problems at the end of each chapter. First, there are exercises in object-oriented analysis and design. Second, there are problems based on the two running case studies, both of which are presented in the fullest detail. Third, there is a team-based term project in which the students perform systems analysis and design from scratch. The instructor has the option of assigning one or more problems of any type.

During the 1990s, there were three major figures in object-oriented technology, namely, Grady Booch (his approach is referred to as "Booch's method"), Ivar Jacobson ("Objectory"), and Jim Rumbaugh ("OMT"). Booch, Jacobson, and Rumbaugh then joined forces at Rational, Inc., and made two landmark contributions to information technology: the Unified Modeling Language (UML) and the Unified Process.

Within a few months of its introduction in 1997, UML version 1.0 literally swept the world. It is inconceivable that a textbook written today would attempt to represent an information system using any other modeling language. UML is now a product of the Object Management Group (OMG), a consortium of the leading software technology firms worldwide. This book uses version 1.4 of UML, the latest version at the time of writing.

Next, Booch, Jacobson, and Rumbaugh developed a methodology that integrated ("unified") their three separate (but similar) methodologies. This unified methodology was first known as the Unified Software Development Process (USDP) or the Rational Unified Process (RUP). Currently it is also called the Unified Process. Just as with UML, there is now no alternative—currently the best methodology for a twenty-first-century textbook on object-oriented analysis and design of information systems is the Unified Process. The other three methodologies are now no longer supported by their respective authors.

The book is divided into three parts. Part 1, as previously stated, has been kept as short as possible. It contains the minimum information needed to enable students to understand object-oriented analysis and design with the Unified Process and UML. Part 2 is on how to perform object-oriented analysis and design using the Unified Process with UML as the modeling language. Part 3 presents nine major topics that should be taught in a course on systems analysis and design, such as project management, planning, and team organization. That is, Part 2 teaches the necessary technical skills, whereas Part 3 stresses the managerial and interpersonal skills that every good systems analyst must have. In addition, further technical skills are taught in Part 3, such as testing and user-interface design. As with the rest of this book, there is an emphasis on the knowledge needed for information systems for the twenty-first century, including portability, reuse, interoperability, the World Wide Web, and process improvement, including CMM. Finally, if an instructor wishes to cover more technical concepts such as modularity and polymorphism and dynamic binding, the last chapter contains introductory-level material on these topics.

As previously mentioned, following the IS'2001 guidelines, programming is not a prerequisite for this book. However, if the class has programming experience, there are three additional problems that can be assigned. More specifically, the term project consists of a number of components that every student can complete, such as determining the requirements and performing the object-oriented analysis. However, the term project also includes three optional components, including a complete implementation, that the instructor may choose to assign if the class has the necessary programming experience.

PROBLEM SETS

There are review questions and problems at the end of each chapter. The review questions can all be answered from the relevant section of the textbook. The problems are of different types. As previously mentioned, there are exercises in object-oriented analysis and design, as well as problems based on the two running case studies. There are also essay-type problems, numerical problems, and problems that test how thoroughly the students understand what was taught in class. Finally, at the end of most chapters there are components of the term project.

The Instructor's Manual has solutions to every problem, including all the components of the term project. There are even implementations of the term project in C++ and Java. The instructor should contact his or her McGraw-Hill representative to obtain the Instructor's Manual.

SUPPLEMENTARY MATERIAL

A complete set of lecture notes in the form of PowerPoint slides are available at the website for this book, www.mhhe.com/schach. In addition, an Instructor CD-Rom is available to adopters. The Instructor CD-Rom contains the PowerPoint lecture notes, together with the following additional resources:

An Instructor's Manual containing suggestions for using the book, teaching suggestions, and answers to all the end of chapter material.

A testbank containing true-false, multiple choice, and fill-in-the-blank questions, as well as a computerized testbank with Brownstone Diploma software offering fully networkable LAN test administration. Tests also can be printed for standard paper delivery or posted to a website for student access.

Acknowledgments

I should like to thank the reviewers who have commented on the various earlier drafts of this book. They are

Thad Crews
Western Kentucky University

Kevin P. Duffy
The University of Texas at Arlington

Jeff Gray
University of Alabama at Birmingham

Kris Howell
University of Southern Colorado

Jon Jasperson
University of Oklahoma

Geoffrey Kennedy
University of Sydney

Sylnovie Merchant
California State University—Sacramento

Megan Murray
Kennesaw State University

Jeffrey Parsons
Memorial University of Newfoundland

David L. Paul
University of Denver

Elizabeth Perry
Binghamton University

Carl Scott
University of Houston

J. Michael Tarn
Western Michigan University

Amir Tomer
The Technion

Steve Walczak
Colorado University at Denver

Each of these reviewers, without exception, provided numerous helpful suggestions that have improved this book, and I am grateful to all of them. Nevertheless, I wish to single out Dr. Kris Howell, whose comments, suggestions, and criticisms were of immeasurable assistance to me.

A special thank you is extended to the following focus group participants:

Jeffrey Parsons
Memorial University of Newfoundland

Parag C. Pendharkar
Penn State University

Carl Scott
University of Houston

Ron Thompson
Wake Forest University
Steve Walczak
Colorado University at Denver

I am indebted to three individuals who also have made significant contributions to many of my earlier books. Dr. Jeff Gray was previously a co-author of four Instructor's Manuals. For this book he has served as a reviewer, and he also was responsible for Appendices B through E; that is, he performed the design and implementation of both the case studies. My son David and my daughter Lauren are two of the co-authors of the Instructor's Manual. Lauren also contributed to the PowerPoint lecture notes. I thank Jeff, David, and Lauren for their usual meticulous work.

Kris Irwin took over Jeff's previous role—she provided a complete solution to the term project, including implementing it in both Java and C++. It was a pleasure working with an information technology professional of Kris's caliber. I also thank Kris for her many suggestions that led to improvements in the term project.

The copyeditor was Betsy Blumenthal. I thank her for her superlative work and her many helpful suggestions.

I turn now to my publisher, McGraw-Hill. The aim of object-oriented analysis is to determine *what* the target information system should do, and the aim of object-oriented design is to determine *how* the information system should do it. From the start of this project, publisher George Werthman and senior editor Rick Williamson made it clear *what* book they wanted me to write, but they left *how* to write it entirely up to me. It has been an eye-opening education to work with George and Rick. It also has been tremendous fun.

I should like to single out project manager Natalie Ruffatto. Natalie was a tower of strength throughout the production process. I deeply appreciate all that she has done.

I am grateful to my development editor, Kelly Delso, for her help from start to finish. I should also like to thank other McGraw-Hill professionals: Paul Ducham, senior sponsoring editor; Greta Kleinert, marketing manager; Greg Bates, media producer; Debra R. Sylvester, production supervisor; Adam Rooke, designer; and Rose Range, supplement coordinator.

I am also grateful to Jade Moran, project manager, and the compositors at Interactive Composition Corporation for their outstanding work. They were always willing to go the extra mile—and more.

I would like to thank the numerous instructors from all over the world who have sent me e-mail about my earlier books. I have used some of their comments, criticisms, and suggestions in this book. I look forward to receiving instructors' feedback on this book, too. My e-mail address is srs@vuse.vanderbilt.edu.

I also want to thank Kai Chen, Fang Fang, David Gannaway, Yun Huang, Kris Irwin (again), Michael Kearney, Johann Klemmack, Tao Lu, Yolanda McMillian, Sarah Miracle, Melissa Nestor, and Glenn Stein, the students in a graduate course on the Unified Process that I recently taught at Vanderbilt University. Their comments and critical analyses have helped to shape my views on the Unified Process, and thereby enriched this book.

I am grateful for the questions and suggestions about earlier books that students have e-mailed to me, and I look forward to receiving student feedback on this book.

I should like to thank Howard Aksen. In 1988 he persuaded me to write my first book, *Software Engineering*. Without Howard's urging, I would never have had 15 years of sheer enjoyment writing textbooks.

Finally, as always, I would like to thank my family for their unfailing support. Once again, writing this book has been a family activity. For the 11th time, it is my privilege to dedicate this book to my wife, Sharon, and my children, David and Lauren, with love.

Stephen R. Schach

Brief Contents

Contents

Introduction to UML and the Unified Process

Part

1

The first part of this book consists of three relatively short chapters. These chapters contain the background information needed to perform systems analysis and design or, more precisely, to perform object-oriented systems analysis and design using UML and the Unified Process. The three chapters explain what systems analysis and design is, what the phrase "object oriented" means, and what UML and the Unified Process are and why they are so important.

Chapter 1, *Introduction to Information Systems,* provides basic information about information systems. The major topic of this chapter is the phases of the traditional information system life cycle.

Chapter 2 is entitled *How Information Systems Are Developed.* Whereas Chapter 1 describes how information systems would be developed in an ideal world, Chapter 2 explains in detail why this does not happen in practice. Most of the chapter is devoted to the iterative and incremental life cycle, the way that information systems are usually developed in the real world.

The Object-Oriented Paradigm, UML, and the Unified Process is the title of Chapter 3. The traditional ("structured") approach to developing information systems has proved to be unsatisfactory for larger information systems. The object-oriented paradigm is the modern approach to developing information systems. It is explained in detail in Chapter 3, which also contains an introduction to UML and the Unified Process.

Chapter 1

Introduction to Information Systems

Learning Objectives

After studying this chapter, you should be able to:

- Define what is meant by systems analysis and design.
- Describe the traditional information system life cycle.
- Discuss the importance of continual planning, testing, and documentation.
- Describe the different types of information systems.
- Describe information services organizations.
- Appreciate the importance of adhering to a code of ethics.

Jethro's Boot Emporium, Inc., in Stambury, Wyoming, is losing money.[1] The majority of Jethro's customers live on isolated ranches three or more hours' drive from Stambury. After the long drive into town, when they shop at Jethro's they expect that the pair of boots they want will be available in their size. Lately, however, more and more customers are finding that Jethro Weatherby, the owner, has forgotten to contact the wholesalers to order a replacement for a pair of boots sold to another customer. Angered by their fruitless expedition to Stambury, when they return to the ranch they order the boots they want by mail order or on the Web, thus cutting into Jethro's turnover and profits.

Jethro decides that what he needs is an automated reordering system. He contacts Western Business Computer Solutions, Inc., a local information system development company. He tells Morgan Cuttler, a systems analyst with Western Business, that whenever a cashier scans the bar code on a pair of boots bought by a customer of Jethro's Boot Emporium, the system must record the details of those boots. At the end of the day, the system must automatically contact all the wholesalers that supply boots to Jethro's and reorder every pair sold that day. When the ordered boots arrive from the wholesalers, they are scanned so that the information system can add them to the database of boots in stock.

---

[1] This story is true. However, for obvious reasons, the names of individuals, organizations, and localities have been changed.

Morgan assures Jethro that this is no problem. In fact, Western Business Computer Solutions had developed such a system some years ago, and he offers to give Jethro a long list of customers in Stambury who will tell Jethro how happy they are that Western Business installed the automated reordering system in their stores.

But Jethro does not consider this standard system to be adequate for his needs. He tells Morgan that, in addition to automated stock reordering, the system has to be able to detect new trends in boot buying. Then, if sales for a particular style of boot suddenly increase from one week to the next, the information system must automatically order additional boots in that style. Jethro shows Morgan the formula that the system must use to compute how many additional pairs to order. The formula that Jethro has developed is complex, but the key point is that the greater the weekly increase in sales, the greater the number of additional boots in that style that must be ordered.

Western Business Computer Solutions develops Jethro's system and installs it. For the first seven months all goes well. The automated reordering system works correctly. Almost every customer finds boots in the right size, and Jethro's Boot Emporium is once again making a healthy profit. However, the portion of the system that detects new trends has not been triggered even once during those seven months.

Then, one fine day, a wealthy ranch owner walks past Jethro's Boot Emporium and notices a pair of boots displayed in the window. His feet are hurting, and the boots on display appear to be very comfortable indeed. He goes in, tries them on, and they are as comfortable as they look. He buys them and walks out of the shop wearing his new boots. He drives back to his ranch, and the entire way home he can think of nothing but his wonderful boots.

During the next week, the automated reordering system ensures that Jethro's Boot Emporium once again has a full range of sizes of that style of boot in stock. This is good, because a week later the rancher's four sons (all of whom work on their father's ranch) drive into Stambury to buy boots. The whole week long the rancher has talked about nothing but his new boots, and his sons think that the only way they will ever get any peace will be if they buy themselves a pair of those boots, too.

As a result, sales of that style of boot jump from just one to four per week. This finally triggers the portion of the system that detects new trends in boot sales, and the system automatically orders enough boots to double the stock of those boots to 132 pairs in various sizes.

Unfortunately, his sons' purchase of those boots does nothing to dampen their father's enthusiasm. In fact, he still thinks so highly of his boots that he resolves that, the next time he is in Stambury, he will buy a pair for each of his many ranch hands. Yes, the cost will be large, but the rancher is sure that this expenditure will soon be recouped via greater productivity and increased job satisfaction. So, when he drives to Stambury a week later to sign a cattle contract, he goes into Jethro's Boot Emporium and buys all 132 pairs of the boots.

Jethro is absolutely delighted. His information system has cost him a considerable amount of money. However, the automated reordering system has already almost paid for itself in increased profits, and the portion of his system that detects future trends and then orders additional stocks on the basis of his formula has been vindicated by the sale of 132 pairs of boots, his single largest sale ever, by far.

Jethro spends the next few days telling everyone he knows about his brilliant formula for ordering boots on the basis of detected future trends—until the end of the week when, as a result of the increase in weekly sales from 4 to 132 for that specific style of boot, 56,943 pairs of boots are delivered to Jethro's Boot Emporium.

There are many lessons to be learned from this story. Perhaps the most important is that our task as systems analysts is to work with our clients to determine the information system that our clients *need,* which is not necessarily the information system that they say they *want.*

1.1   Categories of Information Systems

A *system* is a set of *artifacts* (components) that together achieve some outcome. An *information system* is a system that achieves a business outcome. In more detail, an information system collects, manipulates, stores, and reports information regarding the business activities of an organization, in order to assist the management of that organization in managing the operations of the business.

There are two major categories of computerized information systems: custom information systems and commercial off-the-shelf (COTS) packages. A *custom information system* is an information system that has been developed for one specific client, just as a custom-tailored suit is sewn for one specific individual. For example, the information system developed for Jethro's Boot Emporium is a custom information system—the boot fashion trend detection component is used by no other company.

The three main stakeholders when a custom information system is *developed* (built) are

- The *client,* who is paying for the information system to be developed.
- The future *users* of the information system.
- The *developers* of that information system.

The task of the developers is to determine the needs of the client, and to develop an information system that satisfies those needs and can effectively be utilized by the users. Another example of a custom information system is a management information system for a major car rental company. Custom information systems are expensive, and an organization might be tempted to recoup some of the cost by selling a copy of its custom information system to a competitor. It is unlikely that (say) Hertz operates in exactly the same way as (say) Avis. For this reason, the resale market for custom information systems in general is small. But more importantly, a custom information system incorporates the business model of the organization that commissioned it, and selling a copy of such a custom information system means giving away proprietary information to a competitor. Returning to the example, if Hertz were to allow its custom management information system to be sold to a competitor, that competitor would gain insight into the Hertz business model, and Hertz would lose its business advantage.

In contrast, multiple copies of *commercial off-the-shelf (COTS) packages* are sold. Well-known COTS packages include TurboTax and Microsoft Excel, both used on millions of personal computers. Another popular COTS package is the Peachtree accounting system.

Another name for COTS packages is *shrinkware,* because the diskettes or CDs on which the package used to be supplied were placed in a box together with the manual, and the box was then shrink-wrapped. Nowadays, however, COTS packages are frequently downloaded over the Internet, so the term *clickware* is becoming increasingly common.

There are only two major stakeholders for a COTS package:

- The *developers.*
- The *users.*

A custom information system is developed to satisfy one client's needs, whereas COTS packages are intended to provide functionality that will satisfy the needs of as large a user base as possible.

Some COTS packages are relatively small and cheap, and are intended to satisfy the information system needs of smaller businesses. For example, an accounting package integrated with a tax package will supply most of the information system needs of a small plumbing company or a computer repair shop. In contrast, an *enterprise resource planning*

(ERP) system such as PeopleSoft or SAP is a huge package intended to provide almost all the information needs of a large corporation, including accounting, payroll, inventory, sales, purchasing, personnel, and so on. Such a package often will cost millions of dollars, and it takes months (if not years) to tailor the package to the specific requirements of each organization that purchases it. This tailoring of an ERP is a form of customization. In other words, on the one hand there are pure custom information systems, and on the other hand there are pure COTS packages that are used unchanged. In between lie COTS packages such as ERP systems that need to be tailored to each specific organization that uses them.

1.2   Traditional Information System Development

The *information system life cycle* is the way that an information system is constructed. Because is it almost always easier to perform a sequence of smaller tasks than one large task, the overall life cycle is broken into a series of smaller steps called *phases.* The number of phases varies from organization to organization—there can be as few as four or as many as eight. Typically, there are six phases, as listed in Figure 1.1. Each of these phases is now described in detail.

1.2.1   The Requirements Phase

In the *requirements phase* the client's requirements are extracted. That is, the client and the future users of the information system to be developed interact with the information system development team in order to determine the client's needs. The results of this study are presented in the form of a *requirements document.*

In the case of the information system developed for Jethro's Boot Emporium, the requirements document lists Jethro's needs with regard to automated reordering, as well as his needs with regard to detecting and reacting to new trends in boot fashions. Because Jethro's information system is relatively straightforward, the requirements document is only a few pages long, with the specific needs listed as bullet items.

1.2.2   The Analysis Phase

The second phase is the *analysis phase.* The aim of this phase is to draw up the specification document. The *specification document* (or *specifications*) lays out what the information system has to do. If the delivered information system satisfies the specifications, then the client pays the developers for the information system. If not, the developers have to fix the information system until it satisfies the specifications. The specifications describe *what* the system has to be able to do. Once the specification document has been signed off by the client, the *project management plan* can be drawn up. This detailed plan includes a budget, staffing needs, and a list of what will be delivered to the client and when it will be delivered.

Unlike the relatively informal requirements document, a specification document is essentially a contract between the client and the developers. Thus, in the case of Jethro's

FIGURE 1.1
The Six Phases of the Traditional Information System Life Cycle

1. Requirements phase
2. Analysis phase
3. Design phase
4. Implementation phase
5. Maintenance phase
6. Retirement

Boot Emporium and Western Business Computer Solutions, the specification document spells out in detail what the system will do. It specifies the input (the bar code on the boots) and the various outputs, including the automatically generated orders; reports listing sales to the public; and reports listing purchases from the wholesalers. In addition, the specification document describes precisely how the system is to determine when there is a new trend in boot fashions, and how many additional pairs of boots are to be ordered when a new trend is detected. This latter part of the specification document is based on the formula supplied by Jethro.

1.2.3 The Design Phase

The *design phase* comes next. Here the members of the development team describe *how* the information system is to be developed. Typically, the system is broken into smaller pieces called *modules.* Each module is then designed in detail; the development team has to describe the *algorithms* used by the module (that is, how the module performs its task) and the *data structures* within the module (that is, the data on which the module is to operate). The result is presented in the form of a design document.

Jethro's information system consists of a number of modules. Some of the modules handle the automated reordering based on sales, and some the additional ordering as a consequence of detection of new fashion trends in boots.

In order to appreciate the difference between a specification document and a design document, consider the sales report that Jethro wants to be printed at the end of each week. The specification document states that the report must include the weekly sales of boots from each of the wholesalers, and the overall sales total. That is, the specification document lists *what* is to be printed. The design document, on the other hand, states where on the page the date is to appear (top right-hand corner), what the column headings are to be ("Date," "Wholesaler," and "Sales"), how many characters to use for the name of the wholesaler, how many blank spaces to leave, and then how many digits to use for the total weekly sales from the wholesaler, and so on. In other words, the design of the report states *how* that report is to be printed.

1.2.4 The Implementation Phase

The fourth phase is the *implementation phase.* The designs of the modules are given to the programming team to translate into an appropriate programming language. COBOL is the world's most widely used programming language, whereas modern information systems are often implemented in C++ or Java. The modules are *integrated* (combined) to form the complete information system.

The information system for Jethro's system is in COBOL because the system was implemented over 30 years ago, when the overwhelming majority of information systems were implemented in COBOL.

1.2.5 The Maintenance Phase

After the information system has been installed, it will need to be modified, either to remove any remaining faults from the system or because the system needs to be extended in some way. This fifth phase is called the *maintenance phase.*

In the case of the information system developed for Jethro's Boot Emporium, the first maintenance operation was, not surprisingly, to turn off the part of the program that automatically ordered more boots if a new trend in boot buying was detected. Instead, the system printed a report so that Jethro could decide whether or not there really was a new trend and, if so, he could decide exactly how many additional pairs of boots to order.

1.2.6 Retirement

Finally, after 10 or 15 or more years of maintenance, an information system is retired if it no longer performs a useful service. This sixth and final phase, *retirement,* is shown in Figure 1.1 together with the earlier phases of the information system life cycle.

Three important phases appear to have been omitted. These apparent omissions are addressed in the next three sections.

1.3 Why There Is No Planning Phase

How is it possible to develop a management information system without a plan? The answer is simple: We cannot. But in that case, why is there no *planning phase* at the very beginning of the project?

The key point is that, until we know exactly what we are going to develop, there is no way we can draw up an accurate detailed plan. Thus, there are three types of planning activities that take place when an information system is developed:

• First, at the beginning of the project, preliminary planning takes place so that we can manage the requirements and analysis phases.

• Second, once we know precisely what we are going to develop, we draw up the project management plan. This includes the budget, staffing requirements, and detailed schedule. The earliest we can draw up the project management plan is when the specification document has been approved by the client. Until that time, planning has to be preliminary and partial.

• Third, all through the project, management needs to monitor the project management plan and be on the watch for any deviation from the plan. For example, suppose that the project management plan for a specific project states that the design phase will take four months. However, 12 months have already gone by and the design does not appear to be nearly complete. The project will almost certainly have to be abandoned, and the funds spent to date will then all be wasted. Instead, management should have noticed after at most two months that there was a serious problem with the design phase. At that time, a decision could have been made how best to proceed. The usual initial step in such a situation is to call in a consultant to determine if the project is feasible and whether the design team is competent to carry out their task, or whether the risk of proceeding is too great. Based on the report of the consultant, various alternatives are now considered, including reducing the scope of the target information system and then designing and implementing a less ambitious one. Only if all other alternatives are considered unworkable does the project have to be canceled. In the case of the specific project, this cancellation would have taken place some 10 months earlier if management had monitored the plan closely, thereby saving a considerable sum of money.

In other words, there is no separate planning phase. Instead, planning activities are carried out all through the life cycle. However, there are times when planning activities predominate. These include the beginning of the project (preliminary planning) and directly after the specification document has been signed off by the client (project management plan).

1.4 Why There Is No Testing Phase

Why is there no *testing phase?* Surely it is essential to check an information system carefully after it has been developed.

Unfortunately, checking the information system once it is ready to be delivered to the client is far too late. For instance, if there is a *fault* in the specification document, this fault will have been carried forward into the design and implementation. For example, suppose that the specification document for Jethro's Boot Emporium includes the incorrect statement that, in Wyoming, boots are exempt from sales tax. The design of the information system then would not have included the computation of the sales tax, nor would the implementation. If no checking had been performed until the information system was complete, then, when the fault was finally discovered, major changes would have had to be made to the information system. First, the specification document would have had to be corrected to reflect the fact that sales tax is indeed levied on boots. Second, the design would have had to be changed in the appropriate places. Third, these changes would have had to be made within the code as well. However, if the specification document had been checked before the design was started, only the specification document itself would have had to be changed, and only in that one place where sales tax is mentioned. The obvious conclusion is that, in addition to checking the information system as a whole when it is complete (*validation*), common sense dictates that it also should be checked at the end of each phase (*verification*).

But even this is not enough. What is needed is continual checking of an information system. An information technology professional should not have to be told to breathe while developing an information system. In the same way, careful checking should be an automatic accompaniment of every information system development activity. Conversely, a separate testing phase is incompatible with the goal of ensuring that an information system is as fault-free as possible at all times.

1.5   Why There Is No Documentation Phase

Just as there should never be a separate planning phase or testing phase, there also should never be a separate *documentation phase.* On the contrary, at all times the documentation of the information system must be complete, correct, and up to date. For instance, during the analysis phase, the specification document must reflect the current version of the specifications, and similarly for the other phases.

- One reason why it is essential to ensure that the documentation is always up to date is the large turnover in personnel in the information system industry. For example, suppose that the design documentation has not been kept current and the chief designer leaves to take another job. It will now be extremely hard to update the design document to reflect all the changes that were made while the system was being designed.

- A second reason is that it is almost impossible to perform the steps of a specific phase unless the documentation of the previous phase is complete, correct, and up to date. For instance, an incomplete specification document must inevitably result in an incomplete design and then in an incomplete implementation.

- Third, it is virtually impossible to test whether a program is working correctly unless there are documents that state how that program is supposed to behave. For example, it would not have been possible to test the part of the program that deals with detecting a new trend in boot buying unless the specification document spelled out exactly what constituted a new trend and how many additional pairs of boots were to be ordered.

- Fourth, maintenance is almost impossible unless there is a complete and correct set of documentation that describes precisely what the current version of the system does.

Thus, just as there is no separate planning phase or testing phase, there is no separate documentation phase. Instead, planning, testing, and documentation should be activities that accompany all other activities while an information system is being constructed.

1.6 Systems Analysis and Design

The subject of this book is systems analysis and design. Within the context of traditional information system development, the term *systems analysis* refers to the first two phases (requirements and analysis phases), and *systems design* refers to the third phase, the design phase.

Unfortunately, the terminology of traditional information system development easily can lead to confusion:

- The term *analysis* on its own is used to denote just the second phase. That is, whereas *systems analysis* refers to the first and second phases of traditional information system development, *analysis* refers to just the second phase. There is no question that these two different uses of the word "analysis" are extremely confusing, but it simply is not possible to change the terminology used in information technology for the past 50 years.

- The term *systems analyst* also is used in two different senses. In some organizations, the task of the *systems analysts* is to determine the client's needs in regard to an information system (requirements phase) and then to draw up the specification document to record formally what has to be developed (analysis phase). Then the *systems designers* design the system to be developed. In most organizations, however, there are no separate systems designers. The systems analysts are then responsible for the first three phases, namely, requirements, analysis, and design. In this book, we use the term "systems analyst" in this second sense, because it is still the more commonly used approach in the information systems industry.

It would seem that this book deals only with the first three phases of traditional information system development. However, as will be shown in the next section, this is not the case.

1.7 Maintenance

A commonly held misconception is that only a bad information system has to be modified after installation. On the contrary, bad information systems are thrown away, whereas good information systems are modified for many years. Figure 1.2 is a key diagram. It

FIGURE 1.2

The Average Percentage of Time Devoted to Development and to Maintenance

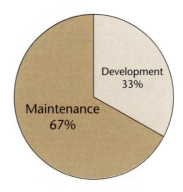

depicts the average percentage of time (= money) devoted to a system before installation (*development*) and after installation (*maintenance*) on the client's computer [Hatton, 1998; Schach, 2002].

Looking at Figure 1.2, it is clear that, on average, for every $1 spent on development, $2 are spent on maintenance. In fact, some experts claim that Figure 1.2 is an understatement, and that for every $1 spent on development, $3 or more are spent on maintenance over the life of the information system [Yourdon, 1992]. Whether the conservative 1:2 ratio between the money spent on development and the money spent on maintenance shown in Figure 1.2 is correct, or whether the actual ratio is 1:3 or more, it is clear that maintenance is the most important phase of the information system life cycle.

There are three main maintenance activities:

- *Corrective maintenance* is the fixing of faults in the information system. Frequently the faults to be fixed are in the code, but corrective maintenance also includes the repair of all other artifacts of an information system, including the specification document, design document, manuals, and so on.
- *Perfective maintenance* consists of changes made to the information system because the client wishes to extend the functionality of the system. For example, the client may want the system to have a shorter response time or to be able to handle pricing in euros in addition to dollars.
- When there is a change in the environment in which the information system operates, the information system has to be modified. This is called *adaptive maintenance*. For example, if the sales tax rate changes, any information system that deals with buying and selling has to be changed accordingly. Furthermore, if the information system has to be changed so that it can be run on a different computer or under a different operating system, this is also adaptive maintenance.

Now consider perfective maintenance and adaptive maintenance, which together are known as *enhancement*. When enhancement is performed, the requirements change. More specifically, in the case of perfective maintenance, the requirements change because the client wants the functionality of the system to be extended; in the case of adaptive maintenance, the requirements change because the environment has changed. In both cases, therefore, there is a change in the requirements, and this change in turn induces changes to the specification document, design document, and implementation.

In other words, each enhancement of an information system can be viewed as a complete life cycle in itself, starting with the requirements phase and ending with implementation. It should go without saying that planning, testing, and documentation are intrinsic aspects of enhancement, as they are of every information system activity, without exception.

As previously stated, the term *systems analysis* refers to the requirements and analysis phases of the information system life cycle, and *systems design* refers to the design phase. But, as previously pointed out, systems analysis and design activities take place not just during development, but also during enhancement. Bearing in mind that, worldwide, one trillion dollars are devoted to information system development and maintenance each year [Seddon, Graeser, and Willcocks, 2000], this means that systems analysis and design activities consume about $350 billion each year.

As reflected in Figure 1.2, twice as much time is spent on maintenance as on all development. Financial implications of this are discussed in Just in Case You Wanted to Know Box 1.1.

In general, maintenance is far more profitable than development. It's not just that, for every dollar spent on development, two or three dollars are spent on maintenance. The key point is that profit margins for maintenance can be much higher than for development.

Consider the following example: XYZ Corporation, Inc., develops and maintains information systems. On average, the hourly cost to XYZ of an information technology professional is $100, including overhead. (The figure of $100 is on the low side, but it makes the arithmetic easier.) Suppose that XYZ is bidding on an information system contract and estimates that the project will take 5,000 person-hours of effort (one *person-hour* is the amount of work that one person can do in one hour). Thus, it will cost XYZ a total of $500,000 to develop the system. Management may decide to put in a bid for developing the new system at its cost price of $500,000, with the expectation that they will be able to charge (say) $150 per hour while maintaining the system in the future. With an expected 10,000 person-hours of maintenance work to be done over the next 10 years or so, they anticipate a net profit of $500,000 on this maintenance. It is true that the client may take their maintenance work elsewhere, but this would mean that the new information system organization would have to spend a considerable amount of time learning all the details of the information system developed by XYZ, and the client would have to pay for that time. Thus, if XYZ does a good job in developing the information system, the client is likely to sign a contract with them to maintain that information system.

Underlying the strategy of XYZ is the belief that a client may well balk at paying a lump sum larger than $500,000 up front but will readily agree to spending a further $1,500,000 in relatively small installments over the next 10 years or so. In other words, XYZ develops information systems for the purpose of acquiring highly profitable future maintenance contracts. For XYZ, development is not an end in itself, but rather a means to making a net profit of 50 percent on future maintenance activities.

1.8   Information Technology Professionals

Software consists of not just the instructions to the computer (the computer program, or code), but also all the documentation that is an intrinsic component of every project. Thus, software includes the specification document, the design document, legal and accounting documents of all kinds, the project management plan, and other management documents, as well as all types of manuals.

Information technology professionals work in two types of organizations. First, there are organizations such as Microsoft, Inc., and Oracle, Inc., whose primary activity is producing software. Such organizations range in size from giants such as Microsoft (at time of writing, the second largest company in the world on the basis of market capitalization), down to individuals who develop software at home.

On the other hand, an organization such as General Motors (GM) has a huge software group within its information services division, and so does General Electric (GE). The difference between GM and GE on the one hand, and Microsoft and Oracle on the other hand, is that software is not a primary product of GM and GE. For example, although it is inconceivable nowadays to think of a GM automobile without computers controlling the engine, it is important to bear in mind that the automobile is a primary product of GM; the software in that automobile is merely a component of the automobile, like the fan belt or the headlights.

Many smaller organizations also have their own systems analysts to perform the first three phases of the information system life cycle within that organization. In particular, virtually every *dot-com* (e-commerce organization), no matter how small, has an information system division to run that aspect of the business.

Thus, information technology professionals are employed by organizations of all sizes, both those where software is the primary product of that organization and where it is merely a component of their products. In addition, in every organization, information systems drive the *mission-critical activities* of that organization. (If a mission-critical activity is terminated, the organization can no longer carry out its core business. For some companies, mission-critical activities include buying or selling; for most companies, keeping the financial records of that organization is mission critical.) For example, an insurance company such as Prudential has a huge information services division that is responsible for the information systems that drive every aspect of their operation, from policy-holder services to maintaining the records of the real estate owned by Prudential.

Most major organizations employ their own systems analysts. A few major organizations and many smaller organizations *outsource;* that is, they contract with other companies (such as EDS) to handle all aspects of their information systems. Some organizations have their own in-house maintenance personnel, but they outsource the development of new information systems; information systems developed by organizations that specialize in developing such new information systems are called *contract information systems*.

The traditional organizational structure for an information services division within a large organization is depicted in Figure 1.3. The entry-level technical position within many information services divisions is *programmer.* After obtaining experience implementing designs in code, the programmer can be promoted to *programmer/analyst,* where he or she will gain experience in systems analysis and design while still being involved in programming activities. The next level is systems analyst; a systems analyst performs systems

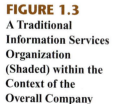

FIGURE 1.3
A Traditional
Information Services
Organization
(Shaded) within the
Context of the
Overall Company

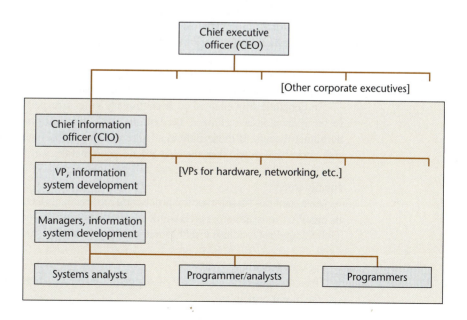

analysis and design. Further promotion is to a managerial position, frequently *manager for information system development.* This is a poor choice of title because, as explained in Section 1.7, the vast majority of his or her activities are maintenance, not development. The managers for information system development report to the *vice president for information system development,* the senior information system manager in the organization. The vice president for system development in turn reports to the *chief information officer* (CIO), who is responsible for all aspects of information technology within the organization, including hardware, software, networking, security, and so on. The CIO, in turn, reports to the *chief executive officer* (CEO).

A systems analyst needs to have a number of different skills. Technical skills are essential—every systems analyst must know the techniques of modern systems analysis and design and be able to apply them effectively. Communication skills are equally important. The systems analyst has to communicate both verbally and in writing with the client and the future users of the information system, as well as with his or her own managers. Also, systems analysts have to be able to program, even though their job usually does not include programming tasks. The reason is that the design of the information system that they produce is the major source of instruction from the systems analysts to the programmers. Unless systems analysts are familiar with programming concepts, written and oral communication with the programmers is likely to be error-prone.

One way of ensuring that systems analysts can program is to promote the best programmers to systems analyst positions, as previously described. Although this is the common practice, many organizations have observed that a good programmer often makes a poor systems analyst. An alternative career path nowadays is for a systems analyst to start as a *business analyst,* that is, a specialist in solving business problems. Once a business analyst has gained some programming experience, perhaps by taking an appropriate course at a two- or four-year college, he or she could be considered for promotion to systems analyst.

Figure 1.3 shows the main job categories within a traditional information services organization. There are usually a number of technical specialists as well. For example, the *database administrator* is responsible for all aspects of the database and the *database management system,* and the *network administrator* is in charge of the local area network (LAN). *Systems programmers* maintain the *operating system* software. Members of the *quality assurance* group are responsible for ensuring that there are no faults in the software. *Software engineers* are specialists in the development and maintenance of software. Systems analysts consult these technical specialists when necessary. That is, systems analysts usually are not specialists in any of these technical areas, but they know enough about each area to be able to utilize the advice of technical specialists effectively.

We conclude this chapter on a cautionary note. Irrespective of how the information services division is organized, the bottom line is that information systems are developed by human beings. If those individuals are hard working, intelligent, sensible, up to date, and, above all, *ethical,* then the chances are good that the way that information systems are developed within that organization will be satisfactory. Unfortunately, the converse is equally true.

Most societies for information processing professionals have a code of ethics to which all its members must adhere. For example, the code of ethics of the Association of Information Technology Professionals (AITP) includes the following paragraphs [AITP, 1997]:

I acknowledge:
That I have an obligation to my College or University, therefore, I shall uphold its ethical and moral principles.

That I have an obligation to my employer whose trust I hold, therefore, I shall endeavor to discharge this obligation to the best of my ability, to guard my employer's interests, and to advise him or her wisely and honestly.

I accept these obligations as a personal responsibility and as a member of this Association. I shall actively discharge these obligations and I dedicate myself to that end.

The codes of ethics of other societies for information processing professionals express similar sentiments. It is vital for the future of our profession that we adhere rigorously to such codes of ethics.

Key Terms

adaptive maintenance, *11*
algorithm, *7*
analysis, *10*
analysis phase, *6*
business analyst, *14*
chief executive officer, 14
chief information officer, *14*
clickware, *5*
client, *5*
commercial off-the-shelf (COTS) package, *5*
contract information system, *13*
corrective maintenance, *11*
custom information system, *5*
data structure, *7*
database administrator, *14*
database management system, *14*
design phase, *7*
developer, *5*
development, *11*
documentation phase, *9*

dot-com, *13*
enhancement, *11*
enterprise resource planning (ERP) system, *5*
fault, *9*
implementation phase, *7*
information system, *5*
information system life cycle, *6*
integration, *7*
maintenance, *11*
maintenance phase, *7*
manager for information system development, *14*
mission-critical activity, *13*
module, *7*
network administrator, *14*
operating system, *14*
outsource, *13*
perfective maintenance, *11*
person-hour, *12*
phase, *6*
planning phase, *8*

programmer, *13*
programmer/analyst, *13*
project management plan, *6*
quality assurance, *14*
requirements document, *6*
requirements phase, *6*
retirement, *8*
software, *12*
software engineer, *14*
specification document, *6*
specifications, *6*
system, *5*
systems analysis, *10*
systems analyst, *10*
systems design, *10*
systems programmer, *14*
testing phase, *8*
user, *5*
validation, *9*
verification, *9*
vice president for information system development, *14*

Review Questions for Chapter 1

1. What are the two major categories of computerized information systems?
2. Distinguish between ERP and COTS.
3. What are the six phases of the traditional information system life cycle?
4. List the documentation that is produced during each phase of the information system life cycle.
5. Briefly describe what is done during each phase of traditional information system development.
6. Why is there no separate planning phase?
7. Why is there no separate testing phase?
8. Why is there no separate documentation phase?
9. Give two different uses of the word *analysis* in the information system context.
10. For every dollar spent on the development of an information system, how much is spent on maintenance over the lifetime of the information system?
11. What are the three main types of maintenance? Briefly describe each one.
12. What are the two major types of organizations in which information technology professionals work?

Problems

1.1   Describe a situation where the client, developer, and user are the same person.

1.2   What advantages can accrue if the client, developer, and user are the same person?

1.3   Consider the requirements phase and the analysis phase. Would it make more sense to combine these activities into one phase than to treat them separately?

1.4   More testing is done during the implementation phase than in any other development phase. Would it be better to divide this phase into two separate phases, one incorporating all the nontesting aspects, the other all the testing?

1.5   To what extent was Morgan Cuttler, the systems analyst at Western Business Computer Solutions, responsible for the delivery of the 56,943 pairs of boots to Jethro's Boot Emporium? How could Morgan have prevented this from happening?

1.6   You are a systems analyst. The executive vice president of a publisher of paperback books wants you to develop an information system that will carry out all the accounting functions of the company and provide online information to the head office staff regarding orders and inventory in the various company warehouses. Computers are required for 15 accounting clerks, 32 order clerks, and 42 warehouse clerks. In addition, 18 managers need access to the data. The president is willing to pay $30,000 for the hardware and the information system together and wants the complete information system in four weeks. What do you tell him? Bear in mind that your company wants his business, no matter how unreasonable his request.

1.7   Look up the word *system* in a dictionary. How many different definitions are there? Write down those definitions that are applicable to information systems.

1.8   Retirement is a rare event. Why do you think this is?

1.9   Due to a fire at Elmer's Information System Developers, Inc., all the documentation for an information system is destroyed shortly before the information system is due to be delivered and installed. What is the impact of the resulting lack of documentation?

References

Association of Information Technology Professionals Code of Ethics. August 27, 1997. Available at www.aitp.org/about/code_of_ethics.html.

Hatton, L. "Does OO Sync with How We Think?" *IEEE Software* 15 (May/June 1998), pp. 46–54.

Schach, S. R. *Object-Oriented and Classical Software Engineering.* 5th ed. New York: WCB/McGraw-Hill, 2002.

Seddon, P.; V. Graeser; and L. Willcocks. "Measuring IS Effectiveness: Senior IT Management Perspectives." Technical Report, Oxford Institute of Information Management, Templeton College, University of Oxford, U.K., 2000.

Yourdon, E. *The Decline and Fall of the American Programmer.* Upper Saddle River, NJ: Yourdon Press, 1992.

2

How Information Systems Are Developed

Learning Objectives

After studying this chapter, you should be able to:

- Describe how information systems are developed in practice.
- Appreciate the importance of not making changes late in the life cycle.
- Distinguish clearly between iteration and incrementation.
- Understand the iterative and incremental life-cycle model.
- Give the modern definition of maintenance.

Chapter 1 describes how information systems would be developed in an ideal world. The main topic of this chapter is what happens in practice. As will soon be explained, there are vast differences between theory and practice.

2.1 Information System Development in Theory

In an ideal world, an information system is developed as described in Chapter 1. As depicted schematically in Figure 2.1, the system is developed from scratch; ϕ denotes the empty set. (See Just in Case You Wanted to Know Box 2.1 if you want to know the origin of the term *from scratch*.) First, the client's **Requirements** are determined, then the **Analysis** is performed. When this phase is complete, the **Design** is produced. This is followed by the **Implementation** of the complete information system, which is then installed on the client's computer.

However, there are two reasons why information system development is very different in practice. First, information technology professionals are human beings and therefore make mistakes. Second, the client's requirements can change while the information system

The term *from scratch,* meaning "starting with nothing," comes from nineteenth-century sports terminology. Before roads (and running tracks) were paved, races had to be held on open ground. In many cases, the starting line was a scratch in the sand. A runner who had no advantage or handicap had to start from that line, that is, "from [the] scratch."

The term *scratch* has a different sporting connotation nowadays. A "scratch golfer" is one whose golfing handicap is zero.

FIGURE 2.1
Idealized Information System Development

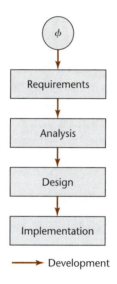

is being developed. In this chapter, both these issues are discussed in some depth, but first a mini case study, based on the case study in Tomer and Schach [2000], is presented that illustrates the issues involved.

2.2 Winburg Mini Case Study

In order to reduce traffic congestion in downtown Winburg, Indiana, the mayor convinces the city to set up a public transportation system. Bus-only lanes are to be established, and commuters will be encouraged to "park and ride," that is, to park their cars in suburban parking lots and then take buses from there to work and back at a cost of one dollar per ride. Each bus is to have a fare machine that accepts only dollar bills. Passengers insert a bill into the slot as they enter the bus. Sensors inside the fare machine scan the bill, and the software in the machine then uses an image recognition algorithm to decide whether the passenger has indeed inserted a valid dollar bill into the slot. It is important that the fare machine be accurate because, once the news gets out that any piece of paper will do the trick, fare income will plummet to effectively zero. Conversely, if the machine regularly rejects valid dollar bills, passengers will be reluctant to use the buses. In addition, the fare machine must be rapid. Passengers will be equally reluctant to use the buses if the machine spends 15 seconds coming to a decision regarding the validity of a dollar bill—it would take even a relatively small number of passengers many minutes to board a bus. Thus, the requirements for the fare machine software include an average response time of less than 1 second, and an average accuracy of at least 98 percent.

Episode 1. The first version of the information system is implemented.

Episode 2. Tests show that the required constraint of an average response time of 1 second for deciding on the validity of a dollar bill is not achieved—in fact, on average it takes 10 seconds to get a response. Senior management discovers the cause. It seems that, in order to get the required 98 percent accuracy, a programmer has been instructed by her manager to use double-precision numbers for all mathematical calculations. That is, instead of using one computer word (storage location) to store a number, she has used two adjoining computer words. As a result, every operation takes at least twice as long as it would with the usual single-precision numbers. The result is that the program is much slower than it should be, resulting in the long response time. Calculations then show that, despite what the manager told the programmer, the stipulated 98 percent accuracy can be attained even if single-precision numbers are used. The programmer starts to make the necessary changes to the implementation.

Episode 3. Before the programmer can complete her work, further tests of the system show that, even if the indicated changes to the implementation were made, the system would still have an average response time of over 4.5 seconds, nowhere near the stipulated 1 second. The problem is the complex image recognition algorithm. Fortunately, a faster algorithm has just been discovered, so the fare machine software is rewritten using the new algorithm. This results in the average response time being successfully achieved.

Episode 4. By now, the project is considerably behind schedule and way over budget. The mayor, a successful information systems entrepreneur, has the bright idea of asking the information system development team to try to increase the accuracy of the dollar bill recognition component of the system as much as possible, in order to sell the resulting package to vending machine companies. A new design is adopted that improves the average accuracy to over 99.5 percent. Management decides to install that version of the software in the fare machines. At this point, development of the information system is complete. The city is later able to sell their system to two small vending machine companies, thereby defraying about one-third of the cost overrun.

Epilogue. A few years later, the sensors inside the fare machine become obsolete and need to be replaced by a newer model. Management suggests taking advantage of the change to upgrade the hardware at the same time. The information technology professionals point out that changing the hardware will mean that new software also will be needed. They suggest rewriting the information system in a different programming language. At the time of writing, the project is six months behind schedule and 25 percent over budget. However, everyone involved is confident that the new system will be more reliable and of higher quality, despite "minor discrepancies" in meeting its response time and accuracy requirements . . .

Figure 2.2 depicts the *evolution tree model* of the mini case study. The leftmost boxes represent Episode 1. As shown in the figure, the system was developed from scratch (ϕ). The requirements (Requirements$_1$), analysis (Analysis$_1$), design (Design$_1$), and implementation (Implementation$_1$) followed in turn. Next, as previously described, trials of the first version of the information system showed that the average response time of one second could not be achieved, and the implementation had to be modified. The modified implementation appears in Figure 2.2 as Implementation$_2$. However, Implementation$_2$ was never completed. That is why the rectangle representing Implementation$_2$ is drawn with a dotted line.

FIGURE 2.2
The Evolution Tree Model for the Winburg Mini Case Study
(The dashed box denotes the implementation that was not completed.)

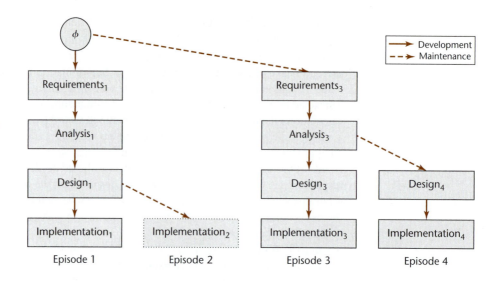

FIGURE 2.3
The Waterfall Model

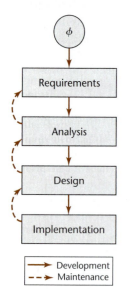

In Episode 3, the requirements had to be changed. Specifically, the faster image recognition algorithm was used. The modified requirements (Requirements$_3$) resulted in modified specifications (Analysis$_3$), modified design (Design$_3$), and modified implementation (Implementation$_3$).

Finally, in Episode 4, the design was changed (Design$_4$) in order to increase the accuracy. Then the implementation had to be changed (Implementation$_4$) to achieve this change in design.

In Figure 2.2, the solid arrows denote development; the dashed arrows denote maintenance. For example, when the design was changed in Episode 4, Design$_4$ replaced Design$_3$ as the design of Analysis$_3$.

The evolution tree model is an example of a *life-cycle model,* that is, the series of steps through which the information progresses as it is developed and maintained. Another life-cycle model that can be used to represent the mini case study is the *waterfall model* [Royce, 1970] depicted in Figure 2.3. This traditional life-cycle model can be viewed as the linear model of Figure 2.1 with feedback loops. Then, if a fault is found during the design phase that was caused by a fault in the requirements, following the dashed upward arrows we can backtrack from the design up to the analysis and hence to the requirements, and make the necessary corrections there. Then we move down to the analysis, correct the specification document to reflect the corrections to the requirements and, in turn, correct the design document. Design activities can now resume where they were suspended when the fault was discovered. Again, the solid arrows denote development, the dashed arrows maintenance.

The waterfall model can certainly be used to represent the Winburg mini case study but, unlike the evolution tree model of Figure 2.2, it cannot show the order of events. The evolution tree model has a further advantage over the waterfall model. At the end of each episode we have a *baseline,* that is, a complete set of artifacts (an *artifact* is a constituent component of an information system, such as a specification document, a code module, or a manual). There are four baselines in Figure 2.2. They are

At the end of Episode 1: Requirements$_1$, Analysis$_1$, Design$_1$, Implementation$_1$.
At the end of Episode 2: Requirements$_1$, Analysis$_1$, Design$_1$, Implementation$_2$.
At the end of Episode 3: Requirements$_3$, Analysis$_3$, Design$_3$, Implementation$_3$.
At the end of Episode 4: Requirements$_3$, Analysis$_3$, Design$_4$, Implementation$_4$.

The first baseline is the initial set of artifacts, the second baseline reflects the modified (but never completed) Implementation$_2$ of Episode 2, together with the unchanged requirements, analysis, and design of Episode 1.

The third baseline is the complete set of new artifacts shown in Figure 2.2. The fourth baseline is the same as the third baseline but with the design and implementation changed. We will revisit the concept of a baseline in Chapters 11 and 14.

2.3   Lessons of the Winburg Mini Case Study

The Winburg mini case study depicts the development of an information system that goes awry for a number of unrelated causes, such as a poor implementation strategy (the unnecessary use of double-precision numbers) and the decision to use an algorithm that was too slow. The good news is that everything worked fine in the end, but the obvious question is: Is information system development really as chaotic in practice? In fact, the mini case study is far less traumatic than many, if not the majority, of information system projects. In the Winburg mini case study, there was only one new version of the information system as a consequence of a fault (the inappropriate use of double-precision numbers), and two new versions because of changes made by the client (the switch to the faster algorithm and the need for increased accuracy).

Why is it that so many changes to an information system are needed? First, an information system is a model of the real world, and the real world is continually changing. This issue is discussed at greater length in Section 2.4. Second, as previously stated, information technology professionals are human and therefore make mistakes. The problem is that, if the resulting fault in the information system is not quickly detected, it will be carried over into the next phase. Fixing the fault then means fixing not just the fault itself, but also the effects of the fault in subsequent phases. Unless a fault is quickly corrected and detected, the cost of that fault will soar—the old proverb "a stitch in time saves nine" is only too true.

This point is illustrated in Figure 2.4, which is based on data in Kan et al. [1994]. The horizontal axis shows the various phases; the vertical axis is the approximate relative cost to detect and correct a fault.

Suppose that it takes $1 to fix a fault in the requirements if the fault is found before the requirements phase is over. Changing the requirements at this stage is easy. Either an eraser and pencil can be used to change handwritten requirements, or a word processor can be used to modify requirements stored as a word processor document.

However, if the fault is detected only at the end of the analysis phase, it will cost $3 to fix: $1 to fix the specification document, $1 to fix the project management plan, and $1 to go back and fix the requirements. Similarly, if that same fault is detected at the end of the design phase, it will cost $4 to fix.

Now, if the fault is detected at the end of the implementation phase, the cost rises steeply to $52. Once the system has been implemented, a change to the information system means changing the code. However, not only does the code itself have to be changed, but the change also needs to be tested. Then the documentation needs to be changed, including manuals and the comments in the code itself.

Worst of all, if the fault is detected only after the information system has been implemented on the client's computer, the cost of fixing the code rockets to $368. After all, the complete system has been installed at the client's site, and the cost of making all the changes there is far greater than on the developer's computer. Worse, the information system may have been installed at a number of different client sites, and the corrected information system needs to be installed at every one of them. In addition, the manuals at the various sites need to be changed as well.

FIGURE 2.4

The Approximate
Relative Cost of
Detecting and
Correcting a Fault
during the Phases of
the Life Cycle

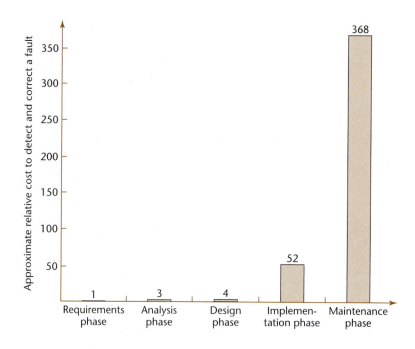

Figure 2.4 is another key diagram. The lesson of Figure 2.4 is clear: It is essential to detect faults early in the information system life cycle and to correct them at that time. Any delay will increase costs, especially if the fault is detected after the information system has been installed.

The early detection of faults is stressed in this section. But what if a mistake is made (say) during the implementation phase? It is clearly impossible to detect this fault during a phase earlier than the implementation phase. The answer is that research has shown that between 60 and 70 percent of all faults detected in delivered large-scale projects are systems analysis faults [Boehm, 1979]. In other words, most of our mistakes are made during the requirements, analysis, and design phases. Figure 2.4 tells us that we must detect and correct those mistakes early, or pay for our carelessness.

2.4 Teal Tractors Mini Case Study

Teal Tractors, Inc., sells tractors in most areas of the United States. The company instructs its information services division to develop a new information system that will be able handle all aspects of their business. For example, the system must be able to handle sales, inventory, and commissions paid to the sales staff, as well as provide all necessary accounting functions. While this information system is being implemented, Teal Tractors buys a Canadian tractor company. Management of Teal Tractors decides that, to save money, the Canadian operations are to be integrated into the U.S. operations. That means that the information system will have to be changed before it has been completed.

• First, it will have to be modified to handle additional sales regions.
• Second, it must be extended to be able to handle those aspects of the business that are handled differently in Canada, such as taxes.
• Third, it must be extended to handle two different currencies, U.S. dollars and Canadian dollars.

Teal Tractors is a rapidly growing company with excellent future prospects. The takeover of the Canadian tractor company is a positive development, one that may well lead to even greater profits in future years. But from the viewpoint of the information services division, the purchase of the Canadian company could be disastrous. Unless the systems analysis and design has been performed with a view to incorporating possible future extensions, the work involved in adding the Canadian sales regions may be so great that it might be more effective to discard everything that has been done to date and start again from scratch. The reason is that changing the system at this stage could be similar to trying to fix an information system late in its life cycle (see Figure 2.4). Extending the information system to be able to handle aspects that are specific to the Canadian market, as well as Canadian currency, may be equally hard.

Even if the information system has been well thought out and the original design is indeed extensible, the design of the resulting patched-together system cannot be as cohesive as it would have been if it had been developed from the very beginning to cater to both the United States and Canada. This can have severe implications for future maintenance.

The information services division of Teal Tractors is a victim of the *moving target problem*. That is, while the information system is being developed, the requirements change. It does not matter that the reason for the change is otherwise extremely worthwhile. The fact is that the takeover of the Canadian company could well be detrimental to the quality of the information system being developed.

In some cases, the reason for the moving target is less benign. Sometimes a powerful senior manager within an organization keeps changing his or her mind regarding the functionality of an information system being developed. Frequent changes, no matter how minor they may seem, are harmful to the health of an information system. It is important that an information system be designed as a set of components that are as independent as possible, so that a change to one part of the information system does not induce a fault in an apparently unrelated part of the code, a so-called *regression fault*. When numerous changes are made, the effect is to induce dependencies within the code. Finally, there will be so many dependencies that virtually any change induces one or more regression faults. At this time, the only thing that can be done is to redesign the entire information system and reimplement it.

Unfortunately, there is no known solution to the moving target problem. With regard to positive changes to requirements, growing companies are always going to change, and these changes will have to be reflected in the mission-critical information systems of the company. And as for negative changes, if the individual calling for those changes has sufficient clout, nothing can be done to prevent those changes from being implemented, to the detriment of the further maintainability of the information system.

2.5   Iteration and Incrementation

As a consequence of both the moving target problem and the need to correct the inevitable mistakes that are made while an information system is being developed, the life cycle of actual information systems resembles the evolution tree model of Figure 2.2 or the waterfall model of Figure 2.3, rather than the idealized chain of Figure 2.1. One consequence of this reality is that it does not make much sense to talk about (say) "*the* analysis phase." Instead, the operations of the analysis phase are spread out over the life cycle. Similarly, Figure 2.2 shows four different versions of the implementation, one of which (Implementation$_2$) was never completed because of the moving target problem.

Consider successive versions of an artifact, for example, the specification document or a code module. From this viewpoint, the basic process is *iterative*. (To "iterate" means to *repeat.*) That is, we produce the first version of the artifact, then we revise it and produce the second version, and so on. Our intent is that each version will be closer to our target than its predecessor, and that finally we will construct a version that is satisfactory.

A second aspect of developing real-world information systems is the restriction imposed on us by *Miller's Law*. In 1956, a professor of psychology named George Miller showed that, at any one time, we human beings are capable of concentrating on only approximately seven chunks (units of information) [Miller, 1956]. However, a typical information system artifact has far more than seven chunks. For example, a client is likely to have considerably more than seven requirements, and a specification document is likely to have many more than seven items. One way we humans handle this restriction on the amount of information we can handle at any one time is to use *stepwise refinement.* That is, we concentrate on those aspects that are currently the most important and postpone until later those aspects that are currently less critical. In other words, every aspect is eventually handled, but in order of current importance. This means that we start off by constructing an artifact that solves only a small part of what we are trying to achieve. Then we consider further aspects of the problem and add the resulting new pieces to the existing artifact. For example, we might construct the requirements document by considering those seven requirements that we consider the most important. Then, we would consider the seven next most important requirements, and so on. This is an *incremental* process. (To "increment" means to *increase.*)

Figure 2.5 schematically shows the difference between *iteration* and *incrementation.* Figure 2.5(a) depicts iteration. First, a complete artifact (represented by the rectangle) is constructed; this is version 1. Each succeeding version (versions 2 through 4) is a modification of its predecessor. In contrast, when an artifact is constructed incrementally, it is constructed piece by piece (or stepwise). Figure 2.5(b) shows the same artifact constructed in five increments, numbered 1 through 5.

In practice, iteration and incrementation are used in conjunction with one another. That is, an artifact is constructed piece by piece (incrementation), and each increment goes through multiple versions (iteration). These ideas are taken further in Figure 2.2, which represents the life cycle for the Winburg mini case study (Sections 2.2 and 2.3). As shown in that figure, there is no single "requirements phase" as such. Instead, the client's requirements were extracted and analyzed twice, yielding the original requirements (Requirements$_1$) and the modified requirements (Requirements$_3$). Similarly, there is no single "implementation phase," but rather four separate episodes in which the code was produced and then modified.

FIGURE 2.5

Schematic Representation of (a) Iteration and (b) Incrementation (The numbers show the order in which the components were added)

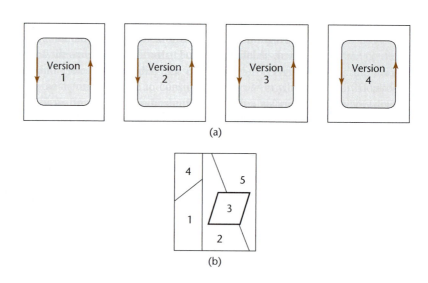

FIGURE 2.6

The Construction of
an Information
System in Four
Increments

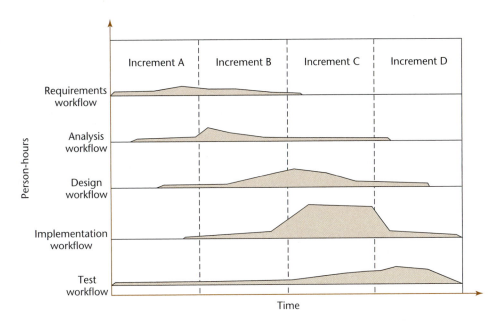

These ideas are generalized in Figure 2.6, which reflects the basic concepts underlying the *iterative and incremental life-cycle model* [Jacobson, Booch, and Rumbaugh, 1999]. The figure shows the development of an information system in four increments, labeled Increment A, Increment B, Increment C, and Increment D. The horizontal axis is time and the vertical axis is person-hours (one person-hour is the amount of work that one person can do in one hour), so the shaded area under each curve is the total effort for that increment.

It is important to appreciate that Figure 2.6 depicts just one possible way that an information system can be decomposed into increments. Another information system may be constructed in just two increments, whereas a third may require 13. Furthermore, the figure is not intended to be an accurate representation of precisely how an information system is developed. Instead, it shows how the emphasis changes from iteration to iteration.

The sequential phases of Figure 2.1 are artificial constructs. Instead, as explicitly reflected in Figure 2.6, we must acknowledge that the requirements *workflow* (activities), analysis workflow, design workflow, implementation workflow, and test workflow are carried out over the entire life cycle. However, there are times when one workflow predominates over the other four.

For example, at the beginning of the life cycle, the information system team extracts an initial set of requirements. In other words, at the beginning of the iterative and incremental life cycle, the requirements workflow predominates. It is certain that the requirements artifacts will be extended and modified during the remainder of the life cycle. It is equally certain that during that later time the other four workflows (analysis, design, implementation, and test) will predominate. In other words, the requirements workflow is the major workflow at the beginning of the life cycle, but its relative importance decreases thereafter. Conversely, the implementation and test workflows occupy far more of the time of the information system development team toward the end of the life cycle than they do at the beginning.

Of course, planning and documentation activities are performed throughout the iterative and incremental life cycle. Furthermore, testing is a major activity during each iteration, and particularly at the end of each iteration. In addition, the information system as a whole is thoroughly tested once it has been completed; at that time, testing and then modifying the implementation in the light of the outcome of the various tests is virtually the sole activity of the software team. This is reflected in the test workflow of Figure 2.6.

Figure 2.6 shows four increments. Consider Increment A, depicted by the column on the left. At the beginning of this increment, the requirements team members determine the client's requirements. Once most of the requirements have been determined, the first version of part of the analysis can be started. When sufficient progress has been made with the analysis, the first version of the design can be started. Even some coding often is done during this first increment, perhaps in the form of a prototype to test the feasibility of part of the proposed information system—prototyping is discussed in greater detail in Chapter 7. Finally, as previously mentioned, planning, testing, and documentation activities start on Day One and continue from then on, until the information system is finally delivered to the client.

Similarly, the primary concentration during Increment B is on the requirements and analysis workflows, and then the design workflow. The emphasis during Increment C is first on the design workflow and then on the implementation workflow and test workflow. Finally, during Increment D, the implementation workflow and test workflow dominate.

Roughly one-fifth of the total effort is devoted to the requirements and analysis workflows (together), another one-fifth to the design workflow, and about three-fifths to the implementation workflow [Grady, 1994]. The relative total sizes of the shaded areas in Figure 2.6 reflect these values.

There is iteration during each increment of Figure 2.6. This is shown in Figure 2.7, which depicts three iterations during Increment B. (Figure 2.7 is an enlarged view of the second column of Figure 2.6). As shown in Figure 2.7, each iteration involves all five workflows, but again in varying proportions.

Again, it must be stressed that Figure 2.7 is not intended to show that every increment involves exactly three iterations. The number of iterations will vary from increment to increment. The purpose of Figure 2.7 is to show the iteration within each increment and to

FIGURE 2.7

The Three Iterations of Increment B of the Iterative and Incremental Model of Figure 2.6

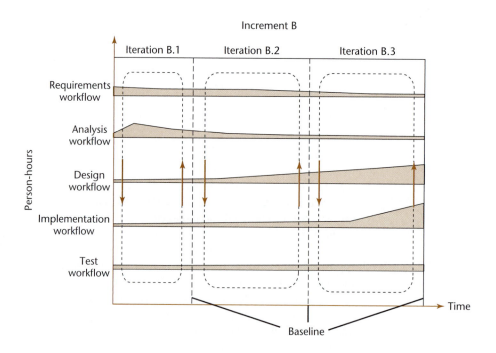

repeat that all five workflows (requirements, analysis, design, implementation, and testing, together with planning and documentation) are carried out during almost every iteration, although in varying proportions each time.

As previously explained, Figure 2.6 reflects the incrementation that is intrinsic to the development of every information system. Figure 2.7 explicitly displays the iteration that underlies incrementation. Specifically, Figure 2.7 depicts three consecutive iterative steps, as opposed to one large incrementation. In more detail, Iteration B.1 consists of requirements, analysis, design, implementation, and test workflows, represented by the leftmost dashed rectangle with rounded corners. The iteration continues until the artifacts of each of the five workflows are satisfactory.

Next, all five sets of artifacts are iterated in Iteration B.2. This second iteration is similar in nature to the first. That is, the requirements artifacts are improved, which in turn triggers improvements to the analysis artifacts, and so on, as reflected in the second iteration of Figure 2.7, and similarly for the third iteration.

The process of iteration and incrementation starts at the beginning of Increment A and continues until the end of Increment D. The completed information system is then installed on the client's computer.

2.6 Iteration: The Newton-Raphson Algorithm

Suppose we are shipwrecked on an uninhabited desert island and we decide to wile away the time waiting to be rescued by computing the square root of some number N to 10 decimal places. Unfortunately, desert islands don't have computers—in fact, the only tool we have at our disposal is a stick with which we can do arithmetic in the sand.

The 300-year-old Newton-Raphson algorithm [Raphson, 1690] can be used to compute the square root of a number using iteration. To show how it works, suppose we want to compute $\sqrt{654321}$. We have to start with an initial estimate. Any positive number will do, so we pick 100. We plug this value into the Newton-Raphson formula

$$\text{newValue} = \frac{1}{2}\left(\text{currentValue} + \frac{N}{\text{currentValue}}\right)$$

where N is the number whose square root we want (654321 in this case), currentValue is our current estimate of $\sqrt{654321}$, and newValue is the new estimate, as returned by the Newton-Raphson formula.

We chose 100 as our initial estimate, so currentValue = 100. We plug this value into the right-hand side of the formula, and we obtain for our first iteration

$$\text{newValue} = \frac{1}{2}\left(100 + \frac{654321}{100}\right) = 3321.605$$

Now our estimate of $\sqrt{654321}$ is 3321.605, so this becomes our next currentValue. We plug the value 3321.605 into the right-hand side of the Newton-Raphson formula. Our second iteration is then

$$\text{newValue} = \frac{1}{2}\left(3321.605 + \frac{654321}{3321.605}\right) = 1759.2972036147$$

That is, our estimate of $\sqrt{654321}$ is now 1759.2972036147, so this becomes our next currentValue. Again we plug this value into the right-hand side of the formula for our third iteration.

Continuing in this way we obtain the following results for newValue:

Third iteration:	newValue = 1065.6095067231
Fourth iteration:	newValue = 839.8220030538
Fifth iteration:	newValue = 809.4703353028
Sixth iteration:	newValue = 808.9013065842
Seventh iteration:	newValue = 808.9011064401
Eighth iteration:	newValue = 808.9011064401

The seventh iteration and the eighth iteration are the same, to 10 decimal places, so the Newton-Raphson algorithm has converged to the square root of 654321 to the desired degree of precision.

The Newton-Raphson algorithm is a good example of iteration because, no matter what positive starting value we choose, the formula soon homes in on the square root of the number we have chosen.

Unfortunately, iteration is not always quite as successful when we build information systems. It sometimes happens that (say) the seventh iteration of the design is worse than the sixth iteration. When this happens, we discard the seventh iteration, go back to the previous (sixth) iteration, and iterate again, obtaining what we hope will be a better seventh iteration—we do not need to start from the beginning.

2.7   The Winburg Mini Case Study Revisited

Figure 2.8 shows the evolution tree model of the Winburg mini case study (Figure 2.2) superimposed on the iterative and incremental life-cycle model (the test workflow is not shown because the evolution tree model assumes continual testing, as explained in Section 1.4.). Figure 2.8 sheds additional light on the concept of incrementation:

- Increment A corresponds to Episode 1, Increment B corresponds to Episode 2, and so on.

- From the viewpoint of the iterative and incremental life-cycle model, two of the increments do not include all four workflows. In more detail, Increment B (Episode 2) includes only the implementation workflow and Increment D (Episode 4) includes only the design workflow and the implementation workflow. It is not a requirement of the iterative and incremental life-cycle model that every workflow be performed during every increment.

- Furthermore, in Figure 2.6 most of the requirements workflow is performed in Increment A and Increment B, whereas in Figure 2.8 it is performed in Increment A and Increment C. Also, in Figure 2.6 most of the analysis is performed in Increment B, whereas in Figure 2.8 the analysis workflow is performed in Increment A and Increment C. This accentuates that neither Figure 2.6 nor Figure 2.8 represents the way every information system is built. Instead, each figure shows the way that one particular information system is built, highlighting the underlying iteration and incrementation.

- The small size and abrupt termination of the implementation workflow during Increment B (Episode 2) of Figure 2.8 shows that Implementation$_2$ was not completed. The more lightly shaded piece reflects the part of the implementation workflow that was not performed.

- The three dashed arrows of the evolution tree model show that each increment constitutes maintenance of the previous increment. More precisely, in this example, each is an instance of corrective maintenance. That is, each increment corrects faults in the

FIGURE 2.8   The Evolution Tree Model for the Winburg Mini Case Study (Figure 2.2) Superimposed on the Iterative and Incremental Life-Cycle Model

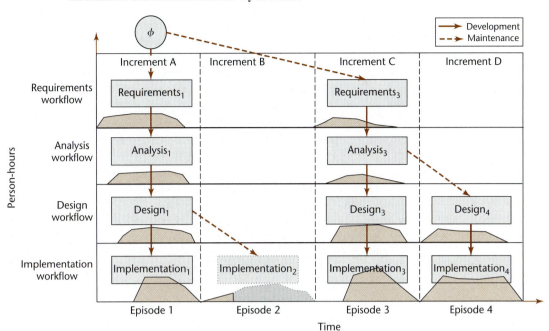

previous increment. As previously explained, Increment B (Episode 2) corrects the implementation workflow by replacing double-precision numbers with the usual single-precision numbers. Increment C (Episode 3) corrects the requirements by stipulating that a faster image recognition algorithm be used. Corresponding changes are then made to the analysis workflow, design workflow, and implementation workflow. Finally, in Increment D (Episode 4) the design is changed to improve the overall accuracy. Corresponding changes have to be made to the implementation workflow.

2.8   Other Aspects of Iteration and Incrementation

Another way of looking at iteration and incrementation is that the project as a whole is divided into smaller mini projects (or increments). Each mini project extends the requirements, analysis, design, implementation, and testing artifacts. Finally, the resulting set of artifacts constitutes the complete information system.

In fact, during each mini project we do more than just extend the artifacts. We check that each artifact is correct (the test workflow) and make any necessary changes to the relevant artifacts. This process of checking and modifying, then rechecking and remodifying, and so on, is clearly iterative in nature. It continues until we are satisfied with all the artifacts of the current mini project (or increment). At this time, we proceed to the next mini project.

Comparing Figure 2.3 (the waterfall model) with Figure 2.7 (view of the iterations within Increment B) shows that each iteration can be viewed as a small but complete waterfall life-cycle model. That is, during each iteration we go through the traditional requirements, analysis, design, and implementation phases on a specific portion of the information system. From this viewpoint, the iterative and incremental life-cycle model of Figures 2.6 and 2.7 can be viewed as a consecutive series of waterfall models.

• One advantage of the iterative and incremental life-cycle model is that there are multiple opportunities for checking that the computerized information system is correct. Every iteration incorporates the test workflow, so every iteration is another chance to check all the artifacts that has been developed up to this point. The later that faults are detected and corrected, the more money it costs, as shown in Figure 2.4. Unlike the traditional waterfall life-cycle model, each of the many iterations of the iterative and incremental life-cycle model offers a further opportunity to find faults and then correct them, thereby saving money.

• A second advantage of the iterative and incremental life-cycle model is that the robustness of the underlying architecture can be determined relatively early in the life cycle. The *architecture* of an information system includes the various component modules and how they fit together. An analogy is the architecture of a cathedral, which might be described as Romanesque, Gothic, or Baroque, among other possibilities. Similarly, the architecture of an information system might be described as object oriented (Chapter 3), pipes and filters (UNIX or Linux components), or client–server (with a central server providing file storage for a network of client computers, as described in Chapter 18). The architecture of an information system that is developed using the iterative and incremental life-cycle model has to have the property that it can be extended continually (and, if necessary, easily changed) to incorporate the next increment. The property of being able to handle such extensions and changes without falling apart is called *robustness*. Robustness is an important quality during development of an information system; it is vital during maintenance. Thus, if an information system is to last through the usual 12, 15, or more years of maintenance, the underlying architecture has to be robust. When an iterative and incremental life-cycle model is used, it soon becomes apparent whether or not the architecture is robust. If, in the course of incorporating (say) the third increment, it is clear that the information system developed to date will have to be drastically reorganized and large parts rewritten, then it is clear that the architecture is not sufficiently robust. The client will have to decide whether to abandon the project or start again from scratch. Another possibility is to redesign the architecture to be more robust and then reuse as much of the current artifacts as possible before proceeding to the next increment. There is another reason why a robust architecture is so important— the moving target problem (Section 2.4). We know that the client's requirements will change, either because of growth within the client's organization or because the client keeps changing his or her mind as to what the target information system has to do. The more robust the architecture, the more resilient to change the information system will be. It is not possible to design an architecture that can cope with too many drastic changes. But if the required changes are reasonable in scope, a robust architecture should be capable of incorporating those changes without having to be drastically restructured.

• A third advantage of the life-cycle model of Figures 2.6 and 2.7 is that an iterative and incremental life-cycle model enables us to mitigate *risks* early. There are always risks involved in software development and maintenance. In the Winburg mini case study, for example, the original image recognition algorithm was not fast enough; there is always the risk that a completed information system will not meet its time constraints. Developing an information system incrementally enables us to mitigate such risks early in the life cycle. For example, suppose that a new local area network (LAN) is being developed, and there is concern that the current network hardware will be inadequate for the new information system. Then, the first one or two iterations will be directed toward constructing those parts of the information system that interface with the network hardware. If it turns out that, contrary to the developers' fears, the network has the necessary capabilities, the developers can proceed with the project, confident that this risk has been mitigated. On the other hand, if the network indeed cannot cope with the additional traffic that the new LAN will generate, this will be reported to the client early in the life cycle, when only a small proportion of the budget has been spent. The client can now decide whether to cancel the project, extend the capabilities of the existing network, buy a new and more powerful network, or take some other action.

• A fourth advantage of the iterative and incremental life-cycle model is that we always have a working version of the information system. Suppose that an information system is developed using the traditional life-cycle model of Figure 2.1. That is, the requirements of the system as a whole are determined, then the specifications of the system as a whole are drawn up, and so on. Only at the very end of the project is there a working version of the information system. In contrast, when the iterative and incremental life-cycle model is used, at the end of each iteration there is a working version of part of the overall target information system. The client and the intended users can experiment with that version and determine what changes are needed to ensure that the future complete implementation will meet their needs. These changes can be made to a subsequent increment, and the client and users can then determine if further changes are needed. A variation on this is to deliver partial versions of the information system not only for the purpose of experimentation, but also to smooth the introduction of the new information system in the client organization. Change is almost always perceived as a threat. All too frequently, users fear that the introduction of a new information system within the workplace will result in their losing their jobs to a computer. However, introducing an information system gradually can have two positive benefits. First, the understandable fear of being replaced by a computer will be diminished. Second, it is generally easier to learn the functionality of a complex information system if that functionality is introduced stepwise over a period of months, rather than as a whole.

2.9   Managing Iteration and Incrementation

At first glance, the iterative and incremental life-cycle model of Figures 2.6 and 2.7 looks totally chaotic. Instead of the orderly progression from requirements to implementation of the waterfall life-cycle model (Figure 2.3), it appears that developers can do whatever they like, perhaps some coding in the morning, an hour or two of design after lunch, and then half an hour of specifying before going home. That is *not* the case. On the contrary, the iterative and incremental life-cycle model is as regimented as the waterfall model because, as previously pointed out, developing an information system using the iterative and incremental life-cycle model is nothing more or less than developing a series of smaller information systems all using the waterfall life-cycle model.

In more detail, as shown in Figure 2.3, developing an information system using the waterfall life-cycle model means successively performing the requirements, analysis, design, and implementation phases (in that order) on the information system as a whole. If a problem is encountered, the feedback loops of Figure 2.3 (dashed arrows) are followed, that is, iteration (maintenance) is performed. Now, if the same information system is developed using the iterative and incremental model, the information system is treated as a set of increments. For each increment in turn, the requirements, analysis, design, and implementation phases (in that order) are repeatedly performed *on that increment* until it is clear that no further iteration is needed. In other words, the project as a whole is broken up into a series of waterfall mini projects. During each mini project, iteration is performed as needed, as shown in Figure 2.7. Thus, the reason that it was stated in the previous paragraph that the iterative and incremental life-cycle model is as regimented as the waterfall model is because the iterative and incremental life-cycle model *is* the waterfall model, applied successively.

In this chapter, the real-world life-cycle model was compared to the idealized life-cycle model of Chapter 1. This chapter is concluded by looking at real-world maintenance, as opposed to the idealized maintenance of Chapter 1.

2.10   Maintenance Revisited

Traditionally, constructing an information system consists of two stages: development, followed by maintenance once the information system has been installed on the client's computer. That is, all information system workflows before installation traditionally are considered development, and everything after installation is considered to be maintenance.

This simplistic view of constructing an information system can have unexpected consequences. For example, suppose that a fault is detected and corrected in an information system one day after the information system was installed. In terms of the traditional definition, this activity constitutes maintenance. But if that same fault had been detected and corrected one day before installation, the identical activity would have to be considered development.

Now suppose that an information system has just been installed, but the client wants the functionality of the information system to be increased. Traditionally, that would be described as "perfective maintenance." However, suppose that the client wants the same change to be made just before the information system is installed, an instance of the moving target problem (Section 2.4). Again, there is no difference whatsoever between the nature of the two workflows, but traditionally the one is considered development, the other perfective maintenance.

The reason for these and similar unexpected consequences is that the traditional definition of maintenance is *temporal*. That is, traditional maintenance is defined in terms of the time at which the activity is performed. In contrast, in 1995 the International Standards Organization and International Electrotechnical Commission defined maintenance *operationally* [ISO/IEC 12207, 1995]. That is, nowadays maintenance is defined as the process that occurs when an information system artifact is modified because of a problem or because of a need for improvement or adaptation. That is, in terms of the ISO/IEC definition, maintenance occurs whenever an information system is modified, regardless of whether this takes place before or after installation of the information system.

Thus, in the rest of this book, *development* refers to the process of creating information system artifacts, whereas *maintenance* refers to modifying those artifacts.

Key Terms

architecture, *30*	life-cycle model, *20*	temporal, *32*
artifact, *20*	Miller's Law, *24*	waterfall model, *20*
baseline, *20*	moving target problem, *23*	workflow, *25*
evolution tree model, *19*	operational, *32*	
incrementation, *24*	regression fault, *23*	
iteration, *24*	risk, *30*	
iterative and incremental	robustness, *30*	
life-cycle model, *25*	stepwise refinement, *24*	

Review Questions for Chapter 2

1. What is an evolution tree model?
2. What is a life-cycle model?
3. Describe the waterfall model.
4. What is an artifact?
5. What is a baseline?
6. Why are so many changes to an information system needed?
7. Why is it important to detect and correct faults early in the life cycle?
8. What is the moving target problem?
9. What is a regression fault?
10. What is Miller's Law?
11. Distinguish clearly between iteration and incrementation.
12. What is a workflow?
13. What is the architecture of an information system?
14. Define robustness.
15. Give four advantages of the iterative and incremental life-cycle model.
16. What is the modern definition of maintenance?

Problems

2.1 Fifteen months after delivery, a fault is detected in the management information system at the Port Cronwick Zoo. The cost of fixing the fault is $18,730. The cause of the fault is an ambiguous sentence in the specification document. Approximately how much would it have cost to have corrected the fault during the analysis phase?

2.2 Suppose that the fault in Problem 2.1 had been detected during the implementation phase. Approximately how much would it have cost to have fixed it then?

2.3 You are the president of an organization that develops large-scale information systems. You show Figure 2.4 to your employees, urging them to find faults early in the information system life cycle. Someone responds that it is unreasonable to expect anyone to remove faults before they have entered the information system. For example, how can anyone remove a fault during the design phase if the fault in question is a coding fault? What do you reply?

2.4 Represent the Winburg mini case study of Section 2.3 using the waterfall model. Is this more or less effective than the evolution tree model? Explain.

2.5 Assume that the programmer in the Winburg mini case study had used single-precision numbers from the beginning. Draw the resulting evolution tree model.

2.6 What is the connection between Miller's Law and stepwise refinement?

2.7 Use a spreadsheet to compute square roots using the Newton-Raphson algorithm. (Hint: Use one column for the successive values of currentValue. The first entry in that column is your initial guess, and each successive entry is computed using the formula in Section 2.6.) Convince yourself that the Newton-Raphson algorithm works no matter how bad your initial guess is, provided that it is positive.

2.8 Does stepwise refinement correspond to iteration or to incrementation?

2.9 How are a workflow, an artifact, and a baseline related?

2.10 What is the connection between the waterfall life-cycle model and the iterative and incremental life-cycle model?

2.11 Is there a way of reconciling the traditional temporal definition of maintenance with the operational definition we now use?

References

Boehm, B. W. "Software Engineering, R & D Trends and Defense Needs." In *Research Directions in Software Technology,* ed. P. Wegner. Cambridge, MA: The MIT Press, 1979.

Grady, R. B. "Successfully Applying Software Metrics." *IEEE Computer* 27 (September 1994), pp. 18–25.

International Organization for Standardization, International Electrotechnical Commission. "ISO/IEC 12207:1995, Information Technology—Software Life-Cycle Processes." Geneva: ISO/IEC, 1995.

Jacobson, I.; G. Booch; and J. Rumbaugh. *The Unified Software Development Process.* Reading, MA: Addison Wesley, 1999.

Kan, S. H.; S. D. Dull; D. N. Amundson; R. J. Lindner; and R. J. Hedger. "AS/400 Software Quality Management." *IBM Systems Journal* 33, no. 1 (1994), pp. 62–88.

Miller, G. A. "The Magical Number Seven, Plus or Minus Two: Some Limits on Our Capacity for Processing Information." *Psychological Review* 63 (March 1956), pp. 81–97. Reprinted at www.well.com/user/smalin/miller.html.

Raphson, J. *Analysis Æquationum Universalis, seu ad Æquationes Algebraicas Resolvendas Methodus Generalis, & Expedita, ex Nova Infinitarum Serierum Methodo, Deducta ac Demonstrata* [Latin]. London: Abel Swalle, 1690. (A more recent reference, in English, is wwwmaths.murdoch.edu.au/units/m161/unitnotes/ch6.pdf.)

Royce, W. W. "Managing the Development of Large Software Systems: Concepts and Techniques." *1970 WESCON Technical Papers, Western Electronic Show and Convention,* Los Angeles, August 1970, pp. A/1-1–A/1-9. Reprinted in *Proceedings of the 11th International Conference on Software Engineering,* Pittsburgh, May 1989, pp. 328–38.

Tomer, A., and S. R. Schach. "The Evolution Tree: A Maintenance-Oriented Software Development Model." *Proceedings of the Fourth European Conference on Software Maintenance and Reengineering (CSMR 2000).* Zürich, Switzerland, February/March 2000, pp. 209–14.

3

The Object-Oriented Paradigm, UML, and the Unified Process

Learning Objectives

After studying this chapter, you should be able to:

- Distinguish in detail between objects and classes.
- Explain inheritance.
- Distinguish between generalization, aggregation, and association.
- Explain the need for information hiding.
- Draw simple UML class diagrams.
- Outline some key ideas underlying the Unified Process.

Thousands of different programming languages have been proposed. However, the vast majority of them have never been used for real-world programs. At the other end of the scale, more programs have been implemented in COBOL (COmmon Business Oriented Language) than in all other languages combined [McClendon, 2002]. Other popular languages include FORTRAN and C. Newer languages such as Java and C++ increasingly are being used.

But regardless of their popularity, all programming languages have one feature in common: They can be used to develop information systems that perform *operations* on *data*. For example, consider a banking information system. If we look at the code in which the program is implemented, we will see data items with names such as accountBalance and operations with names such as deposit and withdraw. Operation deposit increases the value of accountBalance, whereas operation withdraw decreases it. (See Just in Case You Wanted to Know Box 3.1 for an explanation of the unusual way that accountBalance is spelled.)

Now consider a hospital information system. The names of data items within the program include patientName, patientDateOfBirth, patientGender, and so on. Operations include admitPatient, dischargePatient, updatePatientMedicalRecord, and so on.

In almost all programming languages, the name of a data item (or *variable*) cannot include a blank space. Thus, a name like account balance would not be valid. In COBOL, the actual name of that variable would be account-balance. When programming in a traditional programming language like C, the name would be account_balance. C++ and Java programmers would use the name accountBalance; in many object-oriented languages, the convention is to use uppercase letters to mark the beginning of a new part of the name of a data item. The rule forbidding blank spaces in names also applies to the name of an operation in a program.

This is a book on systems analysis and design, not programming. Nevertheless, for both data and operations, the C++ and Java name convention has been used to make it easier to learn object-oriented programming in due course.

The relationship between the operations of a computer program and the data on which that computer program operates is a key aspect of this chapter.

3.1   The Traditional Paradigm versus the Object-Oriented Paradigm

The Computer Age started in the 1940s, so information systems are hardly more than 50 years old. Developing information systems was initially considered a creative skill; individuality was highly prized. However, as larger computers became more affordable, it became possible to run an information system that was too big to be developed by just one person if that information system was to be completed by the deadline specified by the client. Instead, information systems began to be developed by teams. Furthermore, skill specialization became the industry norm. That is, instead of information technology professionals being involved in all the phases, two separate professions arose: programmer and systems analyst. Systems analysts performed the requirements, analysis, and design phases and programmers did the implementation.

Once information system development had become a team activity, it was necessary to decide on a common approach; individuality had become a liability. In this book, the first systematic approach to information system development is called the *traditional methodology* or *traditional paradigm;* it sometimes also is called the *structured methodology* or *structured paradigm.* (For more on the words *methodology* and *paradigm,* see Just in Case You Wanted to Know Box 3.2.)

Initially, the traditional paradigm was extremely successful. After all, this was the first time that information system development had been treated as a methodical discipline rather than a creative activity. The quality of information systems improved, and the delivery of information systems on time and within budget started to become a realistic expectation.

During the 1980s, the cost of hardware continued to decrease as fast as it had done during the preceding decades. As larger computers became more affordable, the size of information systems continued to grow. But the larger the information system, the less successful the traditional paradigm proved to be. Finally, the information system community realized that the traditional paradigm had outlived its usefulness, and something more effective was needed.

What had gone wrong? Why did the traditional paradigm work so well with *small-scale* information systems (that is, implementations with approximately 5,000 lines of code) but

In the 1970s, the word *methodology* began to be used in the sense of "a way of developing an information system"; the word actually means the science of methods. Then, in the 1980s, the word *paradigm* became a major buzzword of the business world, as in the phrase, "It's a whole new paradigm." The information systems industry soon started using the word *paradigm* in the phrases *object-oriented paradigm* and *traditional* (or *classical*) *paradigm* to mean "a style of information system development." This was another unfortunate choice of terminology, because a paradigm means a model or a pattern.

FIGURE 3.1

The Outcomes of 280,000 Development Projects Completed in 2000

not with *medium-scale* (about 50,000 lines of code) or *large-scale* information systems (at least 500,000 lines of code)? The two basic building blocks of an information system are the operations performed by that information system and the data on which the operations are performed. The traditional paradigm essentially ignores the data in favor of the operations. In contrast, the object-oriented paradigm pays equal attention to operations and data.

Just how bad is the current situation? The Standish Group is a research firm that analyzes the development of information systems. Their study of 280,000 development projects completed in 2000, as reported in *SOFTWAREmag.com* [2001], is summarized in Figure 3.1. Only 28 percent of the projects were successfully completed, whereas 23 percent were canceled before completion or were never implemented. The remaining 49 percent of the projects were completed and installed on the client's computer. However, those projects were over budget, late, and/or had fewer features and functionality than initially specified. In other words, during 2000, only about one information system development project in four was successful.

The financial and legal implications of unsuccessful projects are horrendous. A survey conducted by the Cutter Consortium [Cutter, 2002] revealed that an astounding 78 percent of the information technology organizations surveyed have been involved in disputes that ended up in litigation.

For those organizations that reported having entered into litigation:

- In 67 percent of the disputes, the functionality or performance of the information system as delivered did not meet up to the claims of the developers.
- In 56 percent of the disputes, the promised delivery date slipped several times.
- In 45 percent of the disputes, the defects were so severe that the information system was unusable.

Disturbing figures like these are encouraging more and more organizations to change to the object-oriented paradigm.

3.2   Objects and Classes

King George III reigned over Great Britain from 1760 to 1820. Figure 3.2 depicts King George III. Similarly, King Louis XVI ruled France from 1774 to 1792, as shown in Figure 3.3.

Comparing Figures 3.2 and 3.3, it is clear that all kings have something in common. Kings have names; they rule a specific country; and their reign starts in a specific year and ends in a specific year.

Let the set of all kings be called **King Class. King Class** is depicted in Figure 3.4. The four items in the middle box of Figure 3.4—name, country, startOfReign, endOfReign— are called the *attributes* of **King Class.** The bottom box is for operations performed on or by kings. For example, kings reign; if a king wants to stop reigning, he has to abdicate. (In object-oriented programming languages, operations are distinguished from attributes in that operations are followed by a pair of parentheses, ( ), as reflected in Figure 3.4.)

All the *objects* in a class have the same set of attributes and the same set of operations; they differ only in the values of their respective attributes. As shown in Figure 3.2, the attributes of King George III are {King George III, Great Britain, 1760, 1820}. And as shown in Figure 3.3, the attributes of King Louis XVI are {King Louis XVI, France, 1774, 1792}.

We say that King George III *is an instance of* **King Class,** and so is King Louis XVI. That is, a *class* is a set of related objects and, conversely, an *object* is an instance of a class.

Now we consider shoes. A shoe has a color (black, brown); it comes in a size (3, 8½, 9½, 14) and a width (AAA, C, E); it has a style (stiletto heel, wingtip, moccasin, penny loafer); and it is made of some material (leather, plastic). **Shoe Class** is the name of the set of all shoes. Figure 3.5 shows **Shoe Class.** The middle box shows the attributes of a shoe: color, size, width, style, and material. The bottom box shows the operations that can be performed on a shoe. That is, we can putOn a shoe, takeOff that shoe, and shine the shoe.

FIGURE 3.2
King George III of Great Britain

name:	King George III
country:	Great Britain
startOfReign:	1760
endOfReign:	1820

FIGURE 3.3
King Louis XVI of France

name:	King Louis XVI
country:	France
startOfReign:	1774
endOfReign:	1792

FIGURE 3.4
UML Depiction of King Class

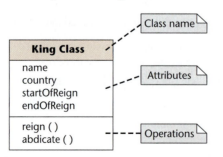

FIGURE 3.5
UML Depiction of Shoe Class

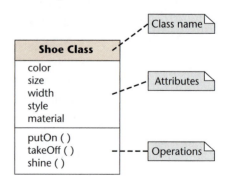

Until recently, the most popular object-oriented analysis and design methodologies were object modeling technique (OMT) [Rumbaugh et al., 1991] and Grady Booch's method [Booch, 1994]. OMT was developed by Jim Rumbaugh and his team at the General Electric Research and Development Center in Schenectady, New York, whereas Grady Booch developed his method at Rational, Inc., in Santa Clara, California. All object-oriented analysis techniques essentially are equivalent, as are all object-oriented design techniques, so the differences between OMT and Booch's method are small. Nevertheless, there always was a friendly rivalry between the supporters of the two camps.

This changed in October 1994 when Rumbaugh joined Booch at Rational. The two methodologists immediately began to work together to develop a methodology that would combine OMT and Booch's method. When a preliminary version of their work was published, it was pointed out that they had not developed a methodology but merely a notation for representing an object-oriented information system. The name *Unified Methodology* was quickly changed to *Unified Modeling Language* (UML). In 1995 they were joined at Rational by Ivar Jacobson, author of the Objectory methodology. Booch, Jacobson, and Rumbaugh, affectionately called "the Three Amigos" (after the 1986 John Landis movie *Three Amigos!* with Chevy Chase and Steve Martin), then worked together. Version 1.0 of UML, published in 1997, took the information system world by storm. Until then, there had been no universally accepted notation for the requirements, analysis, and design of an information system. Almost overnight UML was used all over the world. The Object Management Group (OMG), an association of the world's leading companies in object technology, took the responsibility of organizing an international standard for UML, so that every systems analyst would use the same version of UML, thereby promoting communication between individuals within an organization as well as between companies worldwide. UML [Booch, Rumbaugh, and Jacobson, 1999] is today the unquestioned international standard notation for representing information systems.

An orchestral score shows which musical instruments are needed to play the piece, the notes each instrument is to play, and when it is to play them, as well as a whole host of technical information such as the key signature, tempo, loudness, and so on.

Could this information be given in English rather than a diagram? Probably, but it would be impossible to play music from such a description. For example, there is no way a pianist and a violinist could perform a piece described as follows: "The music is in march time, in the key of B minor. The first bar begins with the A above middle C on the violin (a quarter note). While this note is being played, the pianist plays a chord consisting of seven notes. The right hand plays the following four notes: E sharp above middle C . . ."

It is clear that there are some fields where a textual description simply cannot replace a diagram. Music is one such field; systems analysis and design is another. And for systems analysis and design, the best available modeling language today is UML.

A class is represented in UML (see Just in Case You Wanted to Know Box 3.3) as shown in Figure 3.5. There are three boxes. The top box contains the name of the class, in **Boldface with the Words in the Name Starting with Uppercase Letters.** The middle box contains the names of the attributes of an instance of that class, that is, of an object of that type. The lowest box contains the names of the operations that can be performed by or on an instance of that class, that is, by or on an object of that type.

FIGURE 3.6
Another Way of
Depicting a Class
Using UML

FIGURE 3.7
Yet Another Way of
Depicting a Class Using
UML

As previously stated, **King Class** is the set or *class* of all kings. Conversely, a **king** (object) is a member or instance of **King Class.** (The UML convention is to write the name of an object in **boldface underlined but all in lowercase letters.**) Similarly, a **shoe** is an instance of **Shoe Class.**

As pointed out, Figure 3.5 has three boxes. In fact, UML is an extremely flexible modeling language. If we are not concerned with the attributes and operations of a class, we can represent it as shown in Figure 3.6. And if we are not even concerned about the name of the class, then we can represent it as shown in Figure 3.7.

An important property of classes is inheritance, which is explained in the next section.

3.3   Inheritance

Consider the following example: A maintenance programmer has been assigned the task of modifying an e-commerce information system. Cardholder Clothing Company currently allows individuals to order clothes over the World Wide Web and charge the purchase to a credit card. The information system supports a wide variety of different types of functionality, including communication over the World Wide Web; the intricacies of selling clothing, which usually comes in different sizes and colors; Web security; various shipping options; and the charging of the purchase to a credit card.

Figure 3.8 depicts **Credit Card Class.** It has three attributes (data items): cardNumber, nameOfCardholder, and expirationDate. There are four operations that can be performed on the data: validateTransaction, chargeTransactionToCard, creditPaymentToCard, and printMonthlyStatement. In the interests of clarity, Figure 3.8 has been kept as simple as possible; in an actual credit card information system, there would be many more attributes and many more operations.

If a customer wants to pay for his or her clothing using a credit card, the Cardholder Clothing Company information system sends a message to the information system running on the credit card company's computer requesting to have the purchase approved and payment credited to Cardholder Clothing Company. Suppose that the credit card company now wishes to extend that information system so that it can handle debit cards as well as credit cards. The major difference between a credit card and a debit card is that a credit card allows the cardholder to spend up to the credit limit on that card, whereas a debit card is tied to a bank account, so the cardholder can spend up to the current balance in his or her bank account.

On the other hand, debit card accounts and credit card accounts have many features in common. For example, they both have attributes cardNumber, nameOfCardholder, and

FIGURE 3.8
UML Representation
of Credit Card Class

Credit Card Class
cardNumber nameOfCardholder expirationDate
validateTransaction ( ) chargeTransactionToCard ( ) creditPaymentToCard ( ) printMonthlyStatement ( )

FIGURE 3.9
UML Diagram
Showing That Credit
Card Class Is a
Subclass of Bank
Card Class

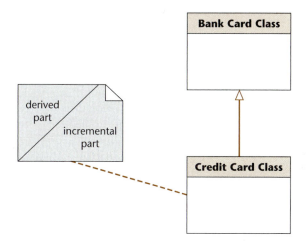

expirationDate. Instead of treating **Debit Card Class** and **Credit Card Class** as two independent classes, it makes more sense to treat each of them as a special case of a more general class, **Bank Card Class.**

Consider Figure 3.9. The figure shows that **Bank Card Class** is a class and that **Credit Card Class** is a subclass of **Bank Card Class.** The open triangle below **Bank Card Class** tells us that **Credit Card Class** inherits from **Bank Card Class.** That is, **Credit Card Class** has all the features of **Bank Card Class** (the *derived part*) but, in addition, has features of its own that are specific to **Credit Card Class** (the *incremental part*), such as a creditLimit.

There are numerous different ways of describing the relationship shown in Figure 3.9. Some of them are

- **Credit Card Class** is a *subclass* of **Bank Card Class.**
- **Bank Card Class** is a *superclass* of **Credit Card Class.**
- **Credit Card Class** is a *specialization* of **Bank Card Class.**
- **Bank Card Class** is a *generalization* of **Credit Card Class.**
- **Credit Card Class** *is a* **Bank Card Class.**
- **Bank Card Class** is the *base class;* **Credit Card Class** is the *derived class*.
- **Bank Card Class** is the *parent class;* **Credit Card Class** is the *child class*.
- **Credit Card Class** *inherits* from **Bank Card Class.**

These ideas can be extended to **Debit Card Class** as well. Consider Figure 3.10, which shows that **Credit Card Class** and **Debit Card Class** are both subclasses of **Bank Card Class.** That is, **Credit Card Class** and **Debit Card Class** both inherit all the

FIGURE 3.10
UML Diagram
Showing That Credit
Card Class and
Debit Card Class
Are Subclasses of
Bank Card Class

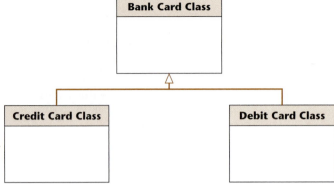

FIGURE 3.11
Inheritance
Hierarchy

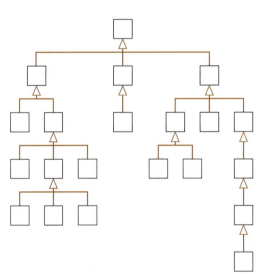

attributes and all the operations of **Bank Card Class,** such as nameOfCardholder and validateTransaction. In addition, however, **Credit Card Class** and **Debit Card Class** have attributes and operations of their own. For example, **Credit Card Class** has attribute creditLimit and **Debit Card Class** has operation determineAccountBalance.

Inheritance is a required feature of object orientation. Consequently, if a programming language does not support inheritance, it cannot possibly be an object-oriented programming language. It therefore follows that all object-oriented programming languages, including Smalltalk, C++, Ada 95, and Java, support inheritance.

Inheritance need not involve just two classes. Consider Figure 3.11, which shows an inheritance hierarchy. An attribute or operation declared in the topmost class in the figure will be inherited by all the other classes in the figure. However, an attribute or operation declared in one of the classes at the lowest level in the figure will be local to that class; inheritance is a top-down relationship.

3.4 Generalization, Aggregation, and Association

In this chapter one relationship between classes, inheritance, has been described. Inheritance is an implementation of the *generalization* relationship. But other kinds of relationships are possible between classes.

For example, a car is constructed from a chassis, engine, wheels, and seats. When performing the object-oriented analysis of a car manufacturing plant, the systems analysts may decide to define classes **Chassis Class, Engine Class, Wheels Class,** and **Seats Class. Car Class** is then defined as the aggregate of the four component classes. This is illustrated in Figure 3.12. The *aggregation* relationship is appropriate when class **X** "consists of" classes **Y** and **Z**. As shown in Figure 3.12, in UML aggregation is represented by an open diamond.

The most general relationship between classes is association (for example, aggregation is a special case of association). *Association* is an arbitrary relationship between two classes. For example, a radiologist may consult a lawyer regarding the interpretation of a contract with a hospital. This example of association is depicted in Figure 3.13 using UML notation. The solid triangle points from the radiologist to the lawyer to show that this UML diagram models a radiologist consulting a lawyer, as opposed to the situation where a lawyer with a broken leg consults a radiologist. This latter situation is depicted in Figure 3.14. Here the solid triangle points in the other direction. Using the solid triangle in this way is called *navigation* in UML.

FIGURE 3.12   **Aggregation Example**

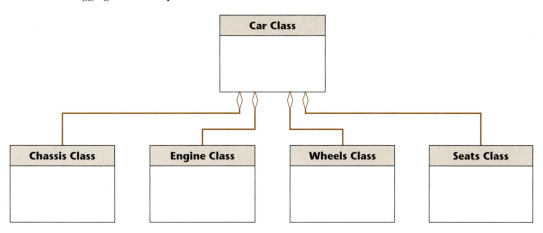

FIGURE 3.13
Association
Example 1
A radiologist consults
a lawyer

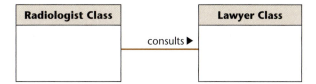

FIGURE 3.14
Association
Example 2
A lawyer consults a
radiologist

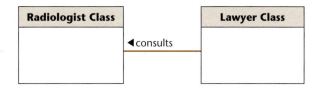

3.5   Examples of UML Class Modeling

The following examples illustrate different relationships between classes.

Example 1   Use UML to model ice cream factories. Here, the only information given is the name of the class to be modeled. Accordingly, Figure 3.15 is an adequate representation. However, if we anticipate that the model will be extended by adding attributes and operations to **Ice Cream Factory Class,** we may prefer to model ice cream factories as shown in Figure 3.16 or Figure 3.17—both are also valid UML models.

Figures 3.4 through 3.17 are all UML class diagrams. In general, a *class diagram* depicts classes and their interrelationships; boxes inside the outer box for the class name, attributes, and operations are optional.

Example 2   Use UML to model human beings. Humans consist of a head, a torso, two arms, and two legs. Because a human being comprises the specified components, aggregation is the relationship needed to model **Human Being Class.** This is shown in Figure 3.18.

Example 3   Extend Example 2 to model the fact that a leg consists of a thigh, a calf, and a foot. Figure 3.19 reflects the additional aggregation. Figure 3.19 shows two types of aggregation. First there is there the aggregation of Example 2 (humans consist of a head, a torso, two arms, and two legs). In addition, the bottom right-hand of the figure exhibits further aggregation, namely, that a leg consists of a thigh, a calf, and a foot.

FIGURE 3.15

A UML Class Diagram for Modeling an Ice Cream Factory

Ice Cream Factory Class

FIGURE 3.16

Another UML Class Diagram for Modeling an Ice Cream Factory

Ice Cream Factory Class

FIGURE 3.17

Yet Another UML Class Diagram for Modeling an Ice Cream Factory

Ice Cream Factory Class

FIGURE 3.18   **A UML Class Diagram Modeling Human Beings Using Aggregation**

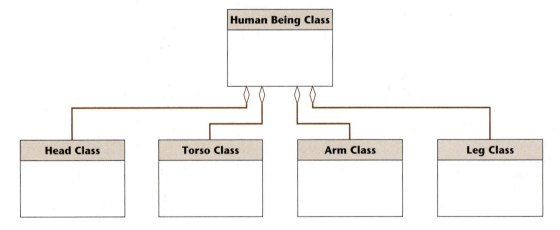

FIGURE 3.19   Extension of Figure 3.18 to Model Additional Aggregation

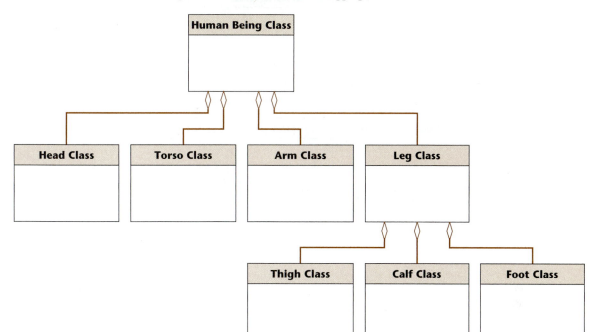

Example 4   Use UML to model human beings, where a human consists of a head, a torso, and four limbs, and a limb is either an arm or a leg.

The fact that a limb is either an arm or leg implies that generalization (inheritance) is needed to model this part of **Human Being Class.** That is, arms and legs have something in common; they are both instances of limbs. On the other hand, they also have specific features of their own. This is the type of situation in which generalization is usually used for modeling a system. The result is shown in Figure 3.20, which reflects both aggregation and generalization.

Figures 3.18 and 3.20 both model human beings. How is it possible to have two different models of the same thing? A model is a representation of reality, and different representations are needed to model different aspects of that reality. Both Figure 3.18 and Figure 3.20 show that a human being consists of a head, torso, arms, and legs. In addition, however, Figure 3.20 reflects the fact that arms and legs are instances of limbs. Again, this does not mean that Figure 3.18 is wrong; only that Figure 3.18 does not model limbs as a class.

There are usually a number of different but correct ways of modeling an information system. In general, all the ways reflect the major aspects of the information system, but each individual model highlights one or more specific details of the system. It is up to the systems analysts to decide which model is most appropriate for the purpose of computerizing that information system.

Example 5   Use UML to model systems analysts listening to the radio. At first sight, there is no relationship between a systems analyst and a radio. However, the example states that the systems analyst is listening to the radio. This is an example of the association relationship. It is modeled in Figure 3.21. The black solid triangle to the right of the association name is superfluous; after all, a radio cannot listen to a systems analyst. Nevertheless, it is good practice to insert the navigation arrow.

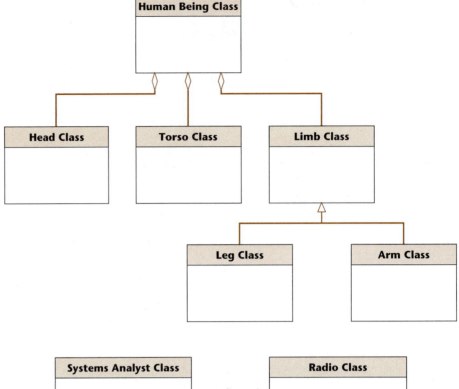

FIGURE 3.20
A UML Class
Diagram for
Modeling Human
Beings Using
Aggregation and
Generalization

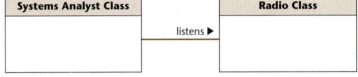

FIGURE 3.21
A UML Class
Diagram Showing
Association and
Navigation

3.6 Information Hiding

The importance of maintenance has repeatedly been stressed. *Information hiding* is a way of enhancing maintainability by making implementation details invisible outside an object.

For example, suppose that accountBalance is an attribute of **Bank Account Class.** There are a number of different ways that accountBalance can be implemented; for example, as an integer (the total amount in cents) or as a dollar amount with two decimal places for the cents. Object-oriented languages allow an attribute to be described as **private,** that is, invisible outside the object. The sole way that accountBalance can then be accessed is via an operation.

For example, suppose that the two operations of **Bank Account Class** are deposit and withdraw, as shown in Figure 3.22. The only way of changing the accountBalance of a **bank account** object is by *sending a message* to one of the two operations of **bank account.**

At first sight, this approach seems to be ridiculous. After all, it seems to be better to modify the account balance directly, rather than to send a message to an operation to make the modification. The critical point is: What happens if, in the course of maintaining the information system, there is a change in the way that accountBalance is stored? If implementation details are invisible outside **Bank Account Class** (that is, if we have information hiding), then changing the implementation cannot affect any other part of the information

FIGURE 3.22
Class Bank Account
with Information
Hiding

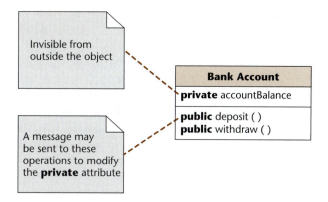

system in any way whatsoever. Recall that a regression fault is a fault in one part of the code caused by making a change in an apparently unrelated part of the code. When there is information hiding, there cannot be regression faults. So, a major advantage of having information hiding is that the resulting information system consists of essentially independent classes that communicate by sending messages to their own operations and the operations of other classes.

Information hiding can be achieved using **private** attributes. When an attribute is declared to be **private,** it can be accessed only from inside the class in which it is declared. Conversely, if an attribute is declared to be **public,** it can be accessed from anywhere inside the information system. The same rules apply to operations. So, by making accountBalance **private** and deposit and withdraw **public,** operations deposit and withdraw can be invoked from anywhere in the information system, but invoking those two operations is the only way of changing the value of attribute accountBalance.

The concept of *responsibility-driven design* goes beyond information hiding. Consider the following situation, derived from an example in Budd [1991]. Suppose that you live in Sacramento, California, and you want to send a Mother's Day bouquet to your mother in Chicago. One strategy would be to consult the Chicago Yellow Pages (on the World Wide Web), determine which florist is located closest to your mother's apartment, and place your order with that florist. A more convenient way is to order the flowers at 1-800-flowers.com, leaving the total responsibility for delivering the flowers to that company. It is irrelevant where 1-800-flowers.com is physically located, or which florist will be given your order to deliver. In any event, the company will not divulge that information, an instance of information hiding.

In the same way, when a message is sent to an object, not only is it totally irrelevant how that request is carried out, but the module that sends the message is not even permitted to know how the attributes of the object are implemented. Furthermore, the total responsibility for carrying out all aspects of the message rests with the object receiving the message. This is the principle of responsibility-driven design.

Now that we know the fundamentals of the object-oriented paradigm, we are ready to learn about the Unified Process, the methodology that we will be using for object-oriented analysis and design.

3.7   The Unified Process

As pointed out earlier in this chapter, problems arose when large information systems were developed using the traditional paradigm, especially when the resulting information systems were maintained. By the mid-1980s it had become clear that a better paradigm was needed. The object-oriented paradigm proved to be the solution. Over the next 10 years, more than 50 different object-oriented methodologies were published. Three of the most successful methodologies were Booch's method, Jacobson's Objectory, and Rumbaugh's OMT.

We have already met Booch, Jacobson, and Rumbaugh within the context of UML (see Just in Case You Wanted to Know Box 3.3). Taking the information system world by storm with UML was not enough for the Three Amigos. Their next endeavor was to publish a complete object-oriented analysis and design methodology that unified their three separate methodologies. This unified methodology was first called the *Rational Unified Process* (RUP); the word "Rational" is in the name of the methodology not because the Three Amigos considered all other approaches to be irrational, but because at that time all three of them were senior managers at Rational, Inc. In their book on RUP [Jacobson, Booch, and Rumbaugh, 1999], the name *Unified Software Development Process* (or *USDP*) was used. The term *Unified Process* is generally used today, for brevity.

The Unified Process is more than just a series of steps that, if followed, will result in the construction of an information system. In fact, no such single "one size fits all" methodology could exist, because there is such a wide variety of different types of information systems. For example, there are many different application domains, such as banking, insurance, or manufacturing. Also, a methodology for rushing a COTS package to market ahead of its competitors will be different from one used for constructing a high-security electronic funds transfer network. In addition, the skills of information technology professionals can vary widely.

The Unified Process can be viewed as an adaptable methodology. That is, it has to be modified for the specific information system to be developed. This book is concerned with information systems that are small enough to be developed by a team of three students during the semester or quarter. Accordingly, that is the version of the Unified Process that is presented here. At the same time, however, mention is made of how the Unified Process has to be modified when using it to develop a large information system. The goal is to get a thorough understanding of how to develop smaller information systems, but also to appreciate the issues that need to be addressed when larger information systems are constructed.

3.8 Iteration and Incrementation within the Unified Process

The Unified Process is a modeling technique. A *model* is a set of UML diagrams that represent one or more aspects of the information system we want to develop. Recall that UML stands for unified *modeling* language. That is, UML is the tool that we use to represent (model) the target information system. A major reason for using a graphical representation like UML is best expressed by the old proverb, namely, a picture is worth a thousand words. UML diagrams enable information technology professionals to communicate with one another more quickly and more accurately than if only verbal descriptions were used.

The Unified Process is an iterative and incremental methodology (iteration and incrementation were discussed in Section 2.5). Each workflow consists of a number of steps, and, in order to carry out that workflow, the steps of the workflow, are repeated until the members of the development team are satisfied that they have an accurate UML model of the information system they want to develop. That is, even the most experienced information technology professionals iterate and reiterate until they are finally satisfied that the UML diagrams are correct. The implication is that systems analysts, no matter how outstanding they may be, almost never get the object-oriented analysis and design right the first time. How can this be?

The nature of information systems is such that everything is developed iteratively and incrementally. After all, we are human beings, and therefore we are subject to Miller's Law (Section 2.5). That is, we cannot think about everything at the same time, so we handle just seven or so chunks (units of information) at once. Then, when we consider the next set of chunks, we gain more knowledge about the information system we want to develop, and we modify our UML diagrams in the light of this additional information. We continue in this way until eventually we are satisfied that all our models for a given workflow are correct. In other words, we start by drawing the best UML diagrams we can using the knowledge we have at the beginning of the workflow. Then, as we gain more knowledge about the real-world system we are modeling, we make our diagrams more accurate (iteration) and we extend them (incrementation). Thus, no matter how experienced and skillful a systems analyst may be, he or she repeatedly iterates and increments again and again until satisfied that the UML diagrams are an accurate representation of the information system to be developed.

It would be nice if, at the end of a course on the Unified Process, every student would be able to perform the systems analysis and design for the large, complex information systems for which the Unified Process was developed. Unfortunately, there are three reasons why this is not feasible.

- First, just as it is not possible to become an expert on calculus or a foreign language in just one course, gaining proficiency in the Unified Process requires extensive study and, more importantly, unending practice in object-oriented analysis and design.

- Second, as previously stated, the Unified Process is intended for use in developing large, complex information systems. In order to be able to handle the many intricacies of such information systems, the Unified Process is itself large. It would be hard for an instructor to cover every aspect of the Unified Process in a single course.

- Third, in a first course on the Unified Process, it is necessary to present a case study that illustrates the features of the Unified Process. In order to illustrate the features that apply to huge information systems, such a case study would have to be huge. For example, the specification document alone might well be over 1,000 pages long.

For these three reasons, in this book most, but not all, of the Unified Process is presented. The material is adequate for performing the systems analysis for the sorts of information systems developed by a professional systems analyst in the first few years of his or her career. That is, the topics covered by this book are sufficient for developing information systems of reasonable size and complexity. In order to work on large-scale information systems, what is needed is experience, followed by training in the more complicated aspects of the Unified Process.

Key Terms

aggregation, *43*	inheritance, *42*	subclass, *41*
association, *43*	is a, *41*	superclass, *41*
attribute, *38*	methodology, *36*	traditional
base class, *41*	model, *48*	methodology, *36*
class diagram, *44*	object, *38*	traditional paradigm, *36*
data, *35*	object-oriented paradigm, *37*	Unified Modeling
derived class, *41*	operation, *35*	Language, *39*
derived part, *41*	paradigm, *36*	Unified Process, *48*
generalization, *41*	responsibility-driven	
incremental part, *41*	design, *47*	
information hiding, *46*	sending a message, *46*	

Review Questions for Chapter 3

1. Why was the traditional paradigm initially so successful?
2. Why did the traditional paradigm prove to be a disappointment?
3. Distinguish carefully between an object and a class.
4. What is the connection between inheritance and generalization?
5. What is the connection between aggregation and association?
6. What is information hiding?
7. What is responsibility-driven design?
8. What is unified by the Unified Process?
9. Is the Unified Process iterative or incremental?

Problems

3.1   People are either left-handed, right-handed, or ambidextrous. Model this using UML. That is, draw a box to represent the class of people in general, another box to represent the class of left-handed people, and so on. Then indicate the relationships between the various classes. Be sure to label your classes.

3.2   Use UML to model personal computers, where a personal computer consists of a CPU, a monitor, a keyboard, and a printer.

3.3   Use UML to model the relationship in which insurance policies insure policyholders.

3.4   Use UML to model the relationship in which policyholders pay their premiums for their insurance policies.

3.5   Use UML to model apartments. A rental unit has a monthly rental; a condominium has a purchase price.

3.6   Use UML to model the following features of books in a public library: The books are categorized into two groups: reserve books (which cannot be borrowed) and circulating books, which can be issued to a borrower and are then returned. Circulating books are classified as children's books or general books. For a children's book, the recommended age range of readers is specified. Every library book has an accession number.

3.7   Use UML to model bank statements. The entries in a bank statement include the balance at the beginning of the period covered by the statement; the number, date, and amount of each check; the date and amount of each deposit; and the balance at the end of the period covered by the statement.

References

Booch, G. *Object-Oriented Analysis and Design with Applications.* 2nd ed. Redwood City, CA: Benjamin/Cummings, 1994.

Booch, G.; J. Rumbaugh; and I. Jacobson. *The UML Users Guide.* Reading, MA: Addison Wesley, 1999.

Budd, T. A. *An Introduction to Object-Oriented Programming.* Reading, MA: Addison Wesley, 1991.

Cutter Consortium. "78% of IT Organizations Have Litigated." *The Cutter Edge,* April 9, 2002. Available at www.cutter.com/research/2002/edge020409.html.

Jacobson, I.; G. Booch; and J. Rumbaugh. *The Unified Software Development Process.* Reading, MA: Addison Wesley, 1999.

McClendon, J. "Is COBOL Dying?" *About Legacy Coding* 4, no. 3 (June 2002). Available at www.legacycoding.com.

Rumbaugh, J.; M. Blaha; W. Premerlani; F. Eddy; and W. Lorensen. *Object-Oriented Modeling and Design.* Englewood Cliffs, NJ: Prentice Hall, 1991.

Schach, S. R. *Software Engineering with Java.* Burr Ridge, IL: Richard D. Irwin, 1997.

SOFTWAREmag.com, February/March 2001. Available at www.softwaremag.com/archive/2001feb/CollaborativeMgt.html (February 26, 2001).

Part 2

UML and the Unified Process

Part 2 of this book consists of seven chapters all with just one aim: to teach you how to perform object-oriented systems analysis and design using UML and the Unified Process. To promote learning, each step is taught three ways. First, an explanation is given of what has to be done. Then, the step is demonstrated by applying it to the Osbert Oglesby case study. And finally it is applied to the MSG Foundation case study.

Chapters 4 and 5 are devoted to *The Requirements Workflow*. More precisely, the steps are explained and applied to the Osbert Oglesby case study in Chapter 4 and to the MSG Foundation case study in Chapter 5.

Similarly, Chapters 6 and 7 describe *The Object-Oriented Analysis Workflow*. Again, each step is explained and then applied to the Osbert Oglesby case study in Chapter 6 and to the MSG Foundation case study in Chapter 7.

The Object-Oriented Design Workflow is the title of Chapter 8. The third workflow is described and then applied to both case studies using the same approach as in Chapters 4 through 7.

Then everything is put together in Chapter 9, *The Workflows and Phases of the Unified Process,* to ensure a thorough understanding of the Unified Process and how to apply it.

The Unified Modeling Language (UML) is the universal graphical language for describing an information system. Enough UML is informally introduced in Chapters 3 through 9 for the purposes of understanding this book and doing all the problems, including the systems analysis and design projects and the term project. However, in order to be a successful information technology professional, a deeper knowledge of UML is needed. That is why Chapter 10, *More on UML,* is included in Part 2.

Chapter 4

The Requirements Workflow I

Learning Objectives

After studying this chapter, you should be able to:

- Perform the requirements workflow.
- Draw up the initial business model.
- Draw up the requirements.

The one sentence that no systems analyst ever wants to hear from a client is: "I know that this is the information system I asked for, but it's not what I wanted." In other words, when performing the *requirements workflow,* the primary task of the systems analysts on the requirements team is to work with the client and future users of the information system to determine what the client needs, which may not be what the client says that he or she wants. (For another insight into this issue, see Just in Case You Wanted to Know Box 4.1.)

4.1 Determining What the Client Needs

At first sight, determining what the client needs is straightforward—we simply ask him or her. However, there are two reasons why this direct approach usually does not work very well.

First, the client may not appreciate what is going on in his or her own organization. For example, it is no use for a client to ask for a faster information system when the real reason why the current information system has such a long response time is that the database is badly designed. What needs to be done is to reorganize and improve the way that data are stored in the current information system. A new information system will be just as slow. Or, if the client operates an unprofitable chain of retail stores, the client may ask for a financial management information system that reflects such items as sales, salaries, accounts payable, and accounts receivable. Such an information system will be of little use if the real reason for the losses is shrinkage (shoplifting and theft by employees). If that is the case, then a stock control system rather than a financial management information system is required.

But the major reason why a client so often asks for the wrong information system is that information systems are complex. It is difficult enough for a systems analyst to visualize an information system and its functionality; the problem is far worse for the client, who usually is not an expert in information technology.

Without the assistance of a skilled systems analyst, the client may be a poor source of information regarding what needs to be developed. On the other hand, unless we communicate with our client, we have no way of finding out what really is needed.

The solution is to obtain initial information from the client and future users of the target information system and to use this initial information as an input to the Unified Process. By following the steps of the Unified Process, the systems analyst will be able to determine the client's real needs.

4.2   Overview of the Requirements Workflow

The Unified Process is iterative [Jacobson, Booch, and Rumbaugh, 1999]. In the case of the requirements workflow, the first step is to gain an understanding of the *application domain* (or *domain,* for short); that is, the specific business environment in which the information system is to operate. The domain could be banking, automobile manufacturing, or book retailing. Once we understand the domain, we build a *business model;* that is, we use UML diagrams to describe the client's business processes. We use the business model to determine what the client's requirements are. Then we iterate (recall from Section 2.5 that to "iterate" means to repeat).

In other words, we start with an initial understanding of the domain and use that information to build the initial business model. This initial business model is then utilized to draw up an initial set of the client's requirements. Then, in the light of what we have learned about the client's requirements, we gain a deeper understanding of the domain and utilize this knowledge to refine our business model and hence the client's requirements. This iteration continues until we are satisfied with the set of requirements we have produced. At this point, the iteration stops. This is expressed in the flowchart of Figure 4.1.

The process of discovering the client's requirements is termed *requirements elicitation* (or *requirements capture*). Once we have drawn up the initial set of requirements, the process of refining and extending them is termed *requirements analysis.*

FIGURE 4.1
Flowchart of the
Requirements
Workflow

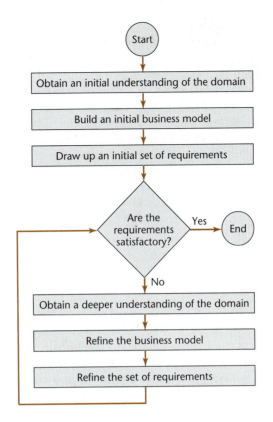

4.3   Understanding the Domain

The first task of every member of the requirements team is to become familiar with the application domain, unless he or she already has experience in that area. It is particularly important to use correct terminology when communicating with the client and potential users of the information system. After all, it is hard to be taken seriously by someone working in a specific domain unless the systems analyst uses the vocabulary of that domain. More importantly, use of an inappropriate word may lead to a misunderstanding, eventually resulting in a faulty information system being delivered. The same problem can arise if the members of the requirements team do not understand the subtleties of the terminology of the domain.

For example, to a layperson words such as *check, draft,* and *money order* may appear to have the same meaning, but to a banker they are distinct terms. If a systems analyst does not appreciate that the banker is using these three terms in a precise way and if the banker assumes that the systems analyst is familiar with the distinctions between the terms, the systems analyst may treat the three terms as equivalent; the resulting banking information system may contain faults that result in violations of banking regulations or serious financial losses for the bank. All information technology professionals hope that the output of every information system will be scrutinized carefully by a human being before decisions are made based on that information system, but the growing popular faith in computers means that it is distinctly unwise to rely on the likelihood of such a review being made. So, it is by no means far-fetched that a misunderstanding in terminology could lead to information technology professionals being sued for negligence.

One way to address the problem with terminology is to construct a *glossary,* a list of technical words used in the domain, together with their meaning. The initial entries are inserted into the glossary while the team members are busy learning as much as they can about the application domain. Then the glossary is updated whenever the members of the requirements team encounter new terminology. Not only does such a glossary reduce confusion between client and systems analysts, it also is useful in lessening misunderstandings between the members of the systems analysis team.

The easiest way to construct a glossary is to use a spreadsheet or word processor. We set up two columns and enter each technical word (in alphabetical order) in the left-hand column, and its meaning in the right-hand column. Every so often, the glossary can be printed out and distributed to team members, or downloaded to a PDA (such as a Palm Pilot).

We see how this first step in the requirements workflow is performed by considering the Osbert Oglesby case study, the first of the two running case studies in this book.

4.4   Initial Understanding of the Domain: Osbert Oglesby Case Study

Osbert Oglesby, the noted art dealer, needs an information system to assist him in buying and selling paintings. Osbert specializes in buying and selling French Impressionist paintings. However, he will buy virtually any painting if he thinks he can make a profit when he sells it in his gallery, *Les Objets d'Orient.*

We will interview Osbert in order to obtain detailed information about every aspect of his business. But before we do this, we need to get domain knowledge, that is, information about paintings and the art business in general. This background information will enable us to understand any technical terms used by Osbert when we meet with him. In addition, if we know something about the art business in general before we meet with him, we will be able to flag any apparently unusual aspects of the way that Osbert does business. We will then ask him about those items. In some instances, we may be able suggest that, by following what most of his competitors are doing, he may be able to increase the profitability of his business. But in other cases, unique aspects of Osbert's business practices may be giving him a competitive edge. It is vital to incorporate all such cases into the computerized information system we will build for him.

In order to learn about paintings and the art business in general we visit the websites of two major art museums and two art dealers. We discover that there are many different ways of categorizing paintings. One is to consider the *medium,* that is, the material with which the artwork was painted. The most popular medium is oil-based paint (oil), but some smaller paintings are done in water-based paint (watercolor). *Other media* are sometimes used, including pencil, pastel, and crayon, but less frequently. We put this information in our glossary, shown in Figure 4.2.

A second way of categorizing a painting is by the *subject.* The most popular subject is a person (portrait). Other common subjects include nature (landscape) and an inanimate object such as a vase of flowers, a bowl of fruit, and so on (still life). This information is added to our glossary.

A third categorization is the *quality* of the painting. A painting of undoubted excellence is termed a masterpiece. A masterwork is an inferior painting by an artist who previously or subsequently has painted a masterpiece. However, the vast majority of paintings are neither masterpieces nor masterworks. This information is also put into the glossary, as shown in Figure 4.2.

FIGURE 4.2

The Initial Glossary of the Osbert Oglesby Information System

Landscape	A painting of a scene in nature.
Masterpiece	A painting of undoubted excellence.
Masterwork	An inferior painting by an artist who previously or subsequently has painted a masterpiece.
Medium	A classification criterion. The material with which an artwork is painted. *See also:* oil, watercolor.
Oil	A medium. Abbreviation for "oil-based paint."
Other painting	A painting that is neither a masterpiece nor a masterwork.
Other subject	A subject that is not a landscape, a portrait, or a still life.
Portrait	A painting of one or more people.
Quality	A classification criterion. A painting is classified as a masterpiece, masterwork, or other painting, depending on its quality.
Still life	A painting of inanimate objects.
Subject	A classification criterion. Subjects include landscape, portrait, and still life.
Watercolor	A medium. Abbreviation for "water-based paint."

4.5   Business Model

Once the requirements team members have acquired familiarity with the domain, the next step is to build the initial business model. A *business model* is a description of the business processes of an organization. For example, some of the business processes of a bank include accepting deposits from clients, loaning money to clients, and making investments.

The reason for building a business model first is that the business model gives us an understanding of the client's business as a whole. With this knowledge we can advise the client as to which portions of the information system to computerize. Alternatively, if our task is to extend an existing computerized information system, we have to understand the existing business as a whole to determine how to incorporate the extension, and to learn what parts, if any, of the existing information system need to be modified in order to add the new piece.

In order to build a business model, a systems analyst needs to obtain a detailed understanding of the various business processes. For instance, the business processes of a catering business include buying ingredients, preparing food, and serving meals. These processes are now *refined;* that is, analyzed in greater detail. For example, the process "buying ingredients" consists of four subprocesses:

- The caterer orders the ingredients from a wholesaler.
- The wholesaler delivers the ingredients to the caterer.
- The wholesaler sends an invoice to the caterer.
- The caterer pays the invoice.

A number of different techniques can be used to obtain the information needed to build the business model, primarily interviewing.

4.5.1   Interviewing

The members of the requirements team meet with members of the client organization until they are convinced that they have elicited all relevant information from the client and future users of the target information system.

There are two basic types of question. A closed-ended question requires a specific answer. For example, the client might be asked how many salespeople the company employs or how fast a response time is required. Open-ended questions are asked to encourage the person being interviewed to speak out. For instance, asking the client, "Why is your current information system unsatisfactory?" may explain many aspects of the client's approach to business. Some of these facts might not come to light if the question were closed-ended.

Similarly, there are two basic types of interview, namely, structured and unstructured. In a *structured interview,* specific preplanned questions are asked, frequently closed-ended. In an *unstructured interview,* the interviewer may start with one or two prepared closed-ended questions, but subsequent questions are posed in response to the answers he or she receives from the person being interviewed. Many of these subsequent questions are likely to be open-ended in nature in order to provide the interviewer with wide-ranging information.

At the same time, it is not a good idea if the interview is too unstructured. Saying to the client, "Tell me about your business" is unlikely to yield much relevant knowledge. In other words, questions should be posed in such a way as to encourage the person being interviewed to give wide-ranging answers, but always within the context of the specific information needed by the interviewer.

Conducting a good interview is not always easy. First, the interviewer must be fully familiar with the application domain. Second, there is no point in interviewing a member of the client organization if the interviewer has already made up his or her mind regarding the client's needs. No matter what the interviewer has previously been told or what he or she has learned by other means, the interviewer must approach every interview with the intention of listening carefully to what the person being interviewed has to say, while firmly suppressing any preconceived notions regarding the client company or the needs of the clients and the potential users of the information system to be developed.

After the interview is concluded, the interviewer must prepare a written report outlining the results of the interview. It is strongly advisable to give a copy of the report to the person who was interviewed; he or she may want to clarify certain statements or add overlooked items.

4.5.2   Other Techniques

Interviewing is the primary technique for obtaining information for the business model. That is, interviewing is always performed, no matter what other techniques may be used in addition. In this section some other techniques are described that may be used in conjunction with interviewing.

One way of gaining knowledge about the activities of the client organization is to send a *questionnaire* to the relevant members of the client organization. This technique is useful when the opinions of, say, hundreds of individuals need to be determined. Furthermore, a carefully thought-out written answer from an employee of the client organization may be more accurate than an immediate verbal response to a question posed by an interviewer. However, an unstructured interview conducted by a methodical interviewer who listens carefully and poses questions that elicit amplifications of initial responses usually yields far better information than a thoughtfully worded questionnaire. Because questionnaires are preplanned, there is no way that a question can be posed in response to an answer.

A different way of eliciting requirements is to examine the various *forms* used by the business. For example, a form in a printing works might reflect press number, paper roll size, humidity, ink temperature, paper tension, and so on. The various fields in this form shed light on the flow of print jobs and the relative importance of the steps in the printing process. Other documents, such as operating procedures and job descriptions, also can be powerful tools for finding out exactly what is done and how. Such comprehensive information regarding how the client currently does business can be extraordinarily helpful in determining the client's needs. Therefore, a good systems analyst will carefully study client documentation, treating it as a priceless source of information that can lead to an accurate assessment of the client's needs.

Another way of obtaining such information is by *direct observation* of the users, that is, by members of the requirements team observing and writing down the actions of the employees while they perform their duties. A modern version of this technique is to set up *videotape cameras* within the workplace to record (with the prior written permission of those being observed) exactly what is being done. One difficulty of this technique is that it can take a long time to analyze the tapes. In general, one or more members of the requirements team has to spend an hour playing back the tape for every hour that the cameras record. This time is in addition to what is needed to assess what was observed. More seriously, this technique has been known to backfire badly because employees may view the cameras as an unwarranted invasion of privacy. It is important that the requirements team have the full cooperation of all employees; it can be extremely difficult to obtain the necessary information if people feel threatened or harassed. The possible risks should be considered carefully before introducing cameras or, for that matter, taking any other action that has the potential to annoy or even anger employees.

4.5.3   Use Cases

As stated in Section 3.8, a *model* is a set of UML diagrams that represent one or more aspects of the information system we want to develop. (The "ML" in UML stands for *modeling language*). A primary UML diagram used in business modeling is the use case.

A *use case* models an interaction between the information system itself and the users of that information system (*actors*). For example, Figure 4.3 depicts a use case from a banking information system. There are two actors, represented by the UML stick figures, namely, the **Customer** and the **Teller.** The label inside the oval describes the business activity represented by the use case, in this instance Withdraw Money.

Another way of looking at a use case is that it shows the interaction between the information system and the environment in which the information system operates. That is, an actor is a member of the world outside the information system, whereas the rectangle in the use case represents the information system itself.

It is usually easy to identify an actor. An actor is frequently a user of the information system. In the case of a banking information system, the users of that information system are the customers of the bank and the staff of the bank, including tellers, managers, and so on. In general, an actor plays a role with regard to the information system. This role may be as a user of the information system. However, an initiator of a use case or someone who plays a critical part in a use case is also playing a role and is therefore regarded as an actor, irrespective of whether that person is also a user of the information system. An example of this is given in Section 4.6.

A user of the system can play more than one role. For example, a customer of the bank can be a **Borrower** (when he or she takes out a loan) or a **Lender** (when he or she deposits money in the bank—a bank makes much of its profits by investing the money deposited by

FIGURE 4.3
The Withdraw
Money Use Case
of the Banking
Information System

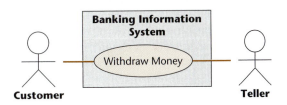

FIGURE 4.4
Generalization of
Medical Staff

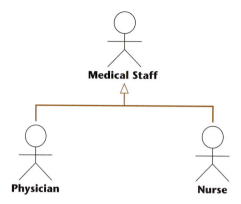

customers). Conversely, one actor can participate in multiple use cases. For example, a **Borrower** may be an actor in the Borrow Money use case, the Pay Interest on Loan use case, and the Repay Loan Principal use case. Also, the actor **Borrower** may stand for many thousands of bank customers.

An actor need not be a human being. Recall that an actor is a user of an information system, and in many cases another information system can be a user. For example, consider Cardholder Clothing Company, the e-commerce information system of Section 3.3 that allows purchasers to pay for clothing with credit cards. The Cardholder Clothing Company information system has to interact with the credit card company information system. That is, the credit card company information system is an actor from the viewpoint of the Cardholder Clothing Company information system. Similarly, the Cardholder Clothing Company information system is an actor from the viewpoint of the credit card company information system.

As previously stated, identification of actors is easy. Generally, the only difficulty that arises in this part of the Unified Process is that an overzealous systems analyst sometimes identifies overlapping actors. For example, in a hospital information system, having a use case with actor **Nurse** and a different use case with actor **Medical Staff** is not a good idea, because all nurses are medical staff, but there are medical staff (such as physicians) who are not nurses. It would be better either to have actors **Physician** and **Nurse**. Alternatively, we can define actor **Medical Staff** with two specializations, **Physician** and **Nurse**. This is depicted in Figure 4.4. In Section 3.4, it was pointed out that inheritance is a special case of generalization. Generalization was applied to classes in Section 3.3. Figure 4.4 shows how generalization applies to actors. The most general actor is **Medical Staff.** Two special cases of **Medical Staff** are **Physician** and **Nurse.**

We now construct the business model of the Osbert Oglesby information system.

4.6   Initial Business Model: Osbert Oglesby Case Study

Osbert Oglesby's business has been successful for many years. Lately, however, Osbert has been losing money. A management consultant has analyzed the business records and concluded that Osbert has been overpaying for paintings. The consultant has advised Osbert to acquire an information system, running on a laptop computer, that he can use to determine the maximum price he should pay for a painting. Osbert can then use the information system in his gallery or take the computer with him when viewing a painting in a customer's home or office. (Osbert refers to his customers as his clients. In this book, however, the word *client* is used for the person who wants an information system to be developed, in this case, Osbert.)

The management consultant has derived an *algorithm* (or formula) that the information system should use to determine the maximum price that Osbert should pay for a painting. At this point in the methodology, it is too soon to look at the formula. After all, Miller's Law applies to all human beings. We are limited in the number of chunks of information we can handle at any one time. At this time all we have to know are Osbert's business processes; the details of the formula can wait until a later iteration.

Osbert wants the information system to compute the maximum price he should offer when buying a painting. Unlike most dealers, Osbert does not believe in bargaining. When he wants to buy a painting, the amount he offers is his final price. Similarly, when he sells a painting, he does not negotiate; the price he names is again the final price.

In addition, Osbert would like the information system to detect new trends in the art market as soon as possible. He is particularly interested in determining when higher prices than expected are consistently paid for a particular artist's work, so that he can buy up paintings by that artist before others notice the trend.

In order to be able to flag when the sales price of a painting is higher than what Osbert expected when he purchased the painting, the information system needs to keep a record of all purchases and all sales. Given that this information will be available on his computer, Osbert might want to utilize it to get additional information about his business. In particular, there are two reports that Osbert currently produces by hand: a report showing all paintings purchased during the past year and another report showing all sales during the past year. At only a small additional cost, the information system will be able to produce these two reports on demand.

In other words, what Osbert *wants* is an information system that computes the highest price that he should pay for a painting and also can detect new art trends. What he *needs* is an information system that, in addition, provides reports on purchases and sales. If the systems analysts had not determined this fact up front, the developers would have had to incorporate the additional functionality after the information system had been delivered. Bearing in mind Figure 2.4, the result would have been that the cost of the information system as modified would have been considerably more than the agreed cost of the original system. Furthermore, Osbert would have been most unhappy with the developers. At best, he would consider them to be incompetent; at worst, he would view the additional charge he would have to pay as evidence of their dishonesty. Alternatively, the developers might have agreed to incorporate the reports free of charge. However, this would have meant that they would have made a significant loss on the information system for Osbert. Fortunately, however, the systems analysts obviated the problem by determining Osbert's real needs.

Now that we have the initial data we need, we can build the initial business model. Osbert has three business activities: he buys paintings, he sells paintings, and he produces reports, all manually. The corresponding Buy a Painting, Sell a Painting, and Produce a Report use cases are shown in Figures 4.5, 4.6, and 4.7. The only person who uses the current (manual) information system is Osbert, so he is an actor in all three use cases.

FIGURE 4.5   **The Buy a Painting Use Case of the Initial Business Model of the Osbert Oglesby Information System**

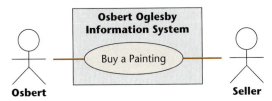

FIGURE 4.6   **The Sell a Painting Use Case of the Initial Business Model of the Osbert Oglesby Information System**

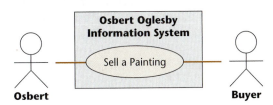

FIGURE 4.7
The Produce a
Report Use Case of
the Initial Business
Model of the
Osbert Oglesby
Information System

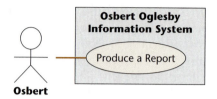

FIGURE 4.8
The Use-Case
Diagram of the Initial
Business Model of the
Osbert Oglesby
Information System

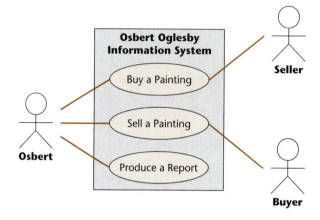

FIGURE 4.9
The Description of
the Buy a Painting
Use Case of the Initial
Business Model of the
Osbert Oglesby
Information System

Brief Description

The `Buy a Painting` use case enables Osbert Oglesby
to buy a painting.

Step-by-Step Description

Not applicable at this initial stage.

FIGURE 4.10
The Description of
the Sell a Painting
Use Case of the Initial
Business Model of the
Osbert Oglesby
Information System

Brief Description

The `Sell a Painting` use case enables Osbert Oglesby
to sell a painting.

Step-by-Step Description

Not applicable at this initial stage.

However, as stated in the previous section, someone who initiates a use case is also an actor, as is someone who plays a critical part. The customer may initiate the Buy a Painting or the Sell a Painting use case, and certainly plays a critical part in both use cases by providing data that are entered into the information system by Osbert. The customer is therefore an actor in both these use cases. It is conceivable that other actors may be added in a subsequent iteration. For conciseness, all three use cases are combined into the *use-case diagram* of Figure 4.8.

Next, we need to annotate the use cases, so we add the initial *use-case descriptions* shown in Figures 4.9 though 4.11.

We are now ready to draw up the initial requirements.

FIGURE 4.11

The Description of the
Produce a Report
Use Case of the Initial
Business Model of the
Osbert Oglesby
Information System

Brief Description
The `Produce a Report` use case enables Osbert Oglesby to obtain information on paintings he has bought or sold in the past year.
Step-by-Step Description
Not applicable at this initial stage.

4.7 Initial Requirements

In order to determine the client's requirements, we start by drawing up initial requirements, based on the initial business model. Then, as we refine our understanding of the domain and the business model on the basis of further discussions with the client, we refine the requirements.

The requirements are dynamic. That is, there are frequent changes not just to the requirements themselves, but also to the attitudes of the requirements team, client, and future users toward each requirement. For example, a particular requirement may first appear to the requirements team to be optional. After further analysis, that requirement may now seem to be critically important. However, after discussion with the client, the requirement is rejected. A good way to handle these frequent changes is to maintain a list of likely requirements, together with use cases of the requirements that have been agreed to by the members of the requirements team and approved by the client.

It is important to appreciate that the loop in the flowchart of Figure 4.1 must not be followed slavishly. That is, we can modify the glossary, the business model, or the requirements at any time. In particular, additions to the requirements list, modifications to items already on the list, and removal of items from the list can be triggered by a wide variety of events, ranging from a casual remark made by a user to a suggestion from the client at a formal meeting of the systems analysts on the requirements team. Any such change may trigger corresponding changes to the business model.

Requirements fall into two categories: functional and nonfunctional. A *functional requirement* is one that specifies an action that the information system must be able to perform. Functional requirements are often expressed in terms of inputs and outputs: Given a specific input, the functional requirement stipulates what the output must be. Conversely, a *nonfunctional requirement* specifies properties of the information system itself, such as *platform constraints* ("The information system must run under Linux"), *response times* ("On average, queries of Type 3B must be answered within 2.5 seconds"), or *reliability* ("The information system must run 99.95 percent of the time").

Functional requirements are handled while the requirements and analysis workflows are being performed, whereas some nonfunctional requirements may have to wait until the design workflow. The reason is that, in order to be able to handle certain nonfunctional requirements, we may need to have detailed knowledge about the target information system, and this knowledge is usually not available until the requirements and analysis workflows have been completed (see Problems 4.2 and 4.3).

4.8 Initial Requirements: Osbert Oglesby Case Study

The initial business model (the three use cases of Figure 4.8) shows how Osbert's business is currently being conducted. The next step is to decide which of these use cases are also requirements of the computerized information system to be built. Then we refine the resulting initial requirements, adding, modifying, and removing requirements, until both Osbert and the requirements team are satisfied with the list of requirements to be implemented by the information system.

All three use cases from the initial business model (Figure 4.8), namely, **Buy a Painting, Sell a Painting,** and **Produce a Report,** will be initial requirements. Furthermore, all three processes will be automated in the target management information system, so the initial descriptions shown in Figures 4.9 though 4.11 are replaced by the initial descriptions of Figures 4.12 through 4.14.

The vagueness of these descriptions is a consequence of the iterative nature of the Unified Process. For example, consider Figure 4.12. Item 1 refers to the "details of the painting [Osbert] is considering buying." We do not yet know what these details are, and we emphatically do not wish to know at this stage. A basic principle is to defer all details to as late as possible. The reason for this deferral is that, when the inevitable changes have to be made in the next iteration, the number of items that have to be modified is as small as possible.

FIGURE 4.12

The Description of the Buy a Painting Use Case of the Initial Requirements of the Osbert Oglesby Information System

---

Brief Description

The `Buy a Painting` use case enables Osbert Oglesby to buy a painting.

Step-by-Step Description

1. Osbert inputs details of the painting he is considering buying.
2. The information system responds with the maximum purchase price he should offer.
3. If the seller accepts Osbert's offer to buy the painting, Osbert enters further details.

Note: Details of the algorithm for determining the maximum price will be obtained later.

FIGURE 4.13

The Description of the Sell a Painting Use Case of the Initial Requirements of the Osbert Oglesby Information System

---

Brief Description

The `Sell a Painting` use case enables Osbert Oglesby to sell a painting.

Step-by-Step Description

1. Osbert inputs details of the painting he has sold.

FIGURE 4.14

The Description of the Produce a Report Use Case of the Initial Requirements of the Osbert Oglesby Information System

---

Brief Description

The `Produce a Report` use case enables Osbert Oglesby to obtain information on paintings he has bought or sold in the past year or to detect new trends in the art market.

Step-by-Step Description

1. Osbert requests a report of the type that he needs. The report is printed.

4.9   Continuing the Requirements Workflow: Osbert Oglesby Case Study

Look at the current versions of each of the descriptions of the use cases (Figures 4.12 through 4.14). It is clear that we need to acquire more details for the next iteration.

First consider the use cases **Buy a Painting** and **Sell a Painting**. In order to refine the description, we have to determine what attributes need to be input when a painting is bought and when a painting is sold. By examining the relevant documentation, namely, Osbert's current manual records, we learn that Osbert will need to record the following data for each painting he buys:

Description of painting:

First name of artist (up to 20 characters, followed by **?** if there is uncertainty).

Last name of artist (up to 20 characters, followed by **?** if there is uncertainty).

Title of work (up to 40 characters, followed by **?** if there is uncertainty).

Date of work (yyyy, followed by **?** if there is uncertainty).

Classification (masterpiece, masterwork, other painting).

Height (cm).

Width (cm).

Medium (oil, watercolor, other medium).

Subject (portrait, still-life, landscape, other subject).

Date of purchase (mm/dd/yyyy).

Name of seller (up to 30 characters).

Address of seller (up to 40 characters).

Maximum purchase price determined by the algorithm (up to $99,999,999).

Actual purchase price (up to $99,999,999).

Target selling price (2.15 times the purchase price).

After a painting has been sold, Osbert must record the following:

Date of sale (mm/dd/yyyy).

Name of buyer (up to 30 characters).

Address of buyer (up to 40 characters).

Actual selling price (up to $99,999,999).

In order to compute the required "Maximum purchase price determined by the algorithm," we now turn to the report from the management consultant. The algorithm developed by the consultant is as follows:

Classify the painting as a masterpiece, a masterwork, or other painting.

- A masterpiece: Scan worldwide auction records over the past 25 years for the most similar work by the same artist, ignoring any question marks in the first or last name of the artist, or in the title or date of the work. (For the definition of similarity, see below.) Use the auction purchase price of the most similar work as the base price. The maximum purchase price is found by adding 8.5 percent to the base price, compounded annually, for each year since that auction.

- A masterwork: First, compute the maximum purchase price as if it were a masterpiece by the same artist. Then, if the picture was painted in the twenty-first century, multiply this figure by 0.25; otherwise multiply it by $(21 - c)/(22 - c)$, where c is the century in which the work was painted ($12 < c < 21$).
- Other painting: Measure the dimensions of the canvas. The maximum purchase price is then given by the formula $F \times A$, where F is a constant for that artist (*fashionability coefficient*) and A is the area of the canvas in square centimeters. If there is no fashionability coefficient for that artist, Osbert will not buy the painting.

In the case of masterpieces and masterworks, the coefficient of similarity between two paintings is computed as follows:

Score 1 for a match on medium, otherwise 0.

Score 1 for a match on subject, otherwise 0.

Add these two numbers, multiply by the area of the smaller of the two paintings, and divide by the area of the larger of the two.

The resulting number is the coefficient of similarity.

If the coefficient of similarity between the painting under consideration and all the paintings in the file of auction data is zero, then Osbert will not buy that masterwork or masterpiece.

The information system must include a list of artists and their corresponding F values. The value of F can vary from month to month, depending on the current fashionability of an artist, so the list must be implemented in a way that will allow Osbert to perform regular updates. Osbert himself determines the value of F on the basis of his knowledge and experience and modifies a coefficient if he observes an increase or decrease in prices paid for a particular artist's work in reports of art sales in newspapers and magazines.

The information system must utilize information on auction sales of masterpieces over the past 25 years worldwide. This information includes name of artist, title of painting, date of painting, date of auction, sale price, and type of work. The type of work consists of three components, namely, medium (oil, watercolor, or other medium), dimensions (height and width), and subject (portrait, still-life, landscape, or *other subject*). Each month Osbert receives a CD with updated worldwide auction prices; these prices are never modified by Osbert.

We update the use-case descriptions to reflect this information. The resulting description of the Buy a Painting use case is shown in Figure 4.15 and of the Sell a Painting use case in Figure 4.16.

Now we consider the reports. There are three reports: purchases during the past year, sales during the past year, and the detection of new trends. Again we look at Osbert's manual records, including the reports that he currently produces manually. We determine that his needs are as follows (question marks in the first or last name of the artist or in the title or date of the work are to be included in all reports).

A report is needed to display all the paintings purchased during the past year. The output should be in the following order:

Classification (masterpiece, masterwork, other painting).

Purchase date.

Last name of artist.

Painting title.

Suggested maximum purchase price.

Actual purchase price.

FIGURE 4.15

The Description of the Buy a Painting Use Case of the Revised Requirements of the Osbert Oglesby Information System

---

Brief Description

The `Buy a Painting` use case enables Osbert Oglesby to buy a painting.

Step-by-Step Description

1. Osbert inputs the details of the painting he is considering buying. These are
    First name of artist
    Last name of artist
    Title of work
    Year of work
    Classification (masterpiece, masterwork, other)
    Height
    Width
    Subject (portrait, still-life, landscape, other)

2. The information system responds with the maximum purchase price Osbert should offer.

2.1 For a masterpiece:
    The information system computes the coefficient of similarity between each painting for which there is an auction record and the painting under consideration for purchase. Question marks in the first or last name of the artist, or in the title or date of the work, are to be ignored.
      The information system scores 1 for a match on medium, otherwise 0.
      The information system scores 1 for a match on subject, otherwise 0.
      It adds these two numbers, multiplies by the area of the smaller of the two paintings, and divides by the area of the larger of the two.
      The resulting number is the coefficient of similarity.
    The information system finds the auctioned painting with the largest nonzero coefficient of similarity. If there is no such painting, Osbert will not buy the painting under consideration.
    The information system computes the maximum purchase price by adding to the auction price of the most similar work 8.5 percent, compounded annually, for each year since that auction.

2.2 For a masterwork:
    The information system first computes the maximum purchase price as if the painting were a masterpiece by the same artist. Then, if the picture was painted in the twenty-first century, it multiplies that figure by 0.25; otherwise it multiplies it by $(21 - c)/(22 - c)$, where c is the century in which the work was painted $(12 < c < 21)$.

2.3 For any other painting:
    The information system computes the maximum purchase price from the formula $F \times A$, where F is a constant for that artist (fashionability coefficient) and A is the area of the canvas in square centimeters. If there is no fashionability coefficient for that artist, Osbert will not buy the painting under consideration.

3. If Osbert buys the painting, he enters further details. These are
    Date of purchase
    Name of seller
    Address of seller
    Actual purchase price

4. The information system then records the following:
    Maximum purchase price determined by the algorithm
    Target selling price

FIGURE 4.16
The Description of
the Sell a Painting
Use Case of the
Revised
Requirements of the
Osbert Oglesby
Information System

Brief Description

The `Sell a Painting` use case enables Osbert Oglesby to sell a painting.

Step-by-Step Description

1. Osbert inputs details of the painting he has sold. These are
   Date of sale
   Name of buyer
   Address of buyer
   Actual selling price

FIGURE 4.17
A Sample Report
Showing Paintings
Bought during the
Past Year

```
                      Report Date: 08/14/2003
                Osbert Oglesby - Collector of Fine Art
                         BOUGHT PAINTINGS
    _____

       CLASSIFICATION: *Masterwork    PURCHASE DATE: 02/08/2003
       LAST NAME: Hatzayar             TITLE: Table_Mountain
       SUGG. PRICE: 54,300             PURCHASE PRICE: 123,000
    _____

       CLASSIFICATION: *Masterwork    PURCHASE DATE: 03/09/2003
       LAST NAME: Hatzayar             TITLE: Walker_Bay
       SUGG. PRICE: 51,580             PURCHASE PRICE:   75,000
    _____

       CLASSIFICATION: Other          PURCHASE DATE: 04/10/2003
       LAST NAME: Amman                TITLE: Apples_and_Oranges
       SUGG. PRICE: 15,400             PURCHASE PRICE: 2,000

       Average ratio: 1.65
```

Any painting purchased for more than the maximum purchase price computed by the algorithm must be flagged (by placing an asterisk before the classification). This report must be sorted by classification and by date of purchase within classification. The average ratio of the actual purchase price to the algorithm's suggested maximum purchase price for all the paintings in the report should be displayed at the end of the report. A sample report is shown in Figure 4.17.

A second report should display the paintings that have been sold during the past year. The output should be in the following order:

Classification.

Sale date.

Last name of artist.

Painting title.

Target selling price.

Actual selling price.

Any painting sold at a price of 5 percent or more below the target selling price must be flagged (by placing an asterisk before the classification). This report must be sorted by classification and by date of sale within classification. The average ratio of the actual selling price to the target selling price for all of the paintings in the report should be displayed at the end of the report. Again, a sample report is shown in Figure 4.18.

FIGURE 4.18
A Sample Report
Showing Paintings
Sold during the
Past Year

```
                    Report Date: 08/14/2003
            Osbert Oglesby - Collector of Fine Art
                       SOLD PAINTINGS

    CLASSIFICATION: Masterwork   SALE DATE: 05/11/2002
    LAST NAME: Hatzayar          TITLE: Table_Mountain
    TARGET PRICE: 264,450        SELLING PRICE: 270,000

    CLASSIFICATION: Masterwork   SALE DATE: 06/12/2002
    LAST NAME: Hatzayar          TITLE: Walker_Bay
    TARGET PRICE: 161,250        SELLING PRICE: 205,000

    CLASSIFICATION: *Other       SALE DATE: 07/13/2002
    LAST NAME: Amann             TITLE:  Apples_and_Oranges
    TARGET PRICE: 4,300          SELLING PRICE: 300

    Average ratio = 1.11
```

FIGURE 4.19
A Sample Report
Showing New Trends
in the Art Market

```
                    Report Date: 08/14/2002
            Osbert Oglesby - Collector of Fine Art
                          TRENDS

                 Artist: David Hatzayar

    CLASSIFICATION: Masterwork    TITLE: Table_Mountain
    SALE DATE: 05/11/2002
    TARGET PRICE: 264,450         SELLING PRICE: 270,000

    CLASSIFICATION: Masterwork    TITLE: Walker_Bay
    SALE DATE: 06/12/2002
    TARGET PRICE: 161,250         SELLING PRICE: 205,000
```

Finally, Osbert is keen to detect new trends in the art market as soon as possible. He is particularly interested in determining when higher prices than expected are consistently paid for a particular artist's work, so that he can buy up paintings by that artist before others notice the trend. He therefore requires a report that shows artists whose works he has sold at a price that has exceeded the target selling price in every instance during the past year. For an artist to appear in this report, at least two of his or her works must have been sold by Osbert during that period. The names of the relevant artists (if any) should be in alphabetical order. Each name should appear on one line of the screen. The various works by that artist that have been sold must then appear, in order of date of sale. For each work, the following must appear:

Classification.

Painting title.

Date of sale.

Target selling price.

Actual selling price.

A sample report is shown in Figure 4.19.

The updated description of the **Produce a Report** use case, incorporating the details listed above, appears in Figure 4.20.

FIGURE 4.20

**The Description of
the Produce a
Report Use Case
of the Revised
Requirements of the
Osbert Oglesby
Information System**

Brief Description

The `Produce a Report` use case enables Osbert Oglesby to obtain information on paintings he has bought or sold in the past year or to detect new trends in the art market.

Step-by-Step Description

1. The following reports must be generated on demand (question marks in the first or last name of the artist or in the title or date of the work must be printed):

1.1 Purchases report:

The system displays all paintings purchased during the past year.

The output is in the order:

   Classification
   Purchase date
   Last name of artist
   Painting title
   Suggested maximum purchase price
   Actual purchase price

Any painting purchased for more than the maximum purchase price computed by the algorithm is flagged (by placing an asterisk before the classification).

This report is sorted by classification and by date of purchase within classification.

The average ratio of the actual purchase price to the algorithm's suggested maximum purchase price for all the paintings in the report is displayed at the end of the report.

1.2 Sales report:

The system displays all paintings sold during the past year.

The output is in the following order:

   Classification
   Sale date
   Last name of artist
   Painting title
   Target selling price
   Actual selling price

Any painting sold at a price of 5 percent or more below the target selling price is flagged (by placing an asterisk before the classification).

This report is sorted by classification and by date of sale within classification.

The average ratio of the actual selling price to the target selling price for all of the paintings in the report is displayed at the end of the report.

1.3 Future trends report:

The system displays all artists whose works have been sold at a price that has exceeded the target selling price in every instance during the past year.

For an artist to appear in this report, at least two of his or her works must have been sold in that period.

The first and last names of the relevant artists (if any) are in alphabetical order by last name.

Each name appears on one line of the screen. The various works sold appear on successive lines, in order of date of sale.

For each work, the output is in the following order:

   Classification
   Painting title
   Sale date
   Target selling price
   Actual selling price

4.10   It Ain't Over Till It's Over

At first sight, the requirements workflow of the Osbert Oglesby information system is complete. Referring to the flowchart of Figure 4.1, all the steps of the Osbert Oglesby case study appear to have been performed. However, this is not the case. We have not done the necessary checking to answer the question in the diamond-shaped decision box, namely, "Are the requirements satisfactory?"

In other words, we have not checked the artifacts of the requirements workflow. In fact, there is a serious omission—we have overlooked a use case. The following paragraph appears in Section 4.9:

> The information system must include a list of artists and their corresponding F values. The value of F can vary from month to month, depending on the current fashionability of an artist, so the list must be implemented in a way that will allow Osbert to perform regular updates.

In other words, we have forgotten to include a use case for updating a fashionability coefficient. We therefore add the use case of Figure 4.21 and its description (Figure 4.22). The second iteration of the use-case diagram, incorporating the missing use case, is shown in Figure 4.23.

It is important to understand precisely what has happened with regard to the requirements workflow. We have detected a fault, namely, a missing use case. This means that another iteration of the loop of Figure 4.1 is needed. The existing artifacts do not need to be changed, but two additional artifacts, namely, a use case and its description, have to be added.

After further checking, it appears that everything is satisfactory, at least for now. However, in the course of performing the object-oriented analysis, further faults may come to light, additional requirements may be needed, or existing requirements may no longer be applicable. The Unified Process is truly iterative and incremental, and systems analysts must always be aware that changes and extensions to the current version of the information system may have to made at any time.

In the interim, we turn to our second running case study. This is described in the next chapter.

But first, you might want to read Just in Case You Wanted to Know Box 4.2.

FIGURE 4.21

The Use Case
**Update a
Fashionability
Coefficient** of
the Revised
Requirements of the
Osbert Oglesby
Information System

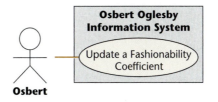

FIGURE 4.22

The Description of
the **Update a
Fashionability
Coefficient** Use Case
of the Revised
Requirements of the
Osbert Oglesby
Information System

Brief description

The `Update a Fashionability` Coefficient use case enables Osbert Oglesby to change the fashionability coefficient F for an artist.

Step-by-Step Description

1. Osbert inputs the new fashionability coefficient for the artist.

Just in Case You Wanted to Know   Box 4.2

The title of this section, "It Ain't Over Till It's Over," is a Yogi-ism; that is, a remark first made by Yogi Berra (Lawrence Peter Berra, 1925–), elected to the National Baseball Hall of Fame in 1972.

Another Yogi-ism is also applicable to the requirements workflow, "I really didn't say everything I said."

FIGURE 4.23
The Second Iteration of the Use-Case Diagram of the Osbert Oglesby Information System

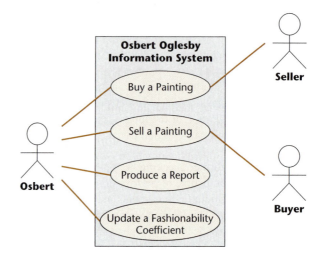

Review Questions for Chapter 4

1. What is the primary task of the systems analyst with regard to the requirements workflow?
2. Why does the client sometimes ask for an inappropriate information system?
3. Distinguish between requirements elicitation and requirements analysis.
4. Why is it essential to construct a glossary?
5. Distinguish between a structured interview and an unstructured interview.
6. What are the drawbacks to videotaping the activities of the workplace?
7. What is a use case?

8. What is an actor?

9. What is the difference between a use case and a use-case diagram?

10. Osbert's customers do not use the information system. So, why are the **Buyer** and the **Seller** actors in the use-case diagram of Figure 4.8?

11. Differentiate between functional and nonfunctional requirements.

Problems

4.1   For the Osbert Oglesby case study, the use-case diagram of the initial business model is also the use-case diagram of the initial requirements model. Will this always be true? Explain your answer.

4.2   Give a nonfunctional requirement that we can handle without having detailed knowledge about the target information system.

4.3   Now give a nonfunctional requirement that has to be handled after the requirements workflow has been completed.

4.4   Jethro Weatherby's formula for ordering boots based on new trends (Chapter 1) had the unexpected consequence of 56,943 pairs of boots being delivered to Jethro's Boot Emporium. Could there also be a mistake in the three-way pricing algorithm the management consultant developed for Osbert Oglesby? What are the possible consequences of such a mistake?

4.5   Jethro Weatherby tried to detect new trends in boot buying. Osbert Oglesby, too, wishes to detect new trends. Could there be a mistake in his formula for detecting a new trend in the art world and, if so, what would be the consequences of such a mistake?

4.6   Osbert Oglesby has decided to expand his business by selling on contingency. That is, he accepts paintings for sale that he will hang in his gallery. If within three months the painting is sold at the price previously agreed between Osbert and the owner of the painting, then Osbert and the owner share the selling price equally. If not, the painting is returned to its owner and no money changes hands. Draw the use case for contingency sales.

4.7   Give the description of the use case you drew for Problem 4.6. Provide as much detail as you can.

4.8   A report of all contingency sales (Problem 4.6) during the past year will have to be generated. Modify Figures 4.7 and 4.20 appropriately to incorporate this additional report.

4.9   You are required to develop an information system for determining whether a bank statement is correct. The data provided include the balance at the beginning of the month; the number, date, and amount of each check; the date and amount of each deposit; and the balance at the end of the month. Draw the use-case diagram and give the descriptions of the use case(s).

Reference

Jacobson, I.; G. Booch; and J. Rumbaugh. *The Unified Software Development Process,* Reading, MA: Addison Wesley, 1999.

Chapter **5**

The Requirements Workflow II

Learning Objectives

After studying this chapter, you should have a deeper understanding than before of how to:

- Perform the requirements workflow.
- Draw up the initial business model.
- Draw up the requirements.

In the previous chapter we performed the requirements workflow of the Osbert Oglesby case study. Now we turn to our other case study, the MSG Foundation. In the Osbert Oglesby case study, the number of use cases grew. In contrast, the number of use cases in the MSG Foundation case study actually shrinks.

5.1 MSG Foundation Case Study

When Martha Stockton Greengage died at the age of 87, she left her entire $2 billion fortune to charity. Specifically, her will set up the Martha Stockton Greengage (MSG) Foundation to assist young couples in purchasing their own homes by providing low-cost loans.

In order to reduce operating expenses, the trustees of the MSG Foundation are investigating computerization. Because none of the trustees has any experience with computers, they decide to commission a small information services organization to implement a pilot project, namely, an information system that will perform the calculations needed to determine how much money is available each week to purchase homes.

The first step, as always, is to understand the application domain, home mortgages in this instance.

Have you ever wondered why the word *mortgage* is pronounced "more gidge" with the accent on the first syllable? The word, which was first used in Middle English in the fourteenth century, comes from the Old French word *mort* meaning "dead" and the Germanic word *gage* meaning "a pledge," that is, a promise to forfeit property if the debt is not paid. Strangely enough, a mortgage is a "dead pledge" in two different senses. If the loan is not repaid, the property is forfeited, or "dead" to the borrower, forever. And if the loan is repaid, then the promise to repay is dead. This two-way explanation was first given by the English judge Sir Edward Coke (1552–1634).

And the strange pronunciation? The final letter in a French word like *mort* is silent—hence the "more." And the suffix "-age" is frequently pronounced "idge" in English. Examples include the words carriage, marriage, disparage, and encourage.

5.2   Initial Understanding of the Domain: MSG Foundation Case Study

Not many people can afford to pay cash to buy a home. Instead, they pay a small percentage of the purchase price out of their own savings and borrow the rest of the money. This type of loan, where real estate is pledged as security for the loan, is termed a *mortgage.* See Just in Case You Wanted to Know Box 5.1 for background information on mortgages.

For example, suppose that someone wishes to buy a house for $100,000. (Many houses nowadays cost much more than that, particularly in the larger cities, but the round number makes the arithmetic easier.) The person buying the house pays a *deposit* of (say) 10 percent, or $10,000, and borrows the remaining $90,000 from a financial institution such as a bank or a savings and loan company in the form of a mortgage for that amount. Thus, the *principal* (or *capital*) borrowed is $90,000.

Suppose that the terms of the mortgage are that the loan is to be repaid in monthly installments over 30 years at an interest rate of 7.5 percent per annum (or 0.625 percent per month). Each month, the borrower pays the finance company $629.30. Part of this amount is the interest on the outstanding balance; the rest is used to reduce the principal. This monthly payment is therefore often referred to as *P & I* (*principal* and *interest*). For example, in the first month the outstanding balance is $90,000. Monthly interest at 0.625 percent on $90,000 is $562.50. The remainder of the P & I payment of $629.30, namely $66.80, is used to reduce the principal. Thus, at the end of the first month, after the first payment has been made, only $89,933.20 is owed to the finance company.

The interest for the second month is 0.625 percent of $89,933.20, or $562.08. The P & I payment is $629.30, as before, and the balance of the P & I payment (now $67.22) again is used to reduce the principal, this time to $89,865.98.

After 15 years (180 months), the monthly P & I payment is still $629.30, but now the principal has been reduced to $67,881.61. The monthly interest on $67,881.61 is $424.26, so the remaining $205.04 of the P & I payment is used to reduce the principal. After 30 years (360 months), the entire loan will have been repaid.

The finance company wants to be certain that it will be repaid the $90,000 it is owed, plus interest. It ensures this in a number of different ways.

- First, the borrower signs a legal document (the mortgage deed) that states that, if the monthly payments are not made, the finance company may sell the house and use the proceeds to pay off the outstanding balance of the loan.

- Second, the finance company requires the borrower to insure the house, so that if (say) the house burns down, the insurance company will cover the loss and the check from the insurance company will then be used to repay the loan. The insurance premium is usually paid once a year by the finance company. To obtain the money for the premium from the borrower, the finance company requires the borrower to pay monthly insurance installments. It deposits the installments in an *escrow account,* essentially a savings account managed by the finance company. When the annual insurance premium is due, the money is taken from the escrow account. Real-estate taxes paid on a home are treated the same way; that is, monthly installments are deposited in the escrow account and the annual real-estate tax payment is made from that account.

- Third, the finance company wants to be sure that the borrower can afford to pay for the mortgage. Typically, a mortgage will not be granted if the total monthly payment (P & I plus insurance plus real-estate taxes) exceeds 28 percent of the borrower's total income.

In addition to the monthly payments, the finance company almost always wants to be paid a lump sum up front in return for lending the money to the borrower. Typically, the finance company will want 2 percent of the principal ("2 *points*"). In the case of the $90,000 loan, this amounts to $1,800.

Finally, there are other costs involved in buying a house, such as legal costs and various taxes. Thus, when the contract to buy the $100,000 house is signed (when the deal is "closed"), the *closing costs* (legal costs, taxes, and so on) plus the points can easily amount to $7,000.

Setting up a glossary of the MSG Foundation domain is left as an exercise (Problem 5.1).

5.3 Initial Business Model: MSG Foundation Case Study

Members of the development organization interview various managers and staff members of the MSG Foundation and discover the way the Foundation operates. At the start of each week, the MSG Foundation estimates how much money will be available that week to fund mortgages. Couples whose income is too low to afford a standard mortgage to buy a home can apply at any time to the MSG Foundation for a mortgage. An MSG Foundation staff member first determines whether the couple qualifies for an MSG mortgage and then determines whether the MSG Foundation still has sufficient funds on hand that week to purchase the home. If so, the mortgage is granted and the weekly mortgage repayment is computed according to the MSG Foundation's rules. This repayment amount may vary from week to week, depending on the couple's current income.

The corresponding part of the business model consists of three use cases: Estimate Funds Available for Week, Apply for an MSG Mortgage, and Compute Weekly Repayment Amount. These use cases are shown in Figures 5.1, 5.2, and 5.3, and the corresponding initial descriptions appear in Figures 5.4, 5.5, and 5.6, respectively.

Look carefully at use case Apply for an MSG Mortgage (Figure 5.2). The actor on the right is **Applicants.** But is **Applicants** really an actor? Recall from Section 4.5.3 that an actor is a user of an information system. However, applicants do not use the information system. They fill in a form. Their answers are then entered into the information system by an MSG staff member. In addition, they may ask questions of the staff member or answer

FIGURE 5.1

The Estimate Funds
Available for Week
Use Case of the
Initial Business
Model of the
MSG Foundation
Information System

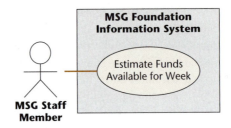

FIGURE 5.2

The Apply for an
MSG Mortgage Use
Case of the Initial
Business Model of the
MSG Foundation
Information System

FIGURE 5.3

The Compute
Weekly Repayment
Amount Use Case of
the Initial Business
Model of the MSG
Foundation
Information System

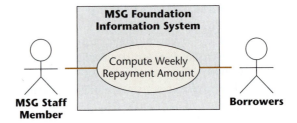

FIGURE 5.4

The Description of
the Estimate Funds
Available for Week
Use Case of the
Initial Business
Model of the MSG
Foundation
Information System

Brief Description

The `Estimate Funds Available for Week` use case
enables an MSG Foundation staff member to estimate how
much money the Foundation has available that week to fund
mortgages.

Step-by-Step Description

Not applicable at this initial stage.

FIGURE 5.5

The Description of
the Apply for an
MSG Mortgage Use
Case of the Initial
Business Model of the
MSG Foundation
Information System

Brief Description

When a couple applies for a mortgage, the `Apply for an MSG Mortgage` use case
enables an MSG Foundation staff member to determine whether they qualify for an
MSG mortgage and, if so, whether funds are currently available for the mortgage.

Step-by-Step Description

Not applicable at this initial stage.

FIGURE 5.6

The Description
of the Compute
Weekly Repayment
Amount Use Case of
the Initial Business
Model of the
MSG Foundation
Information System

Brief Description

The `Compute Weekly Repayment Amount` use
case enables an MSG Foundation staff member to
compute how much borrowers have to repay
each week.

Step-by-Step Description

Not applicable at this initial stage.

FIGURE 5.7

The Manage an
Investment Use
Case of the Initial
Business Model of the
MSG Foundation
Information System

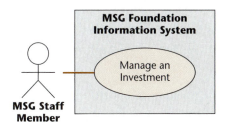

questions put to them by the staff member. But regardless of their interactions with MSG
staff members, applicants never interact with the information system.[1]

However, **Applicants** initiate the use case. That is, if a couple does not apply for a mortgage, this use case never occurs. Second, the information that the **MSG Staff Member**
gives to the information system is provided by **Applicants.** Third, in a sense, the real actor
is **Applicants; the MSG Staff Member** is merely an agent of the **Applicants.** For all
these reasons, **Applicants** is indeed an actor.

Now consider Figure 5.3, which depicts the use case Compute Weekly Repayment
Amount. The actor on the right is now **Borrowers.** Once an application has been granted,
the couple who applied for the mortgage (the **Applicants**) become **Borrowers.** But even
as borrowers they do not interact with the information system. As before, only MSG staff
members can enter information into the information system. Nevertheless, again the use
case is initiated by actor **Borrowers** and again the information entered by the **MSG Staff
Member** is supplied by **Borrowers.** Thus, **Borrowers** is indeed an actor in the use case
shown in Figure 5.3.

Another aspect of the MSG Foundation business model concerns the investments of the
MSG Foundation. At this initial stage details are not yet known regarding the buying and
selling of investments or how investment income becomes available for mortgages, but it is
certainly clear that the use case Manage an Investment shown in Figure 5.7 is an essential part of the initial business model. The initial description appears in Figure 5.8; in a
future iteration, details of how investments are handled will be inserted.

For conciseness, the four use cases of Figures 5.1, 5.2, 5.3, and 5.7 are combined into
the use-case diagram of Figure 5.9.

---

[1] This will change if the MSG Foundation ever decides to accept applications over the World Wide
Web. Specifically, **Applicants** will then become the only actor in Figure 5.3; **MSG Staff Member**
will no longer play a role.

FIGURE 5.8
The Description of
the Manage an
Investment Use
Case of the Initial
Business Model of the
MSG Foundation
Information System

Brief Description

The `Manage an Investment` use case enables an MSG Foundation
staff member to buy and sell investments and manage the
investment portfolio.

Step-by-Step Description

Not applicable at this initial stage.

FIGURE 5.9
The Use-Case
Diagram of the Initial
Business Model of the
MSG Foundation
Information System

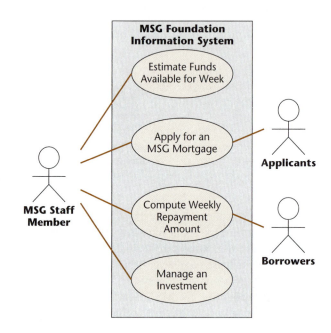

5.4 Initial Requirements: MSG Foundation Case Study

The four use cases of Figure 5.9 comprise the business model of the MSG Foundation.
However, it is not immediately obvious whether they are all requirements of the MSG
Foundation information system that is to be developed. Recall that what the client *wants* is
"a pilot project, namely, an information system that will perform the calculations needed to
determine how much money is available each week to purchase homes." As always, the task
of the systems analysts is to determine, with the aid of the client, what the client *needs*. At
this early stage, however, there is not enough information at the analysts' disposal to be able
to decide whether just this "pilot project" will be what is needed. In situations like this, the
best way to proceed is to draw up the initial requirements on the basis of what the client
wants, and then iterate.

Accordingly, each of the use cases of Figure 5.9 in turn is considered. Use case Estimate
Funds Available for Week is obviously part of the initial requirements. On the other hand,
Apply for an MSG Mortgage does not seem to have anything to do with the pilot project,
so it is excluded from the initial requirements. At first sight, the third use case, Compute
Weekly Repayment Amount, seems equally irrelevant to the pilot project. However, the
pilot project deals with the "money that is available each week to purchase homes." Part of
that money surely comes from the weekly repayment of existing mortgages, so the third use

FIGURE 5.10
The Use-Case
Diagram of the Initial
Requirements of the
MSG Foundation
Information System

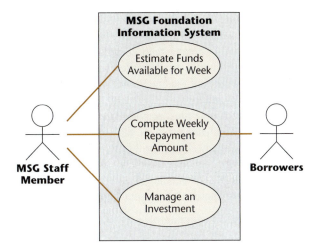

case is indeed part of the initial requirements. The fourth use case, Manage an Investment, is also part of the initial requirements for a similar reason—income from investments also must be used to fund new mortgages.

The initial requirements then consist of three use cases and their descriptions, namely, Estimate Funds Available for Week (Figures 5.1 and 5.4), Compute Weekly Repayment Amount (Figures 5.3 and 5.6), and Manage an Investment (Figures 5.7 and 5.8). These three use cases appear in Figure 5.10.

The next step is to iterate the requirements workflow; that is, we perform the steps again in order to obtain a better model of the client's needs.

5.5 Continuing the Requirements Workflow: MSG Foundation Case Study

Armed with domain knowledge and familiarity with the initial business model, the systems analysts now interview the MSG Foundation managers and staff in greater depth. They discover the following information.

The MSG Foundation grants a 100 percent mortgage to buy a home under the following conditions:

- The couple has been legally married for at least 1 year but not more than 10 years.
- Both husband and wife are gainfully employed. Specifically, proof must be provided that both were employed full time for at least 48 weeks of the preceding year.
- The price of the home must be below the published median price for homes in that area for the past 12 months.
- The installments on a fixed-rate, 30-year, 90 percent mortgage would exceed 28 percent of their combined gross income and/or they do not have sufficient savings to pay 10 percent of the cost of the home plus $7,000. (The $7,000 is an estimate of the additional costs involved, including closing costs and points.)
- The Foundation has sufficient funds to purchase the home; this is described below in more detail.

If the application is approved, then the amount that the couple should pay the MSG Foundation every week for the next 30 years is the total of the principal and interest payment, which never changes over the life of the mortgage, and the escrow payment, which is $\frac{1}{52}$nd of the sum of the annual real-estate tax and the annual homeowner's insurance premium. If this total is greater than 28 percent of the couple's gross weekly income, then the MSG Foundation will pay the difference in the form of a grant. Thus, the mortgage is paid in full each week, but the couple will never have to pay more than 28 percent of their combined gross income.

The couple must provide a copy of their income tax return each year, so that the MSG Foundation has proof of their previous year's income. In addition, the couple may file copies of pay slips as proof of current gross income. The amount the couple has to pay for their mortgage may therefore vary from week to week.

The MSG Foundation uses the following algorithm to determine whether it has the funds to approve a mortgage application:

1. At the beginning of each week, the estimated annual income from its investments is computed and divided by 52.
2. The estimated annual MSG Foundation operating expenses are divided by 52.
3. The total of the estimated mortgage payments for that week is computed.
4. The total of the estimated grants for that week is computed.
5. The amount available at the beginning of the week is then (Item 1) − (Item 2) + (Item 3) − (Item 4).
6. During the week, if the cost of the home is no more than the amount available for mortgages, then the MSG Foundation deems that it has the funds needed to purchase the home; the amount available for mortgages that week is reduced by the cost of that home.
7. At the end of each week, any unspent funds are invested by the MSG Foundation investment advisors.

To keep the cost of the pilot project as low as possible, the information system developers are told that only those data items needed for the weekly funds computation should be incorporated into the information system. The rest can be added later if the MSG Foundation decides to computerize all aspects of its operation. Therefore, only three types of data are needed, namely, investment data, operating expenses data, and mortgage data.

With regard to investments, the following data are required:

Item number (12 digits).

Item name (25 characters).

Estimated annual return (up to $999,999,999.99). (This figure is updated whenever new information becomes available. On average, this occurs about four times a year.)

Date estimated annual return was last updated (mm/dd/yyyy).

With regard to operating expenses, the following data are required:

Estimated annual operating expenses (up to $999,999,999.99). (This figure is currently determined four times a year.)

Date estimated annual operating expenses was last updated (mm/dd/yyyy).

For each mortgage, the following data are required:

Account number (12 digits).

Last name of mortgagees (21 characters). (If husband and wife have different last names, then this field contains the last name of the husband, if necessary truncated to 10 characters, followed by a hyphen, followed by the last name of the wife, if necessary truncated to fit the 21-character field.)

Original purchase price of home (up to $999,999.99).

Date mortgage was issued (mm/dd/yyyy).

Weekly principal and interest payment (up to $9,999.99).

Current combined gross weekly income (up to $999,999.99).

Date combined gross weekly income was last updated (mm/dd/yyyy).

Annual real-estate tax (up to $99,999.99).

Date annual real-estate tax was last updated (mm/dd/yyyy).

Annual homeowner's insurance premium (up to $99,999.99).

Date annual homeowner's insurance premium was last updated (mm/dd/yyyy).

In the course of further discussions with MSG managers, the systems analysts learn that three types of reports are needed:

The results of the funds computation for the week.

A listing of all investments (to be printed on request).

A listing of all mortgages (to be printed on request).

5.6   Revising the Requirements: MSG Foundation Case Study

Recall that the initial requirements model (Section 5.5) includes three use cases, namely Estimate Funds Available for Week, Compute Weekly Repayment Amount, and Manage an Investment. These use cases are shown in Figure 5.10. Now, in the light of the additional information that has been received, the initial requirements can be revised.

The formula given in the previous section for determining how much money is available at the beginning of a week is as follows:

1. The estimated annual income from investments is computed and divided by 52.
2. The estimated annual MSG Foundation operating expenses are divided by 52.
3. The total of the estimated mortgage payments for that week is computed.
4. The total of the estimated grants for that week is computed.
5. The amount available is then (Item 1) − (Item 2) + (Item 3) − (Item 4).

Consider each of these items in turn.

1. *Estimated annual income from investments.* We have to consider all the investments, sum the estimated annual return on each investment, and divide the result by 52. To do this we need an additional use case, namely, Estimate Investment Income for Week. (We still need use case Manage an Investment for adding, deleting, and modifying investments.) This new use case is depicted in Figure 5.11 and described in Figure 5.12. In Figure 5.11, the dashed line with the open arrowhead labeled «include» denotes that use case Estimate

FIGURE 5.11
The Estimate Investment Income for Week Use Case of the Revised Requirements of the MSG Foundation Information System

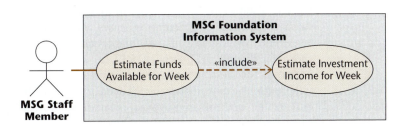

FIGURE 5.12
The Description
of the Estimate
Investment Income
for Week Use Case
of the Revised
Requirements of the
MSG Foundation
Information System

Brief Description

The `Estimate Investment Income for Week` use case enables the `Estimate Funds Available for Week` use case to estimate how much investment income is available for this week.

Step-by-Step Description

1. For each investment, extract the estimated annual return on that investment.
2. Sum the values extracted in Step 1 and divide the result by 52.

FIGURE 5.13
The First Iteration
of the Use-Case
Diagram of
the Revised
Requirements of the
MSG Foundation
Information System
The new use case is
shaded

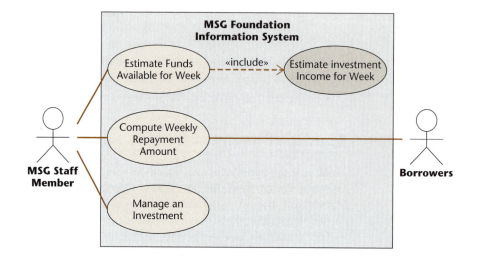

FIGURE 5.14
The Update
Estimated Annual
Operating
Expenses Use Case
of the Revised
Requirements of the
MSG Foundation
Information System

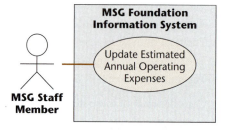

Investment Income for Week is part of use case Estimate Funds Available for Week. The resulting first iteration of the revised use-case diagram is shown in Figure 5.13 with the new use case shaded.

2. *Estimated annual operating expenses.* Up to now, we have not considered the estimated annual operating expenses. To do this we need two additional use cases. Use case Update Estimated Annual Operating Expenses models adjustments to the value of the estimated annual operating expenses and use case Estimate Operating Expenses for Week provides the estimate of the operating expenses that we need. The use cases are shown in Figures 5.14 through 5.17. In Figure 5.16, use case Estimate Operating Expenses for Week is similarly part of use case Estimate Funds Available for Week, as indicated by the dashed line with the open arrowhead labeled «include». The resulting second iteration of the revised use-case diagram is shown in Figure 5.18 with the two new use cases shaded.

FIGURE 5.15
The Description of the
**Update Estimated
Annual Operating
Expenses Use Case**
of the Revised
Requirements of the
MSG Foundation
Information System

Brief Description

The `Update Estimated Annual Operating Expenses`
use case enables an MSG Foundation staff member to update
the estimated annual operating expenses.

Step-by-Step Description

1. Update the estimated annual operating expenses.

FIGURE 5.16
**The Estimate
Operating Expenses
for Week Use Case**
of the Revised
Requirements of the
MSG Foundation
Information System

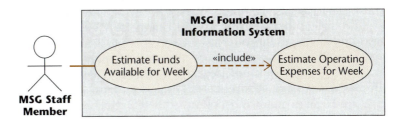

FIGURE 5.17
The Description
of the **Estimate
Operating
Expenses for
Week Use Case**
of the Revised
Requirements of the
MSG Foundation
Information System

Brief Description

The `Estimate Operating Expenses for Week` use case
enables the `Estimate Funds Available for Week` use
case to estimate the operating expenses for the week.

Step-by-Step Description

1. Divide the estimated annual operating expenses by 52.

FIGURE 5.18
**The Second Iteration
of the Use-Case
Diagram of
the Revised
Requirements of the
MSG Foundation
Information System**
The two new use
cases, Estimate
Operating Expenses
for Week and Update
Estimated Annual
Operating Expenses,
are shaded

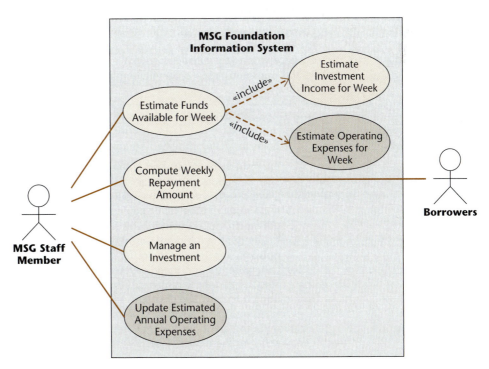

3. *Total estimated mortgage payments for the week* and

4. *Total estimated grant payments for the week.* The weekly repayment amount from use case Compute Weekly Repayment Amount is the total estimated mortgage payment less the estimated total grant payment. In other words, use case Compute Weekly Repayment Amount models the computation of both the estimated mortgage payment and the estimated grant payment for each mortgage separately. Summing these separate quantities will yield the total estimated mortgage payments for the week as well as the total estimated grant payments for the week. However, Compute Weekly Repayment Amount also models the borrowers changing the amount of their weekly income. Accordingly, we need to split Compute Weekly Repayment Amount into two separate use cases, namely, Estimate Payments and Grants for Week and Update Borrowers' Weekly Income. The two new use cases are described in Figures 5.19 through 5.22. Once more, one of the new use cases, namely, Estimate Payments and Grants for Week, is part of use case Estimate Funds Available for Week, as indicated by the dashed line with the open arrowhead labeled «include» in Figure 5.19. The resulting third iteration of the revised use-case

FIGURE 5.19

The Estimate
Payments and
Grants for Week Use
Case of the Revised
Requirements of the
MSG Foundation
Information System

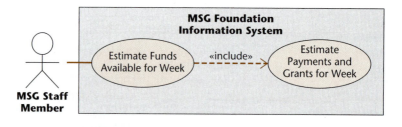

FIGURE 5.20

The Description
of the Estimate
Payments and
Grants for Week
Use Case of
the Revised
Requirements of the
MSG Foundation
Information System

Brief Description

The Estimate Payments and Grants for Week use case enables the Estimate Funds Available for Week use case to estimate the total estimated mortgage payments paid by borrowers to the MSG Foundation for this week and the total estimated grants paid by the MSG Foundation for this week.

Step-by-Step Description

1. For each mortgage:
    1.1 The amount to be paid this week is the total of the principal and interest payment and $\frac{1}{52}$nd of the sum of the annual real-estate tax and the annual homeowner's insurance premium.
    1.2 Compute 28 percent of the couple's current gross weekly income.
    1.3 If the result of Step 1.1 is greater than the result of Step 1.2, then the mortgage payment for this week is the result of Step 1.2, and the amount of the grant for this week is the difference between the result of Step 1.1 and the result of Step 1.2.
    1.4 Otherwise, the mortgage payment for this week is the result of Step 1.1 and there is no grant this week.
2. Summing the mortgage payments of Steps 1.3 and 1.4 yields the estimated mortgage payments for the week.
3. Summing the grant payments of Step 1.3 yields the estimated grant payments for the week.

FIGURE 5.21
The Update Borrowers' Weekly Income Use Case of the Revised Requirements of the MSG Foundation Information System

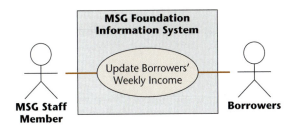

FIGURE 5.22
The Description of the Update Borrowers' Weekly Income Use Case of the Revised Requirements of the MSG Foundation Information System

Brief Description

The `Update Borrowers' Weekly Income` use case enables an MSG Foundation staff member to update the weekly income of a couple who have borrowed money from the Foundation.

Step-by-Step Description

1. Update the borrower's weekly income.

FIGURE 5.23
The Third Iteration of the Use-Case Diagram of the Revised Requirements of the MSG Foundation Information System

The two use cases derived from use case Compute Weekly Repayment Amount are shaded

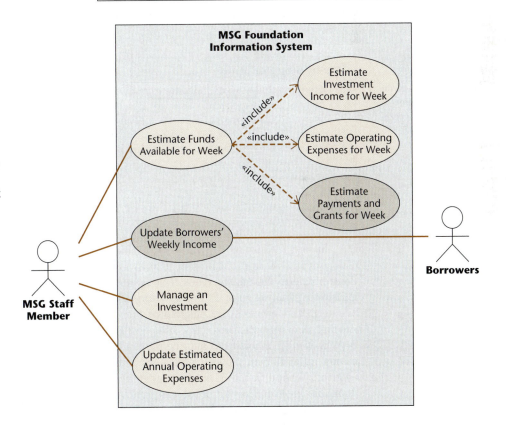

diagram is shown in Figure 5.23 with the two use cases derived from use case Compute Weekly Repayment Amount shaded.

Consider Figure 5.23 again. Use case Estimate Funds Available for Week models the computation that uses the data obtained from three other use cases, namely, Estimate Investment Income for Week, Estimate Operating Expenses for Week, and Estimate

FIGURE 5.24
The Second Iteration
of the Estimate
Funds Available
for Week Use Case
of the Revised
Requirements of the
MSG Foundation
Information System

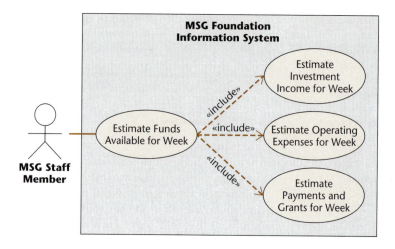

FIGURE 5.25
The Second Iteration
of the Description
of the Estimate
Funds Available
for Week Use Case
of the Revised
Requirements of the
MSG Foundation
Information System

Brief Description

The `Estimate Funds Available for Week` use case enables an MSG Foundation staff member to estimate how much money the Foundation has available that week to fund mortgages.

Step-by-Step Description

1. Determine the estimated income from investments for the week utilizing use case `Estimate Investment Income for Week`.
2. Determine the operating expenses for the week utilizing use case `Estimate Operating Expenses for Week`.
3. Determine the total estimated mortgage payments for the week utilizing use case `Estimate Payments and Grants for Week`.
4. Determine the total estimated grants for the week utilizing use case `Estimate Payments and Grants for Week`.
5. Add the results of Steps 1 and 3 and subtract the results of Steps 2 and 4. This is the total amount available for mortgages for the current week.

Payments and Grants for Week. This is shown in Figure 5.24, which shows the second iteration of the use case Estimate Funds Available for Week; this figure has been extracted from the use-case diagram of Figure 5.23. Figure 5.25 is the corresponding description of the use case.

Why it is so important to indicate the «include» *relationship* in UML diagrams? For example, Figure 5.26 shows two versions of Figure 5.19, the correct version on top, an incorrect version below. The top diagram correctly models use case Estimate Funds Available for Week as part of use case Estimate Payments and Grants for Week. The bottom diagram of Figure 5.26 models use cases Estimate Funds Available for Week and Estimate Payments and Grants for Week as two independent use cases. However, as stated in Section 4.5.3, a use case models an interaction between the information system itself and users of the information system (actors). This is fine for use case Estimate Funds Available for Week. However, use case Estimate Payments and Grants for Week does not interact with an actor and, therefore, cannot be a use case in its own right. Instead, it is a

FIGURE 5.26
Correct (top) and
Incorrect (bottom)
Versions of
Figure 5.19

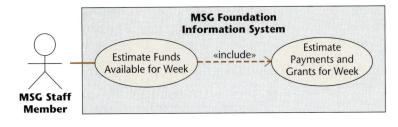

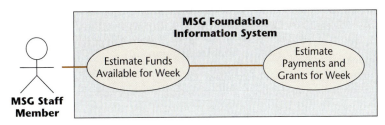

FIGURE 5.27
The Manage an
Investment Use
Case of the Revised
Requirements of the
MSG Foundation
Information System

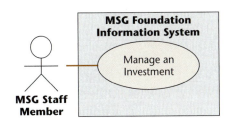

FIGURE 5.28
The Description of
the Manage an
Investment Use
Case of the Revised
Requirements of the
MSG Foundation
Information System

> **Brief Description**
>
> The `Manage an Investment` use case enables an MSG
> Foundation staff member to add and delete investments
> and manage the investment portfolio.
>
> **Step-by-Step Description**
>
> 1. Add, modify, or delete an investment.

portion of use case Estimate Funds Available for Week, as reflected in the top diagram of
Figure 5.26.

A common side-effect of the iterative and incremental life-cycle model is that details
that correctly have been postponed somehow get forgotten. That is one of the many reasons
why continual testing is essential. In this case, we have overlooked the details of the use
case Manage an Investment. This is remedied in Figures 5.27 and 5.28. Further review
brings to light that we have completely forgotten use case Manage a Mortgage to model
the addition of a new mortgage, the modification of an existing mortgage, or the removal
of an existing mortgage, analogous to use case Manage an Investment. Figures 5.29
and 5.30 correct this omission, and the fourth iteration of the revised use-case diagram is
shown in Figure 5.31 with the new use case, Manage a Mortgage, shaded.

FIGURE 5.29
The Manage a
Mortgage Use Case
of the Revised
Requirements of the
MSG Foundation
Information System

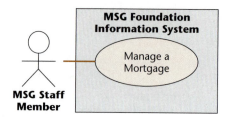

FIGURE 5.30
The Description
of the Manage a
Mortgage Use Case
of the Revised
Requirements of the
MSG Foundation
Information System

Brief Description

The `Manage a Mortgage` use case enables an MSG Foundation
staff member to add and delete mortgages and manage the
mortgage portfolio.

Step-by-Step Description

1. Add, modify, or delete a mortgage.

FIGURE 5.31
The Fourth
Iteration of the
Use-Case Diagram
of the Revised
Requirements of the
MSG Foundation
Information System
The new use case,
Manage a Mortgage,
is shaded

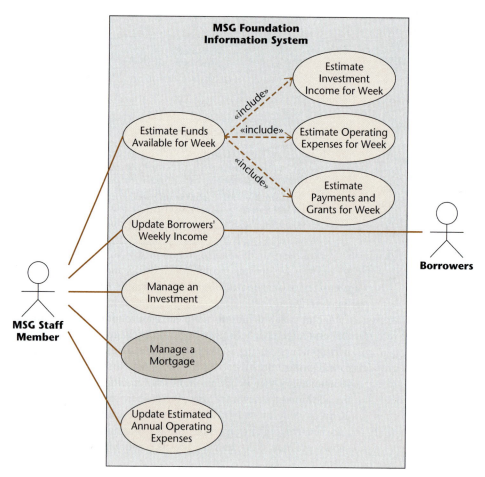

Everything seems fine again, until we notice that we have also overlooked the use case for printing the various reports. We therefore add use case **Produce a Report**, which models the printing of the three reports. The details of the use case appear in Figures 5.32 and 5.33. The fifth iteration of the revised use-case diagram is shown in Figure 5.34 with the new use case, **Produce a Report**, shaded.

FIGURE 5.32

The Produce a Report Use Case of the Revised Requirements of the MSG Foundation Information System

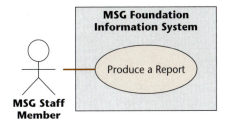

FIGURE 5.33

The Description of the Produce a Report Use Case of the Revised Requirements of the MSG Foundation Information System

---

Brief Description

The `Produce a Report` use case enables an MSG Foundation staff member to print the results of the weekly computation of funds available for new mortgages or to print a listing of all investments or all mortgages.

Step-by-Step Description

1. The following reports must be generated:
1.1 Investments report—printed on demand:
   The information system prints a list of all investments. For each investment, the following attributes are printed:
      Item number
      Item name
      Estimated annual return
      Date estimated annual return was last updated
1.2 Mortgages report—printed on demand:
   The information system prints a list of all mortgages. For each mortgage, the following attributes are printed:
      Account number
      Name of mortgagee
      Original price of home
      Date mortgage was issued
      Principal and interest payment
      Current combined gross weekly income
      Date current combined gross weekly income was last updated
      Annual real-estate tax
      Date annual real-estate tax was last updated
      Annual homeowner's insurance premium
      Date annual homeowner's insurance premium was last updated
1.3 Results of the weekly computation—printed each week:
   The information system prints the total amount available for new mortgages during the current week

FIGURE 5.34

The Fifth Iteration
of the Use-Case
Diagram of
the Revised
Requirements of the
MSG Foundation
Information System
The new use case,
Produce a Report, is
shaded

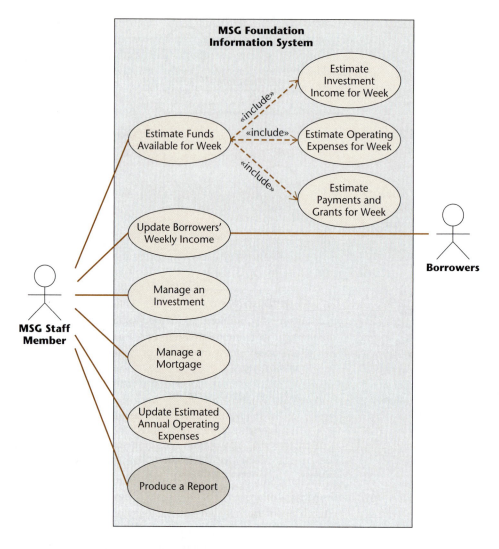

5.7 Refining the Revised Requirements: MSG Foundation Case Study

At this point we check the revised requirements yet again and uncover two new problems. First, we have partially duplicated a use case. Second, two of the use cases need to be reorganized.

The first change we make is to remove the partially duplicated use case. Consider use case **Manage a Mortgage** (Figures 5.29 and 5.30). As stated in Figure 5.30, one of the actions of this use case is to modify a mortgage. Now consider use case **Update Borrowers' Weekly Income** (Figures 5.21 and 5.22). The only purpose of this use case (Figure 5.22) is to update the borrowers' weekly income. But the borrowers' weekly income is an attribute of the mortgage. That is, use case **Manage a Mortgage** already includes the use case **Update Borrowers' Weekly Income**. Accordingly, use case **Update Borrowers' Weekly Income** is superfluous and should be deleted. The result is shown in Figure 5.35, the sixth iteration of the revised use-case diagram.

This is the first iteration that has resulted in a decrement rather than an increment. That is, this is the first time in this book that the result of an iteration has been to delete an artifact

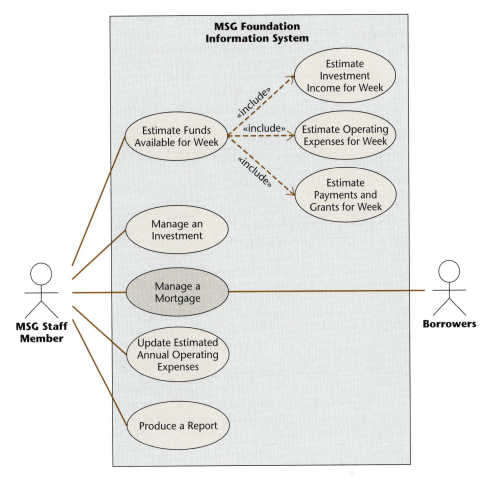

FIGURE 5.35

The Sixth Iteration of the Use-Case Diagram of the Revised Requirements of the MSG Foundation Information System
The modified use case, Manage a Mortgage, is shaded

(the Update Borrowers' Weekly Income use case). In fact, deletion occurs all too often, namely, whenever we have made a mistake. Systems analysts, being human beings, make mistakes. Sometimes we can fix an incorrect artifact, but frequently we have to delete an artifact. The key point is that, when we discover a fault, we do not have to abandon everything we have done to date and start the whole analysis process from scratch. Instead, we first try to fix the current iteration, as we did in this case. If this strategy fails (because the mistake we have made really is serious), we simply backtrack to the previous iteration and try to find a better way to go forward from there.

The second change we make to improve the requirements is by reorganizing two use cases. Consider the descriptions of the use cases Estimate Funds Available for Week (Figure 5.25) and Produce a Report (Figure 5.33). Suppose that an MSG staff member wants to determine the funds available for the current week. Use case Estimate Funds Available for Week models performing the calculation, and Step 1.3 of use case Produce a Report models printing out the result of the computation. This is ridiculous. After all, there is no point in estimating the funds available unless the results are printed out.

In other words, Step 1.3 of Produce a Report needs to be moved from the description of that use case to the end of the description of use case Estimate Funds Available for Week. This does not change the use cases themselves (Figures 5.24 and 5.32) or the current use-case diagram (Figure 5.35), but the descriptions of the two use cases (Figures 5.25 and 5.33) have to be modified. The resulting modified descriptions are shown in Figures 5.36 and 5.37.

FIGURE 5.36

The Second Iteration of the Description of the Produce a Report Use Case of the Revised Requirements of the MSG Foundation Information System

---

Brief Description

The `Produce a Report` use case enables an MSG Foundation staff member to print a listing of all investments or all mortgages.

Step-by-Step Description

1. The following reports must be generated:
   1.1 Investments report—printed on demand:
       The information system prints a list of all investments. For each investment, the following attributes are printed:
           Item number
           Item name
           Estimated annual return
           Date estimated annual return was last updated
   1.2 Mortgages report—printed on demand:
       The information system prints a list of all mortgages. For each mortgage, the following attributes are printed:
           Account number
           Name of mortgagee
           Original price of home
           Date mortgage was issued
           Principal and interest payment
           Current combined gross weekly income
           Date current combined gross weekly income was last updated
           Annual real-estate tax
           Date annual real-estate tax was last updated
           Annual homeowner's insurance premium
           Date annual homeowner's insurance premium was last updated

---

FIGURE 5.37

The Third Iteration of the Description of the Estimate Funds Available for Week Use Case of the Revised Requirements of the MSG Foundation Information System

---

Brief Description

The `Estimate Funds Available for Week` use case enables an MSG Foundation staff member to estimate how much money the Foundation has available that week to fund mortgages.

Step-by-Step Description

1. Determine the estimated income from investments for the week utilizing use case `Estimate Investment Income for Week`.
2. Determine the operating expenses for the week utilizing use case `Estimate Operating Expenses for Week`.
3. Determine the total estimated mortgage payments for the week utilizing use case `Estimate Payments and Grants for Week`.
4. Determine the total estimated grants for the week utilizing use case `Estimate Payments and Grants for Week`.
5. Add the results of Steps 1 and 3 and subtract the results of Steps 2 and 4. This is the total amount available for mortgages for the current week.
6. Print the total amount available for new mortgages during the current week.

Now we can improve the use-case diagram still further. Look at the top four use cases in Figure 5.35. The three use cases on the right, namely **Estimate Investment Income for Week**, **Estimate Operating Expenses for Week**, and **Estimate Payments and Grants for Week**, are part of the use case **Estimate Funds Available for Week**. The usual reason for an «include» relationship is where one use case is part of two or more other use

FIGURE 5.38
Use Case Print
Tax Form Is Part
of Three Other
Use Cases

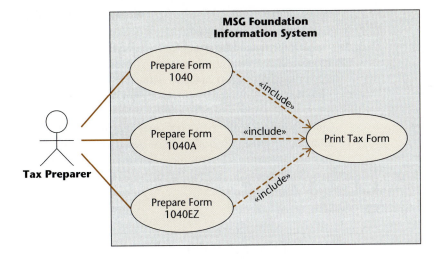

FIGURE 5.39
The Seventh
Iteration of the
Use-Case Diagram
of the Revised
Requirements of the
MSG Foundation
Information System
The modified use case,
Estimate Funds
Available for Week,
is shaded

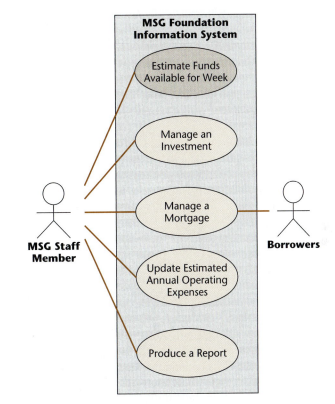

cases. For example, Figure 5.38 shows that use case Print Tax Form is part of use cases Prepare Form 1040, Prepare Form 1040A, and Prepare Form 1040EZ, the three primary U.S. tax forms for individuals. In this situation, it makes sense to retain Print Tax Form as an independent use case. Incorporating the operations of Print Tax Form into the other three use cases would mean triplicating that use case.

With regard to Figure 5.35, however, all of the included use cases are part of only one use case, namely, Estimate Funds Available for Week—there is no duplication. Accordingly, it makes sense to incorporate those three «include» use cases into Estimate Funds Available for Week, as shown in Figure 5.39, the seventh iteration of the use-case diagram.

The resulting fourth iteration of the description of the Estimate Funds Available for Week use case is shown in Figure 5.40.

Now the requirements appear to be correct. First, they correspond to what the client has requested. Second, there do not seem to be any faults. Third, at this stage it would seem that what the client wants coincides with what the client needs. Accordingly, the requirements workflow appears to be complete, for now. Nevertheless, it is certainly possible that, during subsequent workflows, additional requirements may surface. Also, it may be necessary to split one or more of the five use cases into additional cases. For example, in a future iteration the Produce a Report use case described in Figure 5.33 may be split into two separate use cases, one for the investments report, the other for the mortgages report. But for now, everything seems to be fine.

FIGURE 5.40

The Fourth Iteration of the Description of the Use Case Estimate Funds Available for Week of the Revised Requirements of the MSG Foundation Information System

---

Brief Description

The `Estimate Funds Available for Week` use case enables an MSG Foundation staff member to estimate how much money the Foundation has available that week to fund mortgages.

Step-by-Step Description

1. For each investment, extract the estimated annual return on that investment. Summing the separate returns and dividing the result by 52 yields the estimated investment income for the week.
2. Determine the estimated MSG Foundation operating expenses for the week by extracting the estimated annual MSG Foundation operating expenses and dividing by 52.
3. For each mortgage:
   3.1 The amount to be paid this week is the total of the principal and interest payment and $\frac{1}{52}$nd of the sum of the annual real-estate tax and the annual homeowner's insurance premium.
   3.2 Compute 28 percent of the couple's current gross weekly income.
   3.3 If the result of Step 3.1 is greater than the result of Step 3.2, then the mortgage payment for this week is the result of Step 3.2, and the amount of the grant for this week is the difference between the result of Step 3.1 and the result of Step 3.2.
   3.4 Otherwise, the mortgage payment for this week is the result of Step 3.1, and there is no grant this week.
4. Summing the mortgage payments of Steps 3.3 and 3.4 yields the estimated total mortgage payments for the week.
5. Summing the grant payments of Step 3.3 yields the estimated total grant payments for the week.
6. Add the results of Steps 1 and 4 and subtract the results of Steps 2 and 5. This is the total amount available for mortgages for the current week.
7. Print the total amount available for new mortgages during the current week.

Key Term   «include» relationship, *88*

Case Study Key Terms

capital, *76*	escrow account, *77*	P & I, *76*
closing costs, *77*	interest, *76*	points, *77*
deposit, *76*	mortgage, *76*	principal, *76*

Review Questions for Chapter 5

1. Why does the same couple appear as two different actors (**Applicants** and **Borrowers**) in the use-case diagram of Figure 5.9?

2. Noting that only MSG Foundation staff members can use the information system, why do **Applicants** and **Borrowers** appear as actors in the use-case diagram of Figure 5.9?

3. Why does the use case Apply for an MSG Mortgage in Figure 5.9 not appear in Figure 5.10?

4. Refer to Step 1.1 of Figure 5.20. Why is the escrow payment $\frac{1}{52}$nd of the sum of the annual real-estate tax and the annual homeowner's insurance premium?

5. Refer to Steps 1.3 and 1.4 of Figure 5.20. Why is the grant computed that way?

6. Why is the bottom diagram in Figure 5.26 incorrect?

Problems

5.1   Set up a glossary for the MSG Foundation domain.

5.2   Show that, at the end of 30 years, monthly installments of $629.30 will pay off a loan for $90,000 with interest compounded monthly at an annual rate of 7.5 percent. (Hint: Using a spreadsheet, replicate the computation at the beginning of Section 5.2. Extend the computation to 360 months.)

5.3   Suppose that the MSG Foundation decides that it wants its information system to include the mortgage application process. Give the description of the Apply for an MSG Mortgage use case. Give as many details as you can.

5.4   Sections 5.6 and 5.7 describe the restructuring of the use cases of MSG Foundation. How would this restructuring change if, as in Problem 5.3, the Apply for an MSG Mortgage use case of Figure 5.9 had been included in the requirements model?

Systems Analysis and Design Projects

5.5   Consider an automated library circulation system. Every book has a bar code, and every borrower has a card bearing a bar code. When a borrower wishes to check out a book, a librarian enters C at the computer terminal, then scans the bar codes on the book and the borrower's card. Similarly, when a book is returned, a librarian enters R and the book is again scanned. Librarians can add books (+) to the library collection or remove them (−). Librarians and borrowers can go to a terminal and determine all the books in the library by a particular author (the librarian or borrower enters A= followed by the author's name), all the books with a specific title (T= followed by the title), or all the books in a particular subject area (S= followed by the subject area). Finally, if a borrower wants a book currently checked out, a librarian can place a hold on the book so that, when it is returned, it will be held for the borrower who requested it (H= followed by the number of the book). Draw the use-case diagram of the library information system and give descriptions of the use cases.

5.6   Consider an automated teller machine (ATM). The user puts a card into a slot and enters a four-digit personal identification number (PIN). If the PIN is incorrect, the card is ejected. Otherwise, the user may perform the following operations on up to four different bank accounts:

1. Deposit any amount. A receipt is printed showing the date, amount deposited, account number, and account balance before the deposit (the balance is updated once the deposit has been checked.)

2. Withdraw up to $200 in units of $20 (the account may not be overdrawn). In addition to the money, the user is given a receipt showing the date, amount withdrawn, account number, and account balance after the withdrawal.

3. Determine the account balance. This is displayed on the screen.

4. Transfer funds between two accounts. Again, the account from which the funds are transferred must not be overdrawn. The user is given a receipt showing the date, amount transferred, the two account numbers, and the resulting balances.

5. Quit. The card is ejected.

Draw the use-case diagram and give the descriptions of the use cases.

Term Project

5.7   Perform the requirements workflow of the Chocoholics Anonymous term project of Appendix A.

6

The Object-Oriented Analysis Workflow I

Learning Objectives

After studying this chapter, you should be able to:

- Perform the analysis workflow.
- Extract the boundary, control, and entity classes.
- Perform functional modeling.
- Perform class modeling.
- Perform dynamic modeling.

The analysis workflow is a key workflow of the object-oriented paradigm. When this workflow is performed, the classes are extracted. The use cases and the classes are the basis of the object-oriented information system to be developed. (For another insight into the object-oriented paradigm, see Just in Case You Wanted to Know Box 6.1.)

6.1   The Analysis Workflow

There are two aims of the *analysis workflow*. First, we wish to obtain a deeper understanding of the requirements. Second, we wish to describe the requirements in a way that is easy to maintain and provides insights into the structure of the information system to be developed.

The Unified Process [Jacobson, Booch, and Rumbaugh, 1999] is use-case driven. During the analysis workflow, we describe the use cases in terms of the classes of the information system. In the Unified Process, there are three types of classes: entity classes, boundary classes, and control classes. An *entity class* models information that is long lived. In the case of a banking information system, **Account Class** is an entity class because information on accounts has to stay in the information system. For the Osbert Oglesby information system, **Painting Class** is an entity class; again, information on paintings has to be long lived. Finally, **Mortgage Class** and **Investment Class** are entity classes of the MSG Foundation information system, because the mortgages and investments stay in the information system for years, if not decades.

A *boundary class* models the interaction between the information system and its actors. Boundary classes are generally associated with input and output. For example, in the

Most of the major advances in the object-oriented paradigm were made between 1990 and 1995. Because it usually takes some 15 years for new technology to become accepted, widespread adoption of the object-oriented paradigm should have started no sooner than 2005. However, the *millennium bug* or *Y2K problem* changed the expected timetable.

In the 1960s, when computers first started to be used for business on a widespread basis, hardware was far more expensive than it is today. As a result, the vast majority of information systems of that vintage represented a date using only the last two digits for a year; the leading 19 was understood. The problem with this scheme is that the year 00 is then interpreted as 1900, not 2000.

When hardware became cheaper in the 1970s and 1980s, few managers saw any point in spending large sums of money rewriting existing information systems with four-digit dates. After all, by the time the year 2000 arrived, it would be someone else's problem. As a result, *legacy information systems* remained year-2000 noncompliant. However, as the deadline of January 1, 2000, neared, information service organizations were forced to work against the clock to fix their information systems; there was no way to postpone the arrival of Y2K.

Problems facing the maintenance programmers included a lack of documentation for many legacy information systems, as well as information systems written in programming languages that were now obsolete. When modifying an existing information system was impossible, the only alternative was to start again from scratch. Some companies decided to use COTS technology or ERP systems (Section 1.1). Others decided that new custom information systems were needed. For obvious reasons, managers wanted these information systems to be developed using modern technology that had already been shown to be cost effective, and that meant using the object-oriented paradigm. The Y2K problem was therefore a significant catalyst for the widespread acceptance of the object-oriented paradigm.

Osbert Oglesby information system, reports have to be printed listing paintings bought during the previous year and sold during the previous year. This means that boundary classes **Purchases Report Class** and **Sales Report Class** are needed. For the MSG Foundation, the listings of mortgages and investments require classes **Mortgage Report Class** and **Investment Report Class.**

A *control class* models complex computations and algorithms. In the case of the Osbert Oglesby information system, each algorithm for computing the price of a painting type is a control class, namely, **Compute Masterpiece Price Class, Compute Masterwork Price Class,** and **Compute Other Painting Price Class.**

The UML notation for these three types of classes is shown in Figure 6.1. These are *stereotypes,* that is, extensions of UML. One of the many strengths of UML is that it allows us to define additional constructs that are not part of UML but that we need in order to model a system accurately.

FIGURE 6.1
UML Stereotypes
(Extensions of UML)
for Representing
an Entity Class, a
Boundary Class, and
a Control Class

Entity Class **Boundary Class** **Control Class**

As stated at the beginning of this section, during the analysis workflow the use cases are described in terms of the classes of the information system. The Unified Process itself does not describe how classes are to be extracted because users of the Unified Process are expected to have a background in object-oriented analysis and design. Accordingly, we temporarily suspend this discussion of the Unified Process to explain how classes are extracted, and then return (in Section 6.9) to the Unified Process.

First we consider entity classes, that is, classes that model long-lived information.

6.2   Extracting Entity Classes

Entity class extraction consists of three steps that are carried out iteratively and incrementally:

- *Functional modeling.* Present scenarios of all the use cases (a *scenario* is an instance of a use case).
- *Class modeling.* Determine the entity classes and their attributes. Then, determine the interrelationships and interactions between the entity classes. Present this information in the form of a *class diagram.*
- *Dynamic modeling.* Determine the operations performed by or to each entity class or subclass. Present this information in the form of a *statechart.*

These steps are shown in Figure 6.2. However, as with all iterative and incremental processes, the three steps are not necessarily always performed in the order shown in the figure—a change in one model will simply trigger corresponding revisions of the other two models.

We now extract the entity classes of the Osbert Oglesby case study.

FIGURE 6.2

Flowchart for Extracting Entity Classes

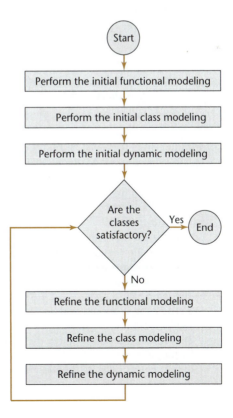

6.3   Initial Functional Model: Osbert Oglesby Case Study

A use-case diagram depicts the interactions between the information system itself and the users of that information system. For example, consider the Osbert Oglesby information system. Although the only user of the information system is Osbert himself, the customer (in the role of **Buyer** or **Seller**) is an actor in the two use cases that model buying or selling a painting. There are four ways that Osbert can use the information system and the resulting four use cases are shown in Figure 4.23, for convenience reproduced here as Figure 6.3.

Consider the use case Buy a Painting, which depicts the interaction when buying a painting between Osbert, the seller, and the information system. One possible instance of this use case is Osbert using the proposed information system to assist him in buying a masterpiece. This instance is shown in the scenario of Figure 6.4. That is, Figure 6.3 (use case) depicts all possible buying interactions, whereas Figure 6.4 (scenario) depicts just one particular buying interaction. A scenario is an instance of a use case, just as an object is an instance of a class.

Look more closely at the scenario of Figure 6.4. There are six paragraphs in the scenario, but only 4 of them are numbered. The reason is that the two unnumbered sentences, namely, Osbert wishes to buy a masterpiece and Osbert makes an offer below the maximum purchase price—the offer is accepted by the seller, have nothing to do

FIGURE 6.3

The Second Iteration of the Use-Case Diagram of the Osbert Oglesby Information System

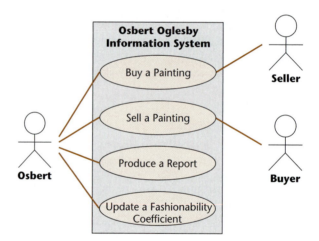

FIGURE 6.4

One Possible Scenario of Buying a Masterpiece

> Osbert Oglesby wishes to buy a masterpiece.
> 1. Osbert enters the description of the painting.
> 2. The information system scans the auction records to find the price and year of the sale of the most similar work by the same artist.
> 3. The information system computes the maximum purchase price by adding 8.5 percent, compounded annually, for each year since the auction of the most similar work.
>   Osbert makes an offer below the maximum purchase price—the offer is accepted by the seller.
> 4. Osbert enters sales information (name and address of seller, purchase price).

with the interaction between Osbert and the information system. These unnumbered paragraphs are essentially comments.

Figures 6.5 and 6.6 show two other scenarios for buying a masterpiece. In the scenario of Figure 6.5 the seller turns down Osbert's offer, and in the scenario of Figure 6.6 the information system cannot find a similar painting by that artist in the auction file. Figure 6.4 represents a *normal scenario,* whereas Figures 6.5 and 6.6 represent *exception scenarios.*

We have seen that, for conciseness, use cases can be combined into one use-case diagram. Similarly, normal and exception scenarios can be combined into an extended scenario, as shown in Figure 6.7.

It should be clear that there are numerous scenarios corresponding to each use case. The systems analysis team investigates as many normal and exception scenarios as time permits, in order to get the deepest possible understanding of the domain, the business model, and, most importantly, the use cases. After all, the use cases are the foundation of the Unified Process.

FIGURE 6.5
A Second Possible Scenario of Buying a Masterpiece

> Osbert Oglesby wishes to buy a masterpiece.
> 1. Osbert enters the description of the painting.
> 2. The information system scans the auction records to find the price and year of the sale of the most similar work by the same artist.
> 3. The information system computes the maximum purchase price by adding 8.5 percent, compounded annually, for each year since the auction of the most similar work.
>   Osbert makes an offer below the maximum purchase price. The seller turns down Osbert's offer.

FIGURE 6.6
A Third Possible Scenario of Buying a Masterpiece

> Osbert Oglesby wishes to buy a masterpiece.
> 1. Osbert enters the description of the painting.
> 2. The information system scans the auction records to find the price and year of the sale of the most similar work by the same artist.
> 3. The information system reports that there are no similar works.
>   Osbert does not make an offer for the painting.

FIGURE 6.7
An Extended Scenario of Buying a Masterpiece

> Osbert Oglesby wishes to buy a masterpiece.
> 1. Osbert enters the description of the painting.
> 2. The information system scans the auction records to find the price and year of the sale of the most similar work by the same artist.
> 3. The information system computes the maximum purchase price by adding 8.5 percent, compounded annually, for each year since the auction of the most similar work.
>   Osbert makes an offer below the maximum purchase price—the offer is accepted by the seller.
> 4. Osbert enters sales information (name and address of seller, purchase price).
>
> **Possible Alternatives**
>
> A. The seller turns down Osbert's offer.
> B. There is no similar painting in the auction file by that artist, so Osbert does not make an offer for the painting.

In this section scenarios of one of the use cases in Figure 6.3 were presented. Extended scenarios of the other three use cases are left as an exercise (see Problems 6.2 through 6.4).

The scenarios are not only used in the functional modeling step, but they are also an important input to the dynamic modeling step, as described in Section 6.5. First, however, we turn to the class modeling step.

6.4   Initial Class Diagram: Osbert Oglesby Case Study

The second step in extracting the entity classes is class modeling. The aim of this step is to extract the entity classes, determine their interrelationships, and find their attributes. Usually, the best way to begin this step is to use the two-stage *noun extraction method.*

In Stage 1 we describe the information system in a single paragraph. In the case of the Osbert Oglesby case study, one possible way of doing this is:

> Reports are to be generated in order to improve the effectiveness of the decision-making process for buying works of art. The reports contain buying and selling information about paintings, which are classified as masterpieces, masterworks, and other paintings.

In Stage 2 we identify the nouns in this paragraph. For clarity, the nouns are printed in sans serif type.

> Reports are to be generated in order to improve the effectiveness of the decision-making process for buying works of art. The reports contain buying and selling information about paintings, which are classified as masterpieces, masterworks, and other paintings.

The nouns are report, effectiveness, process, buying, work of art, selling, information, painting, masterpiece, and masterwork. Effectiveness, process, and information are *abstract nouns* and are therefore unlikely to be entity classes (abstract nouns identify things that have no physical existence).

Nouns buying and selling are nouns derived from the verbs "buy" and "sell," respectively. They will therefore probably be *operations* of some class. Noun report is unlikely to be an entity class, because a report is not long lived. A report is much more likely to be a boundary class. Noun work of art is just a synonym for painting. This leaves four candidate entity classes, namely, **Painting Class, Masterpiece Class, Masterwork Class,** and **Other Painting Class,** as shown in Figure 6.8.

Now we consider the interrelationships between these four entity classes. A masterpiece is a specific type of painting, and so is a masterwork and an "other painting." In terms of the terminology of Section 3.3, that means that **Painting Class** is the base class and

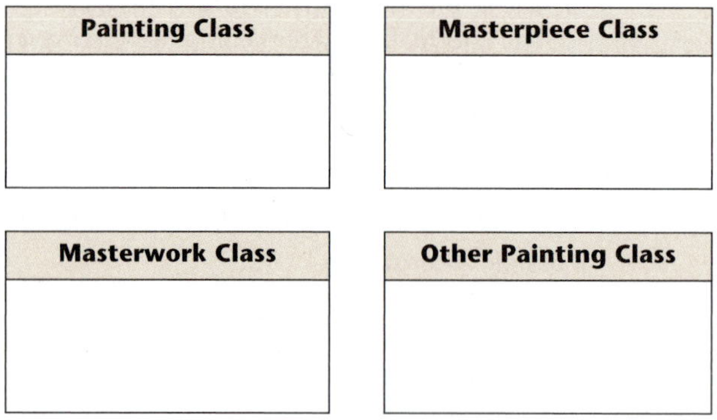

FIGURE 6.8

The First Iteration of the Initial Class Diagram of the Osbert Oglesby Case Study

FIGURE 6.9
The Second Iteration
of the Initial Class
Diagram of the
Osbert Oglesby
Case Study

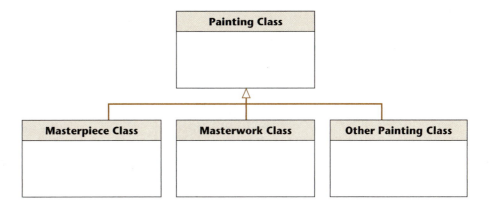

Masterpiece Class, Masterwork Class, and **Other Painting Class** are subclasses
of that base class. This is reflected in Figure 6.9; recall that the open triangle is the UML
representation of inheritance (generalization).

Figure 6.9 is clearly an improvement on Figure 6.8 in that it reflects the interrelationships between the classes. However, as we will see, it does not go far enough—at least one
more iteration is needed. The Unified Process is use-case driven, so studying the use cases
yet again usually leads to additional insights that were not apparent at the level of knowledge we had when we performed the previous iteration.

Reread the algorithm for determining the maximum price that Osbert will pay for a
painting in the description of the Buy a Painting use case of the revised requirements of
the Osbert Oglesby information system (Figure 4.15). From this description, it is apparent
that a number of key aspects of the algorithm have not yet been adequately modeled.

First, according to Figure 6.9, a painting is classified as a masterpiece, a masterwork, or
other painting. Because of the nature of inheritance, this means that all three types inherit
all the attributes of an instance of **Painting Class** and, in addition, may have attributes of
their own. On the other hand, recall paragraph 2.2 of Figure 4.15:

2.2 For a masterwork:
    The information system first computes the maximum purchase price as if the
    painting were a masterpiece by the same artist.

In order to satisfy this paragraph, a masterwork has to have all the attributes of a masterpiece (so that its maximum purchase price can be computed as if it were a masterpiece)
and, in addition, it may have attributes of its own. In other words, the relationship between
the entity classes identified so far is more accurately modeled by Figure 6.10 than by Figure 6.9. According to Figure 6.10, a painting is first classified either as a masterpiece/
masterwork or other painting. If it falls into the first category, it is then further classified as
either a masterpiece or a masterwork.

The second key aspect of the maximum price algorithm that has not yet been modeled
is auctioned paintings. Paragraph 2.1 of Figure 4.15 begins:

2.1 For a masterpiece:
    The information system computes the coefficient of similarity between each
    painting for which there is an auction record and the painting under consideration
    for purchase.

It is clear that **Auctioned Painting Class** is needed so that a masterpiece that Osbert
is considering buying can be compared with paintings auctioned worldwide over the past
25 years. The question is: Where in Figure 6.10 should **Auctioned Painting Class** be

FIGURE 6.10

The Third Iteration
of the Initial Class
Diagram of the
Osbert Oglesby
Case Study

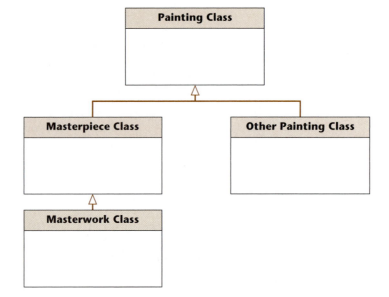

FIGURE 6.11

The Fourth Iteration
of the Initial Class
Diagram of the
Osbert Oglesby
Case Study

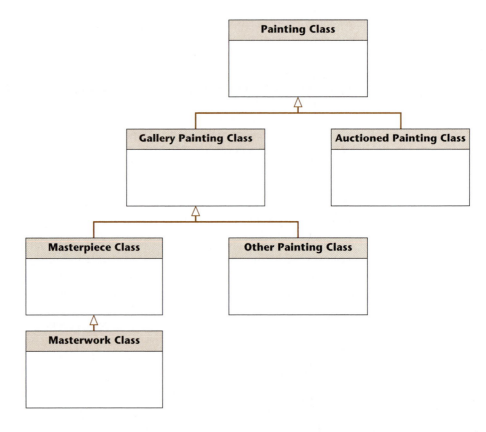

added? An auctioned painting is a painting, so it should be a subclass of **Painting Class.**
But a painting that has previously been sold at an auction somewhere in the world has nothing to do with the paintings currently on display for sale in Osbert's gallery. Accordingly,
what is needed is the class hierarchy of Figure 6.11.

According to the fourth iteration of the class diagram (Figure 6.11), an instance of **Painting Class** is either a painting that Osbert has bought (an instance of **Gallery Painting Class**) or a painting sold at some auction (an instance of **Auctioned Painting Class**). With regard to the paintings that Osbert has bought, they are classified exactly as in the third iteration (Figure 6.10), that is, as a masterpiece/masterwork or other painting.

The third key aspect of the maximum price algorithm that has not yet been modeled is fashionability. Paragraph 2.3 of Figure 4.15 begins:

2.3 For any other painting:
      The information system computes the maximum purchase price from the formula $F \times A$, where F is a constant for that artist (fashionability coefficient) . . .

What is needed, as shown in the bottom right of Figure 6.12, is **Fashionability Class.** A painting of **Other Painting Class** then uses the instance of **Fashionability Class** for that artist to compute the maximum price that Osbert should offer to pay. Figure 6.12 is the fifth iteration of the initial class diagram.

Why was the first iteration of the class diagram so inadequate? The one-paragraph description of what the information system should do did not incorporate the details of the pricing algorithm. After all, the Osbert Oglesby case study appears to be a straightforward data-processing application, so it is surely unreasonable to expect that the computational details of an algorithm would have a major impact on the class diagram. The one-paragraph description, therefore, correctly excluded the details of the algorithm. Unfortunately, the

FIGURE 6.12   **The Fifth Iteration of the Initial Class Diagram of the Osbert Oglesby Case Study**

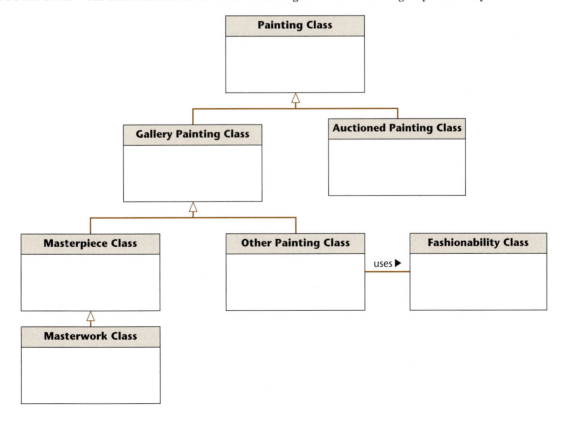

FIGURE 6.13   The Fifth Iteration of the Initial Class Diagram of the Osbert Oglesby Case Study, with Class Attributes Added

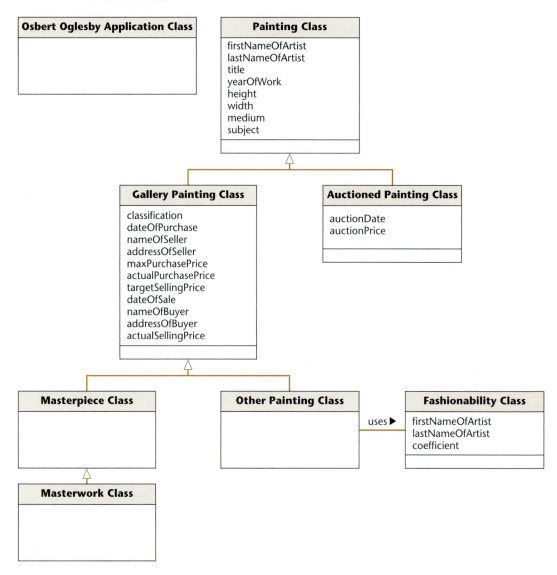

algorithmic details turned out to be critical to the class diagram, so the first iteration of the class diagram was far from adequate. However, a workable class diagram was soon found by repeatedly iterating and incrementing. This demonstrates the power of the iterative and incremental approach.

Finally, we add the *attributes* of each class to the class diagram. For the Osbert Oglesby case study, the result is shown in Figure 6.13. The empty rectangle at the bottom of each box representing a class will later be filled with the operations of that class (but see Problem 6.5).

Figure 6.13 includes a class that was not in Figure 6.12. **Osbert Oglesby Application Class** will contain the operation that starts execution of the whole information system. In other words, all other classes shown in Figure 6.13 contain the attributes and operations of

FIGURE 6.14

The Fifth Iteration of the Initial Class Diagram of the Osbert Oglesby Case Study (Figure 6.13) Redrawn Showing the Stereotypes

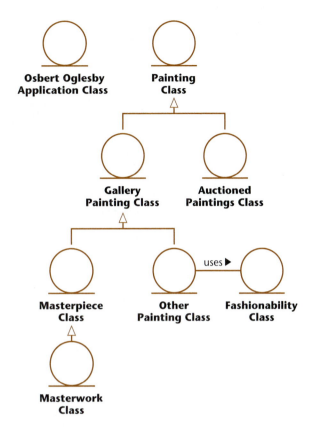

the various types of paintings handled by the Osbert Oglesby information system, whereas **Osbert Oglesby Application Class** contains attributes and operations of the information system as a whole.

Finally, we redraw Figure 6.13 without the attributes, but explicitly reflecting the stereotype of each class (Section 6.1). The result is shown in Figure 6.14. All eight classes in that figure are entity classes, that is, they model long-lived information.

At first sight, Figure 6.14 looks nothing like Figure 6.13. Nevertheless, both are indeed class diagrams. Recall that, as stated in Section 3.5, a class diagram depicts classes and their interrelationships; attributes and operations are optional. The major difference between the class diagram of Figure 6.13 and the class diagram of Figure 6.14 is that the latter does not show attributes. A minor difference is that the names of the classes appear inside the topmost boxes of the rectangles of Figure 6.13 but below the stereotypes of Figure 6.14.

6.5   Initial Dynamic Model: Osbert Oglesby Case Study

The third step in object-oriented analysis is dynamic modeling. In this step, we draw a statechart that reflects all the operations performed by or to the information system. The primary source of information regarding the relevant operations is the scenarios.

To gain an insight into the concept of *state,* consider Microsoft Word (or some other word processing program). When the program starts, we see the initial screen. Now we may select an option from a *menu,* the Font option from the Format menu, say. Selecting an option is an example of an *event.* The effect of the event is that a new screen appears, the

FIGURE 6.15
The Initial Statechart
of the Osbert Oglesby
Information System

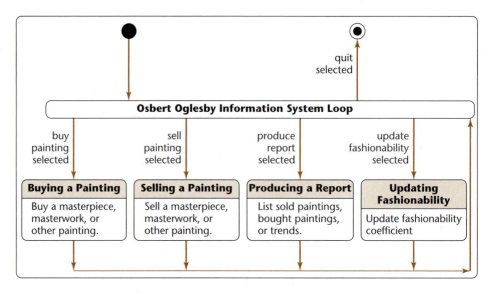

FIGURE 6.16
The Initial Main
Menu in the Target
Osbert Oglesby
Information System

screen that allows us to select a specific font for our document. The initial screen is a representation of the underlying initial state of Word. The Font screen is a representation of the underlying state of Word in which the user is allowed to choose a font. In other words, the state of a computerized information system is a particular set of values of the attributes of that system; the underlying state is often represented by a specific screen. Each event causes the system to move from state to state; that is, an event causes a *transition* between states.

The starting point of the statechart of Figure 6.15 is the solid circle on the top left; the solid circle represents the *initial state*. The arrow from the initial state leads down to the state labeled **Osbert Oglesby Information System Loop** (states other than the initial and final states are represented by rectangles with rounded corners). In state **Osbert Oglesby Information System Loop,** one of five events can occur (an event is something that causes a transition between states). In more detail, Osbert can choose one of five options: buy a painting, sell a painting, print a report, update a fashionability coefficient, or quit. These possibilities are indicated by the five events buy painting selected, sell painting selected, produce report selected, update fashionability selected, and quit selected. So, when the system is in state **Osbert Oglesby Information System Loop,** any one of the five events may occur, depending on which option Osbert selects from the menu of Figure 6.16 (discussed in the next section) that will be incorporated into the target information system.

Suppose that Osbert clicks on *Buy a painting* in the menu. The event buy painting selected (in the middle of the left side of Figure 6.15) has now occurred, so the system moves from its current state, **Osbert Oglesby Information System Loop,** to the state **Buying a Painting.** The operations that Osbert can perform in this state, namely, Buy masterpiece, masterwork, or other painting, appear below the line. From state **Buying a Painting** the arrows lead back to state **Osbert Oglesby Information System Loop.** The behavior of the rest of the statechart is similar. In particular, if Osbert clicks on *Quit,* the system moves to its *final state,* represented by the small black circle inside the white circle.

In summary, the information system moves from state to state when an event occurs. In each state, Osbert performs one of the operations supported by that state. This continues until Osbert clicks on option *Quit* in the menu of Figure 6.16 while the system is in state **Oglesby Information System Loop,** at which time the information system enters the final state (represented by the white circle containing the small black circle). This then terminates execution of the statechart, a model of the execution of the target information system.

Traditionally there is a dynamic model for each class, rather than for the system as a whole, as in this case study. However, within the context of information systems, objects rarely move from one class to another class. Accordingly, a dynamic model for the information system as a whole is appropriate.

Having completed the initial functional modeling, class modeling, and dynamic modeling, we check all three models and determine that the entity classes seem to be correct, at least for now.

Next we determine the boundary classes and control classes.

6.6   Extracting Boundary Classes

Unlike entity classes, boundary classes are usually easy to extract. In general, each input screen, output screen, and printed report is modeled by a class. Recall that a class incorporates attributes (data) and operations. The boundary class modeling (say) a printed report incorporates all the various data items that can be included in the report and the various operations that are carried out in order to print the report.

In the case of the Osbert Oglesby case study, in view of the relative simplicity of the information system, it makes sense to try to have just one screen that Osbert can use for all use cases: buy a painting, sell a painting, print a report, and update a fashionability coefficient. In a subsequent iteration, it may prove necessary to refine this one screen into more screens. In the meantime, however, in our initial class extraction we have only one screen class, **User Interface Class.**

Figure 6.16 depicts the first iteration of the main menu of the user-interface screen. The five commands that appear there correspond precisely to the five events in the statechart of Figure 6.15. If, in a subsequent iteration, additional events were added to the statechart, the corresponding commands would have to be added to the menu. (The implementation of the Osbert Oglesby case study given in Appendix D uses a textual interface rather than a graphical interface (GUI). That is, instead of clicking on a box, as shown in Figure 6.16, the user types in a choice, as shown in Figure 6.17. For example, the user types 1 to Buy a painting, 2 to Sell a painting, and so on. The reason the implementation in Appendix D uses a textual interface, such as Figure 6.17, is that a textual interface can be run on all computers; a GUI generally needs special software.)

There are three reports: the purchases report, the sales report, and the future trends report. Each of these has to be modeled by a separate boundary class because, as reflected in Figure 4.20, the content of each report is distinctly different. The resulting four corresponding initial boundary classes, **User Interface Class, Purchases Report Class, Sales Report Class,** and **Future Trends Report Class,** are listed in Figure 6.18.

FIGURE 6.17

Textual Version of the Graphical Initial Main Menu of Figure 6.16

```
                        MAIN MENU
            OSBERT OGLESBY - COLLECTOR OF FINE ART
                     1. Buy a painting
                     2. Sell a painting
                     3. Produce a report
                     4. Update fashionability
                     5. Quit
               Type your choice and press <ENTER>:
```

FIGURE 6.18
The Initial Boundary
Classes in the Osbert
Oglesby Information
System

| User Interface Class |
| Purchases Report Class |
| Sales Report Class |
| Future Trends Report Class |

FIGURE 6.19
The Initial Control
Classes in the Osbert
Oglesby Information
System

| Compute Masterpiece Price Class |
| Compute Masterwork Price Class |
| Compute Other Painting Price Class |
| Compute Future Trends Class |

6.7 Extracting Control Classes

Control classes are usually as easy to extract as boundary classes. In general, each nontrivial computation is modeled by a control class. In the Osbert Oglesby case study, there are four computations, namely, determining the maximum price that Osbert should offer for a masterpiece, a masterwork, or other painting and determining if there is a new trend in art purchases. This yields four initial control classes: **Compute Masterpiece Price Class, Compute Masterwork Price Class, Compute Other Painting Price Class,** and **Compute Future Trends Class.** They are listed in Figure 6.19.

6.8 Refining the Use Cases

Now we check the three sets of classes: entity, boundary, and control. At this point in the case study, we become aware that further refinement is needed. Recall that in the class diagram of Figure 6.9 (the second iteration) the three types of artwork were treated as subclasses of **Painting Class.** However, by the fifth iteration of the class diagram (Figure 6.12), it was clear that, as a consequence of the pricing algorithm, each of the three types of artwork had to be treated very differently.

Turning to the use cases of Figure 6.3, we now see that the use case Buy a Painting needs to be refined into three separate use cases: Buy a Masterpiece, Buy a Masterwork, and Buy Other Painting. This is reflected in Figure 6.20, the third iteration of the use-case diagram of the Osbert Oglesby information system.

In addition, the Produce a Report use case needs to be refined. Two of the reports, namely, the purchases report and the sales report, are straightforward examples of data extraction. But the future trends report involves a computation. Also, all three reports use their own boundary classes, as shown in Figure 6.18. For both these reasons, the Produce a Report use case needs to be refined into three use cases: Produce a Purchases Report, Produce a Sales Report, and Produce a Future Trends Report. This refinement is also reflected in Figure 6.20.

What changes to the other models do these refinements to the use-case diagram cause? There is no reason to have three separate user interfaces when Osbert wishes to buy a painting. Instead, one of the fields that Osbert will have to supply when using the information system to buy a painting is the classification of the painting. The relevant algorithm will then be invoked. Thus, the only additional change as a consequence of refining the Buy a Painting use case into three separate use cases is to split the description of the Buy a

FIGURE 6.20
The Third Iteration
of the Use-Case
Diagram of the
Osbert Oglesby
Information System

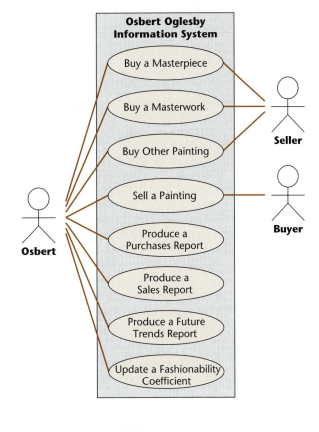

FIGURE 6.21
The Buy a
Masterpiece
Use Case

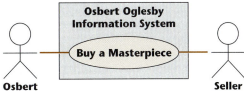

Painting use case (Figure 4.12) into three separate descriptions. The description of use case Buy a Masterpiece (shown separately in Figure 6.21) is given in Figure 6.22; the other two are left as an exercise (Problems 6.6 and 6.7), as are the descriptions of the three report use cases (Problems 6.8 through 6.10).

We now return to the Unified Process [Jacobson, Booch, and Rumbaugh, 1999].

6.9   Use-Case Realization

A use case is a description of an interaction between an actor and the information system. Use cases are first utilized at the beginning of the life cycle, that is, in the requirements workflow. By the end of the life cycle, that is, the implementation workflow, the use cases have been implemented in code. During the analysis and design workflows, more details are added to each use case, including a description of the classes that are involved in carrying out the use case. This process of extending and refining use cases is called *use-case realization.*

FIGURE 6.22
Description of the
Buy a Masterpiece
Use Case

Brief Description

The `Buy a Masterpiece` use case enables Osbert Oglesby to buy a masterpiece.

Step-by-Step Description

1. Osbert inputs the details of the masterpiece he is considering buying. These are
     First name of artist
     Last name of artist
     Title of work
     Date of work
     Height
     Width
     Medium (oil, watercolor, other medium)
     Subject (portrait, still life, landscape, other subject)
2. The information system responds with the maximum purchase price Osbert should offer. In more detail:

     The information system computes the coefficient of similarity between each painting for which there is an auction record and the painting under consideration for purchase. Question marks in the first or last name of the artist or in the title or date of the work are to be ignored.

     The information system scores 1 for a match on medium, otherwise 0.

     The information system scores 1 for a match on subject, otherwise 0.

     It adds these two numbers, multiplies by the area of the smaller of the two paintings, and divides by the area of the larger of the two.

     The resulting number is the coefficient of similarity.

     The information system finds the auctioned painting with the largest nonzero coefficient of similarity. If there is no such painting, Osbert will not buy the painting under consideration.

     The information system computes the maximum purchase price by adding to the auction price of the most similar work 8.5 percent, compounded annually, for each year since that auction.
3. If the seller accepts Osbert's offer, Osbert enters further details. These are
     Date of purchase
     Name of seller
     Address of seller
     Maximum purchase price determined by the algorithm
     Actual purchase price
     Target selling price

This terminology is somewhat confusing, because the verb *realize* can be used in at least three different senses:

- Understand ("Harvey slowly began to realize that he was in the wrong classroom").
- Receive ("Ingrid will realize a profit of $45,000 on the stock transaction").
- Accomplish ("Janet hopes to realize her dream of starting a computer company").

In the phrase "realize a use case," the word *realize* is used in this last sense, that is, it means to *accomplish* (or *achieve*) the use case.

   An *interaction diagram* (*sequence diagram* or *collaboration diagram*) depicts the realization of a specific scenario of the use case. To see how this is done, we first consider the use case Buy a Masterpiece.

FIGURE 6.23

Class Diagram
Showing the Classes
That Realize the **Buy
a Masterpiece** Use
Case of the Osbert
Oglesby Information
System

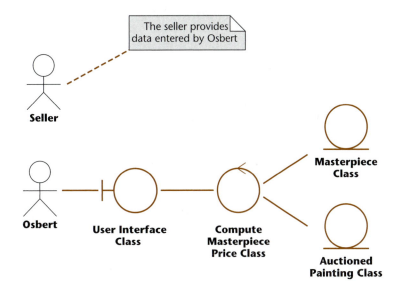

6.9.1 Buy a Masterpiece Use Case

Figure 6.20 is the current use-case diagram for the Osbert Oglesby case study. That is, it is a diagram that incorporates all the use cases of the case study identified at this stage. These include the Buy a Masterpiece use case shown separately in Figure 6.21. Figure 6.22 is the description of the Buy a Masterpiece use case—it specifies in writing the details of the use case.

As shown in the class diagram of Figure 6.23, the classes that enter into this use case include **User Interface Class,** which models the user interface, and **Compute Masterpiece Price Class,** which models the computation of the price Osbert should offer. This computation involves comparing the masterpiece being considered (an instance of **Masterpiece Class**) with the masterpieces that have been previously auctioned (all instances of **Auctioned Painting Class**). The **Seller** does not interact directly with the information system, but rather provides data that Osbert enters into the information system. This is indicated in the note, the rectangle with the top right-hand corner turned over. There is a dashed line from the note to the item to which it refers, the **Seller** in this case.

Figure 6.23 is a class diagram showing the classes that realize (that is, accomplish or achieve) the use case, as well as the relationships between those classes. Figure 6.23 is a class diagram in the style of Figure 6.14 rather than Figure 6.13. That is, Figure 6.23 depicts classes and their interrelationships, but the optional attributes are not shown.

As we have already seen, the artifacts that represent a use case in the requirements workflow are the use case and its description. In the analysis workflow, the use case is represented by a number of different artifacts. One of the analysis workflow artifacts is the class diagram that shows the classes that realize that use case.

Recall that a scenario is one possible instance of a use case. That is, a use case models the set of all interactions between an actor and the information system. Each individual interaction is a scenario (instance) of that use case. For example, Figure 6.4 is one scenario of the Buy a Masterpiece use case; it is reproduced here as Figure 6.24. Thus, the classes in the class diagram of Figure 6.23 have to be able to realize the scenario of Figure 6.24.

A working information system uses *objects* rather than *classes.* Recall that a class is a set of related objects, whereas an object is one instance of that class. Thus, for example, a specific masterpiece cannot be represented by **Masterpiece Class** but rather by an object, a

Osbert Oglesby wishes to buy a masterpiece.
1. Osbert enters the description of the painting.
2. The information system scans the auction records to find the price and year of the sale of the most similar work by the same artist.
3. The information system computes the maximum purchase price by adding 8.5 percent, compounded annually, for each year since the auction of the most similar work.
   Osbert makes an offer below the maximum purchase price—the offer is accepted by the seller.
4. Osbert enters sales information (name and address of seller, purchase price).

FIGURE 6.25   **A Collaboration Diagram of the Realization of the Scenario of Figure 6.24 of the Buy a
Masterpiece Use Case of the Osbert Oglesby Information System**

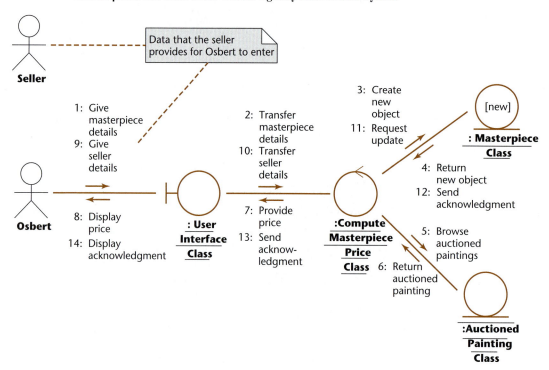

specific instance of **Masterpiece Class.** We denote such an object by **: Masterpiece Class.** (The reason for the colon is explained Chapter 10.) A class diagram such as Figure 6.23 shows the classes in the use case and their relationships; it shows neither the objects nor the sequence of messages as they are sent from object to object. We need something more.

Figure 6.25 is a collaboration diagram; that is, it shows the objects as well as the messages, numbered in the order in which they are sent in a specific scenario, in this case the scenario of Figure 6.24. In paragraph 1 of this scenario, Osbert inputs the details of the masterpiece he is considering buying. In Figure 6.25, this is represented by message 1: Give masterpiece details from **Osbert** to the object **: User Interface Class.** The direction of the arrow shows the direction in which the information flows.

In paragraphs 2 and 3 of this scenario (Figure 6.24), the maximum purchase price is computed by comparing the masterpiece under consideration with masterpieces that have previously been auctioned. This computation is performed by an instance of the control class, namely, object **: Compute Masterpiece Price Class.** In order to do this, the details of the masterpiece under consideration need to be transferred from object **: User Interface Class** to object **: Compute Masterpiece Price Class.** This is modeled by message 2: Transfer masterpiece details.

In order to do the comparison, object **: Compute Masterpiece Price Class** has to create a masterpiece object. It does this by first creating an instance of **Masterpiece Class.** This is modeled by message 3: Create new object from **: Compute Masterpiece Price Class** to **: Masterpiece Class.** The [new] inside the object indicates that it is created as a consequence of the message. The new object is passed back to **: Compute Masterpiece Price Class** (message 4: Return new object).

Now **: Compute Masterpiece Price Class** compares the masterpiece under consideration with each of the previously auctioned masterpieces. That is, it browses through all the instances of **Auctioned Painting Class.** This is modeled by message 5: Browse auctioned paintings from **: Compute Masterpiece Price Class** to **: Auctioned Painting Class** and message 6: Return auctioned painting in the reverse direction.

Having found the best match, **: Compute Masterpiece Price Class** computes the maximum price to be offered and informs Osbert what that price is. In other words, the price is transferred from **: Compute Masterpiece Price Class** to the user interface object **: User Interface Class** so that the price can be displayed. This is modeled by message 7: Provide price. Next the price is displayed for Osbert (message 8: Display price).

Osbert makes an offer for the masterpiece. The comment below Paragraph 3 of the scenario of Figure 6.24 states that the offer is accepted. As stated in Paragraph 4 of the scenario, Osbert now has to enter details provided by the seller. This is modeled by message 9: Give seller details from **Osbert** to object **: User Interface Class.** The note indicates that the data are provided by the seller to Osbert.

The seller data are passed on to object **: Compute Masterpiece Price Class** (message 10: Transfer seller details) to update the details of the masterpiece object **: Masterpiece Class** (message 11: Request update). The latter then sends an acknowledgment to **: Compute Masterpiece Price Class** (message 12: Send acknowledgment). This acknowledgment is then passed on to the user interface object **: User Interface Class** (message 13: Send acknowledgment), which displays it for Osbert (message 14: Display acknowledgment).

Osbert is not going to approve the specification document unless he understands exactly what the proposed information system will do. Accordingly, a written description of the collaboration diagram is needed. This is shown in Figure 6.26, the *flow of events.*

UML supports two different types of interaction diagram. The first is the collaboration diagram, like Figure 6.25. The second is a sequence diagram.

Collaboration diagrams and sequence diagrams contain exactly the same information, but it is displayed in different ways. Figure 6.27 is the sequence diagram equivalent to the

FIGURE 6.26   **The Flow of Events of the Collaboration Diagram of Figure 6.25 of the Realization of the Scenario of Figure 6.24 of the Buy a Masterpiece Use Case of the Osbert Oglesby Information System**

> Osbert inputs the details of the masterpiece he is considering buying (1). The information system then looks through all the masterpieces that have been auctioned to find the one that is closest to the masterpiece under consideration (2–6). It then computes the maximum price that Osbert should offer using the formula provided (7, 8).
>
> Osbert now makes an offer. His offer is accepted, and he supplies details regarding the seller (9), which are then used to update the masterpiece data (10–14).

FIGURE 6.27   The Sequence Diagram of the Realization of the Scenario of Figure 6.24 of the Buy a Masterpiece
Use Case of the Osbert Oglesby Information System, Equivalent to Figure 6.25
(The flow of events of the sequence diagram is therefore also Figure 6.26)

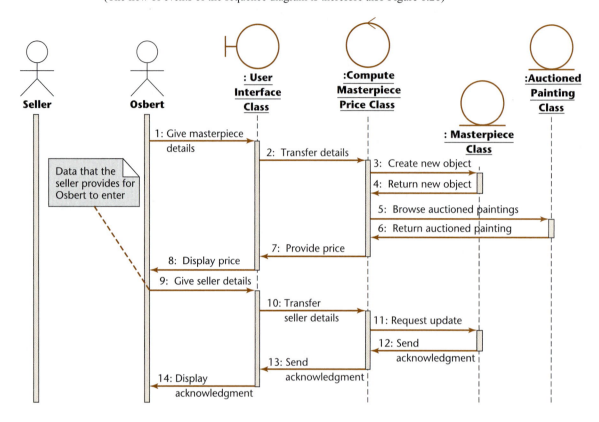

collaboration diagram of Figure 6.25. Instead of the [new] inside the **: Masterpiece Class**
object as in the collaboration diagram, the corresponding object in the sequence diagram
is shifted down so that its *lifeline* (as the vertical lines are called) starts where the object is
created. The narrow rectangle on a lifeline shows when the relevant object is active.

The sequence diagram of Figure 6.27 shows that every message of the scenario of Figure 6.24 involves either the instance of the user interface class **: User Interface Class** or
the instance of the control class **: Compute Masterpiece Price Class.** It also shows that
every transfer of information from object A to object B eventually is followed by a transfer
in the reverse direction. These two facts also are true in the fully equivalent collaboration
diagram (Figure 6.25), but are not as obvious in that format. Information system developers can choose whether to use a sequence diagram or a collaboration diagram, or both, of
each scenario.

The strength of a sequence diagram is that is shows the flow of messages unambigu-
ously. The order of the messages is particularly clear, as are the sender and receiver of each
individual message. So, when the transfer of information is the focus of attention (which is
the case for much of the time when performing systems analysis), a sequence diagram
is superior to a collaboration diagram. On the other hand, the similarity between a class
diagram (such as Figure 6.23) and the collaboration diagram that realizes the relevant
scenario (such as Figure 6.25) is strong. Accordingly, on those occasions when the systems
analysts are concentrating on the classes, a collaboration diagram is generally more useful
than the equivalent sequence diagram.

A point to keep in mind is that Figures 6.21 through 6.27 are all either use cases, instances of use cases, or written descriptions of instances of use case. In more detail:

- Figure 6.21 depicts the use case Buy a Masterpiece.
- Figure 6.22 is the description of that use case; that is, it provides a written account of the details of the Buy a Masterpiece use case of Figure 6.21.
- Figure 6.23 is a class diagram showing the classes that realize the Buy a Masterpiece use case. The class diagram depicts the classes and their interactions for all possible scenarios of the use case.
- Figure 6.24 is a scenario, that is, one instance of the use case of Figure 6.21.
- Figure 6.25 is a collaboration diagram of the realization of the scenario of Figure 6.24; that is, it depicts the objects and the messages sent between them in the realization of that one scenario.
- Figure 6.26 is the flow of events of the collaboration diagram of Figure 6.25. That is, just as Figure 6.22 is a written description of the Buy a Masterpiece use case of Figure 6.21, Figure 6.26 is a written description of the collaboration diagram of Figure 6.25.
- Figure 6.27 is the sequence diagram that is fully equivalent to the collaboration diagram of Figure 6.25. Figure 6.26 is therefore also the flow of events of the sequence diagram of Figure 6.27.

Figures 6.21 through 6.27 use different notations and provide different levels of detail of the same activity, namely, buying a masterpiece. Why do we construct so many related artifacts? The reason we examine this one activity from a variety of different perspectives is to learn enough about it to ensure that the analysis workflow will be correct.

6.9.2   `Buy a Masterwork` Use Case

Consider the class diagram showing the classes that realize the Buy a Masterwork use case (Figure 6.28). Recall that the maximum price of a masterwork is determined by first considering the painting under consideration as if it were a masterpiece and then adjusting the result. In other words, the classes that enter into this use case are first **User Interface Class,** which models the user interface, and **Compute Masterwork Price Class,** which

FIGURE 6.28

Class Diagram Showing the Classes That Realize the Buy a Masterwork Use Case of the Osbert Oglesby Information System

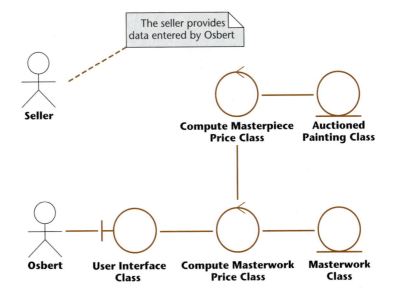

models the computation of the price Osbert should offer. It performs this computation by creating a masterwork object (an instance of **Masterwork Class**) and passing this object onto the **Compute Masterpiece Price Class.** Recall also that, as shown in Figure 6.13, a masterwork *is a* masterpiece (see Section 3.3), so the part of the information system that computes the maximum price Osbert should offer for a masterpiece will work equally well for a masterwork. Thus, the other classes that enter into the computation are **Compute Masterpiece Price Class** and **Auctioned Painting Class.**

Figure 6.29 shows a scenario for the Buy a Masterwork use case, and Figure 6.30 is the equivalent collaboration diagram of the scenario of Figure 6.29. The main difference between collaboration diagrams 6.25 and 6.30 is that in Figure 6.30, object **: Compute Masterwork Price Class** creates a masterwork object (3: Create new object) and passes it to **: Compute Masterpiece Price Class** (5: Transfer masterwork) to compute the maximum asking price as if the painting were a masterpiece. This price is passed back to **: Compute Masterwork Price Class** (8: Provide price), which adjusts the price to

FIGURE 6.29

One Possible Scenario of Buying a Masterwork

> Osbert Oglesby wishes to buy a masterwork painted in the seventeenth century.
> 1. Osbert enters the description of the painting.
> 2. The information system scans the auction records to find the price and year of the sale of the most similar work by the same artist.
> 3. The information system computes the maximum purchase price by adding 8.5 percent, compounded annually, for each year since the auction of the most similar work, and multiplying the result by $(21 - 17) / (22 - 17)$, or 0.8. Osbert makes an offer below the maximum purchase price—the offer is accepted by the seller.
> 4. Osbert enters sales information (name and address of seller, purchase price).

FIGURE 6.30   **A Collaboration Diagram of the Realization of the Scenario of Figure 6.29 of the Buy a Masterwork Use Case of the Osbert Oglesby Information System**

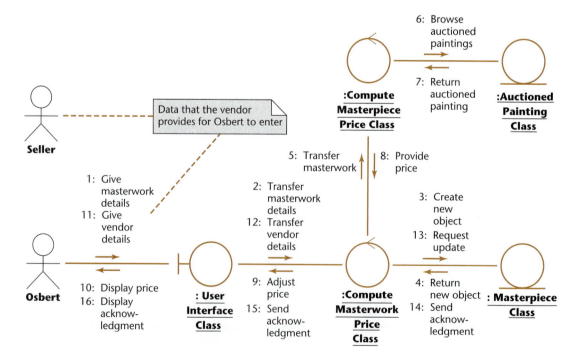

reflect the fact that the painting in question is indeed a masterwork and not a masterpiece (9: Adjust price). The flow of events (written description of the collaboration diagram for the client) appears in Figure 6.31. Figure 6.32 is the sequence diagram equivalent to the collaboration diagram of Figure 6.30; Figure 6.31 is therefore also the flow of events of the sequence diagram.

Comparing the class diagrams of Figures 6.23 and 6.28, we see that many classes are common to both class diagrams. The information system as a whole has only one user interface (an instance of **User Interface Class**) for all three buying use cases. In addition, because the maximum purchase price for a masterwork is first computed as if the painting were a masterpiece, classes **Compute Masterpiece Price Class** and **Auctioned Painting Class** play a role in both use cases.

FIGURE 6.31

The Flow of Events of the Collaboration Diagram of Figure 6.30

> Osbert inputs the details of the masterwork he is considering buying (1). The information system computes the maximum price that Osbert should offer using a two-stage formula. First, the information system computes the price as if the masterwork were a masterpiece (2–8) and then adjusts the price for the masterwork (9, 10).
>
> Osbert now makes an offer. His offer is accepted, and he supplies details regarding the seller (11), which are then used to update the masterwork data (12–16).

FIGURE 6.32   **A Sequence Diagram of the Realization of the Scenario of Figure 6.29 of the Buy a Masterpiece Use Case of the Osbert Oglesby Information System, Equivalent to Figure 6.30**
(The flow of events of the sequence diagram is therefore also Figure 6.31)

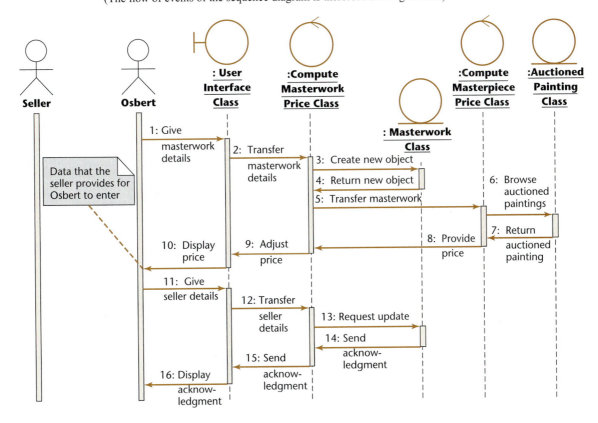

In other words, first we determine the entity classes, boundary classes, and control classes of the information system as a whole. Then we realize scenarios of all the use cases in terms of those classes, bearing in mind that some of those classes may be utilized to realize more than one use case.

We again see use of a common class in the Buy Other Painting use case.

6.9.3 Buy Other Painting Use Case

A class diagram showing the classes that realize the Buy Other Painting use case appears in Figure 6.33. Scenarios and interaction diagrams (collaboration diagram, sequence diagram) and associated flows of events are left as an exercise (Problems 6.11 through 6.14).

It is not surprising that the boundary class **User Interface Class** appears yet again because, as previously explained, the same user interface will be used for buying all three types of painting (and, in fact, by all eight use cases). Accordingly, the main menu of Figure 6.16 has to be modified to reflect buying the three different types of painting explicitly. Thus, *Buy a painting* in Figure 6.16 must replaced by *Buy a masterpiece, Buy a masterwork,* and *Buy other painting.* This will ensure that the correct algorithm is invoked to compute the maximum price that Osbert should offer. The revised screen, shown in Figure 6.34, is generated by **: User Interface Class.** (The corresponding textual interface, as implemented in Appendix D, is shown in Figure 6.35.)

FIGURE 6.33

Class Diagram Showing the Classes That Realize the Buy Other Painting Use Case of the Osbert Oglesby Information System

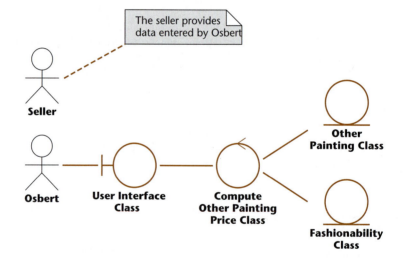

FIGURE 6.34

Second Iteration of the Main Menu in the Target Osbert Oglesby Information System

FIGURE 6.35

Textual Version of the
Graphical Main
Menu of Figure 6.34

```
                 MAIN MENU
  OSBERT OGLESBY - COLLECTOR OF FINE ART
         1.  Buy a masterpiece
         2.  Buy a masterwork
         3.  Buy other painting
         4.  Sell a painting
         5.  Produce a report
         6.  Update fashionability
         7.  Quit
    Type your choice and press <ENTER>:
```

FIGURE 6.36

Class Diagram
Showing the Classes
That Realize the Sell
a Painting Use Case
of the Osbert Oglesby
Information System

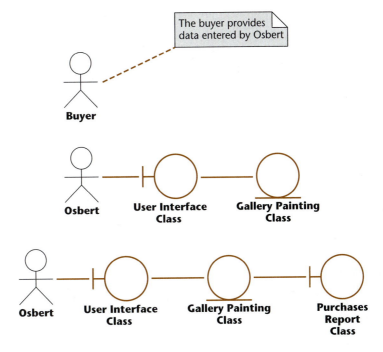

FIGURE 6.37

Class Diagram
Showing the
Classes That Realize
the Produce a
Purchases Report
Use Case of the
Osbert Oglesby
Information System

6.9.4   The Remaining Five Use Cases

Figure 6.36 depicts a class diagram showing the classes that realize the Sell a Painting use case. This realization is straightforward as a consequence of the simplicity of the use case (Figure 4.16).

Turning now to the three report use cases, the class diagrams showing the classes that realize those use cases are shown in Figures 6.37 through 6.39. The first two class diagrams differ only in the output interface class. The third use case, Produce a Future Trends Report, is different from the other two. Use cases Produce a Purchases Report and Produce a Sales Report simply browse through the **Gallery Painting Class,** that is, paintings that Osbert has purchased (and possibly later sold). But use case Produce a Future Trends Report has to perform the computation explained in Paragraph 1.3 of Figure 4.20. This is reflected in the class diagram of Figure 6.39. Details of the realization of this use case are left as an exercise (Problems 6.15 through 6.18).

Finally, a class diagram showing the classes that realize the Update a Fashionability Coefficient use case is shown in Figure 6.40. Again, this use case is straightforward.

FIGURE 6.38
Class Diagram
Showing the Classes
That Realize the
Produce a Sales
Report Use Case of
the Osbert Oglesby
Information System

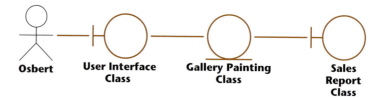

FIGURE 6.39
Class Diagram
Showing the Classes
That Realize the
Produce a Future
Trends Report Use
Case of the Osbert
Oglesby Information
System

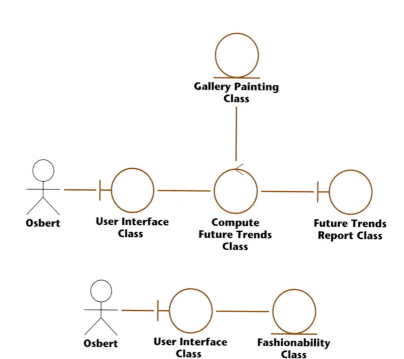

FIGURE 6.40
Class Diagram
Showing the
Classes That Realize
the Update a
Fashionability
Coefficient Use Case
of the Osbert Oglesby
Information System

6.10 Incrementing the Class Diagram

The entity classes were extracted in Sections 6.2 through 6.4, yielding Figure 6.14, which shows eight entity classes. The boundary classes were extracted in Section 6.6, and the control classes in Section 6.7. In the course of realizing the various use cases in Section 6.9, interrelationships between many of the classes became apparent; these interrelationships are shown in the class diagrams of Figures 6.23, 6.28, 6.33, and 6.36 through 6.40. Figure 6.41 combines these class diagrams.

Now the class diagrams of Figures 6.14 and 6.41 are combined to yield the sixth iteration of the class diagram of the Osbert Oglesby case study, shown in Figure 6.42. More specifically, starting with Figure 6.41, the classes **Osbert Oglesby Application Class** and **Painting Class** of Figure 6.14 are added. Then the six relationships in Figure 6.14 are drawn in; they are shown with dashed lines to distinguish them. The result, Figure 6.42, the sixth iteration of the class diagram, is the class diagram at the end of the analysis workflow.

This concludes the analysis workflow of the Osbert Oglesby case study.

FIGURE 6.41   Class Diagram Combining the Class Diagrams of Figures 6.23, 6.28, 6.33, and 6.36 through 6.40

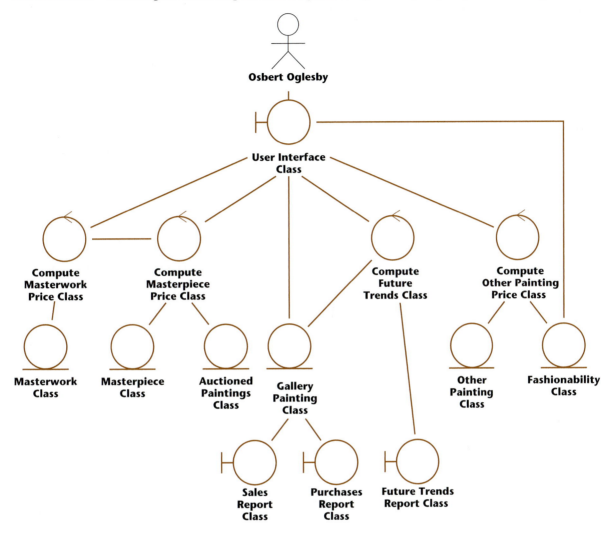

6.11   Where's the Specification Document?

In Section 1.2.2, it was stated that the aim of the analysis workflow is to produce the specification document, but the end of the previous section it was claimed that the analysis workflow is now complete. The obvious question is: Where's the specification document?

The short answer is: The Unified Process is use-case driven. In more detail, the use cases and the artifacts derived from them contain all the information that, in the traditional paradigm, appears in the specification document in text form, and more.

For example, consider the use case Buy a Masterpiece. When the requirements workflow is performed, the Buy a Painting use case (Figure 4.5) and its description (Figure 4.15) are shown to the client. The systems analysts must be meticulous in ensuring that their client, Osbert Oglesby, fully understands these two artifacts and agrees that they accurately model the information system he needs. Then, during the analysis workflow, Osbert is shown the scenarios for buying a painting (Figures 6.4 though 6.6, or the extended scenario of Figure 6.7), the use case Buy a Masterpiece (Figure 6.21), its description (Figure 6.22),

FIGURE 6.42   The Sixth Iteration of the Class Diagram of the Osbert Oglesby Case Study, Obtained by Combining the Class Diagrams of Figures 6.14 and 6.41

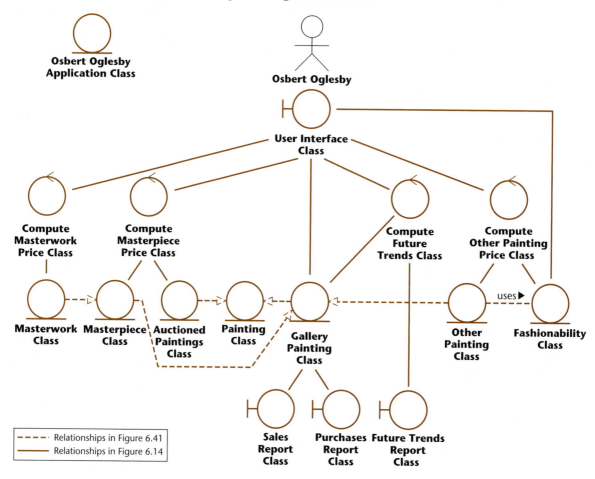

the class diagram showing the classes that realize the use case (Figure 6.23), the interaction diagrams of the realization of a scenario of the use case (Figures 6.25 and 6.27), and the flow of events of these interaction diagrams (Figure 6.26).

The set of artifacts listed in the previous paragraph all appertain to just the use case Buy a Masterpiece. As shown in Figure 6.20, there are eight use cases altogether. The same set of artifacts is produced for each of the other seven use cases. The resulting collection of artifacts, some diagrammatic and some textual, convey to the client more information more accurately than the purely textual specification document of the traditional paradigm possibly could.

The traditional specification document usually plays a contractual role. That is, once it has been signed by both the developers and the client, it essentially constitutes a legal document. If the developers build an information system that satisfies the specification document, the client is obligated to pay for the system and, conversely, if the information system does not conform to its specification document, the developers are required to fix it if they want to get paid. In the case of the Unified Process, the collection of artifacts of the complete set of use cases similarly constitutes a contract. Thus, as claimed at the end of the previous section, the analysis workflow of the Osbert Oglesby case study is indeed complete.

In the next chapter we perform the analysis workflow of the MSG Foundation case study.

Key Terms

abstract noun, *104*
analysis workflow, *99*
attribute, *108*
boundary class, *99*
class diagram, *101*
class modeling, *101*
collaboration diagram, *114*
control class, *100*
dynamic modeling, *101*
entity class, *99*

event, *109*
exception scenario, *103*
flow of events, *117*
functional modeling, *101*
interaction diagram, *114*
legacy information system, *100*
lifeline, *118*
millennium bug, *100*
normal scenario, *103*
noun extraction method, *104*

operation, *104*
realize (in the Unified
   Theory context), *114*
scenario, *101*
sequence diagram, *114*
statechart, *101*
stereotype, *100*
transition, *110*
use-case realization, *113*
Y2K problem, *100*

Review Questions for Chapter 6

1. Distinguish between boundary, control, and entity classes.
2. Why are two of the paragraphs in the scenario of Figure 6.4 unnumbered?
3. Distinguish between functional modeling, class modeling, and dynamic modeling.
4. What is the difference between an exception scenario and an extended scenario?
5. What is an event in UML?
6. What does it mean to "realize a use case"?
7. Distinguish between a sequence diagram, a collaboration diagram, and an interaction diagram.

Problems

6.1   A noun extraction process is described in Section 6.4. Why do we not also extract the verbs? And what about the other six parts of speech (adjectives, adverbs, conjunctions, interjections, prepositions, and pronouns)?

6.2   Give a scenario of the use case Sell a Painting of Figure 6.3.

6.3   Give a scenario of the use case Produce a Report of Figure 6.3.

6.4   Give an extended scenario of the use case Update a Fashionability Coefficient of Figure 6.3.

6.5   Why do you think that the operations of each class are not added to the class diagram while performing the analysis workflow?

6.6   Give the description of the use case Buy a Masterwork of Figure 6.20. Provide as much detail as you can.

6.7   Give the description of the use case Buy Other Painting of Figure 6.20. Provide as much detail as you can.

6.8   Give the description of the use case Produce a Purchases Report of Figure 6.20. Provide as much detail as you can.

6.9   Give the description of the use case Produce a Sales Report of Figure 6.20. Provide as much detail as you can.

6.10 Give the description of the use case Produce a Future Trends Report of Figure 6.20. Provide as much detail as you can.

6.11 Give an extended scenario of the use case Buy Other Painting you gave for Problem 6.7.

6.12 Draw a collaboration diagram of the realization of the normal part of your extended scenario of Problem 6.11. Utilize the class diagram of Figure 6.33.

6.13 Draw a sequence diagram of the realization of the normal part of your extended scenario of Problem 6.11. Utilize the class diagram of Figure 6.33.

6.14 Give the flow of events of your interaction diagrams of Problems 6.12 and 6.13.

6.15 Give an extended scenario of the use case Produce a Future Trends Report of the Osbert Oglesby information system shown in Figure 6.20.

6.16 Draw a collaboration diagram of the realization of your scenario of Problem 6.15. Utilize the class diagram of Figure 6.39.

6.17   Draw a sequence diagram of the realization of your scenario of Problem 6.15. Utilize the class diagram of Figure 6.39.

6.18   Give the flow of events of your interaction diagrams of Problems 6.16 and 6.17.

6.19   Give an extended scenario of your use case for the information system to determine whether a bank statement is correct (Problem 4.9).

6.20   Determine the entity classes for the information system to determine whether a bank statement is correct (Problem 4.9).

6.21   Draw the initial statechart for the information system to determine whether a bank statement is correct (Problem 4.9). (Hint: The statechart should not incorporate the steps of the computation.)

6.22   Determine the boundary and control class(es) for the information system to determine whether a bank statement is correct (Problem 4.9).

6.23   Consider just the normal scenario portion of your answer to Problem 6.19. Give the class diagram showing the classes that realize the use case of the information system to determine whether a bank statement is correct (Problem 4.9).

6.24   Give the interaction diagrams and the flow of events for the normal scenario portion of your answer to Problem 6.19.

Reference

Jacobson, I.; G. Booch; and J. Rumbaugh. *The Unified Software Development Process.* Reading, MA: Addison Wesley, 1999.

Chapter 7

The Object-Oriented Analysis Workflow II

Learning Objectives

After studying this chapter, you should have a deeper understanding than before of how to:

- Perform the analysis workflow.
- Extract the boundary, control, and entity classes.
- Perform functional modeling.
- Perform class modeling.
- Perform dynamic modeling.
- Determine actors and use cases.

In Chapter 6, it was explained how the analysis workflow is performed, and the various steps were applied to the Osbert Oglesby case study. In this chapter the analysis workflow of the MSG Foundation case study is performed step by step. Recall that, during the performance of the requirements workflow of the MSG Foundation in Chapter 5, the number of use cases in the use-case diagram decreased from nine in the fifth iteration (Figure 5.34) to only five in the seventh iteration (Figure 5.39). In this chapter there will be a further decrease.

The Unified Process [Jacobson, Booch, and Rumbaugh, 1999] is use-case driven. Accordingly, the starting point for the analysis of the MSG Foundation case study is the MSG use-case diagram (Figure 5.39), reproduced here as Figure 7.1. The first analysis step is to extract the classes. In the Unified Process there are three types of classes: entity classes, boundary classes, and control classes. We begin by extracting the entity classes, that is, the classes that model long-lived information.

7.1 Extracting Entity Classes: MSG Foundation Case Study

As explained in Section 6.2, entity class extraction is performed by iterating three steps: functional modeling, class modeling, and dynamic modeling. Functional modeling of the MSG Foundation case study comes first.

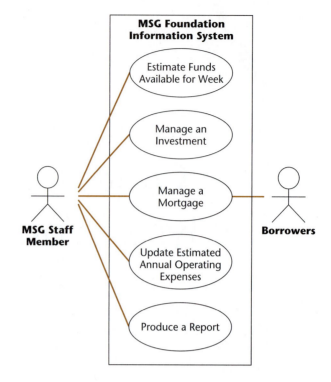

7.2 Initial Functional Model: MSG Foundation Case Study

As described in Section 6.3, functional modeling consists of finding the scenarios of the use cases. Recall that a scenario is an instance of a use case. Consider the use case Manage a Mortgage (Figures 5.29 and 5.30). One possible scenario is shown in Figure 7.2. There is a change in the annual real-estate tax to be paid on a home for which the MSG Foundation has provided a mortgage. Because the borrowers pay this tax in equal weekly payments, any change in the real-estate tax must be entered in the relevant mortgage record, so that the total weekly installment (and perhaps the grant) can be adjusted accordingly. The normal portion of the extended scenario models an MSG staff member accessing the relevant mortgage record and changing the annual real-estate tax. Sometimes, however, the staff member may not be able to locate the correct mortgage stored in the information system because he or she has entered the mortgage number incorrectly. This possibility is modeled by the exception portion of the scenario.

A second scenario corresponding to the Manage a Mortgage use case (Figures 5.29 and 5.30) is shown in Figure 7.3. Here the borrowers' weekly income has changed. They would like this information to be reflected in the MSG Foundation records so that their weekly installment can be correctly computed. The normal portion of this extended scenario shows this operation proceeding as expected. The abnormal portion of this scenario shows two possibilities. First, as in the previous scenario, the staff member may enter the mortgage number incorrectly. Second, the borrowers may not bring with them adequate documentation to support their claim regarding their income.

A third scenario (Figure 7.4) is an instance of use case Estimate Funds Available for Week (Figure 5.39). This scenario is directly derived from the description of the use case (Figure 5.40).

FIGURE 7.2
An Extended Scenario of Managing a Mortgage

> An MSG Foundation staff member wants to update the annual real-estate tax on a home for which the Foundation has provided a mortgage.
> 1. The staff member enters the new value of the annual real-estate tax.
> 2. The information system updates the date on which the annual real-estate tax was last changed.
>
> **Possible Alternative**
>
> A. The staff member enters the mortgage number incorrectly.

FIGURE 7.3
Another Extended Scenario of Managing a Mortgage

> There is a change in the weekly income of a couple who have borrowed money from the MSG Foundation. They wish to have their weekly income updated in the Foundation records by an MSG staff member so that their mortgage payments will be correctly computed.
> 1. The staff member enters the new value of the weekly income.
> 2. The information system updates the date on which the weekly income was last changed.
>
> **Possible Alternatives**
>
> A. The staff member enters the mortgage number incorrectly.
> B. The borrowers do not bring documentation regarding their new income.

FIGURE 7.4
A Scenario of the Estimate Funds Available for Week Use Case

> An MSG Foundation staff member wishes to determine the funds available for mortgages this week.
> 1. For each investment, the information system extracts the estimated annual return on that investment. It sums the separate returns and divides the result by 52 to yield the estimated investment income for the week.
> 2. The information system then extracts the estimated annual MSG Foundation operating expenses and divides the result by 52.
> 3. For each mortgage:
>   3.1 The information system computes the amount to be paid this week by adding the principal and interest payment to $\frac{1}{52}$nd of the sum of the annual real-estate tax and the annual homeowner's insurance premium.
>   3.2 It then computes 28 percent of the couple's current gross weekly income.
>   3.3 If the result of Step 3.1 is greater than the result of Step 3.2, then it determines the mortgage payment for the week as the result of Step 3.2, and the amount of the grant for this week as the difference between the result of Step 3.1 and the result of Step 3.2.
>   3.4 Otherwise, it takes the mortgage payment for this week as the result of Step 3.1, and there is no grant for the week.
> 4. The information system sums the mortgage payments of Steps 3.3 and 3.4 to yield the estimated total mortgage payments for the week.
> 5. It sums the grant payments of Step 3.3 to yield the estimated total grant payments for the week.
> 6. The information system adds the results of Steps 1 and 4 and subtracts the results of Steps 2 and 5. This is the total amount available for mortgages for the current week.
> 7. Finally, the information system prints the total amount available for new mortgages during the current week.

FIGURE 7.5

A Scenario of the
Produce a Report
Use Case

> An MSG staff member wishes to print a list of all
> mortgages.
> 1. The staff member requests a report listing all
>   mortgages.

FIGURE 7.6

Another Scenario
of the Produce a
Report Use Case

> An MSG staff member wishes to print a list of all
> investments.
> 1. The staff member requests a report listing all
>   investments.

The scenarios of Figures 7.5 and 7.6 are instances of use case **Produce a Report**. Again, these scenarios are directly derived from the corresponding description of the use case (Figure 5.36). The remaining scenarios are equally straightforward and are therefore left as an exercise (Problems 7.1 and 7.2).

7.3   Initial Class Diagram: MSG Foundation Case Study

The second step is class modeling. As described in the previous chapter, the aim of this step is to extract the entity classes, determine their interrelationships, and find their attributes. The best way to start this step is usually to use the two-stage noun extraction method.

In Stage 1 we describe the information system in a single paragraph. In the case of the MSG Foundation case study, a way to do this is

> Weekly reports are to be printed showing how much money is available for mortgages. In addition, lists of investments and mortgages must be printed on demand.

In Stage 2 we identify the nouns in this paragraph. For clarity, the nouns are printed in sans serif type.

> Weekly reports are to be printed showing how much money is available for mortgages. In addition, lists of investments and mortgages must be printed on demand.

The nouns are report, money, mortgage, list, and investment. Nouns report and list are not long lived, so they are unlikely to be entity classes (report will surely turn out to be a boundary class), and money is an abstract noun. This leaves two candidate entity classes, namely, **Mortgage Class** and **Investment Class,** as shown in Figure 7.7, the first iteration of the initial class diagram.

Now we consider interactions between these two entity classes. Looking at the descriptions of use cases **Manage an Investment** and **Manage a Mortgage** (Figures 5.28 and 5.30, respectively) it appears that the operations performed on the two entity classes are likely to be very similar, namely, insertions, deletions, and modifications. Also, the second iteration of the description of use case **Produce a Report** (Figure 5.36) shows all the members of both entity classes have to be printed on demand. In other words, **Mortgage Class** and **Investment Class** should probably be subclasses of some superclass. We will call that superclass **Asset Class,** because mortgages and investments are both assets of the MSG Foundation. The resulting second iteration of the initial class diagram is shown in Figure 7.8.

FIGURE 7.7
The First Iteration
of the Initial Class
Diagram of the
MSG Foundation
Case Study

FIGURE 7.8
The Second Iteration
of the Initial Class
Diagram of the
MSG Foundation
Case Study

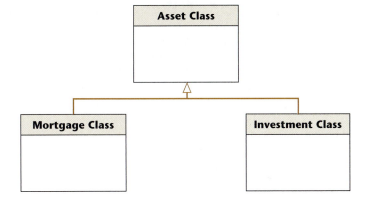

FIGURE 7.9
The Eighth Iteration
of the Use-Case
Diagram of the
MSG Foundation
Information System
The new use case,
Manage an Asset, is
shaded

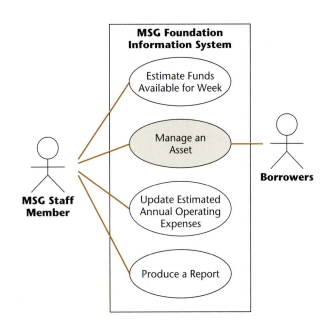

7.4   Back to the Requirements Workflow

A useful side effect of constructing this superclass is that we can once again reduce the number of use cases. As shown in Figure 7.1, we currently have five use cases, including Manage a Mortgage and Manage an Investment. However, if we consider a mortgage or an investment to be a special case of an asset, we can combine the two use cases into a single use case, Manage an Asset. The eighth iteration of the use-case diagram is shown in Figure 7.9. The new use case is shaded. Now the attributes are added, as shown in Figure 7.10.

FIGURE 7.10
Attributes Added to
the Second Iteration
of the Initial Class
Diagram of the
MSG Foundation
Case Study

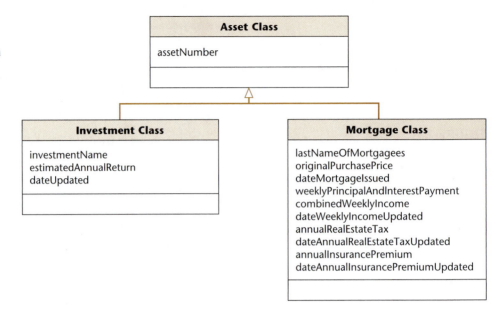

It cannot be stressed too strongly that the phrase "iterate and *in*crement" also includes the possibility that we have to *de*crement what has been developed to date. We have seen two reasons for such a decrease. First, if we make a mistake, the way to correct it may be to *back-track* to an earlier version of the information system and find a better way of performing the step that we incorrectly carried out. When we backtrack, everything that we added in the course of the incorrect step now has to be removed. Second, as a consequence of reorganizing our models to date, one or more artifacts may have become superfluous. Developing an information system is hard. It is therefore important to remove superfluous use cases or other artifacts.

7.5   Initial Dynamic Model: MSG Foundation Case Study

The third step in extracting the entity classes is dynamic modeling. In this step, we draw a statechart that reflects all the operations performed by or to that system, indicating the events that cause the transition from state to state. Our major source of information regarding the relevant operations is the scenarios.

The statechart of Figure 7.11 reflects the operations of the complete MSG Foundation information system. The solid circle on the top left represents the initial state, the starting point of the statechart. The arrow from the initial state leads us to the state labeled **MSG Foundation Information System Loop** (states other than the initial and final states are represented by rectangles with rounded corners). In state **MSG Foundation Information System Loop,** one of five events can occur. In more detail, an MSG staff member can issue one of five commands: estimate funds for the week, manage an asset, update estimated annual operating expenses, produce a report, or quit. These possibilities are indicated by the five events estimate funds for the week selected, manage an asset selected, update estimated annual operating expenses selected, produce a report selected, and quit selected. (An event causes a transition between states.)

When the system is in state **MSG Foundation Information System Loop,** any one of the five events may occur, depending on which option the MSG staff member selects

FIGURE 7.11   The Initial Statechart of the MSG Foundation Information System

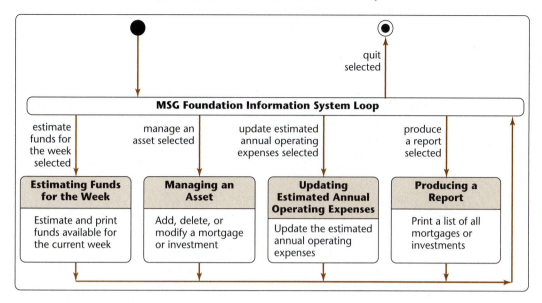

FIGURE 7.12   Menu in the Target MSG Foundation Information System

FIGURE 7.13   Textual Version of the Menu of Figure 7.12

```
                    MAIN MENU
    MARTHA STOCKTON GREENGAGE FOUNDATION
        1.  Estimate funds available for week
        2.  Manage an asset
        3.  Update estimated annual operating expenses
        4.  Produce a report
        5.  Quit
    Type your choice and press <ENTER>:
```

from the menu, shown in Figure 7.12, that will be incorporated in the target information system. (The implementation of the MSG Foundation case study given in Appendix E uses a textual interface rather than a graphical interface (GUI). That is, instead of clicking on a box, as shown in Figure 7.12, the user types in a choice, as shown in Figure 7.13. For example, the user types 1 to Estimate funds available for week, 2 to Manage an asset, and so on. The reason the implementation in Appendix E uses a textual interface such as Figure 7.13 is that a textual interface can be run on all computers; a GUI generally needs special software.)

Suppose that the MSG staff member clicks on the choice *Manage an asset* in the menu of Figure 7.12. The event manage an asset selected (second from the left below the **MSG Foundation Information System Loop** box in Figure 7.11) has now occurred, so the system moves from its current state, **MSG Foundation Information System Loop,** to the state **Managing an Asset.** The operations that the MSG staff member can perform in this state, namely, Add, delete, or modify a mortgage or investment, appear below the line in the box with rounded corners.

Once the operation has been performed, the system returns to the state **MSG Foundation Information System Loop,** as shown by the arrows. The behavior of the rest of the statechart is equally straightforward.

In summary, the information system moves from state to state. In each state, the MSG staff member can perform the operations supported by that state, as listed below the line in the box with rounded corners that represents the state. This continues until the MSG staff member clicks on menu choice *Quit* when the information system is in the state **MSG Foundation Information System Loop.** At this time the information system enters the final state (represented by the white circle containing the small black circle). When this state is entered, execution of the statechart terminates; recall that the statechart is a model of the execution of the target information system.

7.6 Revising the Entity Classes: MSG Foundation Case Study

We have now completed the initial functional model, the initial class diagram, and the initial dynamic model. We check all three models and we find that we have overlooked something.

Look at the initial statechart of Figure 7.11 and consider state **Updating Estimated Annual Operating Expenses** with operation Update the estimated annual operating expenses. This operation has to be performed on data, namely, the current value of the

FIGURE 7.14

The Third Iteration of the Initial Class Diagram of the MSG Foundation Case Study

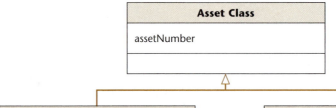

MSG Application Class

estimatedAnnualOperatingExpenses
dateEstimatedAnnualOperatingExpensesUpdated
availableFundsForWeek
expectedAnnualReturnOnInvestments
dateExpectedAnnualReturnOnInvestmentsUpdated
expectedGrantsForWeek
expectedMortgagePaymentsForWeek

Asset Class

assetNumber

Investment Class

investmentName
estimatedAnnualReturn
dateEstimatedReturnUpdated

Mortgage Class

lastNameOfMortgagees
originalPurchasePrice
dateMortgageIssued
weeklyPrincipalAndInterestPayment
combinedWeeklyIncome
dateCombinedWeeklyIncomeUpdated
annualRealEstateTax
dateAnnualRealEstateTaxUpdated
annualInsurancePremium
dateAnnualInsurancePremiumUpdated

FIGURE 7.15
Figure 7.14
**Redrawn to Show
the Stereotypes**

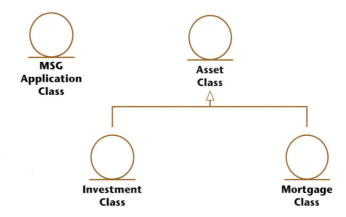

estimated annual operating expenses. But where is the value of the estimated annual operating expenses to be found? Looking at Figure 7.10, we are delighted to see that it is not an attribute of **Asset Class** or either of its subclasses, which would have been a serious error. On the other hand, currently we have only one class (**Asset Class**) and its two subclasses. This means that the only way a value can be stored on a long-term basis is as an attribute of an instance of that class or its subclasses.

The solution is obvious: We need another entity class in which we can store the estimated annual operating expenses. In fact, while we are about it, we check to see if there are any other values that need to be stored. The result is shown in Figure 7.14. We have introduced a new class, **MSG Application Class,** where we will store the various attributes shown in the top box in the figure. As with the Osbert Oglesby case study, in addition the **MSG Application Class** will be assigned the task of starting the execution of the rest of the information system.

Now we redraw the class diagram of Figure 7.14 to reflect the stereotypes. This is shown in Figure 7.15. All four classes are entity classes.

The entity classes seem to be correct, at least for now. The next step is to determine the boundary classes and control classes.

7.7   Extracting Boundary Classes: MSG Foundation Case Study

Extracting entity classes is usually considerably harder than extracting boundary classes. After all, entity classes generally have interrelationships, whereas each input screen, output screen, and printed report is usually modeled by an (independent) boundary class.

In view of the fact that the target MSG Foundation information system appears to be relatively straightforward (at least at this early stage of the Unified Process), we will try to have just one screen that the MSG staff member can use for all four use cases: Estimate Funds Available for Week, Manage an Asset, Update Estimated Annual Operating Expenses, and Produce a Report. As we learn more about the MSG Foundation, it is certainly possible that we may have to refine this one screen into two or more screens. But in our initial class extraction, we will have just one screen class, **User Interface Class.**

There are three reports that have to be printed: the estimated funds for the week report and the two asset reports, namely, the complete listing of all mortgages or of all investments. Each of these has to be modeled by a separate boundary class because the content of each report is different. The four corresponding initial boundary classes are then **User Interface Class, Estimated Funds Report Class, Mortgages Report Class,** and **Investments Report Class.** These four classes are displayed in Figure 7.16.

FIGURE 7.16

The Initial Boundary
Classes of the
MSG Foundation
Information System

> **User Interface Class**
> **Estimated Funds Report Class**
> **Mortgages Report Class**
> **Investments Report Class**

FIGURE 7.17

The Initial Control
Class of the
MSG Foundation
Information System

> **Estimate Funds for Week Class**

FIGURE 7.18

The Estimate Funds
Available for Week
Use Case

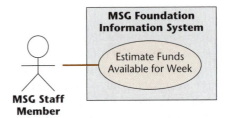

7.8 Extracting Control Classes: MSG Foundation Case Study

Control classes are generally as easy to extract as boundary classes because each nontrivial computation is almost always modeled by a control class. For the MSG Foundation case study, there is just one computation, namely, estimating the funds available for the week. This yields the initial control class **Estimate Funds for Week Class** shown in Figure 7.17.

The next step is to check all three sets of classes: entity classes, boundary classes, and control classes. Careful examination of the classes yields no obvious discrepancies, so we can proceed with the following step.

7.9 Use-Case Realization: MSG Foundation Case Study

A use-case realization is a description of how a use case is performed in terms of its classes, that is, what classes are needed to realize (achieve or accomplish) the use case. We first consider the use case Estimate Funds Available for Week.

7.9.1 Estimate Funds Available for Week Use Case

The use-case diagram of Figure 7.9 shows all the use cases. These include Estimate Funds Available for Week, which is shown separately in Figure 7.18. The description of that use case was given in Figure 5.40, which is reproduced here as Figure 7.19 for convenience. From the description we deduce that, as reflected in the class diagram of Figure 7.20, the classes that enter into this use case are **User Interface Class,** which models the user interface; **Estimate Funds for Week Class,** the control class that models the computation of the estimate of the funds that are available to fund mortgages during that week; **Mortgage Class,** which models the estimated grants and payments for the week; **Investment Class,** which models the estimated return on investments for the week; **MSG**

FIGURE 7.19

The Description of
the Estimate Funds
Available for Week
Use Case

Brief Description

The `Estimate Funds Available for Week` use case enables an MSG Foundation
staff member to estimate how much money the Foundation has available that week to
fund mortgages.

Step-by-Step Description

1. For each investment, extract the estimated annual return on that investment.
   Summing the separate returns and dividing the result by 52 yields the estimated
   investment income for the week.
2. Determine the estimated MSG Foundation operating expenses for the week by
   extracting the estimated annual MSG Foundation operating expenses and dividing
   by 52.
3. For each mortgage:
   3.1 The amount to be paid this week is the total of the principal and interest
       payment and $\frac{1}{52}$nd of the sum of the annual real-estate tax and the annual
       homeowner's insurance premium.
   3.2 Compute 28 percent of the couple's current gross weekly income.
   3.3 If the result of Step 3.1 is greater than the result of Step 3.2, then the mortgage
       payment for this week is the result of Step 3.2, and the amount of the grant for
       this week is the difference between the result of Step 3.1 and the result of Step 3.2.
   3.4 Otherwise, the mortgage payment for this week is the result of Step 3.1, and
       there is no grant this week.
4. Summing the mortgage payments of Steps 3.3 and 3.4 yields the estimated total
   mortgage payments for the week.
5. Summing the grant payments of Step 3.3 yields the estimated total grant payments
   for the week.
6. Add the results of Steps 1 and 4 and subtract the results of Steps 2 and 5. This is the
   total amount available for mortgages for the current week.
7. Print the total amount available for new mortgages during the current week.

FIGURE 7.20

Class Diagram
Showing the Classes
That Realize the
Estimate Funds
Available for Week
Use Case of the
MSG Foundation
Information System

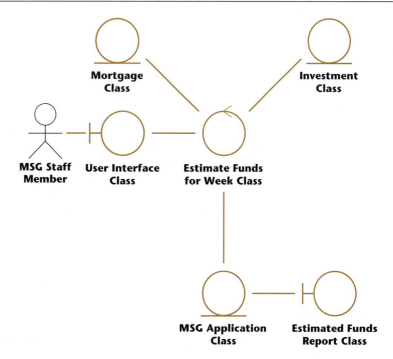

FIGURE 7.21

A Scenario of the
Estimate Funds
Available for Week
Use Case

An MSG Foundation staff member wishes to determine the funds available for mortgages this week.

1. For each investment, the information system extracts the estimated annual return on that investment. It sums the separate returns and divides the result by 52 to yield the estimated investment income for the week.

2. The information system then extracts the estimated annual MSG Foundation operating expenses and divides the result by 52.

3. For each mortgage:

   3.1 The information system computes the amount to be paid this week by adding the principal and interest payment to $\frac{1}{52}$nd of the sum of the annual real-estate tax and the annual homeowner's insurance premium.

   3.2 It then computes 28 percent of the couple's current gross weekly income.

   3.3 If the result of Step 3.1 is greater than the result of Step 3.2, then it determines the mortgage payment for the week as the result of Step 3.2, and the amount of the grant for this week as the difference between the result of Step 3.1 and the result of Step 3.2.

   3.4 Otherwise, it takes the mortgage payment for this week as the result of Step 3.1, and there is no grant for the week.

4. The information system sums the mortgage payments of Steps 3.3 and 3.4 to yield the estimated total mortgage payments for the week.

5. It sums the grant payments of Step 3.3 to yield the estimated total grant payments for the week.

6. The information system adds the results of Steps 1 and 4 and subtracts the results of Steps 2 and 5. This is the total amount available for mortgages for the current week.

7. Finally, the information system prints the total amount available for new mortgages during the current week.

Application Class, which models the estimated operating expenses for the week; and **Estimated Funds Report Class,** which models the printing of the report.

Figure 7.20 is a class diagram. That is, it shows the classes that participate in the realization of the use case and their relationships. A working information system, on the other hand, uses objects rather than classes (an object is an instance of a class). For example, a specific mortgage cannot be represented by **Mortgage Class** but rather by an object, a specific instance of **Mortgage Class,** denoted by **: Mortgage Class.** Also, the class diagram of Figure 7.20 shows the participating classes in the use case and their relationships; it does not show the sequence of events as they occur. We definitely need something more to model a specific scenario such as the scenario of Figure 7.4, reproduced here as Figure 7.21.

Now consider Figure 7.22. This figure is a collaboration diagram. It therefore shows the objects that interact as well as the messages that are sent, numbered in the order in which they are sent. A collaboration diagram depicts a realization of a specific scenario of a use case. In this case, Figure 7.22 depicts the scenario of Figure 7.21. In more detail, in the scenario the staff member wants to compute the funds available for the week. This is represented by message 1: Request estimate of funds available for week from **MSG Staff Member** to **: User Interface Class,** an instance of **User Interface Class.**

FIGURE 7.22   A Collaboration Diagram of the Realization of the Scenario of Figure 7.21 of the Estimate Funds Available for Week Use Case of the MSG Application Information System

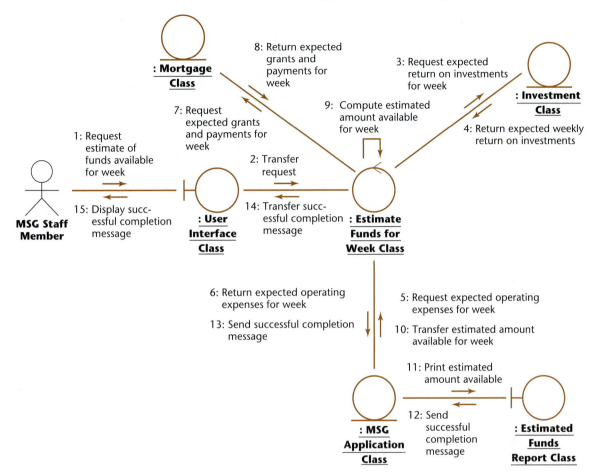

Next, this request is passed on to **: Estimate Funds for Week Class,** an instance of the control class that actually performs the calculation. This is represented by message 2: Transfer request.

Four separate financial estimates are now determined by **: Estimate Funds for Week Class.** In Step 1 of the scenario (Figure 7.21), the estimated annual return on investments is summed for each investment and the result divided by 52. This extraction of the estimated weekly return is modeled in Figure 7.22 by message 3: Request estimated return on investments for week from **: Estimate Funds for Week Class** to **: Investment Class** followed by message 4: Return estimated weekly return on investments in the reverse direction, that is, back to the object that is controlling the computation.

In Step 2 of the scenario (Figure 7.21), the weekly operating expenses are estimated by taking the estimated annual operating expenses and dividing by 52. This extraction of the weekly expenses is modeled in Figure 7.22 by message 5: Request estimated operating expenses for week from **: Estimate Funds for Week Class** to **: MSG Application Class** followed by message 6: Return estimated operating expenses for week in the other direction.

In Steps 3, 4, and 5 of the scenario (Figure 7.21), two estimates are determined, namely the estimated grants for the week and the estimated payments for the week. This is modeled in Figure 7.22 by message 7: Request estimated grants and payments for week from **: Estimate Funds for Week Class** to **: Mortgage Class** and by message 8: Return estimated grants and payments for week in the reverse direction.

Now the arithmetic computation of Step 6 of the scenario is performed. This is modeled in Figure 7.22 by message 9: Compute estimated amount available for week. This is a self call; that is, **: Estimate Funds for Week Class** tells itself to perform the calculation. The result of the computation is stored in **: MSG Application Class** by message 10: Transfer estimated amount available for week.

Next, the result is printed in Step 7 of the scenario (Figure 7.21). This is modeled in Figure 7.22 by message 11: Print estimated amount available from **: MSG Application Class** to **: Estimated Funds Report Class**.

Finally, an acknowledgment is sent to the MSG staff member that the task has been successfully completed. This is modeled in Figure 7.22 by messages 12: Send successful completion message, 13: Send successful completion message, 14: Transfer successful completion message, and 15: Display successful completion message.

No client is going to approve the specification document unless he or she understands precisely what the proposed information system will do. For this reason, a written description of the collaboration diagram is essential. This is shown in Figure 7.23, the flow of events. Finally, the equivalent sequence diagram of the realization of the scenario is shown in Figure 7.24. When constructing an information system, either a collaboration diagram or a sequence diagram may prove to give better insight of a realization of a use case. In some situations, both are needed to get a full understanding of a specific realization of a given use case. That is why, for both case studies in this book, every collaboration diagram is followed by the equivalent sequence diagram.

Summarizing, Figures 7.18 through 7.24 do not depict a random collection of UML artifacts. On the contrary, these figures depict a use case and artifacts derived from that use case. In more detail:

- Figure 7.18 depicts the use case Estimate Funds Available for Week. That is, Figure 7.18 models all possible sets of interactions, between the actor **MSG Staff Member** (an entity that is external to the information system) and the MSG Foundation information system itself, that relate to the action of estimating funds available for the week.

- Figure 7.19 is the description of that use case, that is, it provides a written account of the details of the Estimate Funds Available for Week use case of Figure 7.18.

- Figure 7.20 is a class diagram showing the classes that realize the Estimate Funds Available for Week use case. The class diagram depicts the classes that are needed to model all possible scenarios of the use case, together with their interactions.

FIGURE 7.23   **The Flow of Events of the Collaboration Diagram of Figure 7.22 of the Realization of the Scenario of Figure 7.21 of the Estimate Funds Available for Week Use Case of the MSG Application Information System**

An MSG staff member requests an estimate of the funds available for mortgages for the week (1, 2). The information system estimates the return on investments for the week (3, 4), the operating expenses for the week (5, 6), and the grants and payments for the week (7, 8). Then it estimates (9), stores (10), and prints out (11–14) the funds available for the week.

FIGURE 7.24   **A Sequence Diagram of the Realization of the Scenario of Figure 7.21 of the Estimate Funds Available for Week Use Case of the MSG Application Information System**
This sequence diagram is fully equivalent to the collaboration diagram of Figure 7.22, so its flow of events is also shown in Figure 7.23

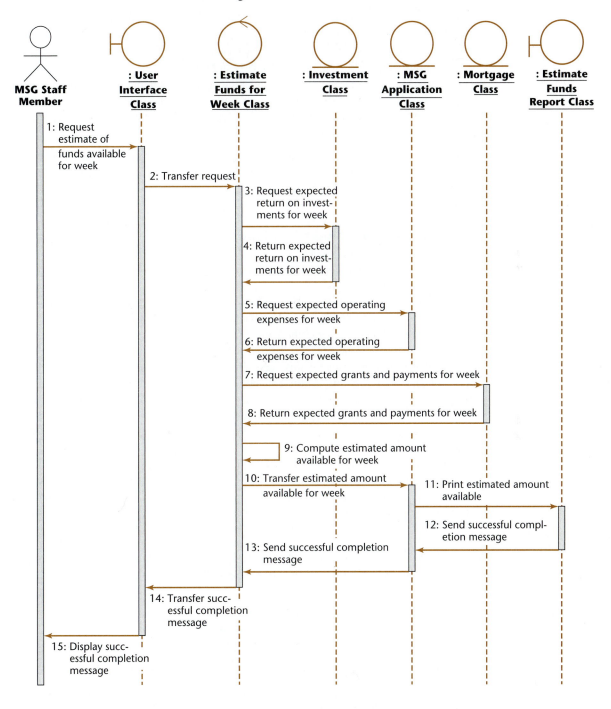

- Figure 7.21 is a scenario, that is, one specific instance of the use case of Figure 7.18.
- Figure 7.22 is a collaboration diagram of the realization of the scenario of Figure 7.21; that is, it depicts the objects and the messages sent between them in the realization of that one specific scenario.
- Figure 7.23 is the flow of events of the collaboration diagram of the realization of the scenario of Figure 7.21. That is, just as Figure 7.19 is a written description of the **Estimate Funds Available for Week** use case of Figure 7.18, Figure 7.23 is a written description of the realization of the scenario of Figure 7.21.
- Figure 7.24 is the sequence diagram that is fully equivalent to the collaboration diagram of Figure 7.22. That is, the sequence diagram depicts the objects and the messages sent between them in the realization of the scenario of Figure 7.21. Its flow of events is therefore also shown in Figure 7.23.

It has been said many times in this book that Unified Process is use-case driven. These bulleted items explicitly state the precise relationship between each of the artifacts of Figures 7.19 through 7.24 and the use case of Figure 7.18 that underlies each of them.

7.9.2 **Manage an Asset** Use Case

The **Manage an Asset** use case is shown in Figure 7.25 and its description in Figure 7.26. A class diagram showing the classes that realize the **Manage an Asset** use case is shown in Figure 7.27.

The normal part of the extended scenario of Figure 7.2 of the use case **Manage a Mortgage** (and hence of **Manage an Asset**) is reproduced as Figure 7.28. In this scenario, an MSG staff member updates the annual real-estate tax on a mortgaged home and the information system updates the date on which the tax was last changed. Figure 7.29 is the collaboration diagram of this scenario. Notice that object **: Investment Class** does not play an active role in this collaboration diagram because the scenario of Figure 7.28 does not involve an investment, only a mortgage. Also, the **Borrowers** do not play a role in this scenario either. The flow of events is left as an exercise (Problem 7.3). The sequence diagram equivalent to the collaboration diagram of Figure 7.28 is shown in Figure 7.30.

Now consider a different scenario of the use case **Manage an Asset** (Figure 7.25), namely the extended scenario of Figure 7.3, the normal part of which is reproduced here as Figure 7.31. In this scenario, at the request of the borrowers, the MSG staff member updates the weekly income of a couple who have an MSG mortgage. As explained in Section 5.3, the scenario is initiated by the **Borrowers,** and their data are entered into the information system by the **MSG Staff Member,** as stated in the note in the collaboration diagram of Figure 7.32. The flow of events is again left as an exercise (Problem 7.4). The equivalent sequence diagram is shown in Figure 7.33.

FIGURE 7.25
The Manage an Asset Use Case

FIGURE 7.26

Description of the
Manage an Asset
Use Case

Brief Description

The `Manage an Asset` use case enables an
MSG Foundation staff member to add and delete
assets and manage the portfolio of assets
(investments and mortgages). Managing a
mortgage includes updating the weekly income
of a couple who have borrowed money from the
Foundation.

Step-by-Step Description

1. Add, modify, or delete an investment or
   mortgage, or update the borrower's
   weekly income.

FIGURE 7.27

Class Diagram
Showing the Classes
That Realize the
Manage an Asset
Use Case of the
MSG Foundation
Information System

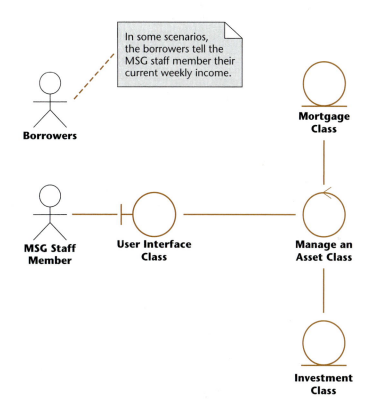

FIGURE 7.28

A Scenario of the
Manage an Asset
Use Case

An MSG Foundation staff member wants to update the annual
real-estate tax on a home for which the Foundation has
provided of a mortgage.
1. The staff member enters the new value of the annual real-
   estate tax.
2. The information system updates the date on which the annual
   real-estate tax was last changed.

FIGURE 7.29

A Collaboration
Diagram of the
Realization of the
Scenario of Figure
7.28 of the Manage
an Asset Use Case of
the MSG Foundation
Information System

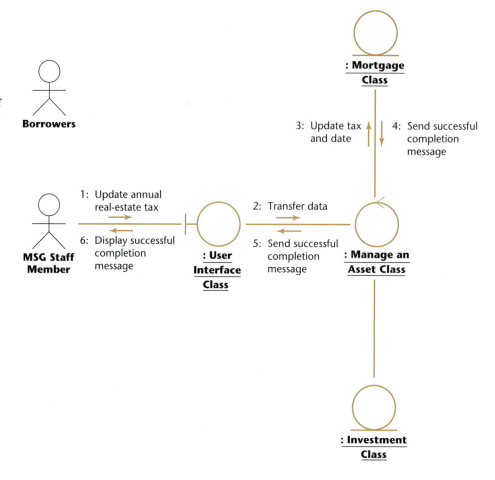

Comparing the collaboration diagrams of Figures 7.29 and 7.32 (or, equivalently, the sequence diagrams of Figures 7.30 and 7.33), we see that, other than the actors involved, the only other difference between the two diagrams is that messages 1, 2, and 3 involve annual real-estate tax in the case of Figure 7.29 (or Figure 7.30) and weekly income in the case of Figure 7.32 (or Figure 7.33). This example highlights the difference between a use case, scenarios (instances of a use case), and collaboration or sequence diagrams of the realization of different scenarios of that use case.

Notice that boundary class **User Interface Class** appears in all the realizations we have seen so far. In fact, the same screen will be used for all commands of the information system. An MSG staff member clicks on the appropriate operation in the revised menu of Figure 7.34. (The corresponding textual interface, as implemented in Appendix E, is given in Figure 7.35.)

7.9.3   Update Estimated Annual Operating Expenses Use Case

The use case Update Estimated Annual Operating Expenses is shown in Figure 5.14 with a description in Figure 5.15. A class diagram showing the classes that realize the Update Estimated Annual Operating Expenses use case appears in Figure 7.36 and a collaboration diagram of a realization of a scenario of the use case in Figure 7.37. The equivalent sequence diagram is shown in Figure 7.38. Details of the scenario and the flow of events are left as an exercise (Problems 7.5 and 7.6).

FIGURE 7.30   A Sequence Diagram of the Realization of the Scenario of Figure 7.28 of the Manage an Asset
Use Case of the MSG Foundation Information System

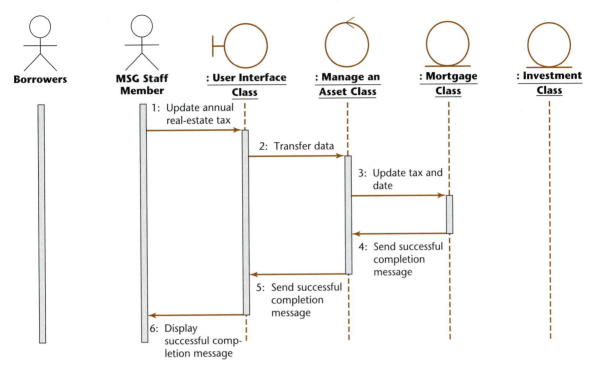

FIGURE 7.31

A Second Scenario
of the Manage an
Asset Use Case

There is a change in the weekly income of a couple who have borrowed money
from the MSG Foundation. They wish to have their weekly income updated in
the Foundation records by an MSG staff member so that their mortgage
payments will be correctly computed.
1. The staff member enters the new value of the weekly income.
2. The information system updates the date on which the weekly income was last
changed.

7.9.4   `Produce a Report` Use Case

Use case `Produce a Report` is shown in Figure 7.39. The description of use case `Produce a Report` of Figure 5.36 is reproduced here as Figure 7.40. A class diagram showing the classes that realize the `Produce a Report` use case is shown in Figure 7.41.

First consider the scenario of Figure 7.5 for listing all mortgages, reproduced here as Figure 7.42. A collaboration diagram of the realization of this scenario is shown in Figure 7.43. This realization models the listing of all mortgages. Accordingly, object **: Investment Class,** an instance of the other subclass of **Asset Class,** plays no role in this realization, and neither does **: Investments Report Class.** The flow of events is left as an exercise (Problem 7.7). The equivalent sequence diagram is shown in Figure 7.44.

Now consider the scenario of Figure 7.6 for listing all investments, reproduced here as Figure 7.45. A collaboration diagram of the realization of this scenario is shown in Figure 7.46. As opposed to the previous realization, Figure 7.46 models the listing of the investments; mortgages are ignored here. The equivalent sequence diagram is shown in Figure 7.47.

FIGURE 7.32

A Collaboration
Diagram of the
Realization of
the Scenario of
Figure 7.31 of the
Manage an Asset
Use Case of the
MSG Foundation
Information System

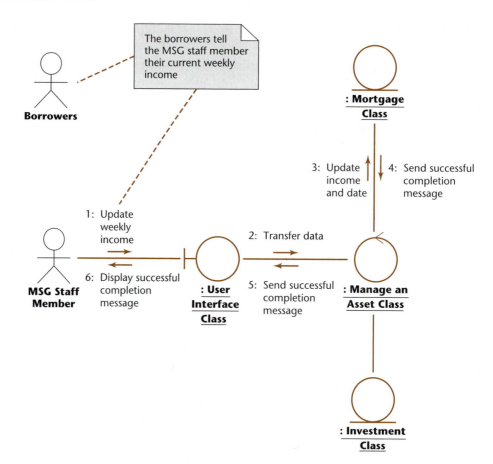

FIGURE 7.33 A Sequence Diagram of the Realization of the Scenario of Figure 7.31 of the Manage an Asset
Use Case of the MSG Foundation Information System

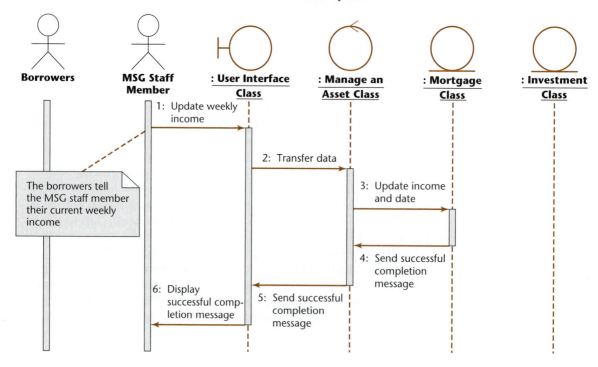

FIGURE 7.34
Revised Menu
of the Target
MSG Foundation
Information System

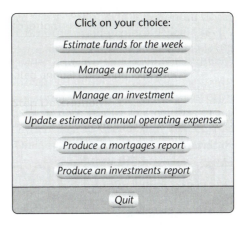

FIGURE 7.35
Textual Version of
the Revised Menu
of Figure 7.34

```
                    MAIN MENU
     MARTHA STOCKTON GREENGAGE FOUNDATION
        1.  Estimate funds available for week
        2.  Manage a mortgage
        3.  Manage an investment
        4.  Update estimated annual operating expenses
        5.  Produce a mortgages report
        6.  Produce an investments report
        7.  Quit
     Type your choice and press <ENTER>:
```

FIGURE 7.36
A Class Diagram
Showing the Classes
That Realize the
Update Estimated
Annual Operating
Expenses Use
Case of the
MSG Foundation
Information System

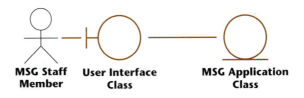

FIGURE 7.37
A Collaboration
Diagram of the
Realization of a
Scenario of the
Update Estimated
Annual Operating
Expenses Use
Case of the
MSG Foundation
Information System

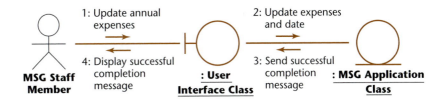

FIGURE 7.38 A Sequence Diagram of the Realization of a Scenario of the Manage Estimated Annual Operating Expenses Use Case of the MSG Foundation Information System

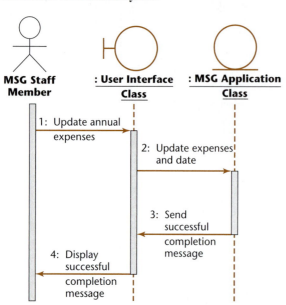

FIGURE 7.39 The Produce a Report Use Case

FIGURE 7.40

Description of the Produce a Report Use Case

Brief Description

The `Produce a Report` use case enables an MSG Foundation staff member to print a listing of all investments or all mortgages.

Step-by-Step Description

1. The following reports must be generated
    1.1 Investments report—printed on demand:
        The information system prints a list of all investments. For each investment, the following attributes are printed:
        Item number
        Item name
        Estimated annual return
        Date estimated annual return was last updated
    1.2 Mortgages report—printed on demand:
        The information system prints a list of all mortgages. For each mortgage, the following attributes are printed:
        Account number
        Name of mortgagee
        Original price of home
        Date mortgage was issued
        Principal and interest payment
        Current combined gross weekly income
        Date current combined gross weekly income was last updated
        Annual real-estate tax
        Date annual real-estate tax was last updated
        Annual homeowner's insurance premium
        Date annual homeowner's insurance premium was last updated

FIGURE 7.41

A Class Diagram
Showing the Classes
That Realize the
Produce a Report
Use Case of the
MSG Foundation
Information System

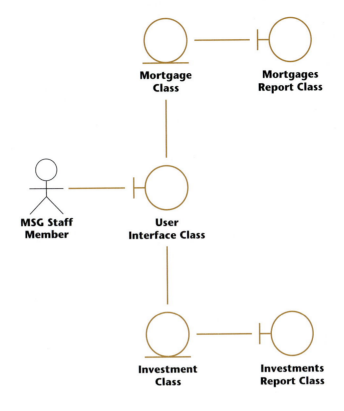

FIGURE 7.42

A Scenario of the
Produce a Report
Use Case

> An MSG staff member wishes to print
> a list of all mortgages.
> 1. The staff member requests a report
>   listing all the mortgages.

7.10   Incrementing the Class Diagram

The entity classes were extracted in Sections 7.1 through 7.5, yielding Figure 7.15, which
shows four entity classes. The boundary classes were extracted in Section 7.7 and the control classes in Section 7.8. In the course of realizing the various use cases in Section 7.9,
interrelationships between many of the classes became apparent; these interrelationships
are reflected in the class diagrams of Figures 7.20, 7.27, 7.36, and 7.41. Figure 7.48 combines these class diagrams.

Now the class diagrams of Figures 7.15 and 7.48 are combined to yield the fourth iteration of the class diagram of the MSG Foundation case study, shown in Figure 7.49. More
specifically, starting with Figure 7.48, **Asset Class** of Figure 7.15 is added. Then the two
inheritance (generalization) relationships in Figure 7.15 are drawn in; they are shown with
dashed lines to distinguish them. The result, Figure 7.49, the fourth iteration of the class
diagram, is the class diagram at the end of the analysis workflow.

This concludes the analysis workflow of the MSG Foundation case study.

In the next two sections, methods for determining actors and use cases are provided.

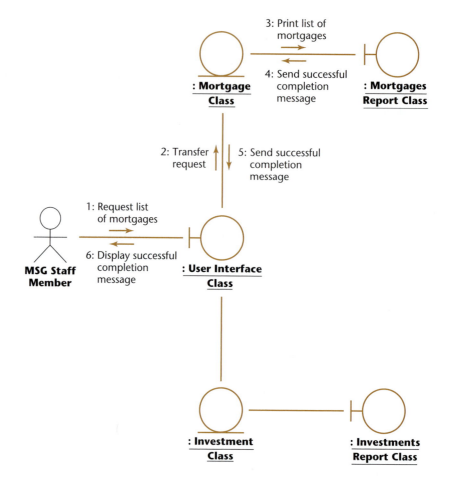

7.11   More on Actors

From Section 4.5.3 we know that a use case depicts an interaction between the information system itself and the actors (the users of that information system). In Chapters 4 through 7 we have seen numerous examples of both actors and use cases. Now that we have some experience with and understanding of actors and use cases, here are some pointers to finding actors and use cases.

To find the actors, we have to consider every *role* in which an individual can interact with the information system. For example, consider a married couple who wish to obtain a low-interest mortgage from the MSG Foundation. When they apply for the mortgage, they are **Applicants,** whereas after their application has been approved and money to buy their home has been loaned to them, they become **Borrowers.** In other words, actors are not so much individuals as roles played by those individuals. Thus, in our example, the actors are not the married couple, but rather first the married couple playing the role of **Applicants** and then the married couple playing the role of **Borrowers.** This means that merely listing all the individuals who will be using the information system is not a satisfactory way of finding the actors. Instead, we need to find all the different roles played by each user (or group of users). From the list of roles we can extract the actors.

In the terminology of the Unified Process, the term *worker* is used to denote a particular role played by an individual. This is a somewhat unfortunate term, because the word *worker*

FIGURE 7.44   A Sequence Diagram of the Realization of the Scenario of Figure 7.42 of the **Produce a Report Use Case** of the MSG Foundation Information System

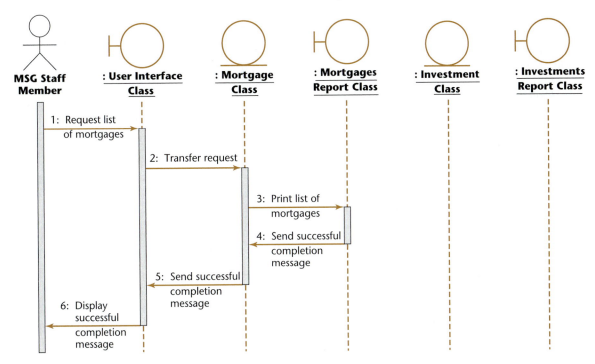

FIGURE 7.45

Another Scenario of the Produce a Report Use Case

An MSG staff member wishes to print a list of all investments.

1. The staff member requests a report listing all the investments.

usually refers to an employee. Thus, in the terminology of the Unified Process, in the case of a married couple with a mortgage from the MSG Foundation, **Applicants** and **Borrowers** are two different workers. In this book, in the interests of clarity, the word *role* will continue to be used in place of *worker*.

Within a business context, the task of finding the roles is generally straightforward. The use-case business model usually displays all the roles played by the individuals who interact with the business, thus highlighting the business actors. We then find the subset of the use-case business model that corresponds to the use-case model of the requirements. In more detail:

- First, construct the use-case business model by finding all the roles played by the individuals who interact with the business.
- Second, find the subset of the use-case diagram of the business model that models the information system we wish to develop. That is, consider only those parts of the business model that correspond to the proposed information system.
- Third, the actors in this subset are the actors we seek.

To see how this works, consider the use-case diagram of the business model of the MSG Foundation shown in Figure 5.9. There are three actors: **MSG Staff Member,**

FIGURE 7.46
A Collaboration
Diagram of the
Realization of the
Scenario of
Figure 7.45 of the
Produce a Report
Use Case of the
MSG Foundation
Information System

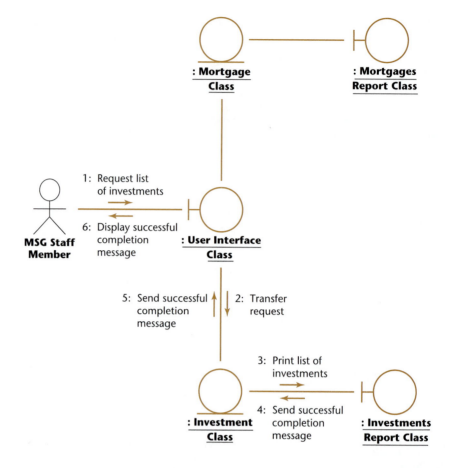

FIGURE 7.47   **A Sequence Diagram of the Realization of the Scenario of Figure 7.45 of the Produce a Report
Use Case of the MSG Foundation Information System**

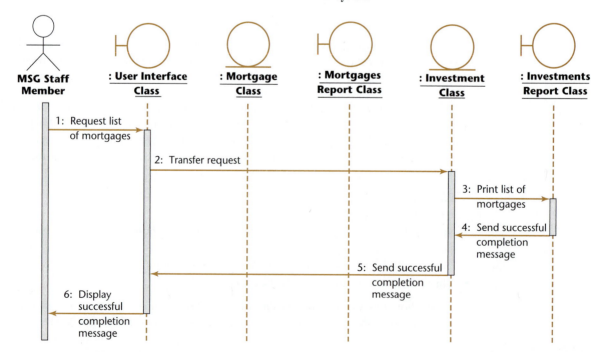

FIGURE 7.48
Class Diagram
Combining the
Class Diagrams
of Figures 7.20, 7.27,
7.36, and 7.41

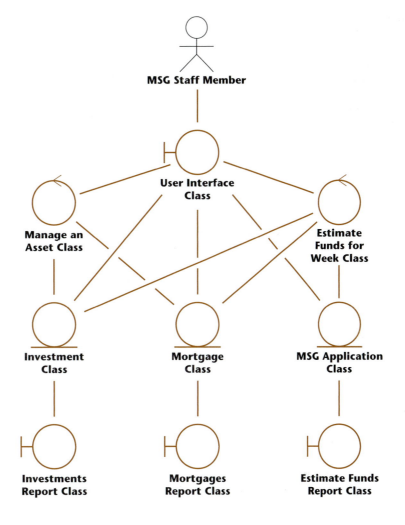

Applicants, and **Borrowers.** These actors are easy to find once we understand the way that the MSG Foundation does business. Now look at the use-case diagram of the requirements shown in Figure 5.10. The use-case diagram of the requirements is a subset of the use-case diagram of the business model, because the business model incorporates all the activities of the MSG Foundation, whereas the information system we have to develop is restricted to "a pilot project, namely, an information system that will perform the calculations needed to determine how much money is available each week to purchase homes." The subset of Figure 5.10 has only two actors: **MSG Staff Member** and **Borrowers.** These two actors are then the actors of the use-case models constructed when following the Unified Process to develop an information system. Looking at the use cases of Figures 7.1 and 7.9, we see that this is precisely what has happened. In those use cases, the actors are indeed **MSG Staff Member** and **Borrowers.**

7.12 More on Use Cases

Again within a business context, finding use cases is generally straightforward. For each role, there will be one or more use cases. Thus, the starting point in finding the use cases of the requirements is finding the actors. This was described in the previous section.

FIGURE 7.49
The Fourth Iteration
of the Class
Diagram of the
MSG Foundation
Case Study, Obtained
by Combining the
Class Diagrams of
Figures 7.15 and 7.48

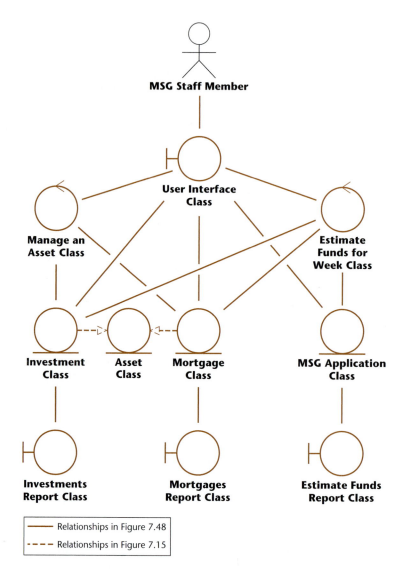

7.13   Risk

A major risk in developing a new information system is that the delivered information system does not meet the client's needs. In the traditional paradigm, this risk was met by constructing a *rapid prototype,* a hurriedly thrown together working program that displays the key functionality of the target information system. This type of prototype is not needed in the Unified Process, because the use cases and their scenarios take the place of the rapid prototype. In order to appreciate why this is so, we first need to look at rapid prototyping in more detail.

7.13.1   Rapid Prototyping

Many approaches have been put forward for ensuring that the client's needs are truly met by the specification document. They all reduce to the systems analysts sitting down with the client, going through the specification document line by line, and asking, "Are you really, really, really sure that this is what you want the proposed information system to do?" None of these methods are foolproof. To see why, consider the following two highly fanciful situations:

The first situation concerns Joe and Jane Johnson, who decide to build a house. They consult with an architect. Instead of showing them sketches, plans, and perhaps a model, the architect gives them a 20-page, single-spaced document describing the house in highly technical terms. Despite the fact that both Joe and Jane have no previous architectural experience and hardly understand any of the document, they enthusiastically sign it and say, "Go right ahead; build the house!"

The second situation concerns Mark Marberry, who buys his suits by mail order. Instead of mailing him pictures of their suits and samples of available cloths, the company sends Mark a catalog containing a written description of the cut and the cloth of their products. Mark then orders a suit solely on the basis of a written description.

Neither of the two preceding situations could possibly happen in real life. Nevertheless, they typify precisely the way an information system is constructed after the client has read through the written specification document. The finished information system is finally delivered to the client a year or so later. The client uses the information system for a few minutes, then turns to the systems analysts and says, "I know that this is the information system I asked for, but it's not what I wanted."

What has gone wrong?

It is hard to imagine how a house will look from a written document, it is hard to imagine how a suit will look from a written description of the cut and the cloth, and it is hard to imagine how an information system will behave from a written document. On the other hand, it is easy to imagine how a house will look from a model of that house, it is easy to imagine how a suit will look from a photograph of another suit with that cut and a piece of the actual cloth from which the suit will be made, and it is easy to imagine how an information system will behave from a rapid prototype.

A rapid prototype is a working program that exhibits the key behavior of that information system. For example, if the target information system is to handle accounts payable, accounts receivable, and warehousing, then the rapid prototype might consist of an information system that performs the screen handling for data capture and prints the reports, but does no database updating or error handling.

Here is another example. Suppose we are asked to develop an information system for managing an apartment complex. The information system must incorporate an input screen that allows the user to enter details of a new tenant and print an occupancy report for each month. These aspects will be incorporated into the rapid prototype. However, error-checking capabilities, routines for updating the database, and complex tax computations will not be included. That is, a rapid prototype reflects the functionality that the client sees, such as input screens and reports, but omits "hidden" aspects such as database updating.

The client and users then experiment with the prototype to determine whether it indeed meets their needs. The rapid prototype can be changed until the client and users are satisfied that it encapsulates the functionality they desire.

The first key point about the rapid prototype is that it must be "rapid." That is, it must be thrown together as quickly as possible. It really does not matter if the rapid prototype crashes every few minutes and the client sees the Windows "blue screen of death." The systems analyst simply types in ALT-CTRL-DEL, the computer starts up again, and the client experiments further with the rapid prototype. The sole use of the rapid prototype is to make sure that, when the complete information system is delivered to the client a year or so later, the functionality of the information system will be precisely what the client needs. One way of doing this is for the client to experiment with a computer program that behaves the same way that the target information system will behave. (For a different way of looking at rapid prototypes, see Just in Case You Wanted to Know Box 7.1.)

The second key point is that after the rapid prototype has been approved by the client, it must be thrown away. This seems bizarre. After all, weeks of programming have gone into the rapid prototype and throwing it away seems like throwing money away. The "obvious" thing to do is to use the rapid prototype as the basis for the information system, fix all the faults, and add all the additional functionality. On the contrary, the rapid prototype must be thrown away. The reason for this can be found in Figure 2.4. Remember that a rapid prototype is a working program. So, making changes to a rapid prototype is terribly expensive. Instead, the rapid prototype should be discarded and the information system constructed from scratch. In fact, there is another reason why we must do this. A rapid prototype is (correctly) thrown together without any sort of specification or design document. Making changes when there is no documentation of any kind is both expensive and foolhardy.

The Unified Process offers an alternative mechanism for determining the client's needs, as described in the next section.

7.13.2   Scenarios and the Client's Needs

As has been stated before, the Unified Process is use-case driven. When using the Unified Process, instead of constructing a rapid prototype, the use cases, or, more precisely, interaction diagrams reflecting the classes that realize the scenarios of the use cases, are shown to the client. The client can understand how the target information system will behave just as well from the interaction diagrams and their written flow of events as from a rapid prototype. After all, a scenario is a particular execution sequence of the proposed information system, as is each execution of the rapid prototype. The difference is that the rapid prototype is discarded, whereas the use cases are successively refined, with more information added each time.

However, there is one area where a rapid prototype is superior to a scenario, and that is the user interface. For example, there is no way that a scenario can describe a screen as well as a rapid prototype can. To see this, suppose that all the screens and reports produced by an organization's current information systems display the date on the top right-hand corner of the screen or page. If a new information system were to display the date on the top left-hand corner, this would be extremely disconcerting for the many users who have become accustomed to the previous format. Now they would have to live with both formats, unless the new information system is changed. Moving the date is usually straightforward, but it is a time-consuming and fault-prone activity. After all, every date output instance has to be located and then changed in the identical way. On the other hand, if a rapid prototype had been constructed, the first person in the client organization to see a screen or report would immediately have noticed the problem, and it would have been corrected before the information system was delivered to the client.

Does this mean that we should construct a rapid prototype just so that specimen screens and reports can be examined by the client and users? Not at all. But we do need to construct specimen screens and reports, preferably with the aid of screen generators and report generators, CASE tools (Chapter 11) that make it easy for us to produce the code for screens and reports. Another approach is to draw specimen screens and reports using a word processor and color printer, but it is generally quicker to use screen and report generators. In addition, the code generated by screen and report generators can usually be utilized when implementing the information system. More on the user interface appears in Chapter 17.

Key Terms

rapid prototype, *156*   role, *152*   worker, *152*

Review Questions for Chapter 7

1. How can a change in the annual real-estate tax affect the weekly grant for a mortgage?
2. What are the potential advantages of treating two related classes as subclasses of some superclass?
3. Give two reasons why we need **MSG Application Class** in Figure 7.14.
4. Why does every interaction diagram need a written description?
5. What are the relationships between a use case, a scenario, a realization, and an interaction diagram?
6. How do we find actors?
7. What is the relationship between the terms *actor, worker,* and *role* within the context of the Unified Process?
8. How do we find use cases?
9. What is a rapid prototype?
10. Why is the rapid prototype of the traditional paradigm not needed in the Unified Process?

Problems

7.1 Give an extended scenario of the use case **Manage an Investment** of Figures 5.27 and 5.28.

7.2 Give an extended scenario of the use case **Update Estimated Annual Operating Expenses** of Figures 5.14 and 5.15.

7.3 Give the flow of events of the interaction diagrams of Figures 7.29 and 7.30.

7.4 Give the flow of events of the interaction diagrams of Figure 7.32 and 7.33.

7.5 Check that your answer to Problem 7.2 is a possible scenario for the interaction diagrams of Figures 7.37 and 7.38. If not, modify your scenario.

7.6 Give the flow of events of the interaction diagrams of Figures 7.37 and 7.38.

7.7 Give the flow of events of the interaction diagrams of Figures 7.43 and 7.44.

Systems Analysis and Design Projects

7.8   Perform the analysis workflow of the library information system of Problem 5.5.

7.9   Perform the analysis workflow of the automated teller machine of Problem 5.6.

Term Project

7.10   Perform the analysis workflow of the Chocoholics Anonymous term project of Appendix A.

Reference

Jacobson, I.; G. Booch; and J. Rumbaugh. *The Unified Software Development Process.* Reading, MA: Addison Wesley, 1999.

Chapter 8

The Object-Oriented Design Workflow

Learning Objectives

After studying this chapter, you should be able to:

- Explain what is performed during the design workflow.
- Determine the formats of attributes.
- Allocate operations to classes.

The client's needs are extracted and refined during the requirements workflow and the analysis workflow. The information system is programmed during the implementation workflow. The design workflow provides the link between extracting the client's needs and implementing them in code.

8.1 The Design Workflow

The input to the *design workflow* is the analysis workflow artifacts (Chapters 6 and 7). During the design workflow, these artifacts are iterated and incremented until they are in a format that can be utilized by the programmers. A major aspect of this iteration and incrementation is the identification of operations and their allocation to the appropriate classes. In addition, many other decisions have to be made as part of the design workflow. One such decision is the selection of the programming language in which the information system will be implemented. This process is described in detail in Chapter 14. Another decision is how much of existing information systems to reuse in the new information system to be developed. Reuse is also described in Chapter 14. Portability is another important design decision; this topic, too, is described in Chapter 14. Also, large information systems are often implemented on a network of computers; yet another design decision is the allocation of each software component to the hardware component on which each is to run.

The major motivation behind the development of the Unified Process was to present a methodology that could be used to develop large-scale information systems, typically, 500,000 lines of code or more. On the other hand, the implementations of the Osbert Oglesby case study and the MSG Foundation case study in Appendices D and E are less than 5,000 lines of Java or C++ in length. In other words, the Unified Process is primarily intended for information systems *at least a hundred times larger* than the case studies presented in this book. Accordingly, many aspects of the Unified Process are inapplicable to the two case studies of this book. For instance, an important part of the analysis workflow is to partition the information system into analysis packages. Each analysis *package* consists of a set of related classes, usually of relevance to a small subset of the actors, that can be implemented as a single unit. For example, accounts payable, accounts receivable, and general ledger are typical analysis packages. The concept underlying analysis packages is that it is much easier to develop smaller information systems than larger information systems. Accordingly, a large information system will be easier to develop if it can be decomposed into relatively independent packages.

This idea of decomposing a large workflow into relatively independent smaller workflows is carried forward to the design workflow. Here the objective is to break up the upcoming implementation workflow into manageable pieces, termed *subsystems*. Again, it does not make sense to break up either of the two case studies into subsystems; they are just too small.

There are two reasons why larger workflows are broken into subsystems. The first is that, as previously explained, it is easier to implement a number of smaller subsystems than one large system. Second, if the subsystems to be implemented are indeed relatively independent, then they can be implemented by programming teams working in parallel. This results in the information system as a whole being delivered sooner. Recall from Section 2.8 that the *architecture* of an information system includes the various component modules and how they fit together. The allocation of components to subsystems is a major part of the architectural task. Deciding on the architecture of an information system is by no means easy and, in all but the smallest information systems, is performed by a specialist, the information system *architect*.

An architect needs to have considerable experience in developing information systems, as well as detailed knowledge of all the relevant technologies, especially programming. However, in addition to being a technical expert, an architect needs to know how to make *trade-offs*. An information system has to satisfy the functional requirements, that is, the use cases. It also needs to satisfy the nonfunctional requirements, including portability (Chapter 14), reliability (Section 13.5.2), robustness (Section 13.5.3), maintainability, security, and so on. But it needs to do all these things within budget and within the time constraint. It is almost never possible to develop an information system that satisfies all its requirements, both functional and nonfunctional, and to finish the project within the cost and time constraints. Some sort of compromises almost always have to be made. The client has to relax some of the requirements, increase the budget, or move the delivery deadline, or do more than one of these. The architect must assist the client's decision making by clearly mapping out the trade-offs.

In some cases the trade-offs are obvious. For example, the architect may point out that a set of security requirements that conform to a new high-security standard are going to take a further three months and $350,000 to incorporate in the information system. If the information system is an international banking network, the issue is moot—there is no way that the client could possibly agree to compromise on security in any way. However, in other instances the client needs to make critical determinations regarding trade-offs, and will have to rely on the technical expertise of the architect to assist in coming to the right business decision. For example, the architect might point out that deferring a particular requirement until the information system has been delivered and is being maintained may save $150,000 now but will cost $300,000 to incorporate later (and if it is unclear why deferring a feature increases the cost of implementing it later, take another look at the right side of Figure 2.4). The decision as to whether or not to defer a requirement can be made by only the client, but he or she needs the technical expertise of the architect to assist him or her in coming to the correct business decision.

The architecture of an information system is a vital factor as to whether the delivered information system will be a success or a failure. And it is while performing the design workflow that the critical decisions regarding the architecture have to be made. If the requirements workflow is badly performed, it is still possible to have a successful project, provided that additional time and money are spent on the analysis workflow. Similarly, if the analysis workflow is inadequate, it is possible to recover by making an extra effort as part of the design workflow. But if the architecture is suboptimal, there is no way to recover; the architecture must immediately be redesigned. It is therefore essential that the development team include an architect with the necessary expertise and people skills.

We now compare the design phase of the traditional paradigm to the design workflow of the object-oriented paradigm.

8.2   Traditional versus Object-Oriented Design

In the traditional paradigm, the design phase consists of two steps. First, the *architectural design* is performed. Here the information system is decomposed into modules. Because classes are modules, much of this step corresponds to class extraction in the analysis workflow. This is depicted by the arrow in Figure 8.1.

The second design step in the traditional paradigm is the *detailed design*. Here, algorithms and data structures are designed for each module. The detailed design is then given to the programmers for implementation. Knowledge of programming is needed for performing much of detailed design because the detailed design includes specific programming features (such as *parameters,* the items that are transferred between modules when they are invoked at run time).

Now look again at Figure 8.1, which depicts a rough correspondence between the traditional paradigm and the object-oriented paradigm. The lowest box on the right reveals that almost all the steps of the object-oriented design workflow require knowledge of programming. However, knowledge of programming is a not a prerequisite for this book. Accordingly, in this chapter a description is given of just one design artifact, the complete class diagram.

FIGURE 8.1
Rough Correspondence between the Traditional Paradigm and the Object-Oriented Paradigm

Structured Paradigm	Object-Oriented Paradigm
1. Requirements phase	**1. Requirements workflow**
... ...	... ...
2. Analysis phase	**2. Object-oriented analysis workflow**
... ...	... Extract the classes ...
3. Structured design phase Architectural design Detailed design (requires knowledge of programming)	**3. Object-oriented design workflow** Various steps, almost all of which require knowledge of programming

8.3   Formats of the Attributes

During the design workflow we have to specify the exact format of each attribute of the class diagram. For instance, a date will usually be represented using 10 characters. For example, December 3, 1947 is represented as 12/03/1947 in the United States (MM/DD/YYYY format) and 03/12/1947 in Europe (DD/MM/YYYY format). But irrespective of which date convention is used, a total of 10 characters is needed.

Why are the formats not determined during the analysis workflow, but rather during the design workflow? As has been stated many times, the object-oriented paradigm is iterative. Each time we iterate, we change part (or all) of what we have already done. For practical reasons, it makes sense to add information to our models as late as we possibly can. Consider, for example, Figures 6.8 through 6.12, which show the first five iterations of the class diagram of the Osbert Oglesby case study. None of those five iterations show the attributes of the classes. If we had determined the attributes earlier, we would probably have had to modify those attributes, as well as move them from class to class, until we were satisfied with the class diagram. Instead, all we had to modify were the classes themselves.

It makes no sense to add an item to a class diagram (or any other UML diagram) before it is absolutely essential to do so, because adding the item will make the next iteration unnecessarily burdensome. In particular, it makes no sense to determine formats before they are strictly needed.

We now show how formats are determined for the attributes of our two case studies. For full details regarding the formats of all attributes of every class, consult Appendix B (Osbert Oglesby) and Appendix C (MSG Foundation). For simplicity, here we consider only the entity classes of Figure 6.13 (fifth iteration of the class diagram of the Osbert Oglesby case study) and Figure 7.14 (third iteration of the class diagram of the MSG Foundation case study).

We begin with the Osbert Oglesby case study.

8.3.1   Formats of the Attributes of the Osbert Oglesby Case Study

Figure 8.2 shows the class diagram of Figure 6.13 with the format of each of the attributes of the classes of the Osbert Oglesby case study added. To understand the notation, refer to the first part of Section 4.9. It is stated there that the first name of an artist is up to 20 characters in length, optionally followed by ? if there is uncertainly. In other words, this attribute must be represented by a string of up to 21 characters. Now look at the first attribute in the **Painting Class** box at the top of Figure 8.2, namely, firstNameOfArtist : 21 chars. The second attribute, lastNameOfArtist, is also a string of at most 21 characters, and the third attribute, title, is up to 40 characters in length, optionally followed by ?, thus 41 chars. The attributes height and width are of type 4 digits because, as stated in the first part of Section 4.9, these quantities are to be measured in centimeters, and four digits will allow for paintings up to 9999 centimeters (99.99 meters) in length or height, just in case Osbert decides to buy a huge mural.

Now consider the **Gallery Painting Class** in Figure 8.2. A dateOfPurchase is of type 10 chars because, as explained in the previous section, dates in most information systems are represented using 10 characters. The three price attributes are of type 8 digits to allow for prices of up to $99,999,999, as stated in the first part of Section 4.9.

Next look at the third attribute of **Fashionability Class.** The coefficient could be a large number or a small number—there is no way of telling from the requirements. Accordingly, the systems analysts compute the actual fashionability coefficients from a

FIGURE 8.2   The Fifth Iteration of the Initial Class Diagram of the Osbert Oglesby Case Study (Figure 6.13), with Attribute Formats Added

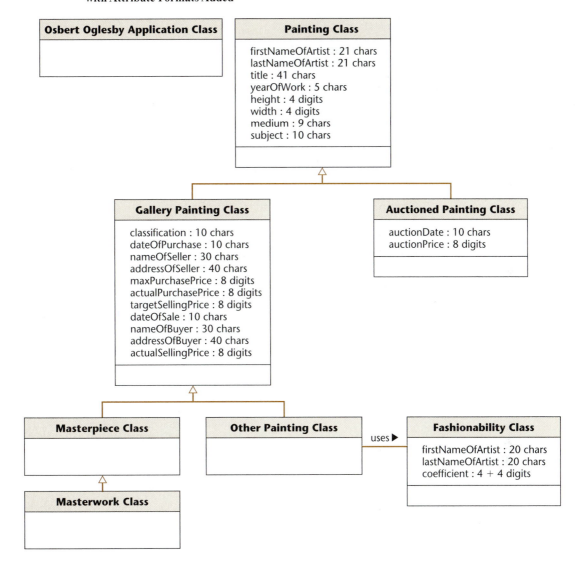

sample of Osbert's sales over the previous year. The coefficients varied from a high of 985 (Rembrandt van Rijn) to a low of 0.064 (Joey T. Dog). So, to be safe, coefficient is of type 4 + 4 digits. The largest value for the coefficient that the information system can handle is then 9999.9999 and the smallest is 0.0001.

8.3.2   Formats of the Attributes of the MSG Foundation Case Study

Figure 8.3 shows the third iteration of the initial class diagram of the MSG Foundation case study (Figure 7.14) with the addition of the attribute formats. First look at **Asset Class.** Attribute assetNumber is inherited by subclasses **Investment Class** and **Mortgage Class** from superclass **Asset Class.** That is, every instance (object) of subclass

FIGURE 8.3   The Third Iteration of the Initial Class Diagram of the MSG Foundation Case Study (Figure 7.14) with the Attribute Formats Specified

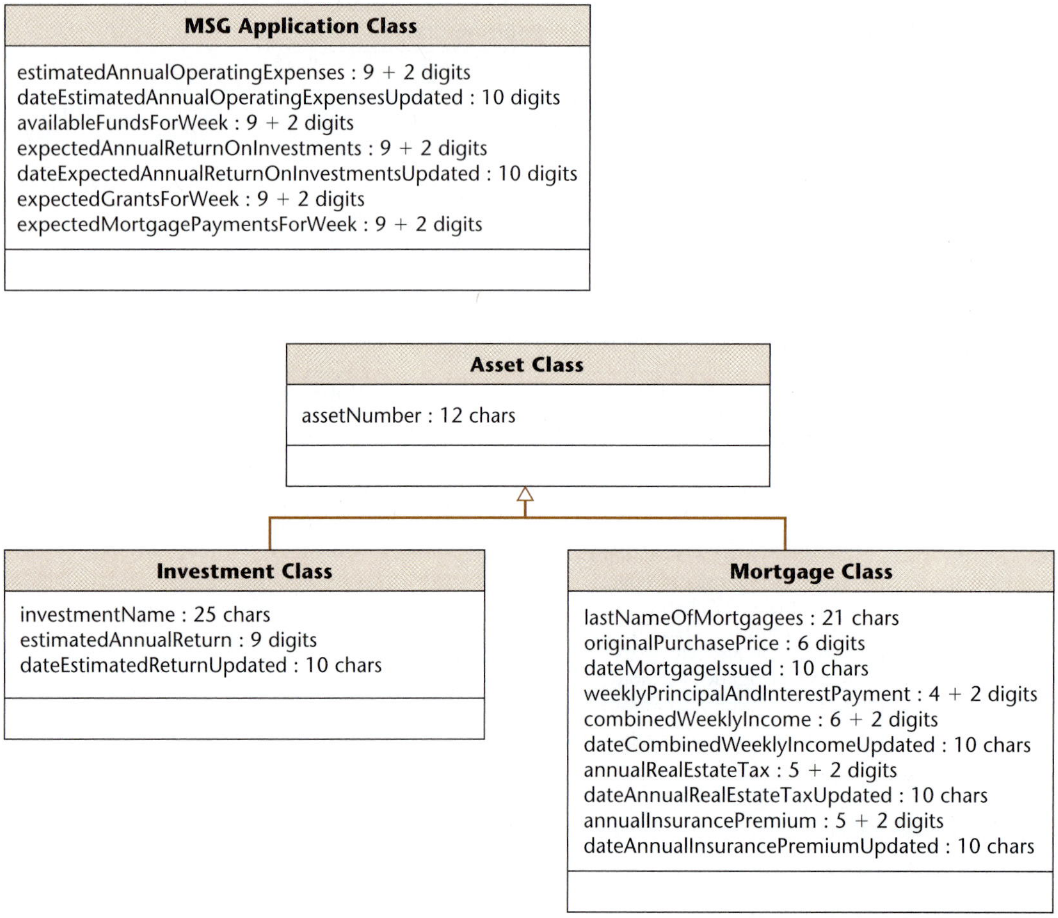

MSG Application Class
estimatedAnnualOperatingExpenses : 9 + 2 digits dateEstimatedAnnualOperatingExpensesUpdated : 10 digits availableFundsForWeek : 9 + 2 digits expectedAnnualReturnOnInvestments : 9 + 2 digits dateExpectedAnnualReturnOnInvestmentsUpdated : 10 digits expectedGrantsForWeek : 9 + 2 digits expectedMortgagePaymentsForWeek : 9 + 2 digits

Asset Class
assetNumber : 12 chars

Investment Class
investmentName : 25 chars estimatedAnnualReturn : 9 digits dateEstimatedReturnUpdated : 10 chars

Mortgage Class
lastNameOfMortgagees : 21 chars originalPurchasePrice : 6 digits dateMortgageIssued : 10 chars weeklyPrincipalAndInterestPayment : 4 + 2 digits combinedWeeklyIncome : 6 + 2 digits dateCombinedWeeklyIncomeUpdated : 10 chars annualRealEstateTax : 5 + 2 digits dateAnnualRealEstateTaxUpdated : 10 chars annualInsurancePremium : 5 + 2 digits dateAnnualInsurancePremiumUpdated : 10 chars

Investment Class and of subclass **Mortgage Class** has attribute assetNumber. Furthermore, the format of an assetNumber is identical in all three classes. More specifically, an assetNumber as defined in superclass **Asset Class** and as inherited by subclasses **Investment Class** and **Mortgage Class** consists of 12 characters, as stated toward the end of Section 5.5. Although assetNumber is the only inherited attribute, we will discover later that numerous operations are also inherited—see Appendix C.

Now consider **MSG Application Class.** It is stated at the end of Section 5.5 that the annual operating expenses are "up to $999,999,999.99." Accordingly, the format of estimatedAnnualOperatingExpenses is specified as 9 + 2 digits. This means that there are nine digits before the decimal point (for the dollar amount, up to $999,999,999) and two digits after the decimal point (for the cents). The other formats are similar.

Next we turn to the allocation of operations to classes. For full details regarding the allocation of all operations to every class, consult Appendix B (Osbert Oglesby) and Appendix C (MSG Foundation). Again, here for simplicity we consider only the entity classes of Figure 8.2 (fifth iteration of the class diagram of the Osbert Oglesby case study) and of Figure 8.3 (third iteration of the class diagram of the MSG Foundation case study).

This time we begin with the MSG Foundation case study.

8.4   Allocation of Operations to Classes

Figure 8.3 depicts the third iteration of the initial class diagram of the MSG Foundation case study with the attributes and their formats added. The operations of the classes are not included in this class diagram, as indicated by the empty rectangle at the bottom of the boxes representing each class.

Why are the operations not added during the analysis workflow, but rather during the design workflow? There are two reasons:

- First, as explained in Section 8.3, as a consequence of the iterative nature of the Unified Process, it is unwise to add an item to a UML diagram before it is strictly necessary to do so.

- Second, the operations to be allocated to the classes are deduced from the interaction diagrams of the realizations of the use cases. In more detail, the messages in interaction diagrams such as Figure 7.22 are used to deduce the operations of the information system. However, these interaction diagrams of realizations of use cases are produced *after* the class diagram. In other words, first we determine the initial class diagram, and later the interaction diagrams of the realizations of the use cases. We then use these interaction diagrams to deduce the operations; only then can we allocate the operations to the classes.

Identifying the operations to be allocated to the various classes is usually straightforward. As explained in the previous paragraph, we deduce the operations from the messages on the interaction diagrams of the realizations of the use cases. This should not come as a surprise. After all, the Unified Process is use-case driven.

The harder part is determining to which class each operation should be allocated. There are three factors that need to be considered. We will describe two of these factors in the next two subsections and illustrate them by applying them to the MSG Foundation case study and then the Osbert Oglesby case study. (There is also a third factor, namely, *polymorphism and dynamic binding*. This is described in Chapter 20.)

8.4.1   Responsibility-Driven Design

The principle of *responsibility-driven design* was described in Section 3.6. It states that, if **Class A** sends a message to **Class B** telling it to do something, it is the responsibility of **Class B** to perform the requested operation.

To see how this is applied in practice, look at Figure 7.24. This sequence diagram of the realization of the scenario of Figure 7.21 of the **Estimate Funds Available for Week** use case of the MSG Foundation case study includes the message 3: **Request estimated return on investments for week**. The weekly return on investments is computed by summing the estimated annual return of each investment and dividing by 52. Thus, the MSG Foundation case study must include the operation getAnnualReturnOnInvestment so that, for each object of **Investment Class**, the estimated annual return on that investment can be determined. It is not important whether the message to determine the estimated annual return is sent from **MSG Application Class, Asset Class**, or any other class. What is important is that **Investment Class** has the responsibility of determining the annual return on an investment. Accordingly, operation getAnnualReturnOnInvestment must be allocated to **Investment Class**, as shown in Figure 8.4.

8.4.2   Inheritance

If an operation is applicable both to an instance of a superclass and to instances of subclasses of that superclass, then it makes sense to allocate that operation to the superclass. In

FIGURE 8.4
Allocation of
Operation
getAnnualReturn-
OnInvestment

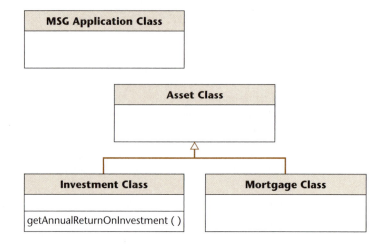

that way, there is just one version of that operation, and it can be used by instances of the superclass and of all its subclasses.

The convention in an object-oriented information system is that associated with each **attribute** of a class are operations

- setAttribute, used to assign a particular value to that **attribute**.
- getAttribute, which returns the current value of that **attribute**.

For example, in the MSG Foundation case study, every asset has an asset number; that is, **Asset Class** has an attribute assetNumber, as shown in Figure 8.3. Operation setAssetNumber is then used to assign the number of the asset to the object that represents that asset. For example, if a staff member of the MSG Foundation invests Foundation funds in General Motors stock, then the information system creates a new object, and operation setAssetNumber is invoked to assign the relevant asset number to that object, which now represents the new investment.

Subsequently, when that staff member wants to print a list of all the assets of the MSG Foundation, each object in the information system in turn is considered, and a message is sent to invoke operation getAssetNumber to obtain the asset number of the asset represented by that object.

The question is then: To which class in Figure 8.3 should operations setAssetNumber and getAssetNumber be allocated? Operation setAssetNumber is considered first.

Before considering the object-oriented paradigm, consider the situation with the traditional paradigm. In the traditional paradigm, we would have to have two different versions of setAssetNumber, one for each of the two types of asset. That is, we would need

set_investment_number
set_mortgage_number

We need two separate functions because the traditional paradigm does not support *inheritance.*

In contrast, consider once again the inheritance hierarchy of Figure 8.3. Class **Asset Class** has an attribute, assetNumber, that represents the number of each asset. The inverted triangle just under the box representing **Asset Class** denotes that classes **Investment Class** and **Mortgage Class** are subclasses of class **Asset Class.** That is, class **Investment Class** and class **Mortgage Class** both inherit attribute assetNumber from class **Asset Class.** Thus, every instance of class **Investment Class** and every instance of class **Mortgage Class**

FIGURE 8.5
Allocation of
Operations
setAssetNumber
and
getAssetNumber

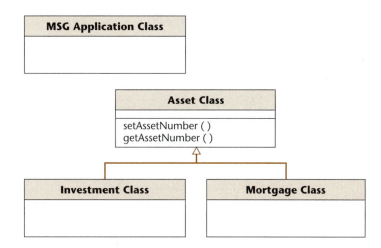

possess an attribute assetNumber that consists of 12 characters. Furthermore, any operation of class **Asset Class** that could be applied to attribute assetNumber of an instance of class **Asset Class** can be applied to attribute assetNumber of every instance of class **Investment Class** or of class **Mortgage Class.**

In other words, in contrast to the two separate operations of the traditional paradigm, in the object-oriented paradigm there is only one operation, namely, setAssetNumber, and it should be allocated to class **Asset Class** (see Figure 8.5). This operation setAssetNumber can then be applied, as a consequence of inheritance, to instances of both subclasses of **Asset Class,** that is, to instances of class **Investment Class** or of class **Mortgage Class.**

Everything stated in this section in regard to operation setAssetNumber applies equally to operation getAssetNumber. Accordingly, getAssetNumber also should be allocated to superclass **Asset Class,** as shown in Figure 8.5.

Finally, the complete class diagram of the MSG Foundation case study is shown in Appendix C.

8.5   Allocation of Operations: Osbert Oglesby Case Study

Figure 8.2 depicts the fifth iteration of the initial class diagram of the Osbert Oglesby case study with the attribute formats added. In this section we indicate how certain operations are allocated to the class diagram.

8.5.1   Responsibility-Driven Design

In the Osbert Oglesby case study, in order to compute the maximum price that Osbert should offer for a masterpiece or a masterwork, one operation that has to be performed is to get the price of an auctioned painting. That is, there has to be an operation getAuctionPrice. It is irrelevant whether the message requesting this auction price is sent from **Osbert Oglesby Application Class** or any other class; class **Auctioned Painting Class** is responsible for determining the relevant auction price. Thus, operation getAuctionPrice should be allocated to **Auctioned Painting Class,** as shown in Figure 8.6.

8.5.2   Inheritance

Every painting has a title. Accordingly, **Painting Class** has an attribute title, as depicted in Figure 8.2. Operation setTitle is then used to assign the name of a painting to a painting

FIGURE 8.6 Allocation of Operation getAuctionPrice

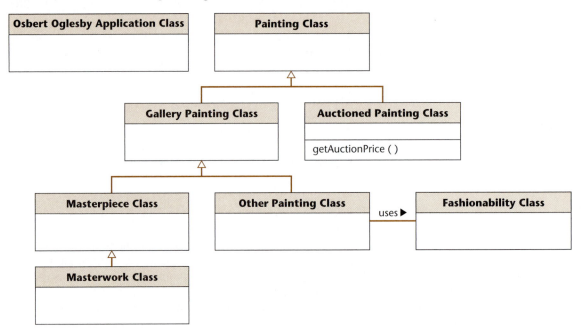

object. For instance, if Osbert buys a new painting, the information system creates a new object, and operation setTitle is invoked to assign the title of the new painting to that object.

If Osbert later wishes to print a list of all the paintings he has bought, each object in the information system in turn is examined, and a message is sent to operation getTitle to obtain the title of the painting represented by that object.

What has to be decided is to which class in Figure 8.2 operations setTitle and getTitle should be allocated. First consider operation setTitle. In the traditional paradigm, there would have to be three different versions of setTitle, one for each type of painting, namely

    set_masterpiece_title
    set_masterwork_title
    set_other_painting_title

But that is because the traditional paradigm does not support inheritance.

In contrast, consider once again the inheritance hierarchy of Figure 8.2. Class **Painting Class** has an attribute title, the title of the painting. The inverted triangle just below the box representing **Painting Class** denotes that classes **Gallery Painting Class** and **Auctioned Painting Class** are subclasses of class **Painting Class.** That is, class **Gallery Painting Class** and class **Auctioned Painting Class** both inherit attribute title from class **Painting Class.** Thus, just as every instance of class **Painting Class** has an attribute title that consists of up to 41 characters, so every instance of class **Gallery Painting Class** and every instance of class **Auctioned Painting Class** also possess that same attribute. Furthermore, any operation of class **Painting Class** that could be applied to attribute title of an instance of class **Painting Class** also can be applied to attribute title of every instance of class **Gallery Painting Class** and of class **Auctioned Painting Class.**

But the consequences of inheritance go much further. Looking again at Figure 8.2, we see that **Masterpiece Class** and **Other Painting Class** are subclasses of **Gallery Painting Class,** and that **Masterwork Class** is a subclass of **Masterpiece Class.** In other words, **Painting Class** is the superclass; **Gallery Painting Class, Auctioned Painting Class, Masterpiece Class, Other Painting Class,** and **Masterwork Class** are all subclasses of **Painting Class.**

In contrast to the three separate operations of the traditional paradigm, in the object-oriented paradigm there is only one operation, namely, setTitle, and it is allocated to class **Painting Class** (see Figure 8.7). This operation can then be applied not only to an instance of class **Painting Class,** but also, as a consequence of inheritance, to instances of every subclass of **Painting Class;** that is, to instances of classes **Gallery Painting Class, Auctioned Painting Class, Masterpiece Class, Other Painting Class,** and **Masterwork Class.**

Note that this approach does not work if operation setTitle is allocated, say, to class **Other Painting Class.** In this case, an object of class **Masterpiece Class** cannot invoke operation setTitle. Inheritance does not work in all directions; it operates only from a superclass down to a subclass of that superclass. By allocating operation setTitle to **Painting Class,** the superclass in the class hierarchy of Figure 8.7, the operation can be used, unchanged, by instances of all five of the subclasses.

Everything stated in this subsection concerning operation setTitle applies equally to operation getTitle. Accordingly, getTitle also should be allocated to the superclass **Painting Class.** This is shown in Figure 8.7.

The complete class diagram of the Osbert Oglesby case study is in Appendix B.

The last section of this chapter describes a useful technique for testing analysis and design artifacts.

FIGURE 8.7   **Allocation of Operations setTitle and getTitle**

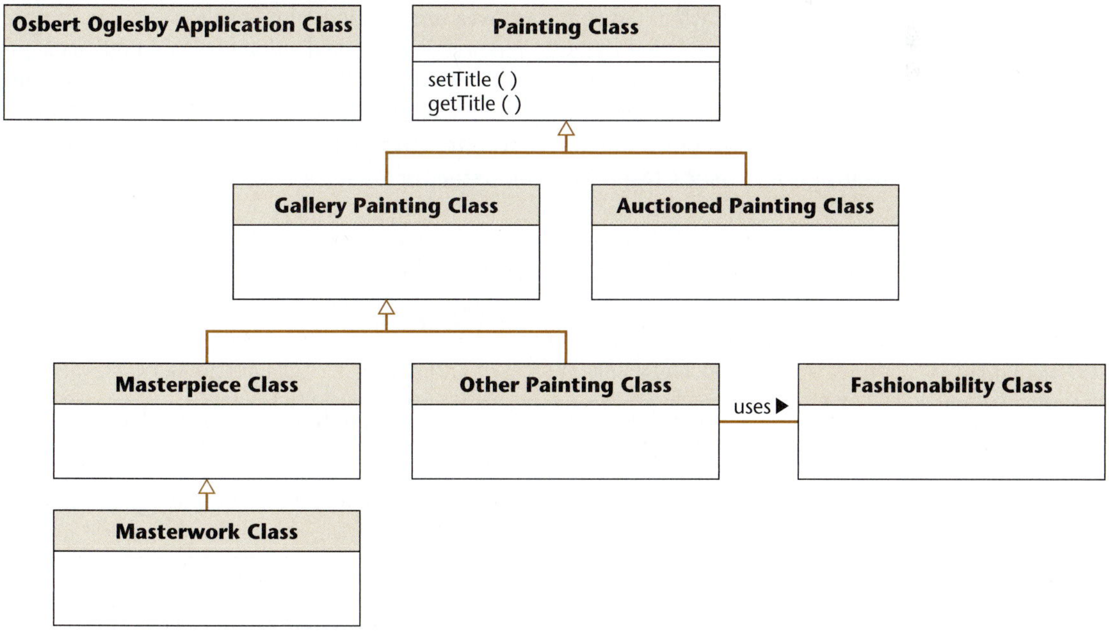

8.6   CRC Cards

Since 1990, class-responsibility-collaboration (CRC) cards have been utilized during object-oriented analysis and design [Wirfs-Brock, Wilkerson, and Wiener, 1990]. For each class, the information system development team fills in a card showing the name of the class, the functionality of that class (its responsibility), and a list of the other classes it invokes in order to achieve that functionality (its collaboration).

CRC cards were originally introduced as a tool for performing requirements elicitation and analysis (Section 4.2). CRC cards are indeed a powerful tool for this purpose, but only when the information technology professionals are familiar with the domain; that is, the specific business environment in which the information system is to operate, such as aerospace, banking, or clothing manufacturing. However, even for information technology professionals who have no domain expertise whatsoever, CRC cards are an extremely effective way of *testing* object-oriented analysis and design artifacts.

An example of a CRC card is shown in Figure 8.8. The data for this figure are obtained from the realizations of all the use cases of the MSG Foundation case study. First look at Figure 7.22 (or 7.24). Message 7: Request estimated grants and payments for week is passed from **: Estimate Funds for Week Class** to **: Mortgage Class,** followed by message 8: Return estimated grants and payments for week in the reverse direction. We conclude that **Mortgage Class** has the responsibility Compute estimated grants and payments for week and, in order to do this, must collaborate with **Estimate Funds for Week Class.** This is reflected in the first entry in the CRC card.

Now consider Figure 7.29. Message 3: Update tax and date is passed from **: Manage an Asset Class** to **: Mortgage Class** after which message 4: Send successful completion message is passed back. However, turning to the class diagram of Figure 7.14, we see that, in addition to attribute annualRealEstateTax, **Mortgage Class** has seven other attributes that might need to be changed by **: Manage an Asset Class,** including combinedWeeklyIncome. Furthermore, all eight attributes are initialized by **: Manage an Asset Class.** In fact, a complete set of scenarios will include all 16 set and get operations. Each of the 16 scenarios in turn requires an interaction diagram of its realization; Figure 7.29 is one of the 16 required interaction diagrams. In addition, managing a mortgage includes two operations not discussed in Chapter 7, namely, adding a new mortgage and deleting an existing mortgage. For brevity, we will combine all these responsibilities into responsibility Initialize, update, and delete mortgages with collaborator **Manage an Asset Class.** This is the second entry in the CRC card (Figure 8.8).

FIGURE 8.8
A CRC Card for
Class Mortgage
Class of the
MSG Foundation
Information System

CLASS	
Mortgage Class	
RESPONSIBILITY	COLLABORATION
Compute estimated grants and payments for week	**Estimate Funds for Week Class**
Initialize, update, and delete mortgages	**Manage an Asset Class**
Generate list of mortgages	**User Interface Class**
Print list of mortgages	**Mortgages Report Class**

Now we turn to Figure 7.32. Here we find message 3: Update income and date passed from **: Manage an Asset Class** to **: Mortgage Class.** Message 4: Send successful completion message is then passed back. As pointed out in the previous paragraph, combinedWeeklyIncome is one of the eight attributes of **Mortgage Class** that might need to be changed by **: Manage an Asset Class.** Thus, this responsibility is already included in Initialize, update, and delete mortgages.

Finally we turn to Figure 7.43. There we see message 2: Transfer request [for list of mortgages] passed from **: User Interface Class** to **: Mortgage Class.** Thus, **Mortgage Class** has the responsibility Generate list of mortgages with collaborator **User Interface Class,** the third entry in the CRC card shown in Figure 8.8. Also, message 3: Print list of mortgages is passed from **: Mortgage Class** to **: Mortgages Report Class.** We deduce that **Mortgage Class** also has the responsibility Print list of mortgages with collaborator **Mortgages Report Class,** the fourth entry in the CRC card shown in Figure 8.8.

As a check, we now examine Figure 7.49 and see that there are five classes with which **Mortgage Class** has a relationship, namely, **User Interface Class, Estimate Funds for Week Class, Mortgages Report Class, Asset Class,** and **Manage an Asset Class.** We know from the realizations that **Mortgage Class** no responsibility with **Asset Class.** We see that all four of the remaining classes are listed in the COLLABORATION column of Figure 8.8. This does not necessarily mean that we have included every responsibility of every collaboration class, but it is likely that all the collaboration classes have been included.

The CRC card technique has subsequently been extended.

- First, a CRC card nowadays often explicitly contains the attributes and operations of the class, rather than just its "responsibility" expressed in some natural language like English. That is, the CRC card essentially contains the information of the complete class diagram (Appendix C).
- Second, the technology has changed. Instead of using cards, some organizations put the names of the classes on Post-it notes that they then move around on a white board; lines are drawn between the Post-it notes to denote collaboration. Nowadays the whole process can be automated; CASE tools (Chapter 11) such as System Architect include modules for creating and updating CRC "cards" on the screen.

The strength of CRC cards is that, when utilized by a team, the interaction between the members can highlight missing or incorrect fields in a class, whether attributes or operations. Also, relationships between classes are clarified when CRC cards are used. One especially powerful technique is to distribute the cards among the team members who then act out the responsibilities of their classes. Thus, someone might say, "I am the **Date** class and my responsibility is to create new date objects." Another team member might then interject that he or she needs additional functionality from the **Date** class, such as converting a date from the conventional format to an integer, the number of days from January 1, 1900, so that finding the number of days between any two dates can easily be computed by subtracting the corresponding two integers (see Just in Case You Wanted to Know Box 8.1). Thus, acting out the responsibilities of CRC cards is an effective means of verifying that the classes are correct.

Just in Case You Wanted to Know   Box 8.1

How do we find the number of days between February 21, 1999, and August 10, 2004? Such subtractions are needed in a great many financial computations, such as calculating an interest payment or determining the present value of a future cash flow. The usual way this is done is to convert each date into an integer, the number of days since a specified starting date. The problem is that we cannot agree what starting date to use.

Astronomers use Julian days, the number of days since noon GMT on January 1, 4713, BCE. This system was invented in 1582 by Joseph Scaliger, who named it for his father, Julius Caesar Scaliger. (If you really, really have to know why January 1, 4713, BCE was chosen, consult the U.S. Naval Observatory web site [USNO, 2000].)

A Lilian date is the number of days since October 15, 1582, the first day of the Gregorian calendar introduced by Pope Gregory XIII. Lilian dates are named for Luigi Lilio, a leading proponent of the Gregorian calendar reform. Lilio was responsible for deriving many of the algorithms of the Gregorian calendar, including the rule for leap years.

Turning to information systems, ANSI COBOL 85 intrinsic functions use January 1, 1601, as the starting date for integer dates. Almost all spreadsheets, however, use January 1, 1900, following the lead of Lotus 1-2-3.

Key Terms

architect, *162*

architectural design, *163*

architecture, *162*

CRC card, *172*

design workflow, *161*

detailed design, *163*

dynamic binding, *167*

inheritance, *168*

package, *162*

parameter, *163*

polymorphism, *167*

responsibility-driven design, *167*

subsystem, *162*

trade-off, *162*

Review Questions for Chapter 8

1. Why is it not possible to cover all aspects of the design workflow in this book?
2. Give two factors for deciding how to allocate operations to classes.
3. How is responsibility-driven design used as a guide for deciding how to allocate operations to classes?
4. How is inheritance used as a guide for deciding how to allocate operations to classes?
5. For what size information systems is the Unified Process primarily intended?
6. Distinguish between packages and subsystems.
7. What is the reason behind breaking up an information system into packages and subsystems?
8. Give an example of a trade-off in the development of an information system.
9. What is the best thing to do if the architecture of an information system is suboptimal?
10. How can the use of CRC cards lead to the detection of missing or incorrect attributes and operations in classes?

Problems

8.1 To which class in the class diagram of Figure 8.3 should operation getDateMortgageIssued be allocated? Justify your answer.

8.2 To which class in the class diagram of Figure 8.3 should operation printAssetNumber be allocated? Justify your answer.

8.3 To which class in the class diagram of Figure 8.3 should operation getEstimatedAnnualOperatingExpenses be allocated? Justify your answer.

8.4   To which class in the class diagram of Figure 8.3 should operation computeEstimatedMortgage-PaymentsForWeek be allocated? (Be careful!)

8.5   To which class in the class diagram of Figure 8.2 should operation setHeight be allocated? Justify your answer.

8.6   To which class in the class diagram of Figure 8.2 should operation getAuctionDate be allocated? Justify your answer.

8.7   To which class in the class diagram of Figure 8.2 should operation setDateOfSale be allocated? Justify your answer.

8.8   To which class in the class diagram of Figure 8.2 should operation printSellingPrice be allocated? Justify your answer.

8.9   Draw a CRC card for class **Investment Class** of the MSG Foundation case study. Utilize Figure 7.49.

8.10   Draw a CRC card for class **Fashionability Class** of the Osbert Oglesby case study. Utilize Figure 6.42.

Systems Analysis and Design Projects

8.11   Draw a CRC card for one class of the library information system of Problem 7.8.

8.12   Draw a CRC card for one class of the ATM information system of Problem 7.9.

Term Project

8.13   Allocate the following operations to your class diagram of the Chocoholics Anonymous term project of Appendix A: getName, addMember, modifyProvider, addVisit, printEFTReport.

8.14   (Knowledge of programming needed) Construct the complete class diagram of the Chocoholics Anonymous term project of Appendix A, including both attributes and methods.

References

Jacobson, I.; G. Booch; and J. Rumbaugh. *The Unified Software Development Process.* Reading, MA: Addison Wesley, 1999.

U.S. Naval Observatory, Astronomical Applications Department. "The 21st Century and the 3rd Millennium—When Will They Begin?" February 22, 2000. Available at aa.usno.navy.mil/AA/faq/docs/millennium.html.

Wirfs-Brock, R.; B. Wilkerson; and L. Wiener. *Designing Object-Oriented Software.* Englewood Cliffs, NJ: Prentice Hall, 1990.

Chapter

9

The Workflows and Phases of the Unified Process

Learning Objectives

After studying this chapter, you should be able to:

- Explain what is performed during all five core workflows.
- List the four phases of the Unified Process.
- Distinguish clearly between the four phases and the five core workflows of the Unified Process.
- Clarify why the Unified Process has both phases and workflows.

The fourth word in the title of this chapter, "Phases," may come as something of a surprise. After all, it was stated in Chapter 2 that the phases of the traditional paradigm correspond to the workflows of the Unified Process. In fact, the Unified Process has both workflows and phases, but the phases of the Unified Process do not correspond to the phases of the traditional paradigm. This chapter is devoted to clarifying precisely what a workflow of the Unified Process is and defining exactly what constitutes a phase of the Unified Process.

First we consider workflows.

9.1 The Workflows of the Unified Process

Our starting point is Figure 2.6, reproduced here as Figure 9.1. The figure shows five workflows, namely, the requirements workflow, analysis workflow, design workflow, implementation workflow, and test workflow. In each increment (there are four increments in Figure 9.1), part of each of these five workflows is carried out. As explained in Chapter 2, the emphasis is on the requirements and analysis workflows in the earlier increments, whereas the implementation workflow is the major focus in the later increments. The test workflow is important throughout the life cycle. However, there is an increased emphasis

FIGURE 9.1
The Core Workflows
of the Unified Process

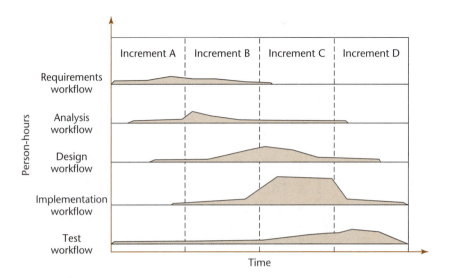

on testing toward the end of the life cycle. In addition to these five *core workflows,* the Unified Process includes other workflows, such as management and planning, that are carried out in parallel with the core workflows. Management issues are the subject of Chapter 14, and planning is described in Chapter 15. In this chapter, therefore, we consider just the five core workflows.

9.1.1 The Requirements Workflow

The aim of the *requirements workflow* is to ensure that the developers build the right information system. This is achieved by describing the target information system sufficiently clearly and accurately that the two main stakeholders, the client and the developers, can agree on what the information system should do and should not do. In order to achieve this, the requirements have to be fully understood by the client. One way to achieve this is to use the Unified Process; the many models of the Unified Process assist the client in gaining the necessary detailed understanding of what is to be developed.

The details of how the requirements workflow is performed were presented in Chapters 4 and 5; there is no need to repeat that material here.

9.1.2 The Analysis Workflow

The purpose of the *analysis workflow* is to analyze and refine the requirements. By doing this we achieve the detailed understanding of the requirements that we must have to develop an information system correctly and to maintain it easily. But why do we have an analysis workflow at all? Surely it would be simpler to develop an information system by continuing with further iterations of the requirements workflow until we obtain the necessary understanding of the target information system.

The key point is that the output of the requirements workflow must be totally comprehensible by the client. In other words, the artifacts of the requirements workflow must be expressed in the language of the client, that is, in a natural (human) language such as English, Armenian, or Zulu. But all natural languages, without exception, are somewhat imprecise and lend themselves to misunderstanding. For example, consider the following paragraph:

A part record and a plant record are read from the database. If it contains the letter A directly followed by the letter Q, then calculate the cost of transporting that part to that plant.

At first sight, this requirement seems perfectly clear. But to what does the "it" (the second word in the second sentence) refer? The part record? The plant record? Or the database?

Ambiguities of this kind cannot arise if the requirements are expressed (say) in a mathematical notation. However, if a mathematical notation is used for the requirements, then the client is unlikely to understand much of the requirements artifacts. Consequently, the information system developed to satisfy these requirements may not be what the client needs.

The solution is to have two separate workflows. The requirements workflow is couched in the language of the client, the analysis workflow in a more precise language that will ensure that the design and implementation workflows are correctly carried out. In addition, more details are added during the analysis workflow, details that are not relevant to the client's understanding of the target information system but are essential for the information technology professionals who will develop the information system. Consider, for example, the initial state of a statechart. This is entirely irrelevant from the viewpoint of the client. However, it is essential to specify the initial state for the information technology professionals so that they can implement the statechart correctly.

Again, details of how the analysis workflow is performed have been given in Chapters 6 and 7.

9.1.3   The Design Workflow

During the *design workflow* we refine the analysis workflow until the material is in a form that can be implemented by the programmers. In addition, a number of requirements need to be finalized at this time, including choice of programming language, as well as reuse and portability issues. The design workflow was discussed in Chapter 8.

9.1.4   The Implementation Workflow

The aim of the *implementation workflow* is to implement the target information system in the selected implementation language. More precisely, as explained in Section 8.1, a large information system is partitioned into smaller subsystems, which are then implemented in parallel by coding teams. The subsystems, in turn, consist of *components* or *code artifacts*.

As soon as a component has been coded, the programmer tests it. Once the programmer is satisfied that the component is correct, it is passed onto the quality assurance group for further testing. This testing by the quality assurance group is part of the test workflow and is described in Chapter 13.

9.1.5   The Test Workflow

The *test workflow* is the responsibility of the quality assurance group. As pointed out at the end of the previous section, each component is tested by the quality assurance group as soon as it has been implemented; this is termed *unit testing*. At the end of each iteration, *integration testing* is performed. Here, the components that have been completed and unit tested are compiled and linked together (*integrated*) and then tested against various test cases. When the product appears to be complete, it is tested as a whole; this is termed *product testing*.

When management believe that the product is fault-free, it is installed on the client's computer. The client now performs *acceptance testing*. That is, the client checks whether the delivered information system satisfies its specifications. If the information system passes the acceptance test, the client pays the developers. If not, the developers have to fix the information system until it passes the acceptance test.

Testing is described in detail in Chapter 13.

9.2 The Phases of the Unified Process

Look at Figure 9.2, which seems to be identical to Figure 9.1. Look more closely—the labels of the increments have changed. Instead of Increment A, Increment B, and so on, the four increments are labeled Inception phase, Elaboration phase, Construction phase, and Transition phase. These are the four phases of the Unified Process and, as we will see, they are particularly aptly named.

In other words, the phases of the Unified Process are the increments. Furthermore, although in theory the development of an information system could be performed in 3, 5, or 16 increments, in practice the development seems to consist of 4 increments. The increments/phases are described in the next four sections, together with the deliverables of each phase; that is, the artifacts that should be completed by the end of that phase.

Every step performed in the Unified Process falls into one of five core workflows and *also* into one of four phases. Thus, the various steps of the four phases below have already been described in Chapters 4 through 8 and in the five subsections of Section 9.1. For example, building a business model is part of the requirements workflow (Chapters 4 and 5). As we will see, it is also part of the inception phase. But why does each step have to be considered twice?

In Chapters 4 and 5, a description was given of building a business model within the context of the requirements workflow. In order to determine the client's needs, one of the steps is to build a business model. In other words, in those chapters, building a business model is presented within a *technical* context. In the next subsection, a description is presented of building a business model within the context of the inception phase; that is, the phase in which management decides whether or not to develop the proposed information system. That is, in this chapter, building a business model is presented within a *business* context.

At the same time, there is no point in presenting each step twice, both times at the same level of detail. Accordingly, the inception phase is described in depth to highlight the difference between the technical context of the workflows and the business context of the phases, but the other three phases are simply outlined.

9.2.1 The Inception Phase

The purpose of the *inception phase* is to determine whether it is worthwhile to develop the target information system. In other words, the primary aim of this phase is to determine whether the proposed information system is economically viable.

FIGURE 9.2

The Core Workflows and Phases of the Unified Process

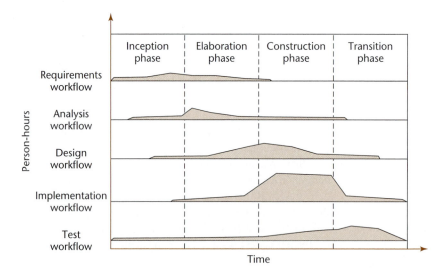

Recall from Chapters 4 and 5 that the first two steps of the requirements workflow are to understand the domain and build a business model. Clearly, there is no way that we can give any kind of opinion regarding a possible future information system unless we first understand the domain in which we are considering developing the target information system. It does not matter if the domain is a television network, a machine tool company, or a hospital specializing in liver disease—if we do not fully understand the domain, no reliance can be placed on anything that we subsequently do. So, the first step is always to obtain domain knowledge. Once we have a full comprehension of the domain, the second step is to build a business model. In other words, first we have to understand the domain, then we have to understand precisely how the client organization does business in that domain.

Now we need to delimit the scope of the proposed project. We saw in Chapter 5 that the use-case diagram of the initial business model of the MSG Foundation information system (Figure 5.9) included four use cases, but only three of them appeared in the use-case diagram of the initial requirements of the MSG Foundation information system (Figure 5.10). Consider a proposed information system for a new highly secure ATM network for a nationwide chain of banks. The use-case diagram of the initial requirements is likely to be large, but will surely be only a fraction of the size of the business model of the banking chain as a whole. In order to be able to determine what the proposed information system should incorporate, we have to focus on only a subset of the business model, namely, the subset that is covered by the proposed information system. Thus, delimiting the scope of the proposed project is obviously the third step.

Now we can begin to make the initial business case. The questions that will need to be answered before proceeding with the project include [Jacobson, Booch, and Rumbaugh, 1999]

- Is the proposed information system cost effective? That is, will the benefits to be gained as a consequence of developing the information system outweigh the costs involved? How long will it take to obtain a return on the investment needed to develop the proposed information system? Alternatively, what will be the cost to the client company if they decide not to develop the proposed information system? If the information system is to be sold in the marketplace, have the necessary marketing studies been performed?

- Can the proposed information system be delivered in time? That is, if the information system is delivered late to the market, will the organization still make a profit, or will a competitive information system obtain the lion's share of the market? Alternatively, if the information system is to be developed to support the client organization's own activities (presumably including mission-critical activities), what will be the impact if the proposed information system is delivered late?

- What are the risks involved in developing the information system, and how can these risks be mitigated? That is, does the team who will develop the proposed information system have the necessary experience? Is new hardware needed for this information system and, if so, is there a risk that it will not be delivered in time? If so, is there a way to mitigate that risk, perhaps by ordering back-up hardware from another supplier? Are software tools (Chapter 11) needed? Are they currently available? Do they have all the necessary functionality? Is it likely that a COTS package with all (or almost all) of the functionality of the proposed custom information system will be put on the market while the project is underway, and how can this be determined?

By the end of the inception phase we will need to have answers to these questions so that we can make the initial business case.

The next step is to identify the use cases and prioritize them. When we extracted the initial requirements of the Osbert Oglesby case study (Section 4.8) and the MSG Foundation case study (Section 5.4), there were only a handful of use cases, so there was no need to prioritize them in any way. However, in a large information system, there will be a large number of risks (Section 14.2), and the use cases need to be prioritized in the order of the risk that they carry. There are three major risk categories:

• Technical risks. Examples of technical risks are listed in the previous bulleted item.

• The risk of not getting the requirements right. This is mitigated by performing the requirements workflow correctly.

• The risk of not getting the architecture right. There is always the risk that the architecture may not be sufficiently robust. (Recall from Section 2.8 that the *architecture* of an information system includes the various component modules and how they fit together, and that the property of being able to handle such extensions and changes without falling apart is called *robustness*.) In other words, while we are developing our information system, there is a risk that trying to add the next piece to what we have developed so far might require the entire architecture to be redesigned from scratch. An analogy would be to build a house of cards, only to find the entire edifice tumbling down when an additional card is added.

In order to mitigate all three classes of risks, the use cases need to be prioritized in order of associated risk, as previously stated, so that the critical risks are mitigated first.

Now that the use cases have been determined and prioritized, the next step is to refine the use cases, as shown in Section 4.9 (Osbert Oglesby case study) and Sections 5.5 through 5.7 (MSG Foundation case study). This concludes the steps of the inception phase that fall under the requirements workflow.

As shown in Figure 9.2, a small amount of the analysis workflow is performed during the inception phase. All that is usually done is that a few *critical use cases* are analyzed, so that the design of the architecture can begin. This design work is also reflected in Figure 9.2.

Turning now to the implementation workflow, frequently no coding is performed during the inception phase. However, on occasion, it is necessary to build a *proof-of-concept prototype* to test the feasibility of part of the proposed information system. This is not a rapid prototype constructed to be certain that the requirements have been accurately determined, as described in Section 7.13.1. After all, rapid prototyping is not part of the Unified Process. Instead, a proof-of-concept prototype is more like an engineering prototype, that is, a scale model constructed to test the feasibility of construction. If the development team is concerned whether a particular part of the proposed information system can be constructed, a proof-of-concept prototype is constructed. For example, we may be concerned whether a particular computation can be performed quickly enough. In that case, we build a prototype to test the timing of just that computation. Or we may be worried that the font we intend to use for all screens will be too small for the average user to read without eyestrain. In this instance we would construct a prototype to display a number of different screens, and determine by experiment whether the users find the font to be uncomfortably small.

The test workflow commences almost at the start of the inception phase. The major aim here is to ensure that the requirements have been accurately determined.

Planning is an essential part of every phase. In the case of the inception phase, we do not have enough information at the beginning of the phase to plan the entire development, so the only planning that is done at the start of the project is the planning for the inception phase itself. For the same reason, namely, a lack of information, the only planning that we can meaningfully do at the end of the inception phase is the plan for just the next phase, the elaboration phase.

Documentation, too, is an essential part of every phase. The *deliverables* of the inception phase include [Jacobson, Booch, and Rumbaugh, 1999]

- The initial version of the domain model.
- The initial version of the business model.
- The initial version of the requirements artifacts (especially the use cases).
- A preliminary version of the analysis artifacts.
- A preliminary version of the architecture.
- The initial list of risks.
- The initial ordering of the use cases.
- The plan for the elaboration phase.
- The initial version of the business case.

Obtaining the last item, the initial version of the business case, is the overall aim of the inception phase. This initial version incorporates a description of the scope of the information system, as well as financial details. If the proposed information system is to be marketed, the business case will include revenue projections, market estimates, and initial cost estimates. If the information system is to be used in-house, the business case will include the initial cost–benefit analysis.

9.2.2   The Elaboration Phase

The aim of the *elaboration phase* is to refine the initial requirements (use cases), refine the architecture, monitor the risks and refine their priorities, refine the business case, and produce the project management plan. The reason for the name "elaboration phase" is obvious; the major activities of this phase are refinements or elaborations of the previous phase.

Referring once more to Figure 9.2, we see that these tasks correspond to all but completing the requirements workflow (Chapters 4 and 5), performing virtually the entire analysis workflow (Chapters 6 and 7), and then starting the design of the architecture (Section 8.1).

The deliverables of the elaboration phase include [Jacobson, Booch, and Rumbaugh, 1999]

- The completed domain model.
- The completed business model.
- The completed requirements artifacts.
- The completed analysis artifacts.
- An updated version of the architecture.
- An updated list of risks.
- The project management plan (for the remainder of the project).
- The completed business case.

9.2.3   The Construction Phase

The purpose of the *construction phase* is to produce the first operational-quality version of the information system, sometimes called the *beta release*. Look again at Figure 9.2. Even though this figure is only a symbolic representation of the phases, it is clear that the emphasis in this phase is on implementation and testing the information system. That is, the various modules in the detailed design are coded and unit tested. The modules are then compiled and linked (integrated) to form subsystems that are integration tested. Finally the subsystems are combined into the overall system, which is product tested.

A real-time system frequently is more complex than most people, even its developers, realize. As a result, there are sometimes subtle interactions that take place among components that even the most skilled testers usually would not detect. An apparently minor change therefore can have major consequences.

A famous example of this is the fault that delayed the first space shuttle orbital flight in April 1981 [Garman, 1981]. The space shuttle avionics are controlled by four identical synchronized computers. Also, an independent fifth computer is ready for backup in case the set of four computers fails. Two years earlier, a change had been made to the module that performs initialization before the avionics computers are synchronized. An unfortunate side effect of this change was that a record containing a time just slightly later than the current time was erroneously sent to the data area used for synchronization of the avionics computers. The time sent was sufficiently close to the actual time for this fault not to be detected. About one year later, the time difference was slightly increased, just enough to cause a 1 in 67 chance of a failure. Then, on the day of the first space shuttle launch, with hundreds of millions of people watching on television all over the world, the synchronization failure occurred, and three of the four identical avionics computers were synchronized one cycle late relative to the first computer. A fail-safe device that prevents the independent fifth computer from receiving information from the other four computers unless they are in agreement had the unanticipated consequence of preventing initialization of the fifth computer, and the launch had to be postponed. An all-too-familiar aspect of this incident was that the fault was in the initialization module, a module that apparently had no connection whatsoever with the synchronization routines.

This phase is carried out largely by the programmers and quality assurance group, although the designers have a role in refining the design. The systems analysts are involved if a fault is detected that requires the earlier workflows to be revisited, or if the moving target problem causes a change in the requirements.

The deliverables of the construction phase include [Jacobson, Booch, and Rumbaugh, 1999]

- The initial user manual and other manuals, as appropriate.
- All the artifacts (beta release versions).
- The completed architecture.
- The updated risk list.
- The project management plan (for the remainder of the project).
- If necessary, the updated business case.

9.2.4 The Transition Phase

The aim of the *transition phase* is to ensure that the client's requirements have indeed been met. This phase is driven by feedback from the sites at which the beta release has been installed. (In the case of a custom information system developed for a specific client, there will be just one such site.) Faults in the information system are corrected. Also, all the manuals are completed. During this phase, it is important to try to discover any previously unidentified risks. (The importance of uncovering risks even during the transition phase is highlighted in Just in Case You Wanted to Know Box 9.1.)

Ideally, this phase should be carried out by the programmers who make the necessary changes and the quality assurance group who test their changes. In practice, however, systems analysts are needed when a fault is highlighted that necessitates a change to the requirements, analysis, or design workflows.

The deliverables of the transition phase include [Jacobson, Booch, and Rumbaugh, 1999]

- All the artifacts (final versions).
- The completed manuals.

9.3   Why a Two-Dimensional Model?

A traditional life cycle (like the waterfall model of Section 2.2) is a one-dimensional model, as represented by the single axis in Figure 9.3(a). The Unified Process is a two-dimensional model, as represented by the two axes in Figure 9.3(b). This latter figure shows both the workflows (technical contexts) and the phases (business contexts).

In more detail, Figure 9.4 shows the waterfall model of the MSG Foundation case study. The boxes are labeled with the section in this book in which the relevant phase was performed. The waterfall model is clearly one dimensional and should be compared to Figure 9.3(a).

In contrast, Figure 9.5 shows the evolution tree model (Section 2.2) of the MSG Foundation case study. This model is two dimensional and should therefore be compared to Figure 9.3(b).

Next, Figure 9.6 shows the evolution tree model of Figure 9.5 superimposed on the Unified Process. Figure 9.6 reflects the two-dimensional nature of the Unified Process and should be compared to Figure 9.3(b).

Are all the additional complications of the two-dimensional model of Figure 9.3(b) necessary? The answer was given in Chapter 2, but this is such an important issue that it is repeated here. When developing an information system, in an ideal world we would first complete the requirements before proceeding to the analysis. Similarly, we would complete all the analysis before starting the design, and so on. In reality, however, all but the most trivial information systems are too large to handle as a single unit. Instead, we have to divide

FIGURE 9.3

Comparison of (a) a Traditional Life Cycle and (b) the Unified Process Life Cycle

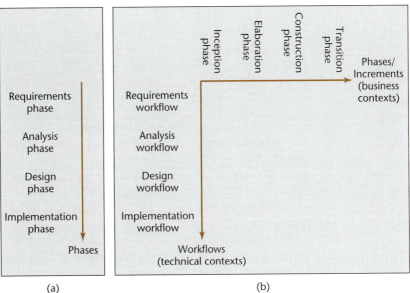

FIGURE 9.4
Waterfall Model of the MSG Foundation Case Study
The boxes are labeled with the sections in the book in which the relevant phase is described

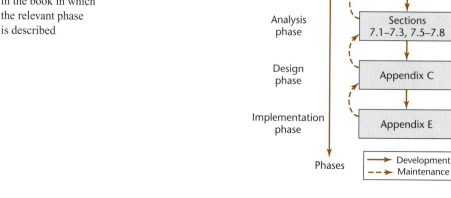

FIGURE 9.5
Evolution Tree Model of the MSG Foundation Case Study
The boxes are labeled with the sections in the book in which the relevant workflow is described

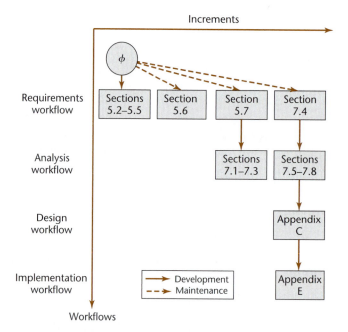

the task into increments (phases), and within each increment we have to iterate until we have completed the task under construction. As human beings, we are limited by Miller's Law, which states that we can actively process only seven concepts at a time. We therefore cannot deal with information systems as a whole, but instead we have to break those systems into subsystems. Even subsystems can be too large at times—modules may be all that we can handle until we have a fuller understanding of all the parts of the information system as a whole.

In other words, we take the first increment and perform the requirements, analysis, design, and implementation workflows on that increment. Then we take the second increment and go through the core workflows again. We continue until we have developed the complete

FIGURE 9.6

The Evolution Tree
Model of the
MSG Foundation
Case Study
Superimposed on
the Unified Process

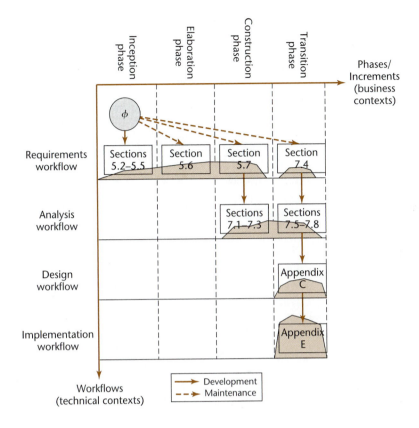

information system. We do it this way because, at the beginning of the process, we simply do not have enough information about the information system as a whole to be able to carry out the requirements workflow for the information system as a whole, and similarly for the other core workflows.

The Unified Process is the best solution we have found to date for treating a large problem as a set of smaller, largely independent subproblems. It provides a framework for incrementation and iteration, the mechanism we use to cope with the complexity of large information systems.

There is another challenge that the Unified Process handles well—the inevitable changes. One aspect of this challenge is changes in the client's requirements while an information system is being developed, the so-called moving target problem (Section 2.4). The real world modeled by the information system is continually changing, so the information system must keep up with those changes by changing as well. A second aspect is that we are human and make mistakes, and these mistakes force us to revisit earlier phases and make changes to the various artifacts to correct our mistakes.

For all these reasons, the Unified Process is currently the best methodology we have. For now, there is no better way to develop an information system than to use the Unified Process. However, in the future, the Unified Process will doubtless be superseded by some new methodology. Today's information technology professionals are looking beyond the Unified Process to the next major breakthrough. After all, in virtually every field of human endeavor, the discoveries of today are often superior to anything that was being put forward in the past. The Unified Process is sure to be superseded, in turn, by the methodologies of the future. The important lesson is that, based on *today's* knowledge, the Unified Process appears to be better than all the other alternatives currently available.

Key Terms

acceptance testing, *179*
analysis workflow, *178*
beta release, *183*
code artifact, *179*
component, *179*
construction phase, *183*
core workflow, *178*
critical use case, *182*

deliverable, *183*
design workflow, *179*
elaboration phase, *183*
implementation
   workflow, *179*
inception phase, *180*
integration, *179*
integration testing, *179*

product testing, *179*
proof-of-concept
   prototype, *182*
requirements workflow, *178*
robustness, *182*
test workflow, *179*
transition phase, *184*
unit testing, *179*

Review Questions for Chapter 9

1. List the five core workflows of the Unified Process.
2. Give two workflows that are not core workflows.
3. What is the main activity of the implementation workflow?
4. What are the main activities of the test workflow?
5. Distinguish between unit, system, and integration testing.
6. List the four phases of the Unified Process.
7. What is the purpose of the inception phase?
8. What is the purpose of the elaboration phase?
9. What is the purpose of the construction phase?
10. What is the purpose of the transition phase?
11. Why does every step of the Unified Process fall into both a workflow and a phase?

Problems

9.1 "The requirements artifacts of the Unified Process are a compromise between precise mathematical requirements that cannot be understood by the client and ambiguous natural language requirements." Discuss this claim.

9.2 The deliverables of the inception phase include an initial list of risks. Give a list of risks associated with the Osbert Oglesby case study. For each risk, explain how it can be mitigated.

9.3 Now give a list of risks associated with the MSG Foundation case study. Explain how each risk can be mitigated.

9.4 Consider the initial business case of the Osbert Oglesby case study. How would you determine whether the proposed information system will be cost effective?

9.5 Consider the initial business case of the MSG Foundation case study. How would you determine whether the proposed information system will be cost effective?

9.6 What sort of manuals will need to be delivered with the Osbert Oglesby information system?

9.7 What sort of manuals will need to be delivered with the MSG Foundation information system?

Term Project

9.8 (Knowledge of programming needed) Perform the implementation workflow of the Chocoholics Anonymous term project of Appendix A.

References

J. R. Garman. "The 'Bug' Heard 'Round the World." *ACM SIGSOFT Software Engineering Notes* 6 (October 1981), pp. 3–10.

Jacobson, I.; G. Booch; and J. Rumbaugh. *The Unified Software Development Process*. Reading, MA: Addison Wesley, 1999.

Chapter **10**

More on UML

Learning Objectives

After studying this chapter, you should be able to:

- Appreciate that UML is a language, *not* a methodology.
- Comprehend typical UML diagrams.
- Describe UML use cases, class diagrams, notes, use-case diagrams, interaction diagrams, statecharts, activity diagrams, packages, component diagrams, and deployment diagrams.

During the course of this book, various elements of UML [Booch, Rumbaugh, and Jacobson, 1999] have been introduced. Specifically, the notation for inheritance, aggregation, and association was described in Chapter 3. In Chapter 4, use cases, use-case diagrams, and notes were introduced; in Chapter 6, class diagrams, statecharts, collaboration diagrams, and sequence diagrams were added.

This subset of UML is adequate for understanding this book and for doing all the exercises, as well as the term project of Appendix A. However, real-world information systems are, unfortunately, much larger and considerably more complex than the Osbert Oglesby and MSG Foundation case studies, or the term project of Appendix A. Accordingly, in this chapter more material on UML is presented, as preparation for entering the real world.

Before reading this chapter, it is necessary to be aware that UML, like all state-of-the-art computer languages, is constantly changing. When this book was written, the latest version of UML was Version 1.4. By this time, however, some aspects of UML may have changed. As explained in Just in Case You Wanted to Know Box 3.3, UML is now under the control of the Object Management Group (OMG). Before proceeding, it would probably be a good idea to check for updates to UML at the OMG website, www.omg.org.

10.1 UML Is Not a Methodology

Before looking at UML in more detail, it is essential to clarify what UML is and, more importantly, what UML is not. *UML* is an acronym for *Unified Modeling Language*. That is, UML is a *language*. Consider a language like English. English can be used to write novels, encyclopedias, poems, prayers, news reports, and even textbooks on systems analysis and design. That is, a language is simply a tool for expressing ideas. A specific language does not constrain the types of ideas that can be described by that language or the way that they can be described.

As a language, UML can be used to describe information systems developed using the traditional paradigm or any of the many versions of the object-oriented paradigm, including the Unified Process. In other words, UML is a notation, not a methodology. It is a notation that can be used in conjunction with any methodology.

In fact, UML is not merely *a* notation; it is *the* notation. It is inconceivable today, for example, to write a book on object-oriented systems analysis and design that does not use UML to describe information systems. UML has become a world standard. A person who is unfamiliar with UML would have difficulty functioning today as an information technology professional.

The title of this chapter is "More on UML." Bearing in mind the central role played by UML, it would seem essential for all of UML to be presented here. However, the manual for Version 1.4 of UML is nearly 600 pages long, so complete coverage would probably not be a good idea. But is it possible to be a competent information technology professional without knowing every single aspect of UML?

Remember that UML is a language. The English language has over 100,000 words, but almost all speakers of English seem to manage fine with just a subset of the complete English vocabulary. In the same way, in this chapter all the types of UML diagrams are described, together with many (but by no means all) of the various options for each of those diagrams. The small subset of UML presented in Chapters 3 through 9 is adequate for the purposes of this book. In the same way, the larger subset of UML presented in this chapter will be adequate for the systems analysis and design of most information systems.

How was it decided what to include and what to leave out of this chapter? UML was designed to be comprehensive; that is, powerful enough to be used for modeling all kinds of software. The subject of this book, however, is systems analysis and design, as opposed to the full life cycle. Furthermore, this book is on information systems, as opposed to other types of software such as scientific software (programs for solving mathematical equations) or real-time control systems such as the software for controlling an internal combustion engine. Those features of UML that are most appropriate for the systems analysis and design of information systems were therefore included in this book.

10.2   Class Diagrams

FIGURE 10.1
Simplest Possible Class Diagram

A *class diagram* depicts classes and their interrelationships. The simplest possible class diagram is shown in Figure 10.1. It depicts the class **Bank Account Class** of Chapter 3. More details of **Bank Account Class** are shown in Figure 10.2. A key aspect of UML is that both Figure 10.1 and Figure 10.2 are valid class diagrams. In other words, in UML you may add as many or as few details as you think are appropriate for the current iteration and incrementation.

Bank Account Class

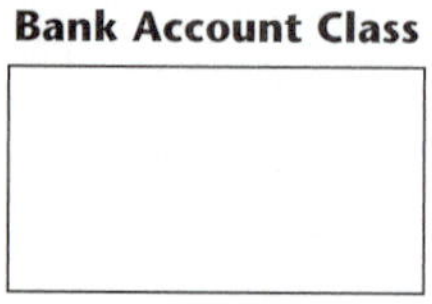

FIGURE 10.2
The Class Diagram of Figure 10.1 with an Attribute and Two Operations Added

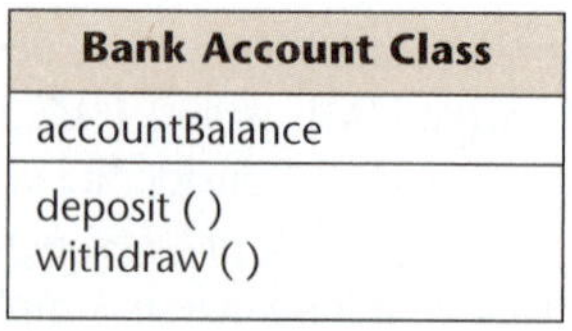

Bank Account Class
accountBalance
deposit ( ) withdraw ( )

This freedom of notation extends to objects. In Section 3.6, the notation **bank account** was informally used for one specific object of this class. The full UML notation is

<u>bank account : Bank Account Class</u>

That is, **<u>bank account</u>** is an object, an instance of a class **Bank Account Class.** In more detail, the underlining denotes that we are dealing with an object, the colon denotes "an instance of," and the bold face and initial uppercase letters in **Bank Account Class** denote this is a class.

However, UML allows us to use a shorter notation when there is no ambiguity. That is why it is valid to use the notation

<u>bank account</u>

in Section 3.6; in that context, **<u>bank account</u>** is clearly an instance of **Bank Account Class** and of no other class.

Now suppose that we wish to model the concept of an arbitrary bank account. That is, we do not wish to refer to one specific object of **Bank Account Class.** The UML notation for this is

<u>: Bank Account Class</u>

As just pointed out, the colon means "an instance of," so **<u>: Bank Account Class</u>** means "an instance of class **Bank Account Class**," which is precisely what we wanted to model. This notation is widely used in Chapters 6 and 7. Conversely, in Figure 6.30, the collaboration diagram for the realization of a scenario of the use case Buy a Masterwork of the Osbert Oglesby information system, the actor is labeled **Osbert** and not **<u>: Osbert</u>** (the labeling of many of the other items in that diagram) precisely because **Osbert** denotes that Osbert is an actor, whereas **<u>: Osbert</u>** would denote "an instance of the [nonexistent] **Osbert Class.**"

In Section 3.6, the concept of information hiding was introduced. In UML, the prefix + indicates that an attribute or operation is **public,** and similarly the prefix – denotes that the attribute or operation is **private.** This notation is used in Figure 10.3. The attribute of **Bank Account Class** is declared to be **private** (so that we can achieve information hiding), whereas both the operations are **public** so that they can be invoked from anywhere in the information system. Just to complicate matters further, there is a third type of visibility, **protected,** with prefix #. If an attribute is **public,** it is visible everywhere; if it is **private,** it is visible only in the class in which it is defined; and if it is **protected,** it is visible either within the class in which it is defined or within subclasses of that class.

Up to now in this chapter, class diagrams containing only one class have been presented. In the next subsection class diagrams with more than one class are considered.

10.2.1   Aggregation

Consider Figure 3.12, reproduced in this chapter as Figure 10.4. This figure models the statement: "A car consists of a chassis, an engine, wheels, and seats." Recall that the open diamonds denote *aggregation.* Aggregation is the UML term for the *part–whole relationship;* the parts of a car are the chassis, engine, wheels, and seats. The diamond is placed

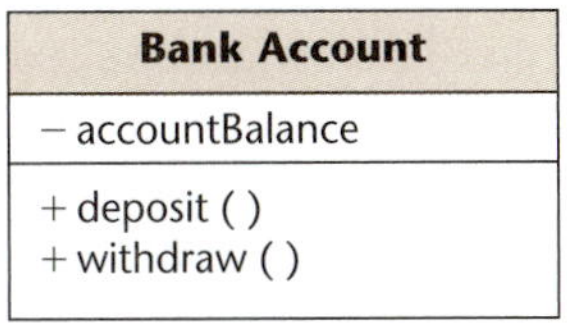

FIGURE 10.3
The Class Diagram of Figure 10.2 with Visibility Prefixes Added

Bank Account
– accountBalance
+ deposit ( )   + withdraw ( )

FIGURE 10.4   **An Aggregation Example**

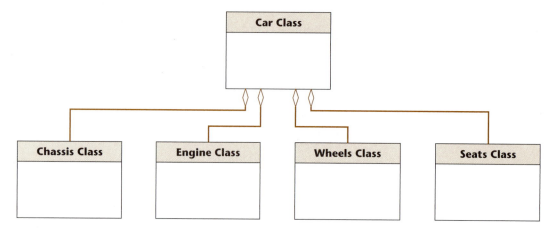

FIGURE 10.5   **Aggregation Example with Multiplicities**

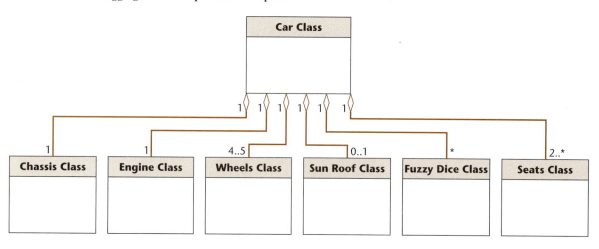

at the "whole" (car) end, not the "part" (chassis, engine, wheels, or seats) end of the line connecting a part to the whole.

10.2.2   Multiplicity

Now suppose that we want to use UML to model the statement: "A car consists of one chassis, one engine, four or five wheels, an optional sun roof, zero or more fuzzy dice hanging from the rear-view mirror, and two or more seats." This is shown in Figure 10.5. The numbers next to the ends of the lines denote *multiplicity,* or the number of times that the one class is associated with the other class.

First consider the line connecting **Chassis Class** to **Car Class.** The 1 at the "part" end of the line denotes that there is one chassis involved in this relationship, and the 1 at the "whole" end denotes that there is one car involved; that is, each car has one chassis. Similar observations hold for the line connecting **Engine Class** to **Car Class.**

Now consider the line connecting **Wheels Class** to **Car Class.** The 4..5 at the "part" end together with the 1 at the "whole" end denotes that each car has from four to five wheels

Just in Case You Wanted to Know Box 10.1

Stephen Kleene laid the foundations of recursive function theory, a branch of mathematical logic that has had a major influence on computer science. The Kleene star (the asterisk that denotes "zero or more" in diagrams like Figure 10.5) is named after him.

The Kleene star is well known among mathematicians and computer scientists. What is considerably less well known is that Kleene pronounced his last name as if it were written "Clay knee" (with the accent on the first syllable), and *not* "Clean knee."

(the fifth wheel is the spare). Because instances of classes come in whole numbers only, this means that the UML diagram models the statement that a car has four or five wheels, as required.

In general, the two dots .. denote a range. Thus 0..1 means zero or one, which is the UML way of denoting "optional." That is why there is the 0..1 next to the line connecting **Sun Roof Class** to **Car Class.**

Now look at the line connecting **Fuzzy Dice Class** to **Car Class.** At the "part" end, the label is *. An asterisk by itself denotes "zero or more." Thus, the * in Figure 10.5 means that a car has zero or more fuzzy dice hanging from the rear-view mirror. (If you want to know more about that asterisk, see Just in Case You Wanted to Know Box 10.1.)

Now look at the line connecting **Seats Class** to **Car Class.** At the "part" end, the label is 2..*. An asterisk by itself denotes "zero or more"; an asterisk in a range denotes "or more." Thus, the 2..* in Figure 10.5 means that a car has two or more seats.

Thus, in UML if we know the exact multiplicity, we just use that number. An example is the 1 that appears in eight places in Figure 10.5. If we know the range, we use the range notation, as with the 0..1 or 4..5 in Figure 10.5. And if the number is unspecified, we use the asterisk. If there is a range where the upper limit is unspecified, we combine the range notation with the asterisk notation, as with the 2..* in Figure 10.5. Finally, if you were wondering where you have seen this notation before, the multiplicity notation of UML is based on the entity-relationship diagrams of traditional database theory.

10.2.3 Composition

Another example of aggregation is shown in Figure 10.6, which models the relationship between a chess board and its squares; every chess board consists of 64 squares. In fact, this relationship goes further; it is an example of *composition,* a stronger form of aggregation. As previously stated, association models the part–whole relationship. When there is composition then, in addition, every part may belong to only one whole and, if the whole is deleted, so are the parts. In our example, if we have a number of different chess boards, each square belongs to only one board and, if we throw away a chess board, all 64 squares on that board go as well. Composition, an extension of aggregation, is depicted with a solid diamond, as in Figure 10.7.

FIGURE 10.6
Another Aggregation Example (but See Figure 10.7)

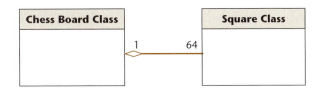

FIGURE 10.7
Composition
Example

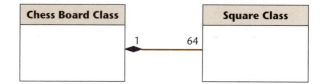

FIGURE 10.8
Generalization
(Inheritance)
Example with
an Explicit
Discriminator

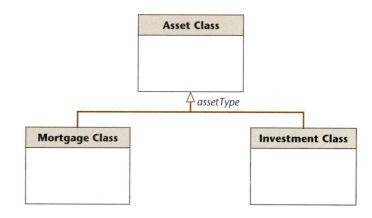

FIGURE 10.9
An Association

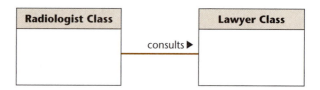

10.2.4 Generalization

Inheritance is a required feature of object orientation. Inheritance is a special case of *generalization*. The UML notation for generalization is an open triangle. Sometimes we choose to label that open triangle with a *discriminator*. An example, based on Figure 7.8, is shown in Figure 10.8. The notation *assetType* next to the open triangle means that every instance of **Asset Class** or its subclasses has an attribute assetType, and that this attribute can be used to distinguish between instances of the subclasses.

10.2.5 Association

In Section 3.4, an example of *association* involving two classes was presented in which the direction of the association had to be clarified by means of a navigation arrow in the form of a solid triangle. Figure 3.13 is reproduced here as Figure 10.9.

In some cases, the association between the two classes may itself need to be modeled as a class. For example, suppose the radiologist in Figure 10.9 consults the lawyer on a number of different occasions, on each occasion for a different length of time. In order to enable the lawyer to bill the radiologist correctly, a class diagram such as that depicted in Figure 10.10 is needed. Now consults has become a class, **Consults Class,** called an *association class* (because it is both an association and a class).

FIGURE 10.10   An Association Class

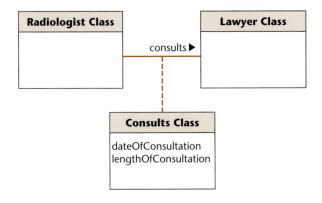

FIGURE 10.11   Generalization of an Actor

10.3   Notes

When we want to include a comment in a UML diagram, we put it in a *note* (a rectangle with the top right-hand corner bent over). We then draw a dashed line from the note to the item to which the note refers. Figure 6.28 shows a note.

10.4   Use-Case Diagrams

As described in Section 4.5.3, a *use case* is a model of the interaction between external users of an information system (*actors*) and the information system itself. More precisely, an actor is a user playing a specific role. A *use-case diagram* is a set of use cases.

In Section 4.6, generalization within the context of actors was described, as depicted in Figure 4.4. Figure 10.11 is another example; it shows that an **MSG Manager** is a special case of an **MSG Staff Member.** As with classes, the open triangle points toward the more general case.

10.5   Stereotypes

For convenience, Figure 5.11 is reproduced here as Figure 10.12. It shows that use case Estimate Funds Available for Week incorporates the use case Estimate Investment Income for Week. The diagram contains the include *relationship,* represented by a stereotype. A *stereotype* in UML is a way of extending UML. That is, if we need to define a construct that is not in UML, we can do it. We have already encountered four stereotypes in Chapter 6, namely, boundary, control, and entity classes and the include stereotype. In general, the names of stereotypes appear between *guillemets,* for example, «this is my own construct». In fact, instead of using the special symbol for a boundary class, we could have used the standard rectangular symbol for a class, but included inside the rectangle the notation «boundary class», and similarly for control and entity classes.

The include relationship shown in Figure 10.12 is treated in UML as a stereotype, hence the notation «include» in that figure to denote common functionality. Another relationship is the extend *relationship,* where one use case is a variation of the standard use

FIGURE 10.12

The Use Case
Estimate Funds
Available for Week
Incorporates the Use
Case Estimate
Investment Income
for Week

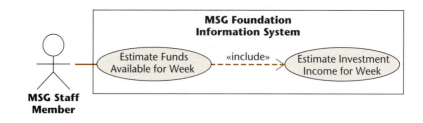

FIGURE 10.13

Use Case Buy
a Masterpiece
Showing the
Variation when the
Customer Turns
Down Osbert's Offer

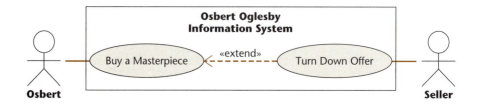

case. For example, we may wish to have a separate use case to model the situation of the potential seller of a painting turning down Osbert's offer. The notation «extend» is similarly used for this purpose, as shown in Figure 10.13. However, for this relationship, the open-headed arrow goes in the other direction.

10.6   Interaction Diagrams

Interaction diagrams show the way that the objects in the information system interact with one another. In Chapter 6, both types of interaction diagram supported by UML were presented: sequence diagrams and collaboration diagrams.

First we consider *sequence diagrams*. In Figure 6.27 it was shown how a sequence diagram looks when an object is dynamically created. Just as objects can be created, they can be destroyed. For example, if Osbert makes an offer for a masterpiece but this offer is turned down, there is no need to keep the masterpiece object that was created for the purpose of performing the computation of the maximum price that Osbert should offer for the masterpiece. Figure 10.14 depicts the creation and subsequent deletion of a masterpiece object. This sequence diagram is loosely based on Figure 6.27, but it contains a number of optional features.

- First, consider the lifelines in Figure 10.14. When an object is active, this is denoted by a thin rectangle (*activation box*) in place of the dashed line. Thus, for example, the **: User Interface Class** object is active from message 1: Give masterpiece details until message 8: Display price, and similarly for the other objects.

- Second, in addition to the creation of the **: Masterpiece Class** object, denoted by the lifeline starting only at the point of dynamic creation, Figure 10.14 shows the destruction of that object after it receives the message 9: Destroy object. The destruction is denoted by the heavy **X**.

- Third, this destruction takes place after a return has taken place, denoted by the dashed horizontal line below event 9, terminated by an open arrow. In all previous sequence diagrams, each message has eventually been followed by a message sent back to the object that sent the original message. In fact, this reciprocity is optional; it is perfectly

FIGURE 10.14

A Sequence Diagram
Showing Dynamic
Creation and
Destruction of an
Object, Return, and
Explicit Activation

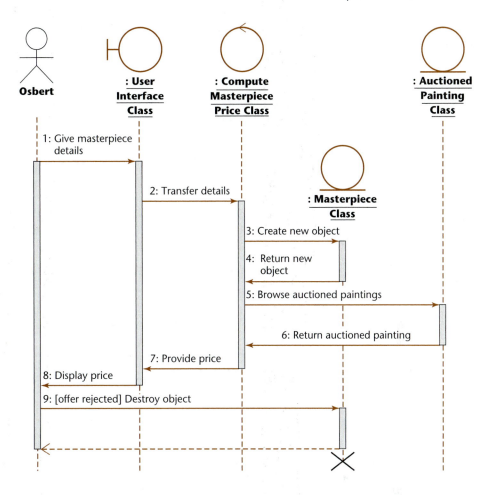

valid to send a message without eventually receiving any sort of reply. Even if there is a return, it is not necessary that a specific new message be sent back. Instead, a dashed line ending in an open arrow is drawn (a *return*) to indicate a return from the original message, as opposed to a new message.

- Fourth, there is a *guard* on message **9: [offer rejected] Destroy object**. That is, only if Osbert's offer is rejected is message 9 sent. A guard (condition) is something that is true or false; only if it is true is the message sent. The purpose of a guard is to ensure that the message is sent only if the relevant condition is true. We will soon see guards in statecharts, but here we see a guard in a sequence diagram.

Many other options are also supported by UML. For example, suppose we are modeling an elevator going up. We do not know in advance which elevator button will be pressed, so we have no idea how many floors up the elevator will go. We model this iteration by labeling the relevant message ***move up one floor**, as shown in Figure 10.15. The asterisk is, once again, the Kleene star (see Just in Case You Wanted to Know Box 10.1). So this message means: "move up zero or more floors."

An object can send a message to itself. This is termed a *self-call*. For example, suppose that the elevator has arrived at a floor. The elevator doors now open and a timer starts. At the end of the timer period, the doors close again. The elevator controller sends a message to itself to start its timer; this self-call is also shown in Figure 10.15. In fact, we have seen an

FIGURE 10.15

A Sequence Diagram
Showing Iteration
and Self-Call

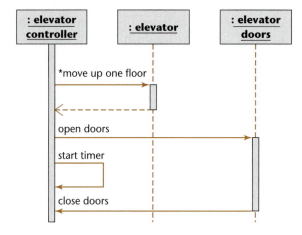

FIGURE 10.16 A Statechart for the MSG Foundation Case Study

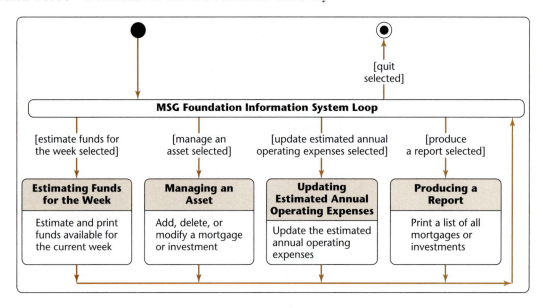

earlier example of a self-call, namely, message **9: Compute estimated amount available for week** in Figures 7.22 and 7.24.

Turning now to *collaboration diagrams,* we have seen in Chapters 6 and 7 that collaboration diagrams are equivalent to sequence diagrams. So, all the features of sequence diagrams presented in this section are equally applicable to collaboration diagrams.

10.7 Statecharts

Consider the *statechart* of Figure 10.16. This is similar to the statechart of Figure 7.11, but modeled using guards instead of events. It shows the start state (the solid circle) with an unlabeled *transition* leading to state **MSG Foundation Information System Loop.** There are five transitions leading from that state, each with a guard, that is, a condition that is true or false. When one of the guards becomes true, the corresponding transition takes place.

An *event* also causes transitions between states. A common type of event is the receipt of a message. Consider Figure 10.17, which depicts a part of a statechart for an elevator.

FIGURE 10.17   A Portion of a
Statechart for an Elevator

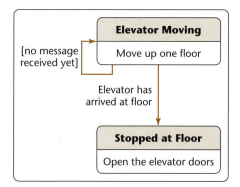

FIGURE 10.18   A Statechart
Equivalent to Figure 10.17

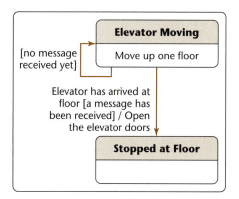

The elevator is in state **Elevator Moving.** It stays in motion, performing operation Move up one floor, while guard [no message received yet] remains true, until it receives the message Elevator has arrived at floor. The receipt of this message (event) causes the guard to be false and also enables a transition to state **Stopped at Floor.** In this state, the activity Open the elevator doors is performed.

So far we have seen transition labels in the form of [guard] or event. In fact, the most general form of a transition label is

event [guard] / action

That is, if event has taken place and [guard] is true, then the transition occurs, and, while it is occurring, action is performed. An example of such a transition label is shown in Figure 10.18, which is equivalent to Figure 10.17. The transition label is Elevator has arrived at floor [a message has been received] / Open the elevator doors. The guard [a message has been received] is true when the event Elevator has arrived at floor has occurred and a message to this effect has been sent. The *action* to be taken, indicated by the instruction following the slash /, is Open the elevator doors.

Comparing Figures 10.17 and 10.18, we see that there are two places where an action can be performed in a statechart. First, as reflected in state **Stopped at Floor** in Figure 10.17, an action can be performed when a state is entered. Such an action is called an *activity* in UML. Second, as shown in Figure 10.18, an action can take place as part of a transition. (Technically, there is a slight difference between an activity and an action. An action is assumed to take place essentially instantaneously, but an activity may take place less quickly, perhaps over several seconds.)

UML supports a wide variety of different types of actions and events in statecharts. For instance, an event can be specified in terms of words like when or after. Thus, an event might stipulate when (cost > 1000) or after (2.5 seconds).

A statechart with a large number of states tends to have a large number of transitions. The many arrows representing these transitions soon start to make the statechart look like a large bowl of spaghetti. One technique for dealing with this is to use a *superstate*. Consider the statechart of Figure 10.19(a). The four states **A, B, C,** and **D** all have transitions to **Next State.** Figure 10.19(b) shows how these four states can be combined into one superstate, **ABCD Combined.** There is only one transition in Figure 10.19(b), as opposed to the four in Figure 10.19(a). This reduces the number of arrows from four to only one. At the same time, states **A, B, C,** and **D** all still exist in their own right, so any existing actions associated

FIGURE 10.19

Statechart
(a) without and
(b) with Superstate

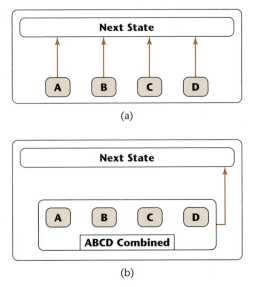

(a)

(b)

FIGURE 10.20   Figure 10.16 with Four States Combined into a Superstate, MSG Combined

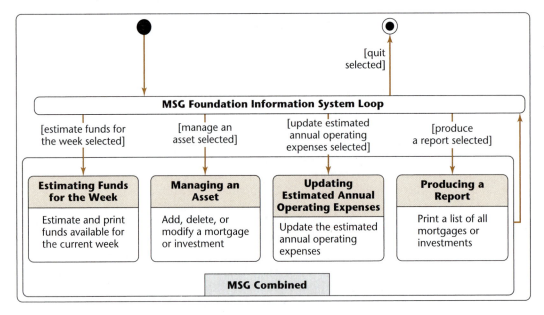

with those states are not affected, nor are any existing transitions into those states. An example of a superstate is shown in Figure 10.20, where the four lower states of Figure 10.16 are unified into one superstate, **MSG Combined,** leading to a cleaner and clearer diagram.

10.8   Activity Diagrams

Activity diagrams show how various events are coordinated. They are therefore used when activities are carried on in parallel. Neither of the case studies we have examined involves parallelism, so here is a different example.

Suppose that a couple seated at a restaurant order their meal. One orders a chicken dish; the other orders fish. The waiter writes down their order and hands the order to the chef so that she knows what dishes to prepare. It does not matter which dish is completed first because the meal is served only when both dishes have been prepared. This is shown in Figure 10.21. The upper heavy horizontal line is called a fork and the lower one is called a join. In general, a *fork* has one incoming transition and many outgoing transitions, each of which starts an activity to be executed in parallel with the other activities. Conversely, a *join* has many incoming transitions, each of which leads from an activity executed in parallel with the other activities, and one outgoing transition that is started when all the parallel activities have been completed.

Activity diagrams are useful for modeling businesses where a number of activities are carried on in parallel. For example, consider a company that assembles computers as specified by the customer. As shown in the activity diagram of Figure 10.22, when an order is received, it is passed on to the **Assembly Department.** It is also passed to the **Accounts Receivable Department.** The order is complete when the computer has been assembled and delivered and the customer's payment has been processed. The three departments involved, the **Assembly Department,** the **Order Department,** and **Accounts Receivable Department,** are each in their own *swimlane.* In general, the combination of forks, joins, and swimlanes shows clearly which branches of an organization are involved in each specific activity, which tasks are carried on in parallel, and which tasks have to be completed in parallel before the next task can be started.

FIGURE 10.21   **An Activity Diagram for a Restaurant Order for Two Diners**

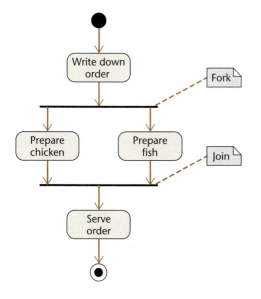

FIGURE 10.22   **An Activity Diagram for a Computer Assembly Company**

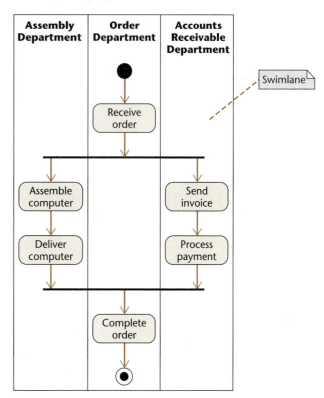

FIGURE 10.23
The UML Notation
for a Package

FIGURE 10.24
The Package of
Figure 10.23 with
More Details Shown

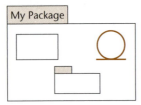

FIGURE 10.25
Component Diagram

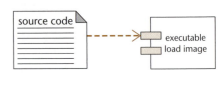

10.9 Package Diagrams

As explained in Section 8.1, the way to handle a large information system is to decompose it into relatively independent packages. The UML notation for a package is a rectangle with a name tag, as shown in Figure 10.23. This figure shows that My Package is a package, but the rectangle is empty. This is a valid UML diagram—the diagram simply models the fact that My Package is a package. Figure 10.24 is more interesting—it shows the contents of My package, including a class, an entity class, and another package. We can continue to supply more details until the *package diagram* is at the appropriate level of detail for the current iteration and incrementation.

10.10 Component Diagrams

A *component diagram* shows dependencies among software components, including source code, compiled code, and executable load images. For example, the component diagram of Figure 10.25 shows source code (represented by a note) and the executable load image created from the source code.

(Programmers write *source code* in an object-oriented language such as C++ or Java. The source code is then translated by a compiler into *compiled code,* the binary code that is the only language a computer understands. Finally, the compiled code for each module is combined with run-time routines to produce an executable load image. Technical details are given in Section 20.1.)

10.11 Deployment Diagrams

A *deployment diagram* shows on which hardware component each software component is installed (or deployed). It also shows the communication links between the hardware components. A simple deployment diagram is shown in Figure 10.26.

10.12 Review of UML Diagrams

A wide variety of different UML diagrams have been presented in this chapter. In the interests of clarity, here is a list of some of the diagram types that might be confused.

- A *use case* models the interaction between actors (external users of an information system) and the information system itself.

FIGURE 10.26
A Deployment
Diagram

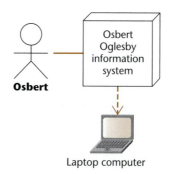

Osbert

Osbert
Oglesby
information
system

Laptop computer

- A *use-case diagram* is a single diagram that incorporates a number of use cases.
- A *class diagram* is a model of the classes showing the static relationships between them, including association and generalization.
- A *statechart* shows states (specific values of attributes of objects), events that cause transitions between states (subject to guards), and actions taken by objects. A statechart is therefore a dynamic model—it reflects the behavior of objects, that is, the way they react to specific events.
- An *interaction diagram* (*sequence diagram* or *collaboration diagram*) shows the way that objects interact with one another as messages are passed between them. This is another dynamic model; that is, it also shows how objects behave.
- An *activity diagram* shows how events that occur at the same time are coordinated. This is yet another dynamic model.

10.13   UML and Iteration

Consider a statechart. The transitions can be labeled with a guard, an event, an action, or all three. Now consider a sequence diagram. The lifelines may or may not include activation boxes, there may or may not be returns, and there may or may not be guards on the messages.

A wide range of options are available for every UML diagram. That is, a valid UML diagram consists of a small required part, plus any number of options. The obvious question is: why?

There are two reasons why UML diagrams have so many options. First, not every feature of UML is applicable to every information system, so there has to be freedom with regard to choice of options. Second, we cannot perform the iteration and incrementation of the Unified Process unless we are permitted to add features stepwise to diagrams, rather than create the complete final diagram at the beginning. That is, UML allows us to start with a basic diagram. We then can add optional features as we wish, bearing in mind that, at all times, the resulting UML diagram is still valid. This is one of the many reasons why UML is so well suited to the Unified Process.

Key Terms

action, *199*
activation box, *196*
activity, *199*
activity diagram, *200*
actor, *195*
aggregation, *191*

association, *194*
association class, *194*
class diagram, *190*
collaboration diagram, *198*
compiled code, *202*
component diagram, *202*

composition, *193*
deployment diagram, *202*
discriminator, *194*
event, *198*
extend relationship, *195*
fork, *201*

Review Questions for Chapter 10

1. Is UML a methodology? If not, what is it?
2. When a class diagram has three boxes, what is inserted in each box?
3. Give three different multiplicity notations in UML.
4. Distinguish between aggregation and composition.
5. What is the difference between generalization and inheritance?
6. Distinguish between an association, a class, and an association class.
7. Distinguish between a use case and a use-case diagram.
8. What are the two types of interaction diagram?
9. Distinguish between actions and activities in statecharts.
10. What is a superstate?
11. Distinguish between forks, joins, and swimlanes.
12. What is a package diagram?

Problems

10.1 Use UML to model stock markets. (Hint: Do not show any more details than are strictly needed to answer the question.)

10.2 Use UML to model cakes. A cake is made with eggs, flour, milk, and, of course, cocoa (see Appendix A). A cake is mixed, baked, frosted, and then eaten. In order to prevent unauthorized individuals from baking a cake, the ingredients are private, as are all but the last operation.

10.3 Use UML to model a dining room. Every dining room has to have a table, four or more chairs, and a sideboard. Optionally, it also may have a fireplace.

10.4 Model the dining room of Problem 10.3 using a combination of aggregation and composition.

10.5 Modify your UML model of Problem 10.3 to reflect that a dining room is a specific type of room.

10.6 Add a note to your diagram of Problem 10.2 pointing out that the cake you have modeled is a chocolate cake.

10.7 Use UML to model John Cage's somewhat controversial 1952 piano composition entitled *4'33"*. The piece consists of three silent movements, of length 30 seconds, 2 minutes 23 seconds, and 1 minute 40 seconds, respectively. (The title of the piece comes from its total length.)

   The pianist walks onto the stage holding a stopwatch and the score (in conventional music notation but with blank measures). The pianist sits down on the piano stool, puts the score and the stopwatch on the piano, opens the score, starts the stopwatch, then signals the start of the first movement by lowering the lid of the piano. At the end of the first movement (that is, after 30 seconds of silence during which the pianist carefully follows the blank score, turning the page when necessary), the lid of the piano is raised to signal the end of the first movement. These actions are repeated for the second movement (2 minutes 23 seconds) and the third movement (1 minute 40 seconds). The pianist then closes the score, picks up the score and the stopwatch, gets up, and leaves the stage.

Reference

Booch, G.; J. Rumbaugh; and I. Jacobson. *The UML Users Guide*. Reading, MA: Addison Wesley, 1999.

Major Topics in Systems Analysis and Design

Part 3

The first nine chapters in Part 3 contain knowledge that is needed to become a professional systems analyst. For example, in the real world, information systems are far too big for the systems analysis and design to be performed by individuals without computer assistance. The tools that information technology professionals use for systems analysis and design of information systems are the topic of Chapter 11, entitled *CASE*. (CASE is an acronym for computer-aided software engineering.)

Also, the large size of real-world information systems means that the systems analysis and design have to be performed by teams. Effective ways of managing teams is the subject of Chapter 12, *Teams*.

It is essential to test that an information system is working correctly. In Chapter 13, *Testing*, an explanation is given regarding what needs to be tested and how to perform testing. This material fleshes out the outline of the test workflow presented in Chapter 9.

Successful management of the development of an information system requires a broad range of skills. These skills form the subject of Chapter 14, *Management Issues*. In this chapter, a wide variety of techniques are presented that are needed to manage the systems analysis and design of an information system.

Two important management skills are the subject of Chapter 15, namely, *Planning and Estimating*. As with any other large construction project, careful planning of the project is a factor that distinguishes success from failure. Every plan incorporates cost, time, and effort estimates. Techniques for obtaining accurate estimates are described in this chapter.

More money is spent on maintenance than any other activity. The importance of maintenance is stressed throughout Chapter 16, *Maintenance*.

In order to communicate with the computer, there has to be a user interface. The design of the user interface is presented in Chapter 17 in two steps. First, user-interface design principles are described. Then an explanation is given of how user interfaces are designed when the Unified Process is used.

Issues raised by the World Wide Web are discussed next. More and more information systems are now implemented on the Web, and the implications of this are described in Chapter 18, *Introduction to Web-Based Information Systems*.

Chapter 19 is entitled *Introduction to Database Management Systems*. Here an explanation is given as to why database management systems are an integral part of most information systems, and object-oriented database management systems are discussed.

The final chapter, Chapter 20, *Technical Topics,* contains introductory-level information on areas such as modularity and polymorphism and dynamic binding so that the instructor can include this material if he or she so wishes.

11

CASE

Learning Objectives

After studying this chapter, you should be able to:

- Describe the scope of CASE.
- Describe version control and configuration control tools.
- Describe CASE environments for information systems.

Computers assist us in almost every human endeavor. For example, we no longer write business correspondence by hand. Instead, we use a word processor. And we no longer add up a column of figures by hand. Instead, we use a spreadsheet. So why should we develop an information system by hand? Surely we should use a computer program of some kind.

The state of the art in computer science is nowhere near the point at which we can instruct a computer to develop an information system for us—that is why we have information technology professionals, including systems analysts. But systems analysts can utilize software tools; that is, computer programs analogous to word processors and spreadsheets that assist teams of information technology professionals in developing and maintaining information systems. These software tools usually are termed *CASE tools* (*CASE* is an acronym that stands for computer-aided software engineering; that is, the development and maintenance of software with the aid of computers).

Computers can help us by carrying out much of the drudge work associated with information system development, including the creation and organization of artifacts of all kinds, such as plans, contracts, specification documents, designs, source code, and management information. Documentation is essential for information system development and maintenance, but the majority of individuals involved in information system development are not fond of creating or updating documentation. Maintaining diagrams on the computer, including UML diagrams, is especially useful as it allows changes to diagrams to be made with ease and without having to redraw the entire diagram.

But CASE is not restricted to assisting with documentation. In particular, computers can assist information technology professionals to cope with the complexity of information system development, especially in managing all the details. At the same time, it is important to remember that CASE stands for computer-*aided* software engineering, and not computer-*automated* software engineering—no computer yet can replace a human being with respect to development or maintenance of information systems. For the foreseeable future, at least, the computer must remain a tool of the information technology professional.

11.1 Taxonomy of CASE

The simplest form of CASE is the software *tool,* a product that assists in just one aspect of the development and maintenance of an information system. CASE tools currently are being used in every workflow of the life cycle. For example, there are a variety of tools on the market, many of them for use with personal computers, that assist in the construction of graphical representations of information systems, such as flowcharts and UML diagrams. CASE tools that help the developer during the earlier workflows of the process (namely, the requirements, analysis, and design workflows) sometimes are termed *upperCASE* or *front-end tools,* whereas those that assist with implementation and maintenance are termed *lowerCASE* or *back-end tools.* Figure 11.1(a) represents a CASE tool that assists with part of the requirements workflow.

One important class of CASE tools is the *data dictionary,* a computerized list of all attributes and methods defined within the information system. (A *method* is an implementation of an operation.) A large information system will contain tens (if not hundreds) of attributes and methods, and the computer is ideal for storing information such as the name of an attribute and the class in which it is defined, and the name of a method, the class in which it is defined, and its parameters. (A *parameter* is data transferred to a method when that method is invoked at run-time.) An important part of every data dictionary entry is a description of the item; for example, Method that takes as input the body weight of the newborn infant and computes the appropriate dosage of the drug or List of arrival times sorted with earliest times first. Typical data dictionary entries for the Osbert Oglesby case study are shown in Figure 11.2.

The power of a data dictionary can be enhanced by combining it with a *consistency checker,* a tool that can check that every data item in the specification artifacts is reflected in the design artifacts and, conversely, that every item in the design artifacts has been defined in the specification artifacts.

Another use of a data dictionary is to provide the data for report generators and screen generators. A *report generator* is used to generate the code needed for producing a report. A *screen generator* is used to assist the information system developer in producing the code for a data capture screen. Suppose that a screen is being designed for entering the weekly sales at each branch of a chain of book stores. The branch number is a four-digit integer in the range 1000 to 4500 or 8000 to 8999, entered on the screen three lines from the

FIGURE 11.1

A Schematic Representation of a Tool, a Workbench, and an Environment

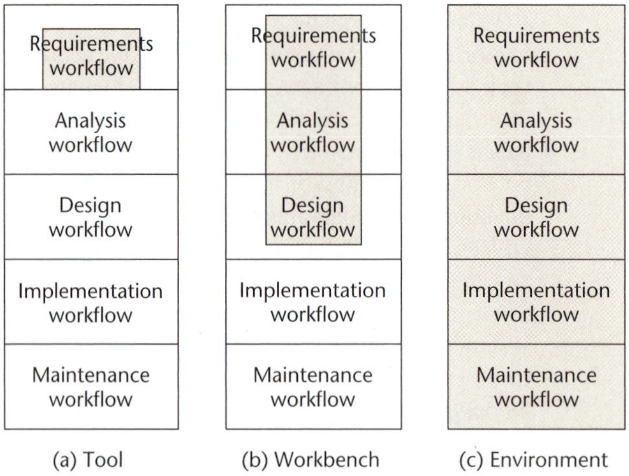

(a) Tool (b) Workbench (c) Environment

FIGURE 11.2   **Typical Data Dictionary Entries for the Osbert Oglesby Case Study**

Name	Description	Narrative
PaintingClass	Class with attributes: firstNameOfArtist lastNameOfArtist title yearOfWork height width medium	This class models a painting.
firstNameOfArtist	21-character string	Attribute of **PaintingClass.** The first name of the artist (up to 20 characters) is optionally followed by ? to denote that there is uncertainty in the name.
printPaintingsSold ( )	Method: Input parameters: startDate endDate	This method takes as input the startDate and endDate of the report and prints every painting sold during that period. The output is in the following order: classification, saleDate, lastNameOfArtist, title, targetSellingPrice, and actualSellingPrice. Any painting sold at a price of 5 percent or more below the target selling price is flagged by placing an asterisk before classification. This report is sorted by classification and by date of sale within classification. The average ratio of actualSellingPrice to targetSellingPrice for all of the paintings in the report is displayed at the end of the report.

top. This information is given to the screen generator. The screen generator then automatically generates code to display the string BRANCH NUMBER _ _ _ _ three lines from the top and position the cursor at the first underline character. As the user enters each digit, it is displayed; and the cursor moves on to the next underline. The screen generator also generates code for checking that the user enters only digits and that the resulting four-digit integer is in the specified range. If the data entered are invalid, or if the user presses the ? key, help information is displayed to assist the user, telling him or her why the data do not match the required format.

Use of such generators can result in information systems being quickly constructed. Furthermore, a graphical representation tool combined with a data dictionary, consistency checker, report generator, and screen generator together constitute a requirements, analysis, and design workbench. Software through Pictures is an example[1] of a commercial workbench that incorporates all these features.

[1] The fact that a specific CASE tool is cited in this book in no way implies any form of endorsement of that CASE tool by the author or the publisher. Each CASE tool mentioned in this book has been included because it is a typical example of the class of CASE tools of which it is an instance.

Another class of workbench is a requirements management workbench. Such a workbench allows systems analysts to organize and track the requirements of an information system development project. RequisitePro is a commercial example of such a workbench.

A CASE *workbench* thus is a collection of tools that together support one or two activities. For example, the coding activity includes editing, compiling, testing, and debugging. An activity is not the same thing as a workflow. In fact, the tasks of an activity can cross workflow boundaries. For example, a project management workbench is used for every workflow of the project, and a coding workbench can be used for rapid prototyping (Section 7.13.1) as well as for the implementation and maintenance workflows. Figure 11.1(b) represents a workbench of upperCASE tools. The workbench includes the requirements workflow tool of Figure 11.1(a), as well as tools for parts of the analysis and design workflows.

Continuing the progression of CASE technology from tools to workbenches, the next item is the CASE environment. Unlike the workbench, which supports one or two activities, an *environment* supports the complete information system development and maintenance life cycle or, at the very least, a large portion of the life cycle [Fuggetta, 1993]; the term *integrated development environment* (IDE) is sometimes used. Figure 11.1(c) depicts an environment that supports all aspects of all workflows of the life cycle. Environments are discussed in greater detail in Section 11.7.

Having set up a CASE taxonomy (tools, workbenches, and environments), the scope of CASE is now considered.

11.2 The Scope of CASE

As mentioned previously, the need to have accurate and up-to-date documentation available at all times is a primary reason for implementing CASE technology. For example, suppose that the artifacts of the analysis workflow are produced manually. A member of the development team has no way of telling whether a particular analysis artifact is the current version or an older version. There is no way of knowing if the handwritten changes on that artifact are part of the current version of the artifact or were merely a suggestion that was rejected later. On the other hand, if the artifacts of the analysis workflow of the information system are produced using a CASE tool, then at any time there is only one copy of the analysis artifacts, the online version accessed via the CASE tool. Then, if there is a change to an analysis artifact, all the members of the development team easily can access the artifact and be sure that they are seeing the current version. In addition, the consistency checker will flag any change made to a design artifact without corresponding changes to the corresponding analysis artifact.

Programmers also need *online documentation*. For example, online help information must be provided for the operating system, text editor, programming language, and so on. In addition, programmers have to consult *manuals* of many kinds, such as text editor manuals and programming manuals. It is highly desirable that, wherever possible, these manuals be available online. Apart from the convenience of having everything at one's fingertips, it generally is quicker to query a manual by computer than to try to find the appropriate manual and plow through it page by page to find the needed item. In addition, it usually is much easier to update an online manual than to try to find all the hard-copy versions of a manual within an organization and make the necessary page changes. As a result, online documentation is likely to be more accurate than hard-copy versions of the same material—another reason for providing online documentation to information technology professionals. For these reasons, CASE tools almost invariably incorporate online documentation.

Communication among team members is vital. *E-mail* is now as much a part of the average office as a computer or a fax machine. There are many advantages to e-mail. From the viewpoint of information system development, if copies of all e-mail relevant to a specific project are stored in a particular mailbox, there will be a written record of the decisions made during the project. This record can be used to resolve conflicts that may arise later. Many CASE environments and some CASE workbenches now incorporate e-mail systems. In other organizations the e-mail system is implemented via a *World Wide Web browser* such as Internet Explorer or Netscape Communicator. Other tools that are equally essential are *spreadsheets* and *word processors.*

The term *coding tools* refers to CASE tools such as text editors and debuggers designed to simplify the programmer's task, reduce the frustration that many programmers experience in their work, and increase programmer productivity. A *structure editor* is a text editor that "understands" the implementation language, in the same way that the spelling checker and grammar checker of a word processing program "understand" English. That is, a structure editor can detect a programming error as soon as it has been keyed in by the programmer, speeding the implementation workflow because time is not wasted on futile compilations. Structure editors exist for a wide variety of languages, operating systems, and hardware. They form part of numerous programming workbenches, such as Visual C++ and JBuilder. Because a structure editor has knowledge of the programming language, it is easy to incorporate a *pretty printer* (or *formatter*) into the editor to ensure that the code always has a good visual appearance.

An essential tool, especially when an information system is developed by a team, is a version-control tool.

11.3 Versions

Whenever an information system is maintained, there will be at least two *versions* of the information system: the old version and the new version. Because an information system is composed of artifacts (including documents and modules), there also will be at least two versions of each of the component artifacts that have been changed.

11.3.1 Revisions

Suppose that an information system is being constructed and a fault is found in an artifact. That artifact now has to be fixed. After appropriate changes have been made, there will be two versions of the artifact, the old version and the new version intended to replace it. The new version is termed a *revision*. The presence of multiple versions apparently is easy to solve—the old version should be thrown away, leaving just the correct one. But that would be most unwise. After all, the "corrected" version may be just as faulty as the original.

Keeping all old versions of artifacts is particularly important when dealing with code artifacts (*modules*). Suppose that the previous version of the module was revision n and that the new version is revision $n + 1$. First, as previously stated, there is no guarantee that revision $n + 1$ will be any more correct than revision n. Even though revision $n + 1$ may have been thoroughly tested by the quality assurance group, both in isolation and linked to the rest of the information system, there may be disastrous consequences when the new version of the information system is run by the user on actual data. But revision n must be kept for a second reason. The information system may have been distributed to a variety of sites and not all of them may have installed revision $n + 1$. If a fault report is received from a site that is still using revision n, then to analyze this new fault, it is necessary to configure the information system in exactly the same way it is configured at the user's site; that is,

FIGURE 11.3

A Schematic
Representation of
Multiple Versions of
Artifacts, Showing
(a) Revisions and
(b) Variations

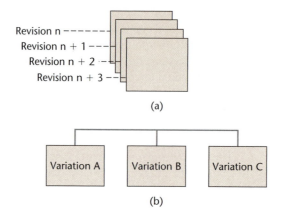

incorporating revision n of the artifact. It therefore is necessary to retain a copy of every revision of each artifact.

Revisions are schematically portrayed in Figure 11.3(a). The revisions all but overlap one another, to indicate that a revision is intended to replace its predecessor.

As described in Section 1.7, perfective maintenance is performed to extend the functionality of an information system. In some instances, new artifacts are constructed. In other cases, current artifacts are extended to incorporate this additional functionality—the resulting artifacts are revisions of existing artifacts. So are artifacts that are changed when we perform adaptive maintenance; that is, changes made to the information system in response to changes in the environment in which the information system operates. As with corrective maintenance, all previous versions must be retained. After all, once an artifact has been constructed, it continually undergoes changes as a consequence of iteration and incrementation. As a result, there will be numerous versions of every artifact, and it is vital to have some sort of control in place to ensure that each member of the development team knows which version is the current version of a given artifact. Before we can present a solution to this problem, a further complication must be taken into account.

11.3.2   Variations

Consider the following example. Most computers support more than one type of printer. For example, a personal computer may support an inkjet printer and a laser printer. The operating system therefore must contain two *variations* of the printer driver, one for each type of printer. Unlike revisions, each of which is written specifically to replace its predecessor, variations are designed to coexist. Another situation where variations are needed is when an information system is to be ported to a variety of different operating systems and hardware; for example, management may want to move an information system running on a network of PCs under Windows to a network of Macintoshes running under Mac OS, as well as to a network of workstations running under Linux. A different variation of many of the artifacts will have to be produced for each operating system–hardware combination.

Versions are schematically portrayed in Figure 11.3, which shows both revisions and variations. As previously stated, the revisions of Figure 11.3(a) all but overlap one another, to indicate that a revision replaces its predecessor. Conversely, variations coexist in parallel, as depicted in Figure 11.3(b).

A complicating factor is that, in general, there will be multiple revisions of each variation. For an information system organization to avoid drowning in a swamp of multiple versions, a CASE tool is needed.

FIGURE 11.4

The Components
of the Executable
Load Image

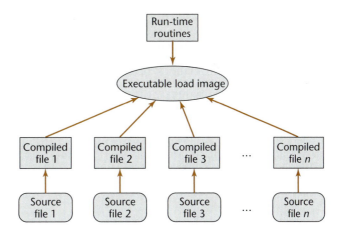

11.3.3 Version-Control Tools

The code for every module exists in three forms. First there is the *source code,* nowadays generally implemented in an object-oriented language such as C++ or Java. Then there is the *compiled code,* produced by compiling the source code; that is, translating it into the binary code that is the only language a computer understands. Finally, the compiled code for each module is *linked* (combined) with run-time routines to produce an executable load image. This process is shown in Figure 11.4; technical details are given in Section 20.1. When generating an executable load image, the programmer must specify the version of each module. The set of the specific versions of the modules from which a given version of the executable load image of the complete information system is developed is called the *configuration* of that version of the information system.

Suppose that a programmer is given a test report from the quality assurance group stating that the information system failed on a specific set of test data. One of the first things that the programmer has to do is attempt to recreate the failure. But how can the programmer determine which revisions of which variations went into the version of the information system that crashed? The obvious way to do this is to look at the executable load image and compare it to the compiled code. Unfortunately, an executable load image is in *binary format.* By grouping binary digits (*bits*) into groups of three bits we get *octal format* and into groups of four bits we get *hexadecimal format.* Examples of binary, octal, and hexadecimal format are shown in Figure 11.5. Clearly, comparing binary images by hand is an extremely laborious and error-prone task, even if the images are in octal or hexadecimal format. And it can take a long time if the information system has dozens (if not hundreds) of modules, each with multiple versions, all of which need to be compared to the executable load image. Therefore, two problems have to be solved when dealing with multiple versions of modules. First, it is necessary to be able to distinguish between versions so that the correct version of each module is compiled and linked to form the information system. Second, there is the inverse problem: Given an executable load image, determine which version of each of its components went into it.

The first item needed to solve these two problems is a *version-control tool.* Many operating systems, particularly for mainframe computers, support *version control.* But many do not, in which case a separate version-control tool is needed. A common technique used in version control is for the name of each artifact to consist of two pieces: the artifact name itself and the revision number. Thus, a module that acknowledges receipt of a message will have revisions acknowledgeMessage / 1, acknowledgeMessage / 2, and so on, as

FIGURE 11.5   Portions of Executable Load Images in (a) Binary, (b) Octal, and (c) Hexadecimal Format

```
1010011011111101110001110101001010101000111011110100000101101001111100110110
1110001010000011101001111011010110010111111111011111011101011000100110111011
0110111001111011101011001101101101101011000110111101111001111111011001011011
1011011111101000111111001000111101011011100110011100101111000110110110010110
0100111110011110010111101101111000101101100100100100001100001001111101001100 11
0000110010110110111111101000100000101110000101111010010011001100110111110001
1100101001110101001101100100111100010000111010000001111011011101100010101110 10
0111101001001110111110111111001101111111010101011000110110111110110111100000 110
1110100111111010111101011111010110101010011011100111010011000101110101100001 111
1010100011101110011011011111011100001011100000011101000111100001011000101010 01
0011010000110110001100100101011101100111001101000011101001111110001011101000 010
0010101100101100011100101111011100110011001111101000100011101111110111100011 10
```

(a)

```
32463344563371760317467124673227717321624535310351265534672372544742316624 4757
37747620307623742373335567642574777033064453306403237016256263033114654635 5153
02746265751454101326204226172472316545505367344474705523516235175750616706 4714
40167443430537120747255370522473736324266663256706161501235404673227262242 3230
42422603106473342056453606425353424013044244163445726112237354360616134025 1434
32232642471744574750174774747422235167756534030776613244521221367564540627 5732
72627061342340654332501657466276373362560431410527772637621553276353260226 2266
16174206302402071046722157234454712641665374473216064104175154035072565011 2760
25116565472326703177201621723060045675467533075515530244440162337452757151 3515
24116752247052216646022626504711101552441675751270555135143634010130227131 5426
23733055735212634543232600572437614701401634222376524757476265322522775141 1753
26456646137135561334267561525343134472146743402611123746071043171647441351 1213
```

(b)

```
728914C1F18195A7113CA104CFD9E951371911CE2C15A17ABA155AF14913E28B9F017EA2A41F23
7103721CFA53CCB4981995519A8FC8BD486133E914B17D17EA312564BC8A1171421A5AE16BD715
316A17B481A81DAE68F40A5541ABBF1129E1111470FD18913ECF195B1211E21891576C19118150
1631591407F71792C199157145FB15AFC1A454291473D1CF18114CB61A181F94A68F1D47BB0102
3A3714E7E1E913C31E87715EC81C911496131132F5F5E814311A1EF731C3147F51DF7D238A18D6
016D145C6192819B1B1B5188A12511D1CE1115611AD0261051C1B2CF151FB91441EF576A5DF957
DDF786185A71AF1496F10524109F9118733149ABD66C11F9A131EFC617F13C195851681B63BCB1
CADFD10A16311B12317A1661CCB61669FD71C2188134FE15116817211819CC71C91A0391B2CE15
6152164173C2182C83F7F8E17117E135C8BE1A711A1E7B64B1BE1A95A6F12E5FD9E715D15A1431
241D2E27C16CAE1DD1CF01101A7C66317711DFF16339115F516AF395F14D1A71EF1DDAF114EF16
6566F1AD5F19112B1D13E1A616023B61701788FB9A114C1A11101181062914D7514AF1A5D619B9
A19814B18B1EC8A23170211A6E1A519929E1553864F1701E2182DE16BDA1821F2B7BA1DDBC1751
```

(c)

depicted in Figure 11.6(a). A programmer then can specify exactly which revision is needed for a given task.

With regard to multiple variations (slightly changed versions that fulfill the same role in different situations), one useful notation is to have a basic artifact name, followed by a variation name in parentheses [Babich, 1986]. Thus, two printer drivers are given the names printerDriver (inkJet) and printerDriver (laser).

Of course, there will be multiple revisions of each variation, such as printerDriver (laser) / 12, printerDriver (laser) / 13, and printerDriver (laser) / 14. This is depicted in Figure 11.6(b).

A version-control tool is the first step toward being able to manage multiple versions. Once it is in place, a detailed record (or *derivation*) of every version of the information system must be kept. The derivation contains the name of each source code element, including the variation and revision; the versions of the various compilers and linkers used; the name of the person who linked together that version of the information system; and, of course, the date and the time at which it was constructed.

FIGURE 11.6

**Multiple Revisions
and Variations**
(a) Four revisions
of module
acknowledge-
Message. (b) Two
variations of module
printerDriver, with
three revisions
of variation
printerDriver (laser)

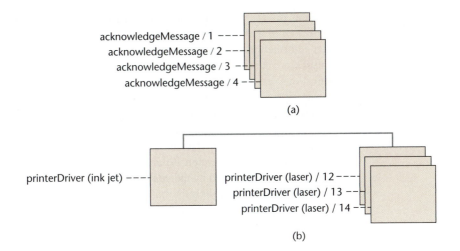

(a)

(b)

Version control is a great help in managing multiple versions of artifacts and of the information system as a whole. But more than just version control is needed because of additional problems that arise when an information system is developed by a team. And every nontrivial information system is developed by a team.

11.4   Configuration Control

The need for *configuration control* exists for artifacts of all kinds. A *configuration-control tool* can handle the problems that can arise when more than one information technology professional is simultaneously working on an information system. For example, suppose two systems analysts are each assigned a different fault report on a Monday morning. By coincidence, both localize the fault they are to fix to different parts of the same artifact **Compute Tax Class.** Each systems analyst makes a copy of the current version of the artifact, namely, **Compute Tax Class / 16,** and they start to work on the faults. The first systems analyst fixes the first fault, has the changes approved, and replaces the artifact, now called **Compute Tax Class / 17,** in the version control system. A day later the second systems analyst fixes the second fault, has the changes approved, and installs artifact **Compute Tax Class / 18** in the version control system. Unfortunately, revision 17 contains the changes of only the first systems analyst, whereas revision 18 contains those of only the second systems analyst. Thus, all the changes of the first systems analyst have been lost.

Although the idea of each systems analyst making individual copies of an artifact is far better than both working together at the same time on the same artifact, it does not help when an information system is being developed by a team. What is needed is some mechanism that allows only one user at a time to change an artifact.

What is needed is a CASE tool installed on a network of computers that incorporates configuration control. All the artifacts in the information system are under the control of this CASE tool. If an information technology professional wants to change an artifact, he or she must *check out* that artifact and, after making changes, *check in* the modified artifact.

The manager must set up a *baseline,* a configuration (set of versions) of all the artifacts in the information system, as described in Section 2.2. When working on an artifact, a systems analyst makes copies of any needed artifacts (using the Copy command of the CASE tool, similar to the Save As command of a word processor) and puts them into his or her *private workspace.*

In this private workspace on his or her own computer, the systems analyst can use the CASE tool to make changes to the artifact without having an impact on the work of any other information technology professional, because all changes are made to the systems analyst's private copy; the baseline version is left untouched. For example, the systems analyst may use the CASE tool to add another attribute to the class diagram or change a message in a collaboration diagram. Both changes are made to a private copy of the relevant artifact, so they cannot impact the information system itself in any way.

Once it has been decided which artifact is to be changed, the systems analyst *freezes* the current version of the artifact that he or she is going to alter. No one may ever make changes to any frozen version. After the systems analyst has made changes to the artifact and they have been tested by the quality assurance group, the new version of the artifact is installed, thereby modifying the baseline. The previous version, now frozen, is retained because it may be needed in the future, as explained previously, but it can never be altered. Once a new version has been installed, any other systems analyst can freeze the new version and make changes to it in turn. The resulting artifact, in turn, will become the next baseline version. A similar procedure is followed if two or more artifacts have to be changed simultaneously.

This scheme solves the problem with artifact **Compute Tax Class.** Both systems analysts make private copies of **Compute Tax Class** / 16 in their own computers and use those copies to analyze the respective faults that they have been assigned to fix. The first systems analyst decides what changes to make, freezes **Compute Tax Class** / 16, and uses the CASE tool on his or her own computer to make the changes to the artifact to repair the first fault. After the changes have been tested, the resulting revision, **Compute Tax Class** / 17, becomes the baseline version. In the meantime, the second systems analyst has found the second fault by experimenting with a private copy of **Compute Tax Class** / 16. However, changes can no longer be made to **Compute Tax Class** / 16 because it has been frozen by the first systems analyst. The baseline version is now **Compute Tax Class** / 17, and any changes to the artifact have to be made to that version. The second systems analyst therefore freezes **Compute Tax Class** / 17 (the current baseline version) and makes changes to **Compute Tax Class** / 17. The resulting artifact is tested, then installed as **Compute Tax Class** / 18, a version that will incorporate the changes of both systems analysts. Revisions **Compute Tax Class** / 16 and **Compute Tax Class** / 17 are retained for possible future reference, but they can never be altered.

Management cannot monitor the development process adequately unless every artifact is subject to configuration control. When configuration control is properly applied, management is aware of the status of every module and can take early corrective action if project deadlines seem to be slipping. PVCS is a popular commercially available configuration-control tool. Microsoft SourceSafe is a configuration-control tool for personal computers. CVS is an open-source configuration management tool. (Open-source software is software that can be downloaded from the World Wide Web free of charge. Examples of open-source software include the Linux operating system and the Apache Web server.)

11.5 Build Tools

If an information system organization does not wish to purchase a complete configuration-control tool, then, at the very least, a *build tool* must be used in conjunction with a version-control tool; that is, a tool that assists in selecting the correct version of each source-code module to be compiled and then linked together to form a specific version of the information system. At any time, there will be multiple variations and revisions of each module of the information system. Any version-control tool will assist users in distinguishing among different versions of modules of source code. But keeping track of compiled code is more difficult, because some version-control tools do not attach revision numbers to compiled versions.

To cope with this, some organizations automatically compile the latest version of each module every night, thereby ensuring that all the compiled code always is up to date. Although this technique works, it can be extremely wasteful of computer time because frequently a large number of unnecessary compilations will be performed. The UNIX tool *make* can solve this problem. For each executable load image, the programmer sets up a Makefile specifying the hierarchy of source and compiled modules that go into that particular configuration; such a hierarchy is shown in Figure 11.4. When invoked by a programmer, the tool works as follows: UNIX, like virtually every other operating system, attaches a date and time stamp to each module. Suppose that the stamp on a source module is Friday, June 6, at 11:24 AM, whereas the stamp on the corresponding compiled module is Friday, June 6, at 11:40 AM. Then it is clear that the source module has not been changed since the compiled module was created by the compiler. On the other hand, if the date and time stamp on the source module is later than that on the compiled module, then *make* calls the appropriate compiler to create a version of the compiled module that corresponds to the current version of the source module.

Next, the date and time stamp on the executable load image are compared to those on every compiled module in that configuration. If the executable load image was created later than all the compiled modules, then there is no need to relink. But if a compiled module has a later stamp than that of the executable load image, then the executable load image does not incorporate the latest version of that compiled module. In this case, *make* calls the linker and constructs an updated executable load image.

In other words, *make* checks whether the executable load image incorporates the current version of every module. If so, then nothing further is done and no computer time is wasted on needless compilations and linkage. But, if not, then *make* calls the relevant system software (compiler or linker in this case) to create an up-to-date version of the information system.

In addition, *make* simplifies the task of constructing an executable load image. There is no need for the user to specify each time what modules are to be used and how they are to be connected, because this information already is in the Makefile. Therefore, a single *make* command is all that is needed to put together an information system consisting of hundreds of modules and ensure that the complete information system is put together correctly.

Tools like *make* have been incorporated into an endless variety of programming environments, including Visual Java and Visual C++. An open-source version of *make* is Ant (a product of the Apache project).

11.6 CASE Environments

As described in Section 11.2, there is a natural progression within CASE. The simplest CASE device is a single tool, such as a build tool. Next, tools can be combined, leading to a workbench that supports one or two activities within the information system life cycle, such as configuration control or coding. However, such a workbench might not provide management information even for the limited portion of the information system life cycle to which it is applicable, let alone for the project as a whole. Finally, an environment provides computer-aided support for most, if not all, aspects of the life cycle.

In 1991, James Gosling of Sun Microsystems developed Java. While developing the language, he frequently stared out the window at a large oak tree outside his office. In fact, he did this so often that he decided to name his new language *Oak*. However, his choice of name was unacceptable to Sun because it could not be trademarked, and without a trademark Sun would lose control of the language.

After an intensive search for a name that could be trademarked and was easy to remember, Gosling's group came up with *Java*. During the eighteenth century, much of the coffee imported into England was grown in Java, the most populous island in the Dutch East Indies (now Indonesia). As a result, *Java* now is a slang word for coffee, the third most popular beverage among information technology professionals. Unfortunately, the names of the Big Two carbonated cola beverages are already trademarked.

To understand why Gosling designed Java, it is necessary to appreciate the source of the weaknesses he perceived in C++. And to do that, we have to go back to C, the parent language of C++.

In 1972, the programming language C was developed by Dennis Ritchie at AT&T Bell Laboratories (now Lucent Technologies). The language was designed to be extremely flexible. But this flexibility made it easy for the programmer to write code that could behave in an unexpected way.

This was not a problem at Bell Labs. After all, C was designed by an experienced software engineer for use by other experienced software engineers at Bell Labs. These professionals could be relied on to use the powerful and flexible features of C in a secure way. A basic philosophy in the design of C was that the person using C knows exactly what he or she is doing. Failures that occurred when C is used by less competent or inexperienced programmers should not be blamed on AT&T; there never was any intent that C should be widely employed as a general-purpose programming language, as it is today.

With the rise of the object-oriented paradigm, a number of object-oriented programming languages based on C were developed, including Object C, Objective C, and C++. The idea behind these languages was to embed object-oriented constructs within C, which

---

Ideally, every information system development organization should utilize an environment. But the cost of an environment can be large—not just the package itself but also the hardware on which to run it. For a smaller organization, a workbench, or perhaps just a set of tools, may suffice. But, if at all possible, an environment should be utilized to support the development and maintenance effort.

11.7   Environments for Information Systems

An important class of environments is used for development of information systems. The emphasis is on ease of use, achieved in a number of ways. In particular, the environment incorporates a number of standard screens, and these can be modified endlessly via a user-friendly *graphical user interface (GUI) generator*. One popular feature of such environments is a code generator. The information system development team produces the detailed design. The detailed design is the input to a code generator that automatically generates code in a language such as C++ or Java. (For some insights into C++ and Java,

by then was a popular programming language. It was argued that it would be easier for programmers to learn a language based on a familiar language than to learn a totally new language. However, only one of the many C-based object-oriented languages became widely accepted and that was C++, developed by Bjarne Stroustrup, also of AT&T Bell Laboratories.

It has been suggested that the reason behind the success of C++ is the enormous financial clout of AT&T. However, if corporate size and financial strength were relevant features in promoting a programming language, today we would all be using PL/I, a language developed and strongly promoted by IBM in the early 1970s. The reality is that PL/I, notwithstanding the prestige of IBM, has retreated into obscurity. The real reason for the success of C++ is that it is a true superset of C. That is, unlike most of the other C-based object-oriented programming languages, virtually any C program is also valid C++. Therefore, organizations realized that they could switch from C to C++ without changing any of their existing information systems implemented in C. They could advance from the traditional paradigm to the object-oriented paradigm without disruption. A remark frequently encountered in the Java literature is "Java is what C++ should have been." The implication is that, if only Stroustrup had been as smart as Gosling, C++ would have turned out to be Java. On the contrary, if C++ had not been a true superset of C, it would have gone the way of the other C-based object-oriented programming languages; that is, it essentially would have disappeared. Only after C++ had taken hold as a popular language was Java designed in reaction to perceived weaknesses in C++. Java is not a superset of C; there are features of C++ (such as "pointer variables") that are not found in Java. Therefore, it would be more accurate to say that "Java is what C++ could not possibly have been."

Finally, it is important to realize that Java, like every other programming language, has weaknesses of its own, and that in some areas (such as "access rules"), C++ is superior to Java [Schach, 1997]. It will be interesting to see, in the coming years, whether C++ continues to be the predominant object-oriented programming language or whether it will be supplanted by Java or some other language entirely.

see Just in Case You Wanted to Know Box 11.1.) This automatically generated code then is compiled; no coding as such is needed.

A number of environments of this type are currently available, including Foundation. Bearing in mind the size of the market for environments for information systems, it is likely that many more environments of this type will be developed in future years.

For object-oriented software engineering, two environments are Rational Rose and System Architect. ArgoUML[2] is an open-source environment of this type.

11.8 Potential Problems with Environments

No one environment is ideal for all information systems and all organizations, any more than one programming language can be considered to be "the best." Every environment has its strengths and its weaknesses, and choosing an inappropriate environment can be worse than

[2] Information on how to install ArgoUML on your computer as well as an introductory tutorial can be found at www.argoUML.org.

using no environment at all. For example, many environments essentially automate a manual methodology. If an organization chooses to use an environment that enforces a methodology that is inappropriate for that organization as a whole or for the current information system under development, then use of that CASE environment will be counterproductive.

11.9 Productivity Gains with CASE Technology

In 1992 an investigation was conducted into productivity gains as a consequence of introducing CASE technology. Data were collected from 45 companies in 10 industries. Half the companies were in the field of information systems, 25 percent in scientific areas, and 25 percent in real-time aerospace. Average annual productivity gains varied from 9 percent (real-time aerospace) to 12 percent (information systems). If only productivity gains are considered, then these figures do not justify the cost of $125,000 per user of introducing CASE technology. However, the companies surveyed felt that the justification for CASE is not merely increased productivity but also shorter development time and improvement in information system quality [Myers, 1992]. In other words, the introduction of CASE environments boosted productivity, although less than some proponents of CASE technology have claimed. Nevertheless, there were other, equally important reasons for introducing CASE technology into an information system organization, such as faster development, fewer faults, better usability, easier maintenance, and improved morale.

Newer results on the effectiveness of CASE technology from over 100 development projects at 15 *Fortune* 500 companies reflect the importance of training within the context of information system development. When teams using CASE were given training in information system development in general as well as tool-specific training, user satisfaction increased and development schedules were met. Also, performance increased by 50 percent when teams used CASE tools in conjunction with an appropriate methodology. However, when training was not provided, information systems were delivered late and users were less satisfied. To put it bluntly, a fool with a tool is still a fool [Guinan, Cooprider, and Sawyer, 1997].

11.10 CASE and Aesthetics

A CASE tool generally does not store UML diagrams as such. Instead, it stores a description of the information system. The tool then uses the stored description to create UML diagrams. For example, a CASE tool stores the name of each class, its attributes, and methods, as well as a description of the relationships between the various classes. Then, when a user needs a class diagram, the CASE tool uses the stored description to create that class diagram.

This approach makes it easy to make changes to the information system. For example, suppose that a user wishes to change the name of a class from **Old Name Class** to **Renamed Class.** The user makes the change by editing the name where it appears in a UML diagram on the screen. The CASE tool implements this change of name by changing the name where it is stored as part of the description of the information system. Now, whenever a UML diagram is needed that includes the renamed class, the UML diagram created by the CASE tool will reflect the name **Renamed Class.** This change will be reflected in every class diagram, interaction diagram, package diagram, and any other diagram in which the renamed class appears.

Similarly, suppose that a new class named **New Class** is added to a UML diagram on the screen. Details of **New Class** are automatically added to the description of the information system stored by the CASE tool. Then, **New Class** will appear in all future UML diagrams, where appropriate.

This ability to handle change is of particular importance when an information system is developed using the Unified Process. After all, a CASE tool has to be able to support the continual iteration and incrementation that is characteristic of the Unified Process.

However, the fact that a CASE tool stores a description of the information system and then creates UML diagrams from that description has consequences regarding the appearance of the resulting UML diagrams. For example, consider the sixth iteration of the class diagram of the Osbert Oglesby case study (Figure 6.42), reproduced here as Figure 11.7. The author has carefully arranged the classes in layers, with a boundary class at the top, then the four control classes, the seven entity classes, and finally the remaining four boundary classes at the bottom. Furthermore, he sorted the classes on each level to minimize the number of crossovers in the lines connecting the classes. Finally, the dashed line from **Masterpiece Class** to **Gallery Painting Class** is drawn in three segments, each carefully placed to avoid overwriting class symbols or class names.

Unfortunately, no CASE tool can draw such a diagram automatically. Instead, the classes are displayed on the screen arranged in some order, and the user can then rearrange the classes to his or her personal taste. While classes are moved about on the screen, the CASE

FIGURE 11.7   The Sixth Iteration of the Class Diagram of the Osbert Oglesby Case Study

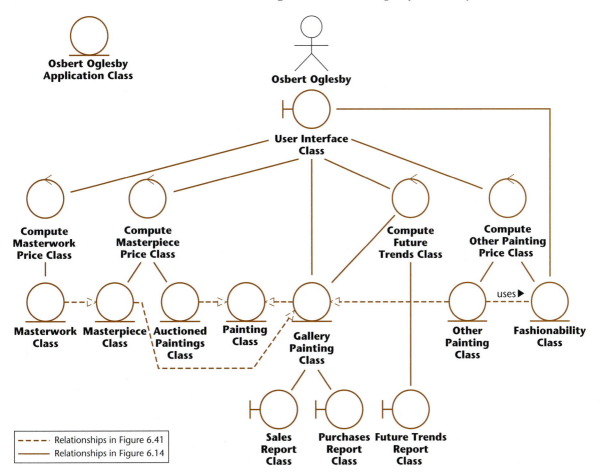

FIGURE 11.8

Figure 11.7 Drawn
Using Rose

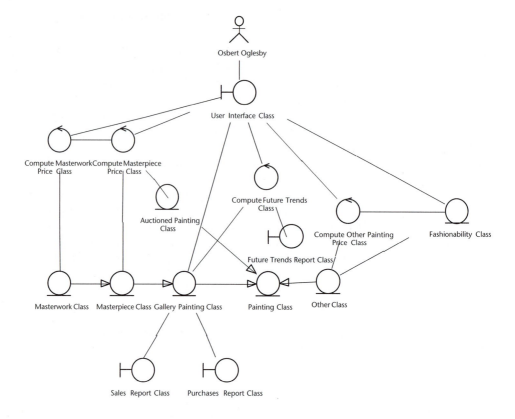

tool automatically adjusts the lines connecting them. However, many CASE tools support only straight lines joining the classes. Figure 11.8 shows Figure 11.7 drawn using Rational Rose. Figure 11.8 is certainly clear in every way, but it is not as aesthetically pleasing as Figure 11.7. On the other hand (and these are the major reasons why CASE tools are essential for developing and maintaining information systems):

- If the classes of the Osbert Oglesby case study are changed, Figure 11.7 has to be re-drawn from scratch, whereas changes can easily be made to Figure 11.8.

- At any time, each member of the development team knows the current classes of the project, namely, the current version of Figure 11.8 as it appears on his or her screen.

- The description stored inside the CASE tool can be used to draw not just Figure 11.8 but all the other UML diagrams as well.

- In the case of environments like Rose, the stored description of the information system can be used to generate code in languages such as C++ and Java.

In other words, the advantages of CASE tools far outweigh the fact that the resulting UML diagrams are not picture perfect.

Some UML diagrams can be adjusted by the user until they are aesthetically pleasing. Consider, for example, Figure 11.9, which shows the use-case diagram of Figure 6.20 drawn using Rational Rose. Figure 11.9 is an example of a good drawing by a CASE tool. Figure 11.10 is a reasonable drawing. It is the Rose representation of the sequence diagram of Figure 6.27.

FIGURE 11.9
The Use-Case
Diagram of
Figure 6.20 Drawn
Using Rose

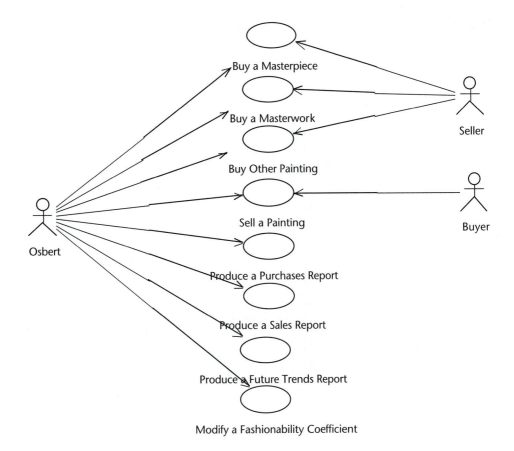

On the other hand, the statechart of Figure 11.11 (Rose version of Figure 6.15) is legible, but is certainly not as clear as Figure 6.15.

We turn now to System Architect, another popular CASE environment. Figure 11.12 is the System Architect version of the use-case diagram of Figure 5.35. This is a clear drawing. On the other hand, Figure 11.13 (System Architect version of the sequence diagram of Figure 7.24), Figure 11.14 (System Architect version of the collaboration diagram of Figure 7.22), and Figure 11.15 (System Architect version of the statechart of Figure 10.16) are less satisfactory, but understandable.

Finally, consider Figures 11.16 and 11.17. Both figures were drawn using ArgoUML, an open-source CASE environment. Figure 11.16 shows the use-case diagram of Figure 5.38 and Figure 11.17 shows the statechart of Figure 6.15.

In general, certain UML diagrams are easier for a CASE tool to draw than others. Use-case diagrams are usually well drawn because of the straightforward nature of most use-case diagrams. On the other hand, statecharts and collaboration diagrams can be complex. This makes it hard for a CASE tool to draw such UML diagrams.

The final figure in this chapter, Figure 11.18, is an alphabetical list of the CASE tools described in this chapter, together with the section in which each is described.

FIGURE 11.10 The Sequence Diagram of Figure 6.27 Drawn Using Rose

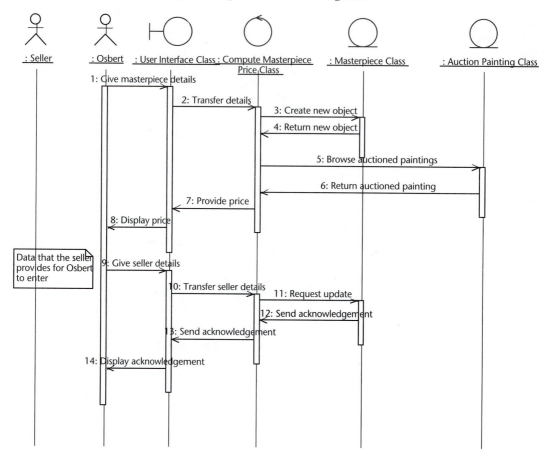

FIGURE 11.11 The Statechart of Figure 6.15 Drawn Using Rose

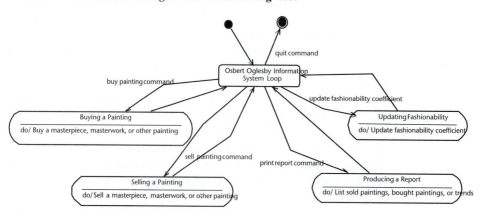

FIGURE 11.12
The Use-Case
Diagram of
Figure 5.35 Drawn
Using System
Architect

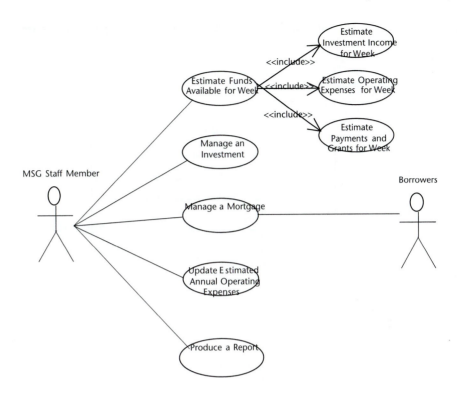

FIGURE 11.13   The Sequence Diagram of Figure 7.24 Drawn Using System Architect

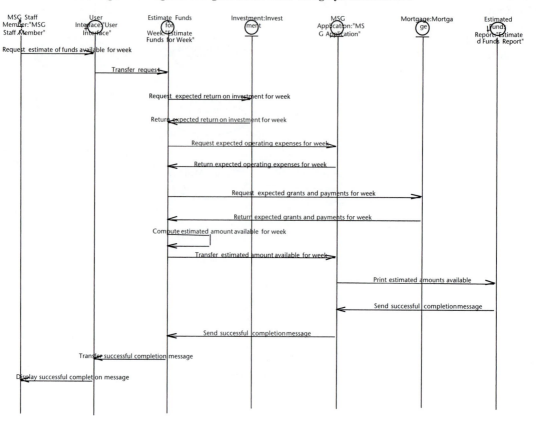

FIGURE 11.14   **The Collaboration Diagram of Figure 7.22 Drawn Using System Architect**

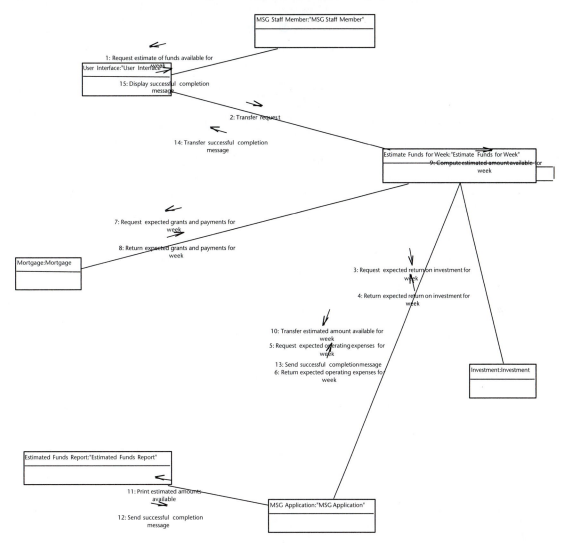

FIGURE 11.15 The Statechart of Figure 10.16 Drawn Using System Architect

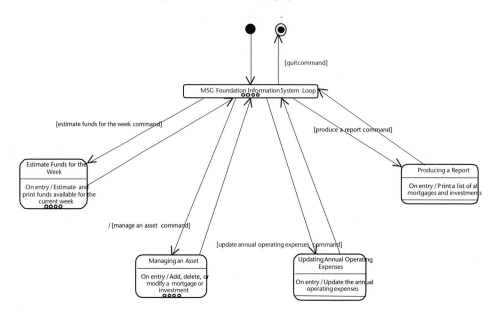

FIGURE 11.16

The Use-Case Diagram of Figure 5.38 Drawn Using ArgoUML

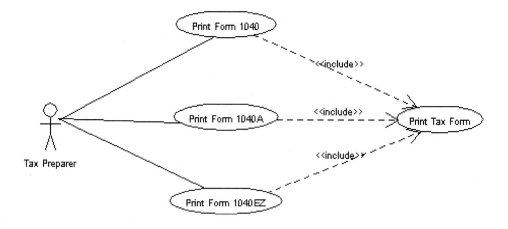

FIGURE 11.17
The Statechart of
Figure 6.15 Drawn
Using ArgoUML

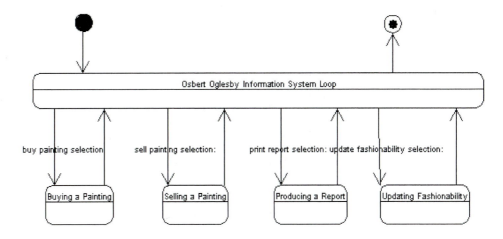

FIGURE 11.18
An Alphabetical List
of the CASE Tools
and Components
of CASE Tools
Presented in This
Chapter and the
Section in Which
Each Is Described

Build tool (Section 11.5)
Coding tool (Section 11.2)
Configuration-control tool (Section 11.4)
Consistency checker (Section 11.1)
Data dictionary (Section 11.1)
E-mail (Section 11.2)
Online documentation (Section 11.2)
Pretty printer (Section 11.2)
Report generator (Section 11.1)
Screen generator (Section 11.1)
Spreadsheet (Section 11.2)
Structure editor (Section 11.2)
Version-control tool (Section 11.3.3)
Word processor (Section 11.2)
World Wide Web browser (Section 11.2)

Key Terms

back-end tools, *208*
baseline, *215*
binary format, *213*
bit, *213*
build tool, *216*
CASE, *207*
CASE tool, *207*
check in/out, *215*
coding tool, *211*
compiled code, *213*
configuration, *213*
configuration control, *215*

configuration-control
   tool, *215*
consistency checker, *208*
data dictionary, *208*
derivation, *214*
e-mail, *211*
environment, *210*
formatter, *211*
freeze, *216*
front-end tool, *208*
graphical user interface
   (GUI) generator, *218*

hexadecimal format, *213*
lowerCASE, *208*
make, *217*
manual, *210*
method, *208*
module, *211*
octal format, *213*
online documentation, *210*
parameter, *208*
pretty printer, *211*
private workspace, *215*
report generator, *208*

Review Questions for Chapter 11

1. Complete the sentence: The acronym CASE stands for _____.
2. Distinguish between a tool, a workbench, and an environment.
3. What is a data dictionary?
4. The data dictionary example of Figure 11.2 refers to "methods" and "parameters." Define these two terms.
5. Why is online documentation an essential aspect of CASE tools?
6. What is the difference between a version, a variation, and a revision?
7. Distinguish carefully between a version and a configuration.
8. What does a build tool do?
9. What is a baseline?
10. What does it mean to "freeze" a version of an artifact?
11. Name three kinds of generators that are widely used CASE tools.
12. What key quality must a CASE environment for information systems have?

Problems

11.1 Does a one-person information system development organization need a version-control tool, and if so, why?

11.2 Does a one-person information system development organization need a configuration-control tool, and if so, why?

11.3 You are the manager in charge of an information system that does the stock control for a statewide chain of 49 computer-theme restaurants. Three different user-reported faults have to be fixed, and you assign one each to Paul, Quentin, and Rachel. A day later you learn that, to implement each of the three fixes, the same four modules must be changed. However, your configuration-control tool is inoperative, so you will have to manage the changes yourself. How will you do it?

11.4 When can old versions of artifacts be discarded? Explain your answer.

11.5 Are a version-control tool and a build tool together equivalent to a configuration-control tool? Explain your answer.

11.6 In your opinion, what are the major reasons why many organizations have not introduced CASE tools?

11.7 You have just been elected mayor of a major city. You discover that no CASE tools are being used to develop information systems for the city. What do you do?

Term Project

11.8 What types of CASE tools would be appropriate for efficient development of the Chocoholics Anonymous information system of Appendix A?

References

Babich, W. A. *Software Configuration Management: Coordination for Team Productivity*. Reading, MA: Addison-Wesley, 1986.

Fuggetta, A. "A Classification of CASE Technology." *IEEE Computer* 26 (December 1993), pp. 25–38.

Guinan, P. J.; J. G. Cooprider; and S. Sawyer. "The Effective Use of Automated Application Development Tools." *IBM Systems Journal* 36, no. 1 (1997), pp. 124–39.

Myers, W. "Good Software Practices Pay Off—or Do They?" *IEEE Software* 9 (March 1992), pp. 96–97.

Schach, S. R. *Software Engineering with Java.* Burr Ridge, IL: Richard D. Irwin, 1997.

12

Teams

Learning Objectives

After studying this chapter, you should be able to:

- Explain the importance of a well-organized team.
- Describe how modern hierarchical teams are organized.
- Give an overview of synchronize-and-stabilize teams.
- Give an outline of extreme programming teams.

Without competent, well-trained information technology professionals, an information system development project is doomed to failure. However, having the right people is not enough; teams must be organized in such a way that the team members can work productively in cooperation with one another. Team organization is the subject of this chapter.

12.1 Team Organization

Most information systems are too large to be completed by a single information technology professional within the given time constraints. As a result, the information system must be assigned to a group of professionals organized as a *team*. For example, consider the analysis workflow. To perform the analysis workflow for the target information system within two months, it may be necessary to assign the task to three systems analysts organized as a team under the direction of the analysis manager.

Suppose now that the analysis workflow of an information system has to be performed within three months, even though one person-year of analysis is involved (a person-year is the amount of work that can be done by one person in one year). The solution is apparently simple: If one systems analyst can perform the analysis workflow in one year, four systems analysts can do it in three months.

This, of course, does not work. In practice, the four systems analysts may take nearly a year, and the quality of the resulting information system may well be lower than if one systems analyst had performed the entire analysis workflow. The reason is that some tasks can be shared, but others must be done individually. For instance, if one farmhand can pick a strawberry field in 10 days, the same strawberry field can be picked by 10 farmhands in

FIGURE 12.1
Communication Paths between Three Information Technology Professionals (Solid Lines) and when a Fourth Professional Joins Them (Dashed Lines)

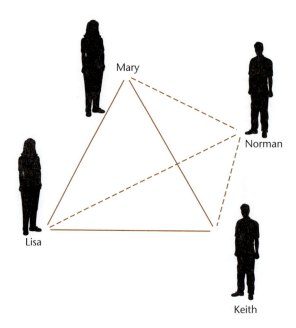

one day. On the other hand, one elephant can produce a calf in 22 months, but this feat cannot possibly be accomplished in one month by 22 elephants.

In other words, tasks such as strawberry picking can be fully shared; others, such as elephant production, cannot be shared at all. Unlike elephant production, it is possible to share analysis tasks between members of a team by distributing the analysis workflow among the team members. However, team analysis also is unlike strawberry picking in that analysis team members have to interact with one another in a meaningful and effective way.

A difficulty that arises from team development of information systems is shown in Figure 12.1. There are three channels of communication between Keith, Lisa, and Mary, the three information technology professionals working on the project. Now suppose that the work is slipping, a deadline is rapidly approaching, and the task is not nearly complete. The obvious thing to do is to add a fourth professional to the team. But the first thing that must happen when Norman joins the team is for the other three to explain in detail what has been accomplished to date and what is still incomplete. In other words, adding personnel to a late information system project makes it even later. This principle is known as *Brooks's Law* after Fred Brooks, who observed it while managing the development of OS/360, an IBM mainframe operating system [Brooks, 1975].

In a large organization, teams perform every workflow of information system development, but especially the implementation workflow, during which programmers work independently on separate modules. Accordingly, the implementation workflow is a prime candidate for sharing the task among several information technology professionals. In some smaller organizations, one individual may be responsible for the requirements, analysis, and design workflows, after which the implementation workflow is performed by a team of two or three programmers. Because teams are most heavily used for the implementation workflow, the problems of team organization are most acutely felt during implementation. In the remainder of this chapter, team organization is therefore presented within the context of implementation, even though the problems and their solution are equally applicable to all the other workflows.

12.2   Traditional Chief Programmer Teams

Consider the four-person team shown in Figure 12.2.

- There are six different ways that Keith, Lisa, Mary, and Norman can meet in groups of two (Keith–Lisa; Keith–Mary; Keith–Norman; Lisa–Mary; Lisa–Norman; Mary–Norman).
- There are four different three-person groups (Keith–Lisa–Mary; Keith–Lisa–Norman; Keith–Mary–Norman; Lisa–Mary–Norman).
- There is one four-person group (Keith–Lisa–Mary–Norman).

That is, the total number of two-, three-, and four-person groups is 11. This large number of communication channels is the major reason why a four-person team organized as in Figure 12.2 is unlikely to be able to perform 24 person-months of work in six months; many hours are wasted in meetings involving two or more team members at a time. (A *person-month* is the amount of work one person can do in one month.)

Now consider the four-person team shown in Figure 12.3. Again there are four programmers, but now there are only three lines of communication, namely, from the chief

FIGURE 12.2

Communication Paths between Four Information Technology Professionals

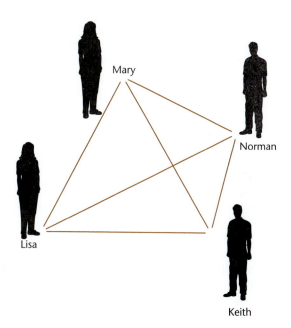

FIGURE 12.3

The Structure of a Traditional Chief Programmer Team

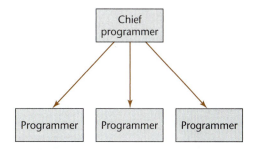

programmer to each of the three programmers, as indicated by the arrows. This is the basic concept behind what now is termed the *chief programmer* team shown in Figure 12.3. The idea was put forward more than 30 years ago [Baker, 1972]. The chief programmer was both a successful manager and a highly skilled programmer who did the design and any critical or complex sections of the code. The other team members worked on the rest of the coding under the direction of the chief programmer; as shown in Figure 12.3, there were no lines of communication between the programmers.

In theory, this seemed to be a good idea. In practice, it was a tremendous success the first time it was used—for computerizing the clippings files of the *New York Times* in 1972. There have subsequently been other successful projects that used chief programmer teams, but none of them reached the heights of the *New York Times* triumph. The reason lay in the skill sets of the chief programmers.

Consider a chief programmer, a combination of a highly skilled programmer and a successful manager. Such individuals are extremely difficult to find: There is a shortage of highly skilled programmers, as well as a shortage of successful managers, and the job description of a chief programmer requires both abilities in equal measure. It also has been suggested that the qualities needed to be a highly skilled programmer are different from those needed to be a successful manager; therefore, the chances of finding a chief programmer are small.

Thus, traditional chief programmer teams are almost impossible to implement in practice. Furthermore, the reason for the limited success of most chief programmer teams was that the person who filled the role of chief programmer was not equally brilliant at both programming and management.

What is needed is a more practical way of organizing programming teams that can be extended to the implementation of larger information systems.

12.3   Modern Hierarchical Teams

As just mentioned, the problem with traditional programmer teams is that it is all but impossible to find one individual who is both a highly skilled programmer and a successful manager. The solution is to use a matrix organizational structure [Kerzner, 2001] and to replace the chief programmer by two individuals: a *team leader*, who is in charge of the technical aspects of the team's activities, and a *team manager*, who is responsible for all nontechnical managerial decisions. The structure of the resulting team is shown in Figure 12.4. It is important to realize that this organizational structure does not violate the fundamental

FIGURE 12.4

The Structure of a Modern Hierarchical Programming Team

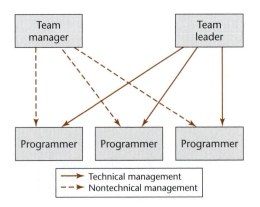

managerial principle that no employee should report to more than one manager. The areas of responsibility are clearly delineated. The team leader is responsible for only technical management. Thus, budgetary and legal issues are not handled by the team leader, nor are performance appraisals. On the other hand, the team leader has sole responsibility on technical issues. The team manager, therefore, has no right to promise, say, that the information system will be delivered within four weeks; promises of that sort have to be made by the team leader.

Before implementation begins, it is important to demarcate clearly those areas that appear to be the responsibility of both the team manager and the team leader. For example, consider the issue of annual leave. The situation can arise that the team manager approves a leave application because leave is a nontechnical issue, only to find the application vetoed by the team leader because a deadline is approaching. The solution to this and related issues is for higher management to draw up a policy regarding those areas that both the team manager and the team leader consider to be their responsibility.

The traditional chief programmer team of Figure 12.3 has one manager, the chief programmer, whereas the modern hierarchical team of Figure 12.4 has two managers: the team manager and the team leader. It would seem that the cost of two managers would make the modern programming team prohibitively expensive. There are two reasons why this is not the case. First, the salary of a chief programmer (assuming that one could be found) is much greater than that of either a team manager or a team leader. Second, each team has its own team leader, but a team manager can usually manage more than one team. Thus, the total cost of the traditional chief programmer team is about the same as that of the modern hierarchical team.

What about larger projects? This approach can be scaled up as shown in Figure 12.5, which shows the technical managerial organizational structure; the nontechnical side is similarly organized. Implementation of the information system as a whole is under the direction of the project leader. The programmers report to their team leaders, and the team leaders report to the project leader. For even larger information systems, additional levels can be

FIGURE 12.5   **Technical Managerial Organizational Structure for Larger Projects**

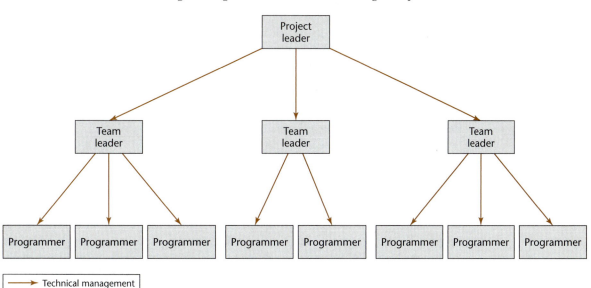

added to the hierarchy. (For simplicity, Figure 12.5 does not show nonprogramming personnel, such as the quality assurance group, described in Chapter 13, who are responsible for the test workflow.)

The figures in this chapter depict teams that consist of three or four information technology professionals in order to achieve clearer, less-cluttered diagrams. In practice, however, teams are often larger than this. For example, when the Unified Process is used, teams of size six to eight are recommended [Jacobson, Booch, and Rumbaugh, 1999].

12.4 Other Ways of Organizing Teams

We conclude this chapter by describing two other ways of organizing teams. One has proved itself to be relatively successful, but so far in only one company; the other is still controversial.

12.4.1 Synchronize-and-Stabilize Teams

Microsoft, Inc., is the world's largest manufacturer of COTS packages. Microsoft develops large-scale products. For example, Windows 2000 consists of more than 30 million lines of code, developed by over 3,000 programmers and testers [Business Week Online, 1999]. Team organization is a vital aspect of the successful construction of a product of this size. The majority of Microsoft COTS packages are developed using a life-cycle model that has been termed the *synchronize-and-stabilize model*. This model has features in common with the Unified Process. In particular, incrementation is heavily used.

The requirements phase is conducted by interviewing numerous potential customers for the COTS package and extracting a list of features prioritized by the customers. A specification document is now drawn up that reflects the customers' responses to the interviews.

Next, the product is designed and implemented. The work is divided into three or four increments (termed *builds* by Microsoft). The first build consists of the most important features. Once the first build is complete, the second build is started. The second build consists of the next most important features, and so on.

Each build is carried out by a number of small teams working in parallel. At the end of each day, all the teams *synchronize;* that is, they put the partially completed components together and test and debug the resulting product. *Stabilization* is performed at the end of each build. Any remaining faults that have been detected so far are fixed and the build is now frozen; that is, no further changes will be made to the specification document.

The repeated synchronization step ensures that the various components always work together. Another advantage of this regular execution of the partially constructed product is that the developers obtain an early insight into the operation of the product and can modify the requirements if necessary during the course of a build. The model can even be used if the initial specification is incomplete.

The success of the synchronize-and-stabilize life-cycle model is largely a consequence of the way the teams are organized. Each of the three or four sequential builds of the synchronize-and-stabilize model is constructed by a number of small teams led by a program manager and consisting of between three and eight developers together with three to eight testers who work one-to-one with the developers. The team is provided the specifications of their overall task; the individual team members then are given the freedom to design and implement their portion of that task as they wish. The reason that this does not rapidly devolve into chaos is the synchronization step performed each day: The partially completed components are tested and debugged on a daily basis. Thus, even though individual creativity and autonomy are nurtured, the individual components always work together.

The strength of this approach is that, on the one hand, individual programmers are encouraged to be creative and innovative. On the other hand, the daily synchronization step ensures that the hundreds of developers are working together toward a common goal.

Microsoft developers must follow very few rules, but one of them is that they must adhere strictly to the time laid down to enter their code into the product database for that day's synchronization. This rule has been likened to telling children that they can do what they like all day but have to be in bed by 9 P.M. [Cusumano and Selby, 1997]. Another rule is that, if a developer's code prevents the product from being compiled for that day's synchronization, the problem must be fixed immediately so that the rest of the team can test and debug that day's work.

Will use of the synchronize-and-stabilize model and associated team organization guarantee that every other software organization will be as successful as Microsoft? This is extremely unlikely. Microsoft, Inc., is more than just the synchronize-and-stabilize model. It is an organization consisting of a highly talented set of managers and software developers with an evolved group ethos. Merely using the synchronize-and-stabilize model will not magically turn an organization into another Microsoft. At the same time, the use of many of the features of the model in other organizations could lead to process improvement. On the other hand, it has been suggested that the synchronize-and-stabilize model is simply a way of allowing a group of hackers to develop large products.

12.4.2 Extreme Programming Teams

Extreme programming [Beck, 1999] is a somewhat controversial new approach to information system development that also utilizes iteration and incrementation. The first step is that the information system development team determines the various features (*stories*) that the client would like the target information system to support. For each such story, the team informs the client how long it will take to implement that story, and how much it will cost. This first step roughly corresponds to the requirements and analysis workflows of the Unified Process.

The client selects the stories to be included in each successive build using cost–benefit analysis; that is, on the basis of the time and the cost estimates provided by the development team as well as the potential benefits of the story to his or her business. The proposed build is broken down into increments, here termed *tasks*. A programmer first draws up test cases for a task. Then, working together with a partner on one computer (*pair programming*), the programmer implements the task, ensuring that all the test cases work correctly. The task is then integrated into the current version of the information system. Ideally, implementing and integrating a task should take no more than a few hours. In general, a number of pairs will be implementing tasks in parallel, so integration can take place essentially continuously. The test cases used for the task are retained and utilized in all further testing.

There are a number of features of extreme programming (XP) that are somewhat unusual:

- The computers of the XP team are set up in the center of a large room lined with small cubicles.
- A client representative works with the XP team at all times.
- No individual can work overtime for two successive weeks.
- There is no specialization. Instead, all members of the XP team work on requirements, analysis, design, code, and testing.
- There is no overall design phase before the various builds are constructed. Instead, the design is modified while the information system is being developed. This procedure is termed *refactoring*. Whenever a test case will not run, the code is reorganized until the team is satisfied that the design is simple and straightforward and runs all the test cases satisfactorily.

The democratic team organization was first described by Gerald Weinberg in 1971 [Weinberg, 1971]. The basic concept underlying the democratic team is *egoless programming*. Weinberg points out that programmers can be highly attached to their code. Sometimes they even name their modules after themselves; they therefore see their modules as an extension of themselves. The difficulty with this is that if a programmer sees a module as an extension of his or her ego, that programmer is certainly not going to try to find all the faults in "his" code or "her" code. And if there is a fault, it is termed a *bug*, like some insect that has crept unasked into the code and could have been prevented if only the code had been guarded more zealously against invasion. Some 35 years ago, when software was still input on punch cards (Section 18.1), that attitude was amusingly lampooned by the marketing of an aerosol spray named Shoo-Bug. The instructions on the label solemnly explained that spraying one's card deck with Shoo-Bug would ensure that no bugs could possibly infest the code.

Weinberg's solution to the problem of programmers being too closely attached to their own code is egoless programming. The social environment must be restructured and so must programmer values. Every programmer must encourage the other members of the team to find faults in his or her code. The presence of a fault must not be considered something bad, but rather a normal and accepted event; the attitude of the person reviewing the code should be appreciation at being asked for advice, rather than ridicule of the programmer for making coding errors. The team as a whole will develop an ethos, a group identity, and modules will belong to the team as a whole rather than to any one individual.

A group of up to 10 egoless programmers constitutes a democratic team. Weinberg warns that management may have difficulty working with such a team. After all, consider the managerial career path. When a programmer is promoted to a management position, his or her fellow programmers are not promoted and must strive to attain the higher level

A particularly unusual feature of XP is pair programming; as previously mentioned, all code is implemented by a team of two programmers sharing a single computer. There are a number of reasons why this is done:

- Programmers first draw up test cases, then implement that task. As explained in Section 13.6, it is highly inadvisable for a programmer to test his or her own code. XP gets around this problem by having one programmer in a team draw up the test cases for a task. These test cases are then used by the other programmer to test the code after they have jointly implemented it.

- In a more conventional life-cycle model, when a developer leaves a project, all the knowledge accumulated by that developer leaves as well. In particular, the information system on which that developer was working may not yet have been documented and therefore may have to be redeveloped from scratch. In contrast, if one member of a pair programming team leaves, the other is sufficiently knowledgeable to continue working on the same part of the information system with a new pair programmer. Furthermore, should the new team member accidentally damage the information system by making an ill-advised modification, the presence of the test cases can assist in highlighting the fault.

- Working closely in pairs enables a less-experienced information technology professional to acquire the skills of the more-experienced team member.

at the next round of promotions. In contrast, a democratic team is a group working for a common cause with no single leader, with no programmers trying to get promoted to the next level. What is important is team identity and mutual respect.

Weinberg tells of a democratic team that developed an outstanding product. Management decided to give a cash award to the team's nominal manager (by definition, a democratic team has no leader). He refused to accept it personally, saying that it had to be shared equally among all members of the team. Management thought that he was angling for more money and that the team (and especially its nominal manager) had some rather unorthodox ideas. Management forced the nominal manager to accept the money, which he then divided equally among the team. Next, the entire team resigned and joined another company as a team.

The major advantage of the democratic team approach is the positive attitude toward the finding of faults. The more that are found, the happier are the members of a democratic team. This positive attitude leads to more rapid detection of faults and hence to high-quality code.

However, there are some major problems. As pointed out, managers may have difficulty accepting egoless programming. In addition, a programmer with, say, 15 years of experience is likely to resent having his or her code appraised by fellow programmers, especially beginners. But the real reason why there are so few democratic teams is that egoless teams have to spring up spontaneously—they cannot be imposed from outside.

It has been my experience that a democratic team works well in an industrial setting when there is a hard problem to solve. On a number of occasions, I have been a member of a democratic team that sprang up spontaneously among information system professionals with research experience. But once the task has been reduced to the implementation of a hard-won solution, the team must then be reorganized in a more hierarchical fashion, such as the modern hierarchical team of Section 12.3.

Thus, even though the idea of two programmers working together on the same computer may seem somewhat unusual, there can be distinct advantages to the practice.

XP has been successfully used on a number of small-scale projects. There also have been a number of failures. It has been suggested that a strength of XP is that it is useful when the client's requirements are vague or changing. However, XP has not yet been used widely enough to determine whether this life-cycle model will fulfill its early promise. Furthermore, even if XP turns out to be good for small-scale information systems, that does not necessarily mean that it can be used for medium- or large-scale information systems, as will be explained.

Extreme programming is one of a number of new paradigms that are collectively referred to as *agile processes*. They are characterized by considerably less emphasis on analysis and design than in the Unified Process, and with implementation starting much earlier in the life cycle.

To appreciate why so many information technology professionals have expressed doubts about agile processes within the context of medium- and large-scale information systems, consider the following analogy by Grady Booch [Booch, 2000]. Anyone can successfully hammer together a few planks to build a doghouse, but it would be foolhardy to build a three-bedroom home without detailed plans. In addition, skills in plumbing, wiring, and roofing are needed to build a three-bedroom home, and inspections are essential. (That is,

FIGURE 12.6
The Ways of Organizing Teams Presented in This Chapter and the Section in Which Each Is Described

Traditional chief programmer teams (Section 12.2)
Modern hierarchical teams (Section 12.3)
Synchronize-and-stabilize teams (Section 12.4.1)
Extreme programming teams (Section 12.4.2)
Democratic teams (Just in Case You Wanted to Know Box 12.1)

being able to build small-scale information systems does not necessarily mean that one has the skills for building medium-scale information systems.) Furthermore, the fact that a skyscraper is the height of 1,000 doghouses does not mean that one can build a skyscraper by piling 1,000 doghouses on top of one another. In other words, building large-scale information systems requires even more specialized and sophisticated skills than those needed to cobble together small-scale information systems.

In conclusion, it seems unlikely that agile processes will prove to be more than a non-traditional way of building small-scale information systems, especially when the client's requirements are changing.

We end this chapter with Just in Case You Wanted to Know Box 12.1. This describes yet another form of team organization, one that cannot be imposed by management on the team members. Figure 12.6 lists the different ways of organizing teams included in this chapter and the section in which each is described.

Key Terms

agile processes, *239*
Brooks's Law, *232*
build, *236*
chief programmer, *234*
extreme programming, *237*
pair programming, *237*
person-month, *233*

refactoring, *237*
stabilize, *236*
story, *237*
synchronize, *236*
synchronize-and-stabilize
   model, *236*
task, *237*

team, *231*
team leader, *234*
team manager, *234*

Review Questions for Chapter 12

1. Why are teams so important when information systems are developed?
2. What is a person-month?
3. State Brooks's Law.
4. Why is the traditional chief programmer team impractical?
5. How do modern hierarchical teams solve the problem of the impracticality of chief programmer teams?
6. Describe the synchronize step used by synchronize-and-stabilize teams.
7. Describe the stabilize step used by synchronize-and-stabilize teams.
8. In what ways are extreme programming teams unusual?
9. Describe pair programming.

Problems

12.1   How would you organize a team to develop a conventional payroll information system? Justify your answer.

12.2   You have just started a new information system company. Almost all your employees are recent graduates; this is their first information technology job. Would it be a good idea to implement synchronize-and-stabilize teams in your organization? Justify your answer.

12.3   A student programming team is organized as a chief programming team. What can be deduced about the students in the team?

12.4   In order to compare two different team organizations, TO_1 and TO_2, within a large information system company, the following experiment is proposed. The same information system will be developed by two different teams, one organized according to TO_1 and the other according to TO_2. The company estimates that each team will take about 18 months to develop the information system. Give three reasons why this experiment is impractical and unlikely to yield meaningful results.

12.5   Why do extreme programming teams have to share a computer?

12.6   Would you like to work in an organization that uses extreme programming teams? Explain your answer.

Term Project

12.7   How should teams be organized for efficient development of the Chocoholics Anonymous information system of Appendix A?

References

Baker, F. T. "Chief Programmer Team Management of Production Programming." *IBM Systems Journal* 11, no. 1 (1972), pp. 56–73.

Beck, K. "Embracing Change with Extreme Programming." *IEEE Computer* 32 (October 1999), pp. 70–77.

Booch, G. "The Future of Software Engineering." Keynote Address, International Conference on Software Engineering, Limerick, Ireland, May 2000.

Brooks, F. P., Jr. *The Mythical Man-Month: Essays in Software Engineering.* Reading, MA: Addison-Wesley, 1975. 20th anniversary ed. Reading, MA: Addison Wesley, 1995.

Business Week Online. February 2, 1999. Available at www.businessweek.com/1999/99_08/b3617025.htm.

Cusumano, M. A., and R. W. Selby. "How Microsoft Builds Software." *Communications of the ACM* 40 (June 1997), pp. 53–61.

Jacobson, I.; G. Booch; and J. Rumbaugh. *The Unified Software Development Process.* Reading, MA: Addison-Wesley, 1999.

Kerzner, H. *Project Management: A Systems Approach to Planning, Scheduling, and Controlling.* 7th ed. New York: Wiley, 2001.

Weinberg, G. M. *The Psychology of Computer Programming.* New York: Van Nostrand Reinhold, 1971.

13

Testing

After studying this chapter, you should be able to:

- Describe quality assurance issues.
- Describe how to perform nonexecution-based testing (inspections) of artifacts.
- Describe the principles of execution-based testing.
- Explain what needs to be tested.

The test workflow was introduced in Section 2.5 and somewhat amplified in Section 9.1.5. In this chapter, testing is described in detail.

13.1   Introduction to Testing

Traditional life-cycle models for developing information systems all too frequently include a separate testing phase, after implementation and before maintenance. Nothing could be more dangerous from the viewpoint of trying to achieve a high-quality information system. Testing is an integral component of the information system development process and an activity that must be carried out throughout the life cycle. While performing the requirements workflow, the requirements must be checked. While performing the analysis workflow, the specification document must be checked; and the information system project management plan must undergo similar scrutiny. The design workflow requires careful checking at every stage. While performing the implementation workflow, each module certainly must be tested, and the information system as a whole needs testing when the implementation is complete. After passing the acceptance test, the information system is installed and post-delivery maintenance begins. And hand in hand with maintenance goes repeated checking of modified versions of the information system.

In other words, it is insufficient to test the artifacts of a workflow merely at the end of that workflow. For example, consider the analysis workflow. The members of the analysis team must carefully check all the artifacts while they develop them. It is not much use for the team to develop the complete specification document only to find, weeks or months later, that they have to rewrite the entire specification because of an error they made early in the process. Therefore, what is needed is continual testing carried out by the development team

On November 9, 1979, the U.S. Strategic Air Command had an alert scramble when the worldwide military command and control system (WWMCCS) computer network reported that the Soviet Union had launched missiles aimed toward the United States [Neumann, 1980]. What actually happened was that a simulated attack was interpreted as the real thing, just as in the movie *WarGames* some five years later. Although the U.S. Department of Defense has understandably not given details of why test data were taken for actual data, it seems reasonable to assume that the problem was a software fault. Either the information system as a whole was not designed to differentiate between simulations and reality or the user interface did not include the necessary checks for ensuring that users of the information system would be able to distinguish fact from fiction. In other words, a software fault, if indeed the problem was caused by software, could have brought civilization as we know it to an unpleasant and abrupt end.

In the case of the WWMCCS network, disaster was averted at the last minute. However, the consequences of other software faults have sometimes been tragic. For example, between 1985 and 1987 at least two patients died as a consequence of severe overdoses of

while it performs each workflow, in addition to more methodical testing at the end of each workflow.

Two terms that are widely used within the context of testing are verification and validation. *Verification* refers to the process of determining whether a specific workflow has been correctly carried out; this takes place at the end of each workflow. On the other hand, *validation* is the intensive evaluation process that takes place just before the information system is delivered to the client. Its purpose is to determine whether the information system as a whole satisfies its specifications. The term *V & V* is often used to denote testing. Nevertheless, the words *verification* and *validation* are used as little as possible in this book. The reason is that the phrase *verification and validation* (or V & V) implies that the process of checking a workflow can wait until the end of that workflow. On the contrary, it is essential that this checking be carried out in parallel with all information system development and maintenance activities. Therefore, in order to avoid the undesirable implications of the phrase *V & V,* the term *testing* is used instead. We use this terminology for consistency with the Unified Process, with its "test workflow."

Essentially there are two types of testing: execution-based testing and nonexecution-based testing. *Execution-based testing* of an artifact means running ("executing") the artifact on a computer and checking the output. For example, if we want to test whether the completed Cardholder Clothing Company e-commerce information system (Section 3.3) can handle debit cards correctly, we run the information system, provide it with test data appertaining to debit cards, and see if the information system produces the correct output. In other words, if we have an artifact that we can run on a computer, we can test whether the output is correct. On the other hand, we cannot run a written specification document on a computer. The only way to check it is to read through it as carefully as possible; this type of checking is termed *nonexecution-based testing*. (Unfortunately, the term *verification* is sometimes also used to mean nonexecution-based testing.)

Clearly, computer code can be tested both ways. We can either execute it on a computer or we can review it carefully. Surprisingly, reviewing code is at least as good a method of testing code as executing it on a computer. In this chapter, principles of both execution-based and nonexecution-based testing are described.

radiation delivered by the Therac-25 medical linear accelerator [Leveson and Turner, 1993]. The cause was a fault in the control software.

During the 1991 Gulf War, a Scud missile penetrated the Patriot antimissile shield and struck a barracks near Dhahran, Saudi Arabia. In all, 28 Americans were killed and 98 wounded. The software for the Patriot missile contained a cumulative timing fault. The Patriot was designed to operate for only a few hours at a time, after which the clock was reset. As a result, the fault never had a significant effect and was therefore not detected during either testing or previous battlefield use. In the Gulf War, however, the Patriot missile battery at Dhahran ran continuously for over 100 hours. This caused the accumulated time discrepancy to become large enough to render the system inaccurate.

During the Gulf War, the United States shipped Patriot missiles to Israel for protection against the Scuds. Israeli forces detected the timing problem after only eight hours and immediately reported it to the manufacturer in the United States. They corrected the fault as quickly as they could, but, tragically, the new software arrived the day after the direct hit by the Scud [Mellor, 1994].

Just how important is testing? Read Just in Case You Wanted to Know Box 13.1 about faults that have led to fatal consequences. Fortunately, in most cases the result of delivering an information system with residual faults is considerably less catastrophic. Nevertheless, the importance of testing cannot be stressed too strongly.

13.2   Quality Issues

The term *quality* frequently is misunderstood when used within the information system context. After all, quality implies excellence of some sort, but this unfortunately is not the meaning intended by information technology professionals. To put it bluntly, the state of the art in information system development is such that merely getting the information system to function correctly is enough—excellence is an order of magnitude more than what is generally possible with our current information system technology. The *quality* of an information system is the extent to which the information system satisfies its specifications (see Just in Case You Wanted to Know Box 13.2).

The task of every information technology professional is to ensure a high-quality information system at all times. However, the information system quality assurance group has additional responsibilities with regard to information system quality.

13.2.1   Quality Assurance

It is the responsibility of each information technology professional to ensure that every aspect of the information system is correct. One component of the job of the quality assurance group is to ensure that this responsibility is carried out. More precisely, once the developers have completed a workflow, members of the quality assurance group have to check that that workflow has been carried out correctly. Also, when the information system is complete, the quality assurance group has to check that the information system as a whole is correct. However, information system quality assurance goes further than just testing (or V & V) at the end of a workflow or at the end of the development process; quality assurance applies to the development process itself. For example, the responsibilities of

The use of the term *quality* to denote "adheres to specifications" (as opposed to "excellent" or "luxurious") is the practice in fields such as manufacturing. Consider, for example, the quality control manager at a Coca-Cola bottling plant. The job of that quality control manager is to ensure that every single bottle or can that leaves the production line satisfies the specifications for Coca-Cola in every way. There is no attempt to produce "excellent" Coca-Cola or "luxurious" Coca-Cola; the sole aim is to be certain that each bottle or can of Coca-Cola stringently adheres to the company's formula (specifications) for that carbonated beverage.

The word *quality* is used identically in the automobile industry. "Quality Is Job One" is a former slogan of the Ford Motor Company. In other words, the aim of Ford is to ensure that every car that comes off a Ford production line adheres rigorously to the specifications for that car; in information technology slang, the car must be "bug free" in every way.

the quality assurance group include setting up the various standards to which the information system must conform as well as the establishment of the monitoring procedures for assuring compliance with those standards. In brief, the role of the quality assurance group is to ensure the quality of the development process and thereby ensure the quality of the information system.

13.2.2 Quality Assurance Terminology

Information technology professionals often refer to an error as a *bug*. For example, if a program does not work correctly, a programmer may say, "There's a bug in the code." The word *bug* has a long and honorable history in this context, as explained in Just in Case You Wanted to Know Box 13.3.

Nowadays, however, the term *bug* is simply a slang word for *error*. Although there generally is no harm in using slang, the word *bug* has overtones that are not conducive to the development of quality information systems. Specifically, instead of saying, "I made an error," a programmer will say, "A bug crept into the code" (not *my* code but *the* code), thereby transferring responsibility for the error from the programmer to the bug. After all, no one blames a programmer for coming down with a case of influenza, because the flu is caused by the flu bug. Referring to an error as a bug is a way of casting off responsibility. In contrast, the programmer who says, "I made an error," is an information technology professional who takes responsibility for his or her actions.

The Institute of Electrical and Electronic Engineers (IEEE) is a major professional society for computer professionals. Because terminology in the computer context can often be confusing, the IEEE has published a standard terminology. A *fault* is the standard IEEE terminology for what is popularly called a *bug,* whereas a *failure* is the observed incorrect behavior of the information system as a consequence of the fault. Finally, an *error* is the mistake made by the programmer [IEEE, 1990] .

13.2.3 Managerial Independence

It is important to have *managerial independence* between the development team and the quality assurance group. That is, development should be under one manager, quality assurance under a different manager, and neither manager should be able to overrule the other. The reason is that, all too frequently, serious faults are found in an information system as the delivery deadline approaches. The information system development organization must now choose between two unsatisfactory options. Either the information system can be released on time but full of faults, leaving the client to struggle with a faulty information system, or the developers can fix the information system but deliver it late. No matter which alternative is chosen, the client probably will lose confidence in the information system development organization. The decision to deliver the faulty information system on time should not be made by the manager responsible for development, nor should the quality assurance manager be able to make the decision to perform further testing and deliver the information system late. Instead, both managers should report to a more senior manager who can decide which of the two choices would be in the best interests of both the development organization and the client.

At first sight, having a separate quality assurance group would appear to add considerably to the cost of information system development. But this is not so. The additional cost is relatively small compared to the resulting benefit, namely, a higher-quality information system. Without a quality assurance group, every member of the information system development organization would have to be involved to some extent with quality assurance activities. Suppose an organization has 100 information technology professionals and that each devotes about 30 percent of his or her time to quality assurance activities. Instead, the 100 individuals should be divided into two groups, with 70 individuals performing information system development and the other 30 people responsible for quality assurance. The same amount of time is devoted to quality assurance, the only additional expense being a manager to lead the quality assurance group. Quality assurance now can be performed by an independent group of specialists, leading to information systems of higher quality than when quality assurance activities are performed throughout the organization.

In the case of a very small development organization (five employees or fewer), it may simply not be economically viable to have a separate quality assurance group. The best that can be done under such circumstances is to ensure that the requirements document be checked by someone other than the person responsible for producing those requirements and similarly for the specification document, design, code, and so on. The reason for this is explained in the next section.

13.3   Nonexecution-Based Testing

Most of us have had the experience of preparing an important document and checking it over and over again until we are absolutely certain that there are no mistakes of any kind. However, when we give the document to someone else to check, he or she immediately finds a mistake that we did not pick up. For this reason, it is not a good idea for the person responsible for drawing up a document to be the only one responsible for reviewing it. We all have blind spots that allow faults to creep into a document, and those same blind spots prevent the faults from being detected on review. Therefore, the review task must be assigned to someone other than the original author of the document. Better still, it should be assigned to a team.

This is the principle underlying the *inspection,* a review technique used to check artifacts of all kinds. In this form of nonexecution-based testing, an artifact (such as a use-case diagram or a collaboration diagram) is carefully checked by a team of information technology professionals with a broad range of skills. The advantage of a review by a team of experts is that the different skills of the participants increase the chances of finding a fault. In addition, a team of skilled individuals working together often generates a synergistic effect. That is, when people work together as a team to achieve a common goal, the result is frequently more effective than if the team members had worked independently as individuals.

13.3.1   Principles of Inspections

An inspection team should consist of from four to six individuals. For example, an analysis workflow inspection team should include at least one systems analyst from the team responsible for the analysis workflow, the manager of the analysis team, a client representative, a representative of the team who will perform the next workflow of the development (in this instance, the design workflow), and a representative of the quality assurance group. The members of the inspection team, as far as possible, should be experienced information technology professionals because they tend to find the important faults; that is, the ones with a major negative impact on the development project.

The inspection team should be chaired by the quality assurance representative because the quality assurance representative has the most to lose if the inspection is performed poorly and faults consequently slip through. In contrast, the systems analyst on the inspection team may be eager to have the specification document approved as quickly as possible in order to be free to start some other task. The client representative may decide that any defects not detected at the review probably will show up during acceptance testing and will therefore be fixed at no cost to the client organization. But the quality assurance representative has the most at stake: The quality of the information system is a direct reflection of the professional competence of the quality assurance group.

The person leading the inspection guides the other members of the inspection team through the artifact to uncover any faults. It is not the task of the team to correct faults, merely to record them for later correction. There are four reasons for this:

- A correction produced by a committee (that is, the inspection team) within the time constraints of the inspection is likely to be inferior in quality to a correction produced by an individual trained in the necessary techniques.
- A correction produced by an inspection team of (say) five individuals will take at least as much time as a correction produced by one person and, therefore, costs five times as much when the salaries of the five participants are considered.
- Not all items flagged as faults actually are incorrect. In accordance with the dictum, "If it ain't broke, don't fix it," it is better for possible faults to be examined carefully and

then corrected only if there really is a problem, rather than have a team attempt to "fix" something that is completely correct.

- There simply is not enough time in an inspection to both detect and correct faults. No inspection should last longer than two hours. The time should be spent detecting and recording faults, not correcting them.

During an inspection, a person responsible for the artifact, either individually or as part of a team, walks the participants through that artifact (for example, a realization of a use case). The reviewers interrupt when they think they have detected a fault. Interestingly enough, the majority of faults at an inspection are spontaneously detected by the presenter. Time after time, the presenter will pause in the middle of a sentence, his or her face will light up, and a fault, one that has remained hidden despite numerous careful readings of the artifact, suddenly will become obvious. A fruitful field for research by a psychologist would be to determine why verbalization so often leads to fault detection during inspections of all kinds, including requirements inspections, specification inspections, plan inspections, design inspections, and code inspections.

The primary task of the inspection leader is to encourage questions about the artifact being inspected and promote discussion. An inspection is an interactive process; it is not supposed to be a lecture by the presenter. Also, it is absolutely essential that the inspection not be used as a means of evaluating the participants. If that happens, the inspection degenerates into a point-scoring session and does not result in the detection of faults, no matter how well the session leader tries to run it.

The sole aim of an inspection is to highlight faults. Now suppose that the systems analyst on the inspection team (one of the information technology professionals who produced the specification document) knows that his or her next performance evaluation will be based on the quality of the specification document, as perceived by the manager of the analysis team, a fellow member of the inspection team. In other words, if the manager thinks that the specification document has too many faults, the systems analyst is not going to get much of a raise this year.

Under these circumstances, the systems analyst will do everything in his or her power to prevent faults coming to light. After all, the more faults there are in the specification document, the lower the perceived quality of that document and, hence, the lower the performance evaluation (and the next raise) of that systems analyst will be. To counteract this, if a member of the inspection team identifies a fault, the systems analyst will either try to argue that the analysis artifact in question is correct or attempt to blame the fault on someone else. In short, inspections must be used for one purpose and one purpose only: to highlight as many faults as possible.

The manager who is responsible for the artifact being reviewed should be a member of the inspection team. If this manager also is responsible for the annual evaluations of the members of the inspection team (and particularly of the presenter), the fault detection capabilities of the team will be fatally weakened, because the primary motive of the presenter will be to minimize the number of faults that show up. To prevent this conflict of interests, the person responsible for a given workflow should not also be directly responsible for evaluating any member of the inspection team for that workflow.

13.3.2 How Inspections Are Performed

An inspection consists of five steps:

- First, an *overview* of the artifact to be inspected is presented to the team by one of the individuals responsible for producing that artifact. At the end of the overview session, the artifact is distributed to the team members.

- In the second step, *preparation,* the participants try to understand the artifact in detail. Lists of fault types found in recent inspections, with the fault types ranked by frequency, are excellent aids. These lists help team members concentrate on the areas where the most faults have occurred.
- The third step is the *inspection.* To begin, one participant walks through the artifact with the inspection team, ensuring that every item is covered and that every alternative is considered. Then fault finding commences. As stated in the previous section, the purpose is to find and document the faults, not to correct them. Within one day the leader of the inspection team (the *moderator*) must produce a written report of the inspection to ensure meticulous follow-through.
- The fourth stage is the *rework,* in which the individual responsible for that artifact resolves all faults and problems noted in the written report.
- The final stage is the *follow-up.* The moderator must ensure that every single issue raised has been resolved satisfactorily, by either fixing the artifact or clarifying items incorrectly flagged as faults. All fixes must be checked to ensure that no new faults have been introduced. If more than 5 percent of the material inspected has been reworked, then the team must reconvene for a 100 percent reinspection.

An essential component of an inspection is the checklist of potential faults. For example, the checklist for a specification inspection should include items such as these: Is each item of the client's requirements adequately and correctly addressed? Are the client's hardware resources adequate for running the target information system, or does more hardware have be leased or purchased?

An important component of the inspection procedure is the record of fault statistics. Faults must be recorded by severity (major or minor; an example of a major fault is one that would cause the information system to terminate in error or damages a database) and fault type. In the case of a specification inspection, typical fault types include omission faults and logic faults. This information can be used in a number of useful ways:

- The number of faults in a given information system can be compared with averages of faults detected in those same artifact types in comparable information systems, giving management an early warning that something is wrong and allowing timely corrective action to be taken.
- If inspecting (say) the design of two or three modules results in the discovery of a disproportionate number of faults of a particular type in the design artifacts, management can begin checking other modules and take corrective action.
- If the inspection of the detailed design of a particular module reveals far more faults than were found in any other module in the information system, then there usually is a strong case for redesigning that module from scratch.
- Information regarding the number and types of faults detected at a detailed design inspection will aid the team performing the code inspection of the same module at a later stage.

Over the past 25 years, numerous experiments have been conducted on inspections to measure their effectiveness in finding faults, as well as their cost effectiveness. For full details of a wide variety of these experiments, consult Schach [2002]. In summary, the results of experiments on inspections have been overwhelmingly positive. Typically, 75 percent or more of all the faults detected over the lifetime of an information system are detected during inspections before execution-based testing of the modules is started. An experiment conducted at the Jet Propulsion Laboratory (JPL) in Pasadena, California, showed that, on average, each two-hour inspection exposed 4 major faults and 14 minor faults. Translated into dollar terms, this meant a saving of approximately $25,000 *per inspection*. Bearing in mind that the cost of a two-hour inspection by a team of four information technology professionals is about $1,000, the JPL inspections were exceedingly cost effective. Further proof of the cost effectiveness of inspections comes from another experiment at JPL that showed that inspections lead to early detection of faults. The vital importance of earlier detection is reflected in Figure 2.4.

Having discussed nonexecution-based testing, the next topic is execution-based testing.

13.4   Execution-Based Testing

The first Unified Process workflow is the requirements workflow. The artifacts of this workflow are diagrams and documents. Accordingly, the requirements artifacts have to undergo nonexecution-based testing—there is no way that, say, a use-case description could be executed on a computer.

Next comes the analysis workflow. Again the artifacts of this workflow are diagrams and documents, and again nonexecution-based testing is the only alternative.

The third workflow is the design workflow. Yet again the artifacts are diagrams and documents, and yet again these artifacts have to undergo nonexecution-based testing.

Now comes the implementation workflow. Here the programmers translate the design into computer code, which can be executed. Thus, execution-based testing is an important part of the implementation workflow. However, implementation is the responsibility of programmers, not systems analysts. Thus, it would appear that nonexecution-based testing is the responsibility of systems analysts, whereas execution-based testing is solely the province of programmers. However, this is not so.

13.4.1   The Relevance of Execution-Based Testing

Systems analysts need to have knowledge of execution-based testing because not all information systems are developed from scratch. The task of the systems analyst is to determine what the client really needs. In some cases, the client's needs may be met by a COTS package (see Section 1.1) at considerably lower cost than the development of a custom information system from scratch.

Now, in order to determine whether a COTS package is appropriate, the systems analyst has to test it. That is, in order to provide his or her client with adequate information about a COTS package that could possibly meet the client's needs, the systems analyst has to know about execution-based testing.

Programming is not a prerequisite for this book. Accordingly, the material presented in the remainder of this chapter has been written in such a way that the essentials of execution-based testing can be appreciated without actually doing it.

13.4.2   Principles of Execution-Based Testing

It has been claimed that testing is a demonstration that faults are not present. Even though some organizations spend 50 percent or more of their information system budget on testing, delivered "tested" information systems are notoriously unreliable. The reason for this contradiction is simple: Execution-based testing can be used to show the presence of faults, but it can never be used to show their absence.

For example, suppose we take an information system and run it with a specific set of test data. If the output is wrong, then the information system definitely contains a fault. But, if the output is correct, then there still may be a fault in the information system; the only conclusion we can deduce from that particular test is that the information system runs correctly on that specific set of test data.

In other words, if we choose our test data cleverly, we should be able to highlight faults. But if we choose poorly, we will learn nothing about the information system.

We now examine test cases for execution-based testing.

13.5   The Two Basic Types of Test Cases

When execution-based testing is performed, two basic types of test cases are used. The first type is drawn up by looking at only the specifications. For example, if the specifications state that the information system has to be able to handle three different types of discount, then there needs to be a set of test cases to check that the information system handles each of these three types of discount correctly. Test cases drawn up purely on the basis of the specifications are called *black-box test cases,* because the program is treated as a black box—we do not look inside the "box."

The second basic type of test case is drawn up by carefully examining the code and finding a set of test cases that, when executed, will together ensure that every line of code is executed at least once. These are called *glass-box test cases,* because now we look inside the "box" and examine the code itself to draw up the test cases. (These test cases used to be called *white-box test cases* until someone realized that it is just as hard to see inside a box that is painted white as one that is painted black.)

13.6   What Execution-Based Testing Should Test

Suppose that a systems analyst is considering advising the client to buy a COTS package. Before making a recommendation, the systems analyst needs to test the COTS package. The obvious question is: What should be tested in the course of this execution-based testing? The obvious answer is: correctness—there is no point in buying a COTS package that does not function correctly. However, correctness is by no means enough. There are four other qualities that need to be tested: utility, reliability, robustness, and performance [Goodenough, 1979].

13.6.1   Utility

Utility is the measure of the extent to which an information system meets the user's needs. The systems analyst may test, for example, how easy the information system is to use, whether the information system performs useful functions, and whether the information system is cost effective compared to competing information systems. Irrespective of whether the information system is correct or not, these vital issues have to be tested. If the information system is not cost effective, then there is no point in buying it. And unless the information system is easy to use, it will not be used at all or it will be used incorrectly. Therefore, when considering buying an existing information system (including a COTS package), the utility of the information system should be tested first and, if the information system fails on that score, testing should stop.

13.6.2   Reliability

Another aspect of an information system that must be tested is its reliability. *Reliability* is a measure of the frequency and criticality of information system failure. In other words, it is necessary to know how often the information system fails (*mean time between failures*) and how bad the effects of that failure can be. When an information system fails, an important issue is how long it takes, on average, to repair it (*mean time to repair*). But often more important is how long it takes to repair the results of the failure.

This last point frequently is overlooked. Suppose that an information system fails, on average, only once every six months; but when it fails, it completely wipes out a database. At best the database can be reinitialized to its status when the last checkpoint dump was taken (that is, when the last complete backup copy was made); the audit trail (the list of all transactions that have taken place since the checkpoint dump) can then be used to restore the database to its state before the failure. But, if this recovery process takes the better part of two days, during which time the information system is totally out of action, then the reliability of the information system is low, notwithstanding that the mean time between failures is six months.

13.6.3   Robustness

Another aspect of every information system that requires testing is its robustness. Although it is difficult to come up with a precise definition, *robustness* essentially involves a number of factors, such as the range of operating conditions, the possibility of unacceptable results with valid input, and the acceptability of effects when the information system is given invalid input. For example, when the information system solicits a name, the tester may reply with a stream of unacceptable characters, such as control-A escape-% ?$#. If the computer responds with a message such as Incorrect data—Try again or, better, informs the user as to why the data do not conform to what was expected, it is more robust than an information system that crashes whenever the data deviate even slightly from what is required.

13.6.4   Performance

Performance is another aspect of the information system that must be tested. For example, it is essential to know the extent to which the information system meets its constraints with regard to response time or space requirements. For example, if the specification document states that the average response time has to be under two seconds, then it is necessary to test whether or not that constraint is met.

In the case of information systems, what usually is important is average response time. On the other hand, a hard real-time system is characterized by hard time constraints; that is, time constraints of such a nature that, if a constraint is not met, information is lost. For example, a nuclear reactor control system may have to sample the temperature of the core and process the data every 100th of a second. If the system is not fast enough to be able to handle interrupts from the temperature sensor every 100th of a second, then data will be lost, and there is no way of ever recovering the data; the next time that the system receives temperature data, they will be the current temperature, not the reading that was missed. If the reactor is on the point of a meltdown, then it is critical that all relevant information be both received and processed as laid down in the specification document. With all hard real-time systems, the performance must meet every hard time constraint listed in the specification document. (An insight into one of the challenges of real-time systems was given in Just in Case You Wanted to Know Box 9.1.)

13.6.5   Correctness

An information system is *correct* if it satisfies its specifications. That is another reason why the specification document is so important—without a specification document, there is no way of determining whether an information system is correct. Clearly, every information system has to be correct. But in addition, we need to perform execution-based testing of utility, reliability, robustness, and performance.

13.7 Who Should Perform Execution-Based Testing?

It was explained in Section 13.4.2 that, if a test case executes correctly, we learn nothing. However, if there is a failure, we can immediately deduce that there is a fault, and we can then detect and correct the fault. In other words, when we test, we try to come up with test cases that will highlight faults. Testing is therefore a destructive process.

Now suppose that a programmer is asked to test a module that he or she has implemented. As just stated, testing is a destructive process. On the other hand, the programmer doing the testing ordinarily does not wish to destroy his or her own work. If the attitude of the programmer toward the code is the usual protective one, then the chances of that programmer using test data that will highlight faults is considerably lower than if the major motivation were truly destructive. A programmer who is asked to test a module he or she has implemented is being asked to execute the module in such a way that a failure (incorrect behavior) ensues. This goes against the creative instincts of programmers.

An inescapable conclusion is that programmers should not test their own modules. After a programmer has been *con*structive and constructed a module, testing that module requires the creator to perform a *de*structive act and attempt to destroy that creation. A second reason why execution-based testing should be done by someone else is that the programmer may have misunderstood some aspect of the design or specification document. If testing is done by someone else, such faults may be discovered. Nevertheless, debugging (finding the fault that is the cause of the failure and correcting the fault) is best done by the original programmer, the person most familiar with the code.

The statement that a programmer should not test his or her own code must not be taken too far. Consider the programming process. The programmer begins by reading the detailed design of the module. Then the programmer *desk checks* the design. That is, seated at his or her desk, the programmer traces through the detailed design with various test cases to check that each test case is executed correctly. When the programmer is satisfied that the detailed design is correct, he or she translates the module into the appropriate programming language.

Then the programmer executes the module using test data, probably the same test data that were used to desk check the design. Next, if the module executes correctly when correct test data are used, the programmer tries out incorrect data to test the robustness of the module. When the programmer is satisfied that the module is operating correctly, systematic execution-based testing commences. It is this *systematic testing* that should not be performed by the programmer.

If the programmer is not to perform this systematic testing, who is to do it? As stated in Section 13.2.3, independent testing must be performed by the quality assurance group. The key word here is *independent*. Only if the quality assurance group truly is independent of the development team can its members fulfill their mission of ensuring that the information system indeed satisfies its specifications, without development managers applying pressures such as deadlines that might hamper the work of the quality assurance group. Quality assurance professionals must report to their own managers and thus protect their independence.

How is systematic execution-based testing performed? An essential part of a test case is a statement of the expected output before the test is executed. It is a complete waste of time for the tester to sit at a terminal, execute the module, enter haphazard test data, and then peer at the screen and say, "I guess that looks right." Equally futile is for the tester to plan test cases with great care and execute each test case in turn, look at the output, and say, "Yes, that certainly looks right." It is far too easy to be fooled by plausible results. If programmers

A successful test is one that highlights a fault. That means that if a module passes a test, then the test has failed. Conversely, if the module fails the test, then the test has succeeded!

FIGURE 13.1

The Testing Techniques Described in This Chapter
The number of the section in which each is presented appears in parentheses

---

Nonexecution-Based Testing (13.3)

Inspections (13.3.1–13.3.2)

Execution-Based Testing (13.4–13.7)

Black-box test cases (13.5)
Glass-box test cases (13.5)
What execution-based testing should test (13.6)
      Utility (13.6.1)
      Reliability (13.6.2)
      Robustness (13.6.3)
      Performance (13.6.4)
      Correctness (13.6.5)
Who should perform execution-based testing (13.7)

---

are allowed to test their own code, then there always is the danger that the programmer will see what he or she wants to see. The same danger can occur even when the testing is done by someone else. The solution is for management to insist that, before a test is performed, both the test data and the expected results of that test be recorded. After the test has been performed, the actual results should be recorded and compared with the expected results.

Even in small organizations and with small information systems, it is important that this recording be done in machine-readable form, because test cases should never be thrown away. The reason for this is maintenance. While the information system is being maintained, *regression testing* must be performed. Stored test cases that the information system has previously executed correctly must be rerun to ensure that the modifications made to add new functionality to the information system have not destroyed the information system's existing functionality. That is, it is vital to determine that no regression faults (Section 2.4) have been induced.

Figure 13.1 summarizes the testing techniques presented in this chapter. It includes the section in which each is described.

13.8 When Testing Stops

After an information system has been successfully maintained for many years, it eventually may lose its usefulness and be superseded by a totally different information system, in much the same way that the horse and buggy was replaced by the automobile. So, finally, the information system is decommissioned and removed from service. Only at that point, when the information system has been irrevocably discarded, is it time to stop testing.

For an amusing final thought about testing, look at Just in Case You Wanted to Know Box 13.4.

Key Terms

black-box test case, *252*
bug, *246*
correctness, *253*
desk check, *254*
error, *246*
execution-based
   testing, *244*
failure, *246*
fault, *246*
glass-box test case, *252*

inspection, *248*
managerial independence, *246*
mean time between
   failures, *252*
mean time to repair, *253*
moderator, *250*
nonexecution-based
   testing, *244*
performance, *253*
quality, *245*

regression testing, *255*
reliability, *252*
robustness, *253*
systematic testing, *254*
testing, *244*
utility, *252*
V & V, *244*
validation, *244*
verification, *244*
white-box test case, *252*

Review Questions for Chapter 13

1. Distinguish between verification and validation.
2. Distinguish between execution-based testing and nonexecution-based testing.
3. Define *quality* within the information system context.
4. Why should we not use the word *bug*?
5. Distinguish between an error, a fault, and a failure.
6. Why is managerial independence between the development team and the quality assurance group so important?
7. What principles underlie inspections by a team?
8. Why should an inspection team detect faults but not correct them?
9. What are the five steps of an inspection?
10. What five qualities of an information system should be tested?
11. Who should perform execution-based testing?
12. When can testing of an information system stop?

Problems

13.1   How are the terms *verification* and *validation* used in this book?

13.2   An information system development organization currently employs 83 information technology professionals, including 17 managers, all of whom do development as well as testing of information systems. Latest figures show that 28 percent of their time is spent on testing. The average annual cost to the company of a manager is $140,000, whereas nonmanagerial professionals cost $104,000 a year on average; both figures include overhead. How much would it cost to set up a separate quality assurance group within the organization?

13.3   Repeat the calculation of Problem 13.2 for a firm with only seven information technology professionals, including two managers. Assume that the other figures remain unchanged.

13.4   You are a member of the quality assurance group at Ye Olde Fashioned Information Systems Organization. You suggest to your manager that inspections be introduced. He responds that he sees no reason why four people should waste their time looking for faults when one person can run test cases on the same piece of code. How do you respond?

13.5   You are the quality assurance manager at Tex–Tenn Taxes, a tax preparation franchise with 154 branches, all in Texas and Tennessee. The owners of the franchise are considering buying a new type of tax preparation package for use throughout the organization. Before authorizing the purchase of the package, you decide to test it thoroughly. What properties of the package do you investigate?

13.6   All 154 branches of Tex–Tenn Taxes are now to be connected by a communications network. A representative offers you a four-week free trial to experiment with the communications package he is trying to sell. What sort of tests would you perform and why?

13.7   You are a major general of the army of the Republic of Mowbray in charge of developing an information system that stores the current addresses and contact telephone numbers of reservists so that they can be quickly called up in the event of an emergency. The information system has been delivered to you for acceptance testing. What properties of the information system do you test?

Term Project

13.8 Explain how you would test the utility, reliability, robustness, performance, and correctness of the Chocoholics Anonymous information system of Appendix A.

13.9 (Knowledge of programming needed) Construct a set of test data for your implementation of the Chocoholics Anonymous term project of Appendix A. Check that your implementation executes each test case correctly, modifying the source code and other relevant artifacts, if needed.

References

Boehm, B. W. "Verifying and Validating Software Requirements and Design Specifications." *IEEE Software* 1 (January 1984), pp. 75–88.

Garman, J. R. "The 'Bug' Heard 'Round the World." *ACM SIGSOFT Software Engineering Notes* 6 (October 1981), pp. 3–10.

Goodenough, J. B. "A Survey of Program Testing Issues." In *Research Directions in Software Technology,* ed. P. Wegner, pp. 316–40. Cambridge, MA: The MIT Press, 1979.

Institute of Electrical and Electronic Engineers. "A Glossary of Software Engineering Terminology." IEEE 610.12-1990, New York: IEEE, 1990.

Josephson, M. *Edison, A Biography*. New York: John Wiley & Sons, 1992.

Leveson, N. G., and C. S. Turner. "An Investigation of the Therac-25 Accidents." *IEEE Computer* 26 (July 1993), pp. 18–41.

Mellor, P. "CAD: Computer-Aided Disaster." Technical Report, Centre for Software Reliability, City University, London, UK, July 1994.

Neumann, P. G. Letter from the Editor. *ACM SIGSOFT Software Engineering Notes* 5 (July 1980), p. 2.

Schach, S. R. *Object-Oriented and Classical Software Engineering*. 5th ed. New York: WCB/McGraw-Hill, 2002.

Shapiro, F. R. "The First Bug." *Byte* 19 (April 1994), p. 308.

Chapter 14

Management Issues

Learning Objectives

After studying this chapter, you should be able to:

- Appreciate some of the skills needed for managing information systems.
- Describe how to perform cost–benefit analysis.
- Appreciate the importance of risk analysis and the role it plays in the Unified Process.
- Describe process improvement initiatives, especially CMM.
- Understand CPM/PERT charts.
- Describe how to promote reuse.
- Describe how to promote portability.

Successful management of the development of an information system requires a broad range of skills. These skills form the subject of this chapter.

14.1 Cost–Benefit Analysis

It is poor business practice to develop an information system that is not cost effective. To put it bluntly, it is not a good idea to develop a new information system if it is going to cost $1 million but is going to save the client only $5,000 per year.

There are a number of different approaches to deciding whether a particular proposed course of action will be cost effective. One of the most popular techniques is to compare estimated future benefits against projected future costs. This is termed *cost–benefit analysis*.

As an example of cost–benefit analysis within the information system context, consider how Krag Central Electric Company (KCEC) decided in 1965 whether or not to computerize its billing system. Billing was being done manually by 80 clerks who mailed bills every two months to KCEC customers. Computerization would require KCEC to buy or lease the necessary information system and the hardware on which to run it, including data-capture equipment for recording the input data on punch cards or magnetic tape.

One advantage of computerization would be that bills could be mailed monthly instead of every two months, thereby improving the company's cash flow considerably. Furthermore, the 80 billing clerks would be replaced by 11 data-capture clerks. Salary savings were estimated to be $1,575,000 and improved cash flow was projected to be worth $875,000. The total benefits, therefore, were estimated at $2.45 million. On the other hand, a complete data processing department would have to be set up, staffed by well-paid computer professionals. Over a seven-year period, costs were estimated as follows. The cost of the information system itself and the hardware on which it would run, including maintenance, was estimated to be $1.25 million. In the first year, there would be a conversion cost of $350,000, and the cost of explaining the new system to customers was estimated at an additional $125,000. Total costs were estimated at $1,725,000, about $750,000 less than the estimated benefits. KCEC immediately decided to computerize.

Cost–benefit analysis is not always straightforward. On the one hand, a management consultant can estimate salary savings, an accountant can project cash flow improvements, net present value (NPV) can be used to handle the change in the cost of money, and an information technology consultant can estimate the costs of hardware, information system, and conversion. But how are we to determine the cost of dealing with customers trying to adjust to computerization? Or how can we measure the benefits of inoculating an entire population against measles?

The point is that tangible benefits are easy to measure, but intangible benefits can be hard to quantify directly. A practical way of assigning a dollar value to intangible benefits is to make *assumptions*. These assumptions always must be stated in conjunction with the resulting estimates of the benefits. After all, managers have to make decisions. If no data are available, then making assumptions from which such data can be determined usually is the best that can be done under the circumstances. This approach has the further advantage that, if someone else reviewing the data and the underlying assumptions can come up with better assumptions, then better data can be produced and the associated intangible benefits can be computed more accurately. The same technique can be used for intangible costs.

Cost–benefit analysis is a fundamental technique in deciding whether a client should computerize his or her business and, if so, in what way. The costs and benefits of various alternative strategies are compared. For example, an information system for storing the results of drug trials can be implemented in a number of different ways, including a variety of database management systems (Chapter 19). For each possible strategy, the costs and benefits are computed and the one for which the difference between benefits and costs is the largest is selected as the optimal strategy.

14.2 Risk Analysis

A *risk* is an event or condition that can cause the delivery of an information system to be canceled, delayed, or over budget or not to meet its requirements. We have encountered a number of examples of risks earlier in the book, including the following:

- There is always the risk that a completed information system will not meet its time constraints. We encountered this risk in the Winburg mini case study (Section 2.2), where the original image recognition algorithm was not fast enough.
- The moving target problem (Section 2.4) can lead to widespread changes in the product while the project is underway, with the risk of time and cost overruns.
- In Section 7.13 it was pointed out that a major risk in developing a new information system is that the delivered information system will not meet the client's real needs.
- Section 9.2.1 contains a list of typical risks of the inception phase. These include the risk that the team who will develop the proposed information system may not have the necessary expertise; the hardware may not be delivered in time; the CASE tools may not be available or may not have all the necessary functionality; or a COTS package with the functionality of the proposed custom information system may be put on the market while the project is underway.

However, merely listing the risks in a project is just the first step. *Risk management* is the process of determining what the risks are and then attempting to *mitigate* them. In other words, first we identify each risk and then we try to minimize its impact.

- For example, in Section 9.2.1, we pointed out that one way of mitigating the risk that part of a proposed information system will not work is to build a proof-of-concept prototype. We may build such a proof-of-concept prototype to determine whether a particular computation can be performed quickly enough, or whether the lettering on a screen will be large enough for the average user to read without eyestrain.
- A common risk is that the development team will not have the necessary skills for a particular aspect of the project. This risk can be mitigated by providing training in the relevant area.

Risks are like diseases. Sometimes they go away spontaneously. They often get better or worse without intervention. Minor ones merely need to be watched, but major ones need to be cured (mitigated).

Accordingly, we need to maintain a *risk list*. For each risk on the list, the following items are recorded:

- A description of the risk.
- The priority of the risk (critical, significant, or routine). The priority of a risk can change, in either direction.
- The way the project is impacted by the risk.
- The name of the person responsible for monitoring the risk.
- The action to be taken if the risk materializes.

Risk analysis is an integral part of the Unified Process [Jacobson, Booch, and Rumbaugh, 1999]. We have previously described the Unified Process as use-case driven, but it is equally risk driven:

- During the inception phase, as previously described in Section 9.2.1, the risk list is drawn up and we attempt to mitigate the critical risks. Also, the use cases are prioritized according to their associated risks.
- During the elaboration phase (Section 9.2.2), the risks are monitored and the risk list is updated, particularly with regard to the priorities of the remaining risks.
- During the construction phase (Section 9.2.3), the risk list is again updated.
- During the transition phase (Section 9.2.4), it is important to try to discover any previously unidentified risks.

Finally, risk analysis does not terminate when the product is delivered to the client. On the contrary, the risk list needs to be maintained over the entire life cycle of the product.

14.3   Improving the Process

Our global economy is critically dependent on computers and hence on information systems. For this reason, the governments of many countries are concerned about the *process* whereby information systems are developed; that is, the activities, techniques, and tools used to produce information systems. For example, in 1987 a task force of the U.S. Department of Defense reported: "After two decades of largely unfulfilled promises about productivity and quality gains from applying new software methodologies and technologies, industry and government organizations are realizing that their fundamental problem is the inability to manage the software process" [Brooks et al., 1987].

In response to this and related concerns, the Department of Defense founded the *Software Engineering Institute* and set it up at Carnegie Mellon University in Pittsburgh on the basis of a competitive procurement process. One of the major successes of the Software Engineering Institute has been the capability maturity model (CMM) initiative. Related process improvement efforts include the ISO 9000-series standards of the International Standards Organization and ISO/IEC 15504, an international software improvement initiative involving more than 40 countries. We begin by describing CMM.

14.3.1 Capability Maturity Models

The *capability maturity models* (*CMMs*) of the Software Engineering Institute are a related group of strategies for improving the process for developing information systems, irrespective of the actual life-cycle model used. (The term *maturity* is a measure of the goodness of the process itself.) The Software Engineering Institute has developed CMMs for software (SW–CMM), for management of human resources (P–CMM; the *P* stands for "people"), for systems engineering (SE–CMM), for integrated product development (IPD–CMM), and for software acquisition (SA–CMM). There are some inconsistencies between the models and an inevitable level of redundancy. Accordingly, in 1997 it was decided to develop a single integrated framework for maturity models, capability maturity model integration (CMMI). Four of these five existing capability maturity models have been integrated into CMMI, and SA–CMM is due to be incorporated later. Additional disciplines may be added in the future.

For reasons of space, only one capability maturity model, SW–CMM, is presented here. SW–CMM was first put forward in 1986 by Watts Humphrey [1989]. It incorporates both technical and managerial aspects of the development of an information system. Underlying the SW–CMM is the belief that the use of new techniques in itself will not result in increased productivity and profitability, because our problems are caused by how we manage the process. The strategy of the SW–CMM is to improve the management of the process in the belief that improvements in techniques will be a natural consequence. The resulting improvement in the process as a whole should result in better-quality information systems and fewer information system projects that suffer from time and cost overruns.

Bearing in mind that improvements in the process cannot occur overnight, the SW–CMM induces change incrementally. More specifically, five different levels of maturity are defined, and an organization advances slowly in a series of small evolutionary steps toward the higher levels of process maturity. To understand this approach, the five levels now are described.

Maturity Level 1: Initial Level   At this the lowest level, essentially no sound information system management practices are in place in the organization. Instead, everything is done on an ad hoc basis. A specific project that happens to be staffed by a competent manager and a good information system development team may be successful. However, the usual pattern is time and cost overruns caused by a lack of sound management in general and planning in particular. As a result, most activities are responses to crises rather than preplanned tasks. In level 1 organizations, the process is unpredictable, because it depends totally on the current information technology professionals; as the professionals change, so does the process. As a consequence, it is impossible to predict with any accuracy such important items as the time it will take to develop an information system or the cost of that information system.

It is unfortunate that the vast majority of information system development organizations all over the world are still level 1 organizations.

Maturity Level 2: Repeatable Level   At this level, basic information system project management practices are in place. Planning and management techniques are based on experience with similar information systems; hence, the name repeatable. At level 2, measurements are taken, an essential first step in achieving an adequate process. Typical measurements include the careful tracking of costs and schedules. Instead of functioning in crisis mode as in level 1, managers identify problems as they arise and take immediate corrective action to prevent them from becoming crises. The key point is that, without measurements, it is impossible to detect problems before they get out of hand. Also, measurements taken during one project can be used to draw up realistic duration and cost schedules for future projects.

Maturity Level 3: Defined Level   At level 3, the process for information system development is fully documented. Both the managerial and technical aspects of the process are clearly defined, and continual efforts are made to improve the process wherever possible. Inspections (Section 13.2) are used to achieve information system quality. At this level, it makes sense to introduce new technology such as CASE environments (Section 11.7) to increase quality and productivity further. In contrast, "high tech" only makes the crisis-driven level 1 process even more chaotic.

Although a number of organizations have attained maturity levels 2 and 3, not many have reached levels 4 or 5. For most companies, therefore, the two highest levels are targets for the future.

Maturity Level 4: Managed Level   A level 4 organization sets quality and productivity goals for each project. These two quantities are measured continually and corrective action is taken when there are unacceptable deviations from the goal. Statistical quality controls [Deming, 1986] are in place to enable management to distinguish a random deviation from a meaningful violation of quality or productivity standards. (A simple example of a statistical quality control measure is the number of faults detected per 1,000 lines of code. A corresponding objective is to reduce this quantity over time.)

Maturity Level 5: Optimizing Level   The goal of a level 5 organization is continuous process improvement. Statistical quality and process control techniques are used to guide the organization. The knowledge gained from each project is utilized in future projects. The process thus incorporates a positive feedback loop, resulting in a steady improvement in productivity and quality.

These five maturity levels are summarized in Figure 14.1. To improve its process, an organization first attempts to gain an understanding of its current process, then formulates the intended process. Next, actions that will achieve this process improvement are determined and ranked in priority. Finally, a plan to accomplish this improvement is drawn up and executed. This series of steps then is repeated, with the organization successively improving its process; this progression from level to level is reflected in Figure 14.1. Experience with

FIGURE 14.1
The Five Levels of the Capability Maturity Model

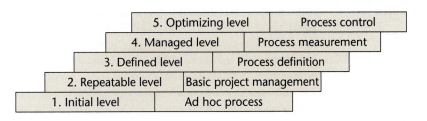

the capability maturity model has shown that advancing a complete maturity level usually takes from 18 months to three years, but moving from level 1 to level 2 can sometimes take up to five years. This is a reflection of how difficult it is to instill a methodical approach in an organization that up to now has functioned on a purely ad hoc and reactive basis.

For each maturity level, the Software Engineering Institute has highlighted a series of *key process areas* that an organization should target in its endeavor to reach the next maturity level. For example, the key process areas for level 2 (repeatable level) include configuration control (Chapter 11), quality assurance (Chapter 12), project planning (Chapter 14), project tracking (Chapter 14), and requirements management (Chapters 4 and 5). These areas cover the basic elements of information system management: Determine the client's needs (requirements management), draw up a plan (project planning), monitor deviations from that plan (project tracking), control the various pieces that make up the information system (configuration management), and ensure that the information system is fault free (quality assurance). Within each key process area is a group of between two and four related goals that, if achieved, result in the next maturity level being attained. For example, one project planning goal is the development of a plan that appropriately and realistically covers the activities of information system development.

At the highest level, maturity level 5, the key process areas include fault prevention, technology innovation, and process change management. Comparing the key process areas of the two levels, it is clear that a level 5 organization is far in advance of one at level 2. For example, a level 2 organization is concerned with quality assurance, that is, with detecting and correcting faults (information system quality is discussed in more detail in Chapter 12). In contrast, the process of a level 5 organization incorporates fault prevention; that is, trying to ensure that no faults are in the information system in the first place. To aid an organization to reach the higher maturity levels, the Software Engineering Institute has developed a series of questionnaires that form the basis for an assessment by a Software Engineering Institute team. The purpose of the assessment is to highlight current shortcomings in the organization's process and to indicate ways in which the organization can improve its process.

The CMM program of the Software Engineering Institute was sponsored by the U.S. Department of Defense. One of the original goals of the CMM program was to raise the quality of defense software by evaluating the processes of contractors who produce systems for the Department of Defense and awarding contracts to those contractors who demonstrate a mature process. The U.S. Air Force stipulated that any system development organization that wished to be an Air Force contractor had to conform to SW–CMM level 3 by 1998, and the Department of Defense as a whole subsequently issued a similar directive. Thus, pressure is put on organizations to improve the maturity of their process. However, the SW–CMM program has moved far beyond the limited goal of improving Department of Defense software and is being implemented by a wide variety of information system development organizations that wish to improve quality and productivity.

14.3.2 Other Process Improvement Initiatives

A different attempt to improve information system quality is based on the *International Standards Organization* (ISO) 9000-series standards, a series of five related standards applicable to a wide variety of industrial activities, including design, development, production, installation, and servicing; *ISO 9000* certainly is not just an information system standard. Within the ISO 9000 series, standard ISO 9001 for quality systems [ISO, 1987] is the standard most applicable to information system development. Because of the broadness of ISO 9001, ISO has published specific guidelines to assist in applying ISO 9001 to information systems: ISO 9000-3 [ISO, 1991].

ISO 9000 is by no means the same thing as CMM. ISO 9000 stresses documenting the process in both words and pictures in order to ensure consistency and comprehensibility. Also, the ISO 9000 philosophy is that adherence to the standard does not guarantee a high-quality information system but rather reduces the risk of a poor-quality information system. ISO 9000 is only part of a quality system. Also required are management commitment to quality, intensive training of workers, and setting and achieving goals for continual quality improvement.

ISO 9000-series standards have been adopted by over 60 countries, including the United States, Japan, Canada, and the countries of the European Union. This means, for example, that if a U.S. information system development organization wishes to do business with a European client, the U.S. organization must first be certified as ISO 9000 compliant. A certified registrar (auditor) has to examine the company's process and certify that its process complies with the ISO standard.

Following their European counterparts, more and more U.S. organizations are requiring ISO 9000 certification. For example, General Electric Plastic Division insisted that 340 vendors achieve the standard by June 1993 [Dawood, 1994]. It is unlikely that the U.S. government will follow the lead of the European Union and require ISO 9000 compliance for non-U.S. companies that wish to do business with organizations in the United States. Nevertheless, pressures both within the United States and from its major trading partners ultimately may result in significant worldwide ISO 9000 compliance.

ISO/IEC 15504 is an international process improvement initiative, like ISO 9000. The initiative was formerly known as *SPICE,* an acronym formed from Software Process Improvement Capability dEtermination. Over 40 countries actively contributed to the SPICE endeavor. SPICE was initiated by the British Ministry of Defence with the long-term aim of establishing SPICE as an international standard (the Ministry of Defence is the U.K. counterpart of the U.S. Department of Defense, which initiated the CMM). The first version of SPICE was completed in 1995. In July 1997, the SPICE initiative was taken over by a joint committee of the International Standards Organization and the International Electrotechnical Commission. For this reason, the name of the initiative was changed from SPICE to ISO/IEC 15504, or 15504 for short.

14.3.3   Costs and Benefits of Process Improvement

Does implementing information system process improvement lead to increased profitability? Preliminary results indicate that this indeed is the case. For example, the Software Engineering Division of Hughes Aircraft in Fullerton, California, spent nearly $500,000 between 1987 and 1990 for assessments and improvement programs. During this three-year period, Hughes Aircraft moved up from maturity level 2 to level 3, with every expectation of future improvement to level 4 and even level 5. As a consequence of improving its process, Hughes Aircraft estimates its annual savings to be of the order of $2 million. These savings have accrued in a number of ways, including decreased overtime hours, fewer crises, improved employee morale, and lower turnover of information technology professionals [Humphrey, Snider, and Willis, 1991]. Comparable results have been reported at other organizations. For example, the Equipment Division at Raytheon moved from level 1 in 1988 to level 3 in 1993. A twofold increase in productivity has resulted, as well as a return of $7.70 for every dollar invested in the process improvement effort [Dion, 1993].

As a consequence of published studies such as those described in this section and many others [Schach, 2002], more and more organizations worldwide are realizing that process improvement is cost effective.

14.3.4 CMM and CASE

As pointed out in Section 11.9, many CASE environments essentially automate a manual process. So, if an organization selects an environment that enforces a process that is not appropriate for that organization, then use of that CASE environment would be counterproductive.

A worse situation occurs when an organization at CMM level 1 or 2 uses a CASE environment. Of course, every organization should use CASE tools, and there generally is little harm in using a workbench. However, an environment imposes an automated process on an organization that uses it. If an appropriate process is being used, that is, the organization is at level 3 or higher, then use of the environment will assist in all aspects of information system production by automating that process. But if the organization is at the crisis-driven level 1 or even at level 2, then no process as such is in place. Automation of this nonexistent process, that is, the introduction of a CASE environment (as opposed to a CASE tool or CASE workbench), can lead only to chaos.

The next management technique is the use of metrics to monitor and control the process.

14.4 Metrics

A key point of Section 14.3.1 is that measurements (or *metrics*) are essential if we wish to detect problems early in the information system process, before they get out of hand. Metrics thus can serve as an early warning system for potential problems. A wide variety of metrics can be used. For example, *lines of code* (*LOC*) is one way of measuring the size of an information system. If LOC measurements are taken at regular intervals, they provide a measure of how fast the project is progressing. In addition, the number of faults per 1,000 lines of code is a measure of information system quality. After all, it is of little use if a programmer consistently turns out 2,000 lines of code a month but half of them have to be thrown away because they are unacceptable. Thus, LOC in isolation is not a very meaningful metric.

Once the information system has been installed on the client's computer, a metric such as mean time between failures provides management with an indication of its reliability. If a certain information system fails every other day, its quality is clearly lower than that of a similar information system that on average runs for nine months without a failure.

Certain metrics can be applied throughout the information system life cycle. For example, for each workflow and for each phase, we can measure the effort in person-months (one person-month is the amount of work done by one person in one month). Personnel turnover is another important metric. High turnover will adversely affect current projects because it takes time for a new employee to learn the relevant facts about the project (Brooks's Law—Section 12.1). In addition, new employees may have to be trained in aspects of the information system methodology; if new employees are less educated in information system development than the individuals they replace, then the project as a whole may suffer. Of course, cost is an essential metric that also must be monitored continually throughout the entire life cycle.

A number of different metrics are described in this book. Some are *product metrics;* that is, they measure some aspect of the information system itself, such as its size or its reliability. In contrast, others are *process metrics;* these metrics are used by the developers to deduce information about their development process. A typical metric of this kind is the efficiency of fault detection during development; that is, the ratio of the number of faults detected during development to the total number of faults detected in the information system over its lifetime.

Many metrics are specific to a given phase or workflow. For example, lines of code cannot be used before implementation begins, and the number of faults detected per hour in specification inspections is relevant to only the analysis workflow.

A cost is involved in gathering the data needed to compute the values of metrics. Even if the data gathering is fully automated, the CASE tool (Chapter 11) that accumulates the required information is not free, and interpreting the output from the tool consumes human resources. Bearing in mind that hundreds (if not thousands) of different metrics have been put forward, an obvious question is, What should an information system organization measure? There are five essential, fundamental metrics:

- Size (in lines of code or, better, in a more meaningful metric such as those of Section 15.2.1).
- Cost (in dollars).
- Duration (in months).
- Effort (in person-months).
- Quality (number of faults detected).

Each of these metrics must be measured by phase or workflow. On the basis of the data from these fundamental metrics, management can identify problems within the information system organization, such as high fault rates during the design workflow, or code output that is well below the industry average. Once problem areas have been highlighted, a strategy to correct these problems can be put into place. To monitor the success of this strategy, more detailed metrics can be introduced. For example, it may be deemed appropriate to collect data on fault rates of each programmer or to conduct a survey of user satisfaction. Thus, in addition to the five fundamental metrics, more detailed data gathering and analysis should be performed only toward a specific objective.

14.5   CPM/PERT

While developing an information system, more general types of management information are also needed. An example of this is *critical path management* (*CPM*), otherwise known as *program evaluation review techniques* (*PERT*).

Many hundreds of activities have to be performed in the course of developing an information system, such as projecting cash flow or checking that the user manual is an accurate reflection of the current version of the information system. Some activities have to precede others; for instance, a module cannot be coded until it has been designed. Other activities can be carried on in parallel. For example, implementation of the various modules can be assigned to different members of the programming team.

Suppose that two activities are started at the same time and can be performed in parallel, but that both have to be completed before proceeding with the project as a whole. If the first takes 12 days, while the second needs only 3 days, then the first activity is critical. Any delay in the first activity will cause the project as a whole to be delayed. However, the second activity can be delayed up to 9 days without adversely impacting the project; there is a *slack* of 9 days associated with the second activity. When using PERT/CPM, the manager inputs the activities, their estimated durations, and any precedence relations, that is, the activities that have to be completed before a specific activity can be started. The PERT/CPM package then will determine which of the hundreds of activities are critical, and it will also compute the slack for each of the noncritical activities. Most packages also print out a PERT chart showing the precedence relationships between the activities and

FIGURE 14.2 **A PERT Chart Showing Estimated Durations of the Activities and the Critical Path**

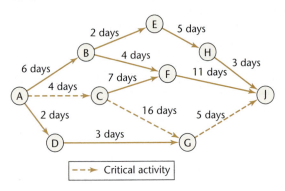

FIGURE 14.3 **The Updated PERT Chart of Figure 14.2 at Day 17**
The actual durations of completed activities are <u>underlined</u>

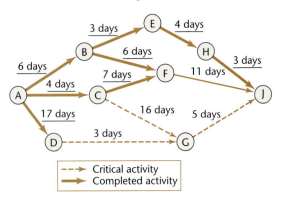

highlighting the *critical path,* the path through the chart that consists of critical activities only. If any activity on the critical path is delayed, then so is the project as a whole.

A simple PERT chart is shown in Figure 14.2. There are 12 activities and 9 milestones. (A *milestone* is an event used to measure progress, such as the completion of an activity or set of activities.) Starting with milestone A, activities AB, AC, and AD can be started in parallel. Activity FJ cannot be started until both BF and CF are finished. The project as a whole is complete when activities HJ, FJ, and GJ are all complete. Completing the whole project will take at least 25 days. The critical path is ACGJ; if any one of the critical activities, namely, AC, CG, or GJ, is delayed in any way, the project as a whole will be delayed. On the other hand, if activity AD is delayed by up to 15 days, the project as a whole will not be delayed, because there is a slack of 15 days associated with activity AD.

Now suppose that activity AD is in fact delayed by 15 days. The situation at day 17 is shown in Figure 14.3. Actual durations of completed activities are underlined; activities that have been completed cannot be critical. There are now two critical paths, and activity DG has become critical. In other words, simply printing out a PERT chart showing the expected duration of each activity is in itself of little use. Data regarding actual durations must be input continually, and the PERT chart updated.

An important issue is: Who is responsible for the continual updating of the PERT data? After all, unless the information for the PERT chart is up to the minute, management will be unable to determine which activities are currently critical and take appropriate action. What is needed is for all the information system development tools to be integrated, and for information of all kinds, including source code, designs, documentation, contracts, and management information, to be stored in an information system development database. The CASE tool that generates the PERT chart can then obtain its information directly from the database. In other words, what is needed is a CASE environment, as explained in Chapter 11.

For more information on PERT, see Just in Case You Wanted to Know Box 14.1.

14.6 Choice of Programming Language

In most cases, the issue of which programming language management should choose for the implementation simply does not arise. Suppose the client wants an information system to be implemented in, say, *Smalltalk,* an early object-oriented programming language that was used for implementing some information systems around 1990. Perhaps, in the opinion

PERT was developed in 1957 by the U.S. Navy to plan and schedule the development of the Polaris missiles. When applied to the missile program, the technique was found to yield overly optimistic results, and the missiles were delivered late. Afterwards it was discovered that the PERT network had many paths that were almost critical. When some of the activities on the almost-critical paths had actual durations that were longer than predicted, those paths then became critical. The project managers had concentrated their efforts on ensuring that the original critical activities would be completed on time. The project as a whole was then slowed by the newly critical activities that had not received the same managerial monitoring as the original critical activities.

The solution to this problem is to replace the single value for a predicted duration by an appropriate statistical distribution. Then the PERT network is simulated. For each simulation run, the value of the duration will be a random value selected from the distribution, rather than a fixed value as before. The critical activities flagged in each simulation run are recorded. Any activity that is flagged as critical in a large percentage of the runs is then closely monitored by management; such an activity has a high probability of turning out to be critical in the actual project. This statistical technique yields more accurate predictions than deciding which activities are critical on the basis of a single estimated duration.

---

of the development team, Smalltalk is entirely unsuitable for the information system. Such an opinion is irrelevant to the client. Management of the development organization has only two choices: implement the information system in Smalltalk or turn down the job.

A more common situation is that all the client's existing information systems have been implemented in, say, C++. The client organization has a large information system division, staffed by able C++ programmers as well as systems analysts with considerable experience in C++. Under these circumstances there is no alternative. Any new information system will surely be implemented in C++.

From the business viewpoint, a more interesting question is this: The contract specifies that an information system is to be implemented in "the most suitable" programming language. What language should be chosen? To answer this question, consider the following mini case study. For over 25 years, QQQ Corporation has been developing information systems in *COBOL,* the world's most widely used programming language (see *Just in Case You Wanted to Know* Box 14.2). The entire 200-member technical staff of QQQ Corporation, from the most junior programmer to the vice president for information system development, has COBOL expertise. How could the most suitable programming language be anything but COBOL? The introduction of a new language, Java, for example, would mean having to hire new programmers or, at the very least, existing staff would have to be intensively retrained in a totally different language. Having invested all that money and effort in Java training, management might well decide that future information systems also should be implemented in Java. Nevertheless, all the existing COBOL information systems would have to be maintained. There then would be two classes of programmers: COBOL maintenance programmers and Java programmers developing the new information systems. Quite undeservedly, maintenance almost always is considered inferior to developing new information systems, so there would be distinct unhappiness among the ranks of the COBOL programmers. This unhappiness would be compounded by the fact that Java programmers usually are paid more than COBOL programmers because Java programmers are in short supply. Although QQQ Corporation has excellent development tools for COBOL, a Java

Far more code has been implemented in COBOL than all other programming languages put together. Surveys conducted around 1998 to estimate the effort needed to fix all Y2K-noncompliant code showed that between 60 and 80 percent of all code used at that time was written in COBOL [McClendon, 2002].

COBOL is the most widely used language primarily because COBOL is a product of the U.S. Department of Defense. Developed under the direction of the late Rear Admiral Grace Murray Hopper, COBOL was approved by the Department of Defense in 1960. Thereafter, the Department of Defense would not buy hardware for running information systems unless that hardware had a COBOL compiler [Sammet, 1978]. The Department of Defense was, and still is, the world's largest purchaser of computer hardware; and in the 1960s, a considerable proportion of Department of Defense software was written for information systems. As a result, COBOL compilers were constructed as a matter of urgency for virtually every computer. This widespread availability of COBOL, at a time when the only alternative language usually was assembler, resulted in COBOL becoming the world's most popular programming language.

Languages such as C++ and Java undoubtedly are growing in popularity for new information systems. Nevertheless, maintenance still is the major activity for information technology professionals, and this maintenance is being performed on existing COBOL information systems. In short, the Department of Defense put its stamp onto the world's information systems via its first major programming language, COBOL.

Another reason for the popularity of COBOL is that COBOL frequently was the best traditional language for implementing an information system. In particular, COBOL generally was the language of choice when money was involved. Financial books have to balance, so rounding errors cannot be allowed to creep in. Therefore, all computations have to be performed using integer arithmetic. COBOL supports integer arithmetic on very large numbers (that is, billions of dollars). In addition, COBOL can handle very small numbers, such as fractions of a cent. Banking regulations require interest computations to be calculated to at least four decimal places of a cent, and COBOL can do this arithmetic with ease as well. Finally, COBOL probably has the best formatting, sorting, and report generation facilities of any traditional language. All these reasons made COBOL an excellent choice for implementing a traditional information system.

compiler would have to be purchased, as well as appropriate Java CASE tools. Additional hardware may have to be purchased or leased to run these new development tools. Perhaps most serious of all, QQQ Corporation has accumulated hundreds of person-years of COBOL expertise, the kind of expertise that can be gained only through hands-on experience, such as what to do when a certain cryptic error message appears on the screen or how to handle the quirks of the compiler. In brief, it would seem that, as far as QQQ Corporation is concerned, "the most suitable" programming language could only be COBOL—any other choice would be financial suicide, either from the viewpoint of the costs involved or as a consequence of plummeting staff morale leading to poor-quality code.

The solution to this apparent dilemma is simple. The 2002 standard for COBOL is for an object-oriented programming language named OO-COBOL. QQQ Corporation must ensure that every member of their technical staff receives training in the object-oriented paradigm in general, and in OO-COBOL in particular. After all, OO-COBOL is essentially an object-oriented incrementation of COBOL. Once an information technology professional who knows COBOL has learned about the object-oriented paradigm, transitioning to OO-COBOL is not too hard. It is certainly true that the object-oriented paradigm is a different way of looking at the world compared to the traditional paradigm, so it can take many months for information technology professionals to "think object-oriented." But after the transition to the object-oriented paradigm has been made, QQQ Corporation can develop new information systems in OO-COBOL and maintain existing information systems in traditional COBOL, at a cost that should ensure a good return on investment, and with minimal dislocation.

In cases where there is no clear-cut reason for choosing one programming language over another, the issue of which language to use often can be decided by using cost–benefit analysis (Section 14.1). That is, management must compute the dollar cost of an implementation in each of the languages under consideration, as well as the dollar benefits, present and future, of using that language. This computation must be repeated for every language under consideration. The language with the largest expected gain, that is, the largest difference between estimated benefits and estimated costs, is then the appropriate implementation language.

Another way of deciding which programming language to select is to use risk analysis. For each language under consideration, a list is made of the potential risks and ways of mitigating them. The language for which the overall risk is the smallest then is selected.

Currently, information system development organizations are under pressure to develop new information systems in an object-oriented language—*any* object-oriented language. The question that arises is: Which is the appropriate object-oriented language? Twenty years ago, there really was only one choice, Smalltalk. Today, however, the most widely used object-oriented programming language is *C++* [Borland, 2002], with Java in second place. There are a number of reasons for the popularity of C++. One is the widespread availability of C++ compilers.

But, as explained in Just in Case You Wanted to Know Box 11.1, the real explanation for the popularity of C++ is its similarity to C. This is unfortunate, in that a number of managers view C++ simply as a superset of C and, therefore, conclude that any programmer who knows C can quickly pick up the additional pieces. Indeed, at first glance, C++ appears to be a superset of C. After all, any C program can be compiled using a C++ compiler. Conceptually, however, C++ is totally different from C. C is a product of the traditional paradigm, whereas C++ is for the object-oriented paradigm. Using C++ makes sense only if object-oriented techniques have been used and if the information system is organized around objects and classes.

Therefore, before an organization adopts C++, it is essential that the relevant information technology professionals be trained in the object-oriented paradigm. Unless it is clear to all involved, and particularly to management, that the object-oriented paradigm requires a different way of developing information systems and what the precise differences are, the traditional paradigm just will continue to be used but with the code implemented in C++ rather than C. When organizations are disappointed with the results of switching from C to C++, a major contributory factor is a lack of education in the object-oriented paradigm.

Now suppose that an organization currently using a traditional programming language decides to adopt Java. In that case it is not possible to move gradually from the traditional paradigm to the object-oriented paradigm. *Java is a pure object-oriented programming language;* it does not support the functions and procedures of the traditional paradigm. Unlike a *hybrid object-oriented programming language* such as C++, Java programmers have to use the object-oriented paradigm (and only the object-oriented paradigm) from the very beginning. Because of the necessity of an abrupt transition from the one paradigm to the other, education and training are even more important when adopting Java (or other pure object-oriented language such as Smalltalk) than if the organization were to switch to a hybrid object-oriented language such as C++ or OO-COBOL.

What of the future? Will Java become the most important object-oriented programming language because of its suitability for Web applications? Will C# replace Visual Basic as the most widely used Microsoft language?

The huge volume of COBOL legacy code (see Just in Case You Wanted to Know Box 14.2) will certainly ensure that COBOL remains the most widely used language in *existing* information systems for many years. The most widely used language for *new* information systems in five years' time will surely be object oriented, but whether it will be C++, Java, or C# remains to be seen.

The next management topic is reuse.

14.7   Reuse

If reinventing the wheel were a criminal offense, many information technology managers would today be languishing in jail. For example, there are tens of thousands (if not hundreds of thousands) of different payroll programs, all doing essentially the same thing. Surely, all that the world needs is just one payroll program that can run on a variety of hardware and can be tailored, if necessary, to cater to the specific needs of an individual organization. However, instead of utilizing previously developed payroll programs, myriad organizations all over the world have developed their own payroll program from scratch.

In this section we investigate why information technology professionals delight in continually reinventing the wheel, and what can be done to develop information systems using reusable artifacts. We begin by defining reuse.

14.7.1   Reuse Concepts

Reuse refers to using artifacts of one information system to facilitate developing a different information system with different functionality. A reusable artifact need not necessarily be a module or a code fragment—it could be a design artifact, a part of a manual, a set of test data, or a duration and cost estimate.

For example, many artifacts from an information system for a car dealership could be reused in developing an information system for a company that buys and sells boats. The graphical user interface from a billing information system for a group of dermatologists could surely be reused in a billing information system for audiologists. (For a different view on reuse, see Just in Case You Wanted to Know Box 14.3.)

There are two types of reuse: accidental reuse and deliberate reuse. If the developers of a new information system realize that an artifact of a previously developed information system can be reused in the new information system, then this is *accidental reuse* or *opportunistic reuse*. On the other hand, utilization of information system artifacts constructed specifically for possible future reuse is *deliberate reuse* or *systematic reuse*. One potential advantage of deliberate reuse over accidental reuse is that artifacts specially constructed for use in future information systems are more likely to be easy and safe to reuse; such artifacts generally are robust, well documented, and thoroughly tested. In addition, they usually display a uniformity of style that makes maintenance easier. The other side of the coin is that implementing deliberate reuse within an organization can be expensive; for example, it takes time to specify, design, implement, test, and document an artifact. However, there can be no guarantee that such an artifact will ever be reused and thereby recoup the money invested in developing that potentially reusable artifact.

Reuse is not restricted to information systems. For example, lawyers nowadays rarely draft wills from scratch. Instead, they use a word processor to store wills they have previously drafted and then make appropriate changes to an existing will. Other legal documents, like contracts, are usually drafted in the same way from existing documents.

Classical composers frequently reused their own music. For example, in 1823 Franz Schubert wrote an entr'acte for Helmina von Chezy's play *Rosamunde, Fürstin von Zypern* (Rosamunde, Princess of Cyprus) and the following year he reused that material in the slow movement of his String Quartet No. 13. Ludwig van Beethoven's Opus 66, *Variations for Cello on Mozart's "Ein Mädchen oder Weibchen,"* is a good example of one great composer reusing the music of another great composer; Beethoven simply took the aria "A Girlfriend or Little Wife" from Scene 22 of Wolfgang Amadeus Mozart's opera *Der Zauberflöte* (The Magic Flute) and wrote a series of seven variations on that aria for the cello with piano accompaniment.

In my opinion, the greatest reuser of all time was William Shakespeare. His genius lay in reusing the plots of others—I cannot think of a single story line he made up himself. For example, his historical plays heavily reused parts of Raphael Holinshed's 1577 work, *Chronicles of England, Scotland and Ireland.* Then, Shakespeare's *Romeo and Juliet* (1594) is borrowed, on an almost line-for-line basis, from Arthur Brooke's lengthy poem *The Tragicall Historye of Romeus and Iuliet* published in 1562, two years before Shakespeare was born.

But this reuse saga didn't begin there. In fact, the earliest known version appeared around 200 CE in *Ephesiaka* (Ephesian tale) by the Greek novelist Xenophon of Ephesus. In 1476, Tommaso Guardati (more commonly known as Masuccio Salernitano) reused Xenophon's tale in novella 33 in his collection of 50 novellas, *Il Novellino.* In 1530, Luigi da Porto reused that story in *Historia Novellamente Ritrovata di Due Nobili Amanti* (A Newly Found Story of Two Noble Lovers), for the first time setting it in Verona, Italy. Brooke's poem reuses parts of *Giulietta e Romeo* (1554) by Matteo Bandello, a reuse of da Porto's version.

And this reuse saga didn't end with *Romeo and Juliet,* either. In 1957, *West Side Story* opened on Broadway. The musical, with book by Arthur Laurents, lyrics by Stephen Sondheim, and score by Leonard Bernstein, reused Shakespeare's version of the story. The Broadway musical was then reused in a Hollywood movie, which won 10 Academy Awards in 1961.

No matter how high the quality of an information system may be, it will not sell if it takes four years to get it onto the market when a competitive information system can be delivered in only two years. The length of the development process is critical in a market economy. All other criteria as to what constitutes a "good" information system are irrelevant if the information system cannot compete timewise. For an organization that has repeatedly failed to get an information system to market first, reuse offers a tempting technique. After all, if an existing artifact is reused, then there is no need to specify, design, implement, test, and document that artifact. The key point is that, on average, only about 15 percent of any information system serves a truly original purpose [Jones, 1984]. The other 85 percent of the information system in theory could be standardized and reused in future information systems. The figure of 85 percent is essentially a theoretical upper limit for the reuse rate; nevertheless, reuse rates on the order of 40 percent can be achieved in practice, as described in Section 14.8. This leads to an obvious question: If such reuse rates are attainable in practice and reuse is by no means a new idea, why do so few organizations employ reuse to shorten the development process?

14.7.2 Impediments to Reuse

There are a number of impediments to reuse:

- All too many information technology professionals would rather rewrite an artifact from scratch than reuse an artifact written by someone else, the implication being that an artifact cannot be any good unless they wrote it themselves. This phenomenon is known as the *not invented here (NIH) syndrome* [Griss, 1993]. NIH is a management issue and, if management is aware of the problem, it can be solved, usually by offering financial incentives to promote reuse.

- Many information technology professionals would be willing to reuse an artifact, provided they could be sure that the artifact in question would not introduce faults into the information system. This attitude toward information system quality is perfectly easy to understand. After all, every information technology professional has seen faulty information systems written by others. The solution here is to subject potentially reusable artifacts, especially code modules, to exhaustive testing before making them available for reuse.

- A large organization may have hundreds of thousands of potentially useful artifacts. How should these artifacts be stored for effective later retrieval? For example, a reusable artifacts database might consist of 20,000 items, 125 of which are sort routines. The database must be organized so that the designer of a new information system can quickly determine which (if any) of those 125 sort routines is appropriate for the new information system.

- Reuse is expensive. A number of different costs are involved. First, there is the cost of implementing a reuse process within an organization. Then, once the process is in place, there is a cost to making an artifact reusable. After all, a reusable artifact has to be extremely thoroughly tested and documented. Finally, there is a cost associated with reusing an artifact, namely, the cost of testing the artifact once it has been integrated into the new information system. Of course, this reuse cost is much less than if the artifact were constructed from scratch rather than reused, but it is a cost nonetheless.

The preceding four impediments can be overcome, at least in principle. The fifth impediment is more problematic.

- There are legal issues that arise with a contract information system (an information system developed by an outside organization that specializes in developing such information systems). In terms of the type of contract usually drawn up between a client and an information system development organization, the information system belongs to the client. Therefore, if the information system development organization reuses an artifact of one client's information system while developing an information system for a different client, this constitutes theft of the first client's intellectual property. For internal information systems, that is, when the developers and client are members of the same organization, this problem does not arise.

So, other than certain legal issues, in theory there are no major impediments to implementing reuse within an information system development organization. In practice, however, it is not always that easy—for example, see Just in Case You Wanted to Know Box 14.4.

The World Wide Web is a great source of "urban myths"; that is, apparently true stories that somehow just do not stand up under scrutiny when they are investigated closely. One such urban myth concerns code reuse.

The story is told that the Australian Air Force set up a virtual reality training simulator for helicopter combat training. To make the scenarios as realistic as possible, programmers included detailed landscapes and (in the Northern Territory) herds of kangaroos. After all, the dust from a herd disturbed by a helicopter might reveal the position of that helicopter to the enemy.

The programmers were instructed to model both the movements of the kangaroos and their reaction to helicopters. To save time, the programmers reused code originally used to simulate the reaction of infantry to attack by a helicopter. Only two changes were made: They changed the icon from a soldier to a kangaroo and they increased the speed of movement of the figures.

One fine day, a group of Australian pilots wanted to demonstrate their prowess with the flight simulator to some visiting American pilots. They "buzzed" (flew very low over) the virtual kangaroos. As expected, the kangaroos scattered, then reappeared from behind a hill and launched Stinger missiles at the helicopter. The programmers had forgotten to remove that part of the code when they reused the virtual infantry implementation.

However, as reported in *The Risks Digest*, it appears that the story is not totally an urban myth—much of it actually happened [Green, 2000]. Dr. Anne-Marie Grisogono, head of the Simulation Land Operations Division at the Australian Defence Science and Technology Organisation, told the story at a meeting in Canberra, Australia, on May 6, 1999. Although the simulator was designed to be as realistic as possible (it even included over two million virtual trees, as indicated on aerial photographs), the kangaroos were included for fun. The programmers indeed reused Stinger missile detachments so that the kangaroos could detect the arrival of helicopters, but the behavior of the kangaroos was set to "retreat" so that the kangaroos, correctly, would flee if a helicopter approached. However, when the information system team tested their simulator in their laboratory (not in front of visitors), they discovered that they had forgotten to remove both the weapons and "fire" behavior. Also, they had not specified what weapons were to be used by the simulated figures, so when the kangaroos fired on the helicopters, they fired the default weapon, which happened to be large multicolored beachballs.

Grisogono confirmed that the kangaroos were immediately disarmed and therefore it is now safe to fly over Australia. But notwithstanding this happy ending, information technology professionals still must take care when reusing code not to reuse too much of it.

14.8 Reuse Case Studies

The following six case studies show how reuse has been achieved in practice. They span the 25-year period from 1976 to 2000.

14.8.1 Raytheon Missile Systems Division

In 1976, a study was undertaken at Raytheon's Missile Systems Division to determine whether deliberate reuse of design and code artifacts was feasible [Lanergan and Grasso,

1984]. Over 5,000 COBOL information systems in use in the Missile Systems Division were analyzed and classified. It was discovered that, in the Raytheon information systems, only six basic actions were performed: sort data, edit or manipulate data, combine data, explode data, update data, and report on data. As a result, between 40 and 60 percent of designs and code modules could be standardized and reused. For the next six years, a concerted attempt was made to reuse both design artifacts and code artifacts wherever possible.

The Raytheon information technology professionals constructed over 3,200 reusable code artifacts, such as an edit routine, a tax computation routine, and a date aging routine for accounts receivable. Use of the reusable code artifacts resulted in information systems that, on average, consisted of 60 percent reused code. Information systems that used these artifacts were found to be more reliable, and less testing of the information system as a whole was needed.

By 1983, design artifacts had been used over 5,500 times in developing new information systems. About 60 percent of the code consisted of reused artifacts, so design, coding, unit testing, and documentation time also were reduced by 60 percent, leading to an estimated 50 percent increase in productivity in information system development. But, for Raytheon, the real benefit of the technique lay in the hope that the readability and understandability resulting from the consistent style would reduce the cost of maintenance by between 60 and 80 percent. Unfortunately, Raytheon closed the division before the necessary maintenance data could be obtained.

14.8.2 Toshiba Software Factory

In 1977, the Toshiba Corporation started the Fuchu Software Factory at the Toshiba Fuchu Works in Tokyo. At the Fuchu Works, industrial process control systems are manufactured for, among other areas, electric power networks, nuclear power generators, factory automation, and traffic control; at the Software Factory, software is developed for the computers that control those systems [Matsumoto, 1987].

By 1985, the Software Factory employed a total of 2,300 technical and managerial personnel. Output from the Software Factory in 1985 was 1.8 million lines of code. Information systems ranged in size from 250,000 lines to over 5 million lines, with an average size of 1 million lines of code.

Software was developed using the waterfall model, with detailed inspections at the end of each phase. Productivity was the driving force behind the Software Factory. It was monitored on both a projectwide basis and an individual basis. Annual productivity increases for the factory as a whole have been on the order of 8 to 9 percent. One item measured when appraising performance was the individual's fault rate. In the case of a programmer, for example, the number of faults per 1,000 lines of code was expected to decrease over time as a consequence of training and experience. Quality was an important aspect of the factory and was achieved through a number of different mechanisms, including inspections and quality circles (groups of workers who met on a regular basis to find ways to improve quality).

Improvements in both productivity and quality have been attributed to reuse of existing actifacts, that is, to accidental reuse [Matsumoto, 1987]. These reused artifacts included not only code modules but also designs, specifications, contracts, and manuals. A committee was responsible for deciding which artifacts should be placed in the reusable artifacts database where they were indexed by keyword for later retrieval. Careful statistics were maintained on the reuse rate of every artifact in the database. In 1985, the documentation reuse rate, that is, the number of reused pages divided by the total number of pages of documentation produced, was 32 percent. With regard to design, the reuse rate was 33 percent, whereas 48 percent of code was reused. In addition, statistics are kept on the sizes of reused artifacts; about 55 percent were under 2,500 lines of code in size and 36 percent were in the 2,500 to 25,000 lines of code range.

Corresponding statistics for 25 systems developed by NASA follow in the next section.

14.8.3 NASA Software

There has been considerable accidental reuse of code modules in a NASA group that produces ground support software for unmanned spacecraft control [Selby, 1989]. Altogether 25 systems were involved. They ranged in size from 3,000 to 112,000 lines of source code. The 7,188 modules involved were classified into four categories. Group 1 consisted of modules that were reused with no changes. Group 2 were those modules reused with slight revisions; that is, less than 25 percent of the code was changed. Modules falling into group 3 were reused with major revisions; 25 percent or more of the code was changed. Group 4 modules were developed from scratch.

A total of 2,954 FORTRAN modules in the sample were studied in detail. On average, 45 percent of these modules were reused in modified or unmodified form. More specifically, 28 percent fell into group 1, 10 percent into group 2, and 7 percent into group 3. In general, the reused modules were small and well documented, and performed little input or output.

These results are not really surprising. Small, well-documented modules are easier to comprehend than large modules with poor documentation, and therefore more likely to be reused. In addition, a large module is likely to perform a number of different actions, or perhaps one rather specialized action, and therefore less likely to be reused than its smaller counterpart. Input and output can be somewhat application specific and therefore less reusable.

A more constructive way of looking at the NASA results is to utilize them to ensure that code artifacts can be reused in future information systems. Management should ensure that a specific design objective should be small code artifacts. Input and output should be localized to a few code artifacts. All code artifacts must be properly documented.

There are considerable differences between the NASA group and the Fuchu Software Factory. In particular, the decision to reuse was the personal choice of the NASA staff members themselves; there were no managerial directives of any kind. The NASA staff members reused code modules simply because they believed that reuse is a worthwhile practice, despite the fact that there were no CASE tools to assist with the reuse process. This situation is in stark contrast to the reuse-oriented management of the Fuchu works and the sophisticated artifact retrieval mechanisms employed there. Despite this, surprisingly high reuse rates have been obtained at NASA.

The fourth case study highlights the effect of strong management commitment to reuse.

14.8.4 GTE Data Services

A successful accidental reuse scheme was implemented at GTE Data Services [Prieto-Díaz, 1991]. Unlike the NASA case study, a key aspect of the GTE scheme was full management commitment to the reuse of code modules. To promote reuse, a cash incentive of between $50 and $100 was paid for a module accepted for possible reuse, and royalties were paid when the module actually was reused. In addition, managers' budgets were increased when the information systems they managed achieved a high level of reuse. There was even a Reuser of the Month award.

The results of this scheme were as follows. In 1988 a reuse level of 14 percent was achieved; this saved the company an estimated $1.5 million. The following year, it was estimated that the reuse level rose to 20 percent, and a 50 percent level was predicted for

1993. One reason that GTE pushed its reuse scheme so strongly was that it had anticipated overall savings of well over $10 million by that date.

The GTE reuse program reveals a number of interesting aspects. First, the total number of modules available for reuse dropped from 190 in 1988 to 128 in 1990, even though new modules were added. It appears that, at least in organizations such as GTE Data Services, it is not necessary to assemble a huge inventory of reusable artifacts. Second, the emphasis was on larger modules (10,000 lines of code or more) because of the greater payoff. In contrast to the NASA experience, where smaller modules tended to be reused, GTE succeeded in reusing larger modules. This disparity emphasizes the importance of having management commitment to any reuse program.

14.8.5   Hewlett-Packard

Hewlett-Packard has implemented reuse programs in a number of different divisions of the company [Lim, 1994]. In general, these programs have been successful from the viewpoint of improved quality as a consequence of reuse. Three specific programs are described here.

First, since 1983 a program for the accidental reuse of code modules has been in place in the manufacturing productivity section of the software technology division. This section develops information systems for resource planning by manufacturers. The fault rate for new code is 4.1 faults per 1,000 lines of code (KLOC) but only 0.9 faults per KLOC for the reused code. As a consequence of reuse, the overall fault rate dropped to only 2.0 faults per KLOC, a 51 percent reduction. Productivity increased 57 percent, to 1.1 KLOC per person-month in 1992. The program cost $1 million but saved $4.1 million between 1983 and 1992. Amazingly, the project broke even in its second year.

Turning now to the second program at Hewlett-Packard, since 1987 there has been a planned reuse program in the San Diego Technical Graphics (STG) division. This division develops and maintains software for running plotters and printers. The gross cost of the reuse program between 1987 and 1994 (1994 data estimated) was $2.6 million, and savings were $5.6 million. There was a 24 percent reduction in the fault rate to 1.3 faults per KLOC. Also, productivity increased by 40 percent to 0.7 KLOC per person-month. Finally, the delivery time decreased by 24 percent.

The costs of the STG reuse program are also interesting. The cost of developing a reusable artifact was only 11 percent more than the cost of a similar nonreusable artifact. Then, each time the artifact was reused, the cost was only about one-fifth the cost of developing that artifact from scratch.

Third, Hewlett-Packard manufactures a broad variety of printers, and new models constantly are being developed. Hewlett-Packard now endeavors to have common software, as far as possible, in all printer models. The results have been impressive. For example, between 1995 and 1998, the effort to develop the code for a new printer model decreased by a factor of four and the time to develop the code decreased by a factor of three. Also, reuse has increased. For more recent printers, over 70 percent of the components of the code are reused, almost unchanged, from earlier products [Toft, Coleman, and Ohta, 2000].

The overall lesson of these five case studies is that reuse is possible in practice and can result in significant cost savings. However, the major push for reuse must come from management.

The final case study is a cautionary tale, rather than a success story.

14.8.6   European Space Agency

On June 4, 1996, the European Space Agency launched the *Ariane 5* rocket for the first time. As a consequence of a software fault, the rocket crashed about 37 seconds after liftoff. The cost of the rocket and payload was about $500 million, making this the most costly software fault to date [Jézéquel and Meyer, 1997]. (Clearly, no financial value can be attached to faults that cause a loss of human life, such as those listed in Just in Case You Wanted to Know Box 13.1.)

The primary cause of the failure was an attempt to convert a number from one format into another format. The number being converted was too large for this conversion to be possible, so a run-time failure occurred. This caused the on-board computers to crash, which, in turn, caused the *Ariane 5* rocket to crash.

Ironically, the conversion that caused the failure was unnecessary. Certain computations are performed before liftoff to align the inertial reference system. These computations should stop nine seconds before liftoff. However, if there is a subsequent hold in the countdown, resetting the inertial reference system after the countdown has recommenced can take several hours. To prevent that happening, the computations continue for 50 seconds after the start of flight mode, that is, well into the flight (notwithstanding that, once liftoff has occurred, there is no way to align the inertial reference system). The failure occurred during this futile continuation of the alignment process.

The European Space Agency uses a careful development process that incorporates effective quality assurance. Then, why did the code not check whether the attempted conversion could be done before performing the conversion? The code in question was 10 years old. It had been reused, unchanged and without any further testing, from the code controlling the *Ariane 4* rocket (the precursor of the *Ariane 5*). Mathematical analysis had proven that the computation in question was totally safe for the *Ariane 4.* However, the analysis was performed on the basis of certain assumptions that were true for the *Ariane 4* but not for the *Ariane 5.* Therefore, the analysis no longer was valid, and additional code was needed to be sure that the number conversion could be safely performed.

The major lesson of this reuse experience is that artifacts developed in one context must be retested when reused in another context. That is, a reused artifact does not need to be retested by itself, but it must be retested after it has been integrated into the new information system in which it is reused.

14.9 Portability

It is vital that every information system can be easily adapted to run on a variety of different hardware–operating system combinations, that is, every information system must be *portable*. The reason for developing an information system that can be implemented without difficulty on other computers is that, every four years or so, the organization that uses that information system will purchase new hardware, and all its information systems will then have to be converted to run on the new hardware. For this reason, it is important for an information system to be portable; that is, it should be significantly less expensive to adapt the information system to run on the new computer than to write a new information system from scratch.

Overall, the problem of porting information systems is nontrivial because of incompatibilities between different hardware configurations, operating systems, and compilers. Each of these aspects is briefly examined in turn.

14.9.1 Hardware Incompatibilities

A diskette formatted for a PC cannot be read by a Macintosh computer, and conversely. Data written in Extended Binary Coded Decimal Interchange Code (*EBCDIC*) cannot be read by a computer than expects characters in American Standard Code for Information Interchange (*ASCII*), and vice versa. Other hardware incompatibilities can arise from inconsistent tape drives, or printers that are incompatible with the Universal Serial Bus (USB), a way of connecting input and output devices to a computer.

Although the original reason for these differences is historical (that is, researchers working independently for different manufacturers developed different ways of doing the same thing), there are definite economic reasons for perpetuating them. Suppose that an information system runs on computer C_A that is made by manufacturer M_A and costs \$10,000. Manufacturer M_B now announces that the company is selling a computer C_B that is just as powerful as computer C_A but costs only \$5,000. However, converting the information system to run on computer C_B will cost \$25,000. In other words, instead of saving \$5,000, moving the information system to C_B will result in a loss of \$20,000. It is therefore strongly in the interests of manufacturer M_A to keep their more expensive computer C_A incompatible with computer C_B, thereby ensuring that their customers will not switch to the cheaper C_B computer because of the high conversion costs.

Moving from the preceding imaginary situation to the real world, the most successful line of computers to date has been the IBM System/360-370 series [Gifford and Spector, 1987]. The success of this line of computers is due largely to full compatibility between machines; an information system that runs on an IBM System/360 Model 30 built in 1964 will run unchanged on an IBM zSeries 900 built in 2003. However, the information system that runs on the IBM System/360 Model 30 under OS/360 may require considerable modification before it can run on a totally different 2003 machine, such as a Sun Fire 6800 under Solaris. Part of the difficulty may be due to hardware incompatibilities. But part may be caused by operating system incompatibilities, our next topic.

14.9.2 Operating System Incompatibilities

An information system that runs under Windows will not run under Linux. It certainly will not run on a Macintosh under Mac OS, let alone under a mainframe computer operating system such as OS/370. In other words, porting an information system from one operating system to another usually requires considerable modification by a maintenance programmer who is experienced in both operating systems.

Problems also can arise when upgrading the same operating system. For example, information systems that ran successfully for many years under Windows 3.0 usually required changes to run under later versions of the Windows family of operating systems. An information system is rarely truly portable. Some modifications are usually needed when porting an information system to a new operating system.

14.9.3 Compiler Incompatibilities

Portability is difficult to achieve if an information system is implemented in a language for which few compilers now exist. For example, if the information system has been implemented in a language such as PL/I, it may be necessary to rewrite it in a different language if the target computer does not have a compiler for that language. (PL/I was a language that was enthusiastically promoted by IBM in the 1970s but is almost unknown today.) On the other hand, if an information system is implemented in a popular language such as COBOL, C, C++, or Java, the chances are good that a compiler for that language can be found for a target computer (and see Just in Case You Wanted to Know Box 14.5 for remarks on the correct spelling of the names of programming languages).

Unfortunately, even when an information system has been implemented in a popular programming language, there can still be portability problems. Many compilers do not adhere strictly to the standards of the language they translate. Instead, they support extensions to the language, as well as nonstandard versions of standard features. For example, a manufacturer of COBOL compilers may decide to include additional features not usually found in COBOL so that the marketing division can tout a "new, extended COBOL compiler." As a result, when an information system is ported to a computer that has a standard COBOL compiler, parts of the information system will have to be modified. This type of problem can be averted if management insist that programmers use only standard language features in all their information systems.

14.10   Why Portability?

In light of the many barriers to porting information systems, the reader might well wonder if it is worthwhile to port information systems at all. Is it not a waste of time and money to engineer portability into an information system when it is designed?

The answer to this question is an emphatic *No*. The major reason why portability is essential is that the life of an information system generally is far longer than the life of the hardware for which it was first implemented. Good information systems have a life of 15 or 20 years or more, whereas hardware frequently is changed every four years. Therefore, a good information system will be implemented, over its lifetime, on three or more different hardware configurations.

One way to solve this problem is to buy truly upwardly compatible hardware and operating systems. The only expense is then the cost of the new hardware and operating systems; the information system will not need to be changed. Nevertheless, in some cases it may be economically more sound to port the information system to different hardware entirely. For example, the first version of a certain information system was implemented 15 years ago on a mainframe. Although it was possible 10 years ago to buy a new mainframe on which the information system could run with no changes, it was considerably less expensive to implement multiple copies of the information system on a network of personal computers, one on the desk of each user. Now it seems to be financially desirable to reimplement the information system as a Web-based system. In instances such as these, if the information system has been implemented in a way that promotes portability, then porting the information system to a new hardware–operating system environment becomes economically viable.

FIGURE 14.4
The Management Issues Presented in This Chapter and the Section in Which Each Is Described

Cost–benefit analysis (Section 14.1)
Risk analysis (Section 14.2)
Process improvement (Section 14.3)
Risk analysis (Section 14.4)
CPM/PERT (Section 14.5)
Choice of programming language (Section 14.6)
Reuse (Sections 14.7–14.8)
Portability (Sections 14.9–14.10)

But there are other kinds of information systems. For example, many organizations that develop software for personal computers make their money by selling multiple copies of COTS packages. For instance, the profit on a spreadsheet package is small and cannot possibly cover the cost of development. To make a profit, 10,000 (or even 100,000) copies may have to be sold. After this point, additional sales are pure profit. So, if the software can be ported to other types of hardware with ease, even more money can be made.

Of course, an information system is not just the code; there also is the documentation, including the manuals. Porting an information system to other hardware means changing the documentation as well. Thus, portability also means being able to change the documentation easily to reflect the new environment, instead of having to write new documentation from scratch. Considerably less training is needed if a familiar, existing information system is ported to a new computer than if a completely new information system were to be developed.

For all these reasons, portability should be strongly encouraged by all information technology managers, especially top management.

Figure 14.4 lists the management issues presented in this chapter and the section in which each is described.

Key Terms

accidental reuse, *272*
ASCII, *279*
assumption, *260*
C++, *271*
capability maturity model, *262*
CMM, *262*
COBOL, *269*
cost–benefit analysis, *259*
CPM, *267*
critical path, *268*
critical path management, *267*
defined level, *263*
deliberate reuse, *272*
EBCDIC, *279*
hybrid object-oriented programming language, *271*
initial level, *262*
International Standards Organization, *264*
ISO 9000, *264*
ISO/IEC 15504, *265*
Java, *271*
key process area, *264*
lines of code, *266*
LOC, *266*
managed level, *263*
maturity, *262*
metric, *266*
milestone, *268*
mitigation of risks, *261*
not invented here (NIH) syndrome, *274*
opportunistic reuse, *272*
optimizing level, *263*
PERT, *267*
portable, *279*
process, *261*
process metric, *266*
product metric, *266*
program evaluation review techniques, *267*
pure object-oriented programming language, *271*
repeatable level, *263*
reuse, *272*
risk, *260*
risk analysis, *261*
risk list, *261*
risk management, *261*
slack, *267*
Smalltalk, *268*
Software Engineering Institute, *262*
SPICE, *265*
systematic reuse, *272*

Review Questions for Chapter 14

1. Explain what is meant by cost–benefit analysis.
2. What is the aim of CMM?
3. Name the five maturity levels of CMM and briefly describe each one.
4. What is ISO 9000?
5. What is ISO/IEC 15504?
6. What are the five essential, fundamental metrics that need to be monitored when developing an information system?
7. For what does the acronym CPM/PERT stand?
8. What is a critical path?
9. Name the two most widely used object-oriented programming languages and the most widely used of all programming languages.
10. What is the difference between accidental reuse and deliberate reuse?
11. What are the five major impediments to reuse?
12. Distinguish between reuse and portability.
13. List three sources of incompatibilities that can hamper portability.
14. Why is portability so important?

Problems

14.1 A new form of gastrointestinal disease is sweeping the country of Concordia. Like histoplasmosis, it is transmitted as an airborne fungus. Although the disease is almost never fatal, an attack is very painful and the sufferer is unable to work for about two weeks. The government of Concordia wishes to determine how much money, if any, to spend on attempting to eradicate the disease. The committee charged with advising the Department of Public Health is considering four aspects of the problem: health care costs (Concordia provides free health care to all its citizens), loss of earnings (and hence loss of taxes), pain and discomfort, and gratitude toward the government. Explain how cost–benefit analysis can assist the committee. For each benefit or cost, suggest how a dollar estimate for that benefit or cost could be obtained.

14.2 You have just purchased Medieval Software Developers, an organization on the verge of bankruptcy because the company is at maturity level 1. What is the first step you will take to restore the organization to profitability?

14.3 Section 14.3.4 states that it makes little sense to introduce CASE environments within organizations at maturity level 1 or 2. Explain why this is so.

14.4 What is the effect of introducing CASE tools (as opposed to environments) within organizations with a low maturity level?

14.5 Which of the three paths through the PERT chart of Figure 14.5 from activity A to activity J is critical?

14.6 What are the critical activities of the PERT chart of Figure 14.6?

FIGURE 14.5 **PERT Chart for Problem 14.5**
The estimated duration of each activity is marked

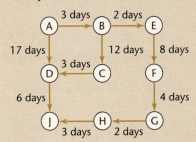

FIGURE 14.6 **PERT Chart for Problem 14.6**
The estimated duration of each activity is marked

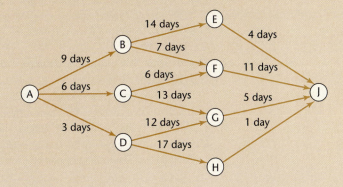

14.7   A code artifact is reused, unchanged, in a new information system. In what ways does this reuse reduce the overall cost of the information system? In what ways is the cost unchanged?

14.8   Suppose that a code artifact is reused with one change, namely, an addition operation is changed to a subtraction. What impact does this minor change have on the savings of Problem 14.7?

14.9   How early in the life cycle could the developers have caught the fault in the *Ariane 5* code (Section 14.8.6)?

14.10   Consider the automated library circulation system of Problem 5.5. Explain how you would ensure a high percentage of reusable artifacts.

14.11   Consider the information system of Problem 4.9 that checks whether a bank statement is correct. Explain how you would ensure that as many artifacts as possible can be reused in future information systems.

14.12   Consider the automated teller machine (ATM) of Problem 5.6. Explain how you would ensure that as many artifacts as possible can be reused in future information systems.

14.13   What management lesson can we learn about reuse from each of the six reuse case studies in Section 14.8?

14.14   Explain how you would ensure that the automated library circulation system of Problem 5.5 is as portable as possible.

14.15   Explain how you would ensure that the information system of Problem 4.9 that checks whether a bank statement is correct is as portable as possible.

14.16   Explain how you would ensure that the software for the automated teller machine (ATM) of Problem 5.6 is as portable as possible.

Term Project

14.17   Suppose that the Chocoholics Anonymous information system of Appendix A has been constructed. What parts of the information system could be reused in future information systems?

References

Borland. "Press Release: Borland Unveils C++ Application Development Strategy for 2002." http://www.borland.com/news/press_releases/2002/01_28_02_cpp.strategy.html, January 28, 2002.

Brooks, F. P., Jr.; V. Basili; B. Boehm; E. Bond; N. Eastman; D. L. Evans; A. K. Jones; M. Shaw; and C. A. Braket. "Report of the Defense Science Board Task Force on Military Software." Washington, DC: Department of Defense, Office of the Under Secretary of Defense for Acquisition, September 1987.

Dawood, M. "It's Time for ISO 9000." *CrossTalk,* March 1994, pp. 26–28.

Deming, W. E. *Out of the Crisis.* Cambridge, MA: MIT Center for Advanced Engineering Study, 1986.

Dion, R. "Process Improvement and the Corporate Balance Sheet." *IEEE Software* 10 (July 1993), pp. 28–35.

Gifford, D., and A. Spector. "Case Study: IBM's System/360-370 Architecture." *Communications of the ACM* 30 (April 1987), pp. 292–307.

Green, P. "FW: Here's an Update to the Simulated Kangaroo Story." *The Risks Digest* 20, no. 76 (January 23, 2000). Available at catless.ncl.ac.uk/Risks/20.76.html.

Griss, M. L. "Software Reuse: From Library to Factory." *IBM Systems Journal* 32, no. 4 (1993), pp. 548–66.

Humphrey, W. S. *Managing the Software Process.* Reading, MA: Addison Wesley, 1989.

Humphrey, W. S.; T. R. Snider; and R. R. Willis. "Software Process Improvement at Hughes Aircraft." *IEEE Software* 8 (July 1991), pp. 11–23.

International Organization for Standardization. "ISO 9000-3, Guidelines for the Application of ISO 9001 to the Development, Supply, and Maintenance of Software." Geneva: ISO, 1991.

International Organization for Standardization. "ISO 9001, Quality Systems—Model for Quality Assurance in Design/Development, Production, Installation, and Servicing." Geneva: ISO, 1987.

Jacobson, I.; G. Booch; and J. Rumbaugh. *The Unified Software Development Process.* Reading, MA: Addison Wesley, 1999.

Jézéquel, J.-M., and B. Meyer. "Put It in the Contract: The Lessons of Ariane." *IEEE Computer* 30 (January 1997), pp. 129–30.

Jones, T. C. "Reusability in Programming: A Survey of the State of the Art." *IEEE Transactions on Software Engineering* SE-10 (September 1984), pp. 488–94.

Lanergan, R. G., and C. A. Grasso. "Software Engineering with Reusable Designs and Code." *IEEE Transactions on Software Engineering* SE-10 (September 1984), pp. 498–501.

Lim, W. C. "Effects of Reuse on Quality, Productivity, and Economics." *IEEE Software* 11 (September 1994), pp. 23–30.

Matsumoto, Y. "A Software Factory: An Overall Approach to Software Production." In *Tutorial: Software Reusability,* ed. P. Freeman, pp. 155–78. Washington, DC: Computer Society Press, 1987.

McClendon, J. "Is COBOL Dying?" *About Legacy Coding* 4, no. 3 (June 2002), available at www.legacycoding.com.

Prieto-Díaz, R. "Implementing Faceted Classification for Software Reuse." *Communications of the ACM* 34 (May 1991), pp. 88–97.

Schach, S. R. *Object-Oriented and Classical Software Engineering.* 5th ed. New York: WCB/McGraw-Hill, 2002.

Selby, R. W. "Quantitative Studies of Software Reuse." In *Software Reusability.* Volume 2. *Applications and Experience,* ed. T. J. Biggerstaff and A. J. Perlis, pp. 213–33. New York: ACM Press, 1989.

Toft, P.; D. Coleman; and J. Ohta. "A Cooperative Model for Cross-Divisional Product Development for a Software Product Line." In *Software Product Lines: Experience and Research Directions,* ed. P. Donohoe, pp. 111–32. Boston: Kluwer Academic Publishers, 2000.

Chapter 15

Planning and Estimating

Learning Objectives

After studying this chapter, you should be able to:

- Explain the importance of planning.
- Describe how to estimate the size and cost of an information system.
- Draw up a project management plan.

There is no easy solution to the difficulties of constructing an information system. To put together a large information system takes time and resources. And, like any other large construction project, careful *planning* at the beginning of the project perhaps is the single most important factor that distinguishes success from failure. This initial planning, however, by no means is enough. Planning, like testing, must continue throughout the development and maintenance life cycle. Notwithstanding the need for continual planning, these activities reach a peak after the specification document has been drawn up but before design activities commence. At this point in the life cycle, meaningful duration and cost estimates are computed and a detailed plan for completing the project produced.

In this chapter, we distinguish these two types of planning, the planning that proceeds throughout the project and the intense planning that must be carried out once the specification document is complete at the end of performing the analysis workflow.

15.1 Planning and the Information System Life Cycle

Ideally, we would like to plan the entire information system project at the very beginning of the life cycle, then follow that plan until the target information system finally has been delivered to the client. This is impossible, however, because we lack enough information during the initial workflows to be able to draw up a meaningful plan for the complete project. For example, while performing the requirements workflow, any sort of planning (other than just for the requirements workflow itself) is futile.

Suppose that the developers have completed the requirements workflow and the client feels that the requirements artifacts indeed encapsulate the key functionality of the target information system. It might seem that at this stage it would be possible to provide reasonably

FIGURE 15.1

A Model of the Relative Range of Cost Estimates for Each Life-Cycle Workflow

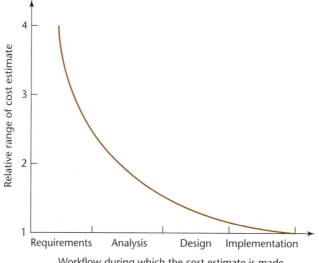

accurate duration and cost estimates for the project. Unfortunately, that is not true. There is a world of difference between the information at the developers' disposal at the end of the requirements workflow and at the end of the analysis workflow, analogous to the difference between a rough sketch and a detailed blueprint. By the end of the requirements workflow, the developers at best have an informal understanding of what the client needs. In contrast, by the end of the analysis workflow, at which time the client usually signs a document stating precisely what is going to be developed, the developers have a detailed appreciation of most (but usually still not all) aspects of the target information system. This is the earliest point in the life cycle at which accurate duration and cost estimates can be determined.

Nevertheless, in some situations, an organization may be required to produce duration and cost estimates before the specification document can be drawn up. In the worst case, a client may insist on a bid on the basis of an hour or two of preliminary discussion. Unfortunately, this happens all too often. Figure 15.1 shows how problematic this can be. Based on a model in Boehm et al. [2000], it depicts the relative range of cost estimates for the various workflows of the life cycle. For example, suppose that, when an information system passes its acceptance test at the end of the implementation workflow and is delivered to the client, its cost is found to be $1 million.

- If a cost estimate had been made midway through the requirements workflow, then at that time (from the curve in Figure 15.1), the relative range for the cost estimate was 4. This means that the cost estimate was probably in the range ($1 million / 4, $1 million × 4), or ($0.25 million, $4 million).
- If a cost estimate had been made midway through the analysis workflow where, from Figure 15.1, the relative range for the cost estimate was 2, the range of likely estimates would have shrunk to ($1 million / 2, $1 million × 2), or ($0.5 million, $2 million).
- Finally, if a cost estimate had been made at the end of the analysis workflow, that is, at the earliest possible appropriate time, then, from Figure 15.1, the relative range at this point was 1.5. The estimate probably would have been in the still relatively wide range of ($1 million / 1.5, $1 million × 1.5), or ($0.67 million, $1.5 million).

In other words, cost estimation is not an exact science. And a premature duration or cost estimate, that is, an estimate made before the specification document has been signed off by the client, is likely to be even less accurate than an estimate made at the correct time.

We now examine techniques for estimating duration and cost. The assumption throughout the remainder of this chapter is that the analysis workflow has been completed; that is, meaningful estimating and planning now can be carried out.

15.2   Estimating Duration and Cost

The budget is an integral part of any project management plan. Before development commences, the client wants to know how much he or she will have to pay for the information system. If the development team underestimates the actual cost, the development organization can lose money on the project. On the other hand, if the development team overestimates, then the client may decide that, on the basis of cost–benefit analysis or return on investment, there is no point in having the information system developed. Alternatively, the client may give the job to another development organization whose estimate is more reasonable. Either way, it is clear that accurate cost estimation is critical.

In fact, two types of *costs* are associated with information system development. The first is the *internal cost,* the cost to the developers; the second is the *external cost,* the cost to the client. The internal cost includes the salaries of the development teams, managers, and support personnel involved in the project; the cost of the hardware and software for developing the information system (including CASE tools—see Chapter 11); and the cost of overhead such as rent, utilities, and salaries of senior management. Although the external cost generally is based on the internal cost plus a profit margin, in some cases economic and psychological factors are important. For example, developers who desperately need the work may be prepared to charge the client the internal cost or less. A different situation arises when a contract is to be awarded on the basis of bids. The client may reject a bid that is significantly lower than all the other bids on the grounds that the quality of the resulting information system probably also would be significantly lower. A development team therefore may try to come up with a bid that will be slightly, but not significantly, lower than what they believe will be their competitors' bids.

Another important part of any plan is estimating the *duration* of the project. The client certainly wants to know when the finished information system will be delivered. If the development organization is unable to keep to its schedule, then at best the organization loses credibility; at worst penalty clauses are invoked. In all cases, the managers responsible for the project management plan have a lot of explaining to do. Conversely, if the development organization overestimates the time needed to develop the information system, then there is a good chance that the client will go elsewhere.

Unfortunately, it is by no means easy to estimate duration and cost accurately. Too many variables are involved to be able to get an accurate handle on either duration or cost. One big difficulty is the human factor. Over 30 years ago Sackman and his co-workers observed differences of up to 28 to 1 between pairs of programmers [Sackman, Erikson, and Grant, 1968]. It is easy to try to brush off their results by saying that experienced programmers always outperform beginners, but Sackman and his colleagues compared matched pairs of programmers.

They observed, for example, two programmers with 10 years of experience on similar types of projects and measured the time it took them to perform tasks such as coding and debugging. Then they observed, say, two beginners who had been in the profession for the same short length of time and had similar educational backgrounds. Comparing worst and best performances, they observed the following:

- A difference of 6 to 1 in information system size. That is, the best performer constructed an information system that was six times smaller than that of the worst performer.

- A difference of 8 to 1 in information system execution time. That is, the best performer constructed an information system that was eight times faster than that of the worst performer.
- A difference of 9 to 1 in development time. That is, the best performer developed an information system nine times faster than the worst performer.
- A difference of 18 to 1 in coding time. That is, the best performer coded an information system 18 times faster than the worst performer.
- A difference of 28 to 1 in debugging time. That is, the best performer found the faults in an information system 28 times faster than the worst performer.

A particularly alarming observation is that the best and worst performances on one information system were by two programmers, each of whom had 11 years of experience. Even when the best and worst cases were removed from Sackman et al.'s sample, observed differences were still on the order of 5 to 1. On the basis of these results, clearly we cannot hope to estimate information system duration or cost with any degree of accuracy (unless we have detailed information regarding all the skills of all our employees, which would be most unusual). It has been argued that, on a large project, differences among individuals tend to cancel out, but this perhaps is wishful thinking; the presence of one or two very good (or very bad) team members causes marked deviations from schedules and significantly affects the budget.

Another human factor that can affect estimation is that, in a free country, there is no way of ensuring that a critical staff member will not resign during the project. Time and money then are spent attempting to fill the vacated position and integrate the replacement into the team, or in reorganizing the remaining team members to compensate for the loss. Either way, schedules slip and estimates come unstuck.

Underlying the cost estimation problem is another issue: How is the size of an information system to be measured?

15.2.1 Metrics for the Size of an Information System

The most common metric for the size of an information system is the number of lines of code. Two different units commonly are used: *lines of code* (*LOC*) and *thousand delivered source instructions* (*KDSI*). Many problems are associated with the use of lines of code as a size metric [van der Poel and Schach, 1983]:

- Creation of source code is only a small part of the total information system development effort. It seems somewhat far-fetched that the time required for requirements, analysis, planning, designing, implementing, documenting, and testing can be expressed solely as a function of the number of lines of code of the delivered information system.
- Implementing the same information system in two different languages will result in versions with different numbers of lines of code.
- It often is unclear exactly how to count lines of code. For example, should comments in the code be counted? If not, there is a danger that programmers will be reluctant to spend time on what they perceive to be "nonproductive" commenting, but if comments are counted, then the opposite danger is that programmers will write reams of comments in an attempt to boost their apparent productivity. Another problem is how changed lines or deleted lines are counted—in the course of enhancing an information system to improve its performance, sometimes the number of lines of code is decreased. And what if code is not written, but rather inherited from a parent class (Section 3.3)? In short, the apparently straightforward metric of lines of code is anything but straightforward to count.

- Not all the code written is delivered to the client. It is not uncommon for half the code to consist of tools needed to support the development effort.
- Suppose that an information system developer uses a code generator, such as a report generator, a screen generator, or a graphical user interface (GUI) generator. After a few minutes of design activity on the part of the developer, the tool may generate many thousands of lines of code.

An additional problem arises when lines of code is used as the basis of an estimate of the size of the completed information system. The number of lines of code in the final information system can be determined only after the information system has been completely finished. Therefore, basing cost estimation on lines of code is doubly dangerous. To start the estimation process, the number of lines of code in the finished information system must be estimated. Then, this estimate is used to estimate the cost of the information system. Not only is there uncertainty in every costing technique, but if the input to an uncertain cost estimator itself is uncertain, namely, the number of lines of code in an information system that has not yet been developed, then the reliability of the resulting cost estimate is unlikely to be very high.

Because the number of lines of code is so unreliable, other metrics must be considered. So-called *software science* [Halstead, 1977] proposes a variety of measures of information system size. These are derived from the fundamental metrics of software science, namely, the number of operands and operators in the information system and the number of unique operands and unique operators. As with lines of code, these numbers can be determined only after the information system has been completed, severely reducing the predictive power of the metrics. Also, numerous studies have cast the strongest doubt on the validity of software science [Shepperd and Ince, 1994].

An alternative approach to estimating the size of an information system is the use of metrics based on measurable quantities that can be determined early in the information system development life cycle. To explain this concept, a simple metric for the size of a traditional information system is described. The *FFP metric* was designed for cost estimation of medium-scale information systems; that is, information systems that take between 2 and 10 person-years to complete [van der Poel and Schach, 1983]. The three basic elements of a traditional information system are its files, flows, and processes; the name FFP is an acronym formed from the initial letters of those elements. A *file* is defined as a collection of logically or physically related records permanently resident in the information system; transaction and temporary files are excluded. A *flow* is a data interface between the information system and the environment, such as a screen or a report. A *process* is a functionally defined logical or arithmetic manipulation of data; examples include sorting, validating, or updating. Given the number of files Fi, flows Fl, and processes Pr in an information system, its size S and cost C are given by

$$S = Fi + Fl + Pr$$
$$C = d \times S$$

(15.1)

where d is a constant that will vary from organization to organization. Constant d is a measure of the *efficiency* (*productivity*) of the information system development process within that organization. The size of an information system simply is the sum of the number of files, flows, and processes, a quantity that can be determined once the design is complete. The cost then is proportional to the size, the constant of proportionality d being determined from cost data relating to information systems previously developed by that organization. Unlike metrics based on the number of lines of code, the cost can be estimated before coding begins.

FIGURE 15.2
**Technical Factors
for Computing
Function Points**

1. Data communications
2. Distributed data processing
3. Performance criteria
4. Heavily utilized hardware
5. High transaction rates
6. Online data entry
7. End-user efficiency
8. Online updating
9. Complex computations
10. Reusability
11. Ease of installation
12. Ease of operation
13. Portability
14. Maintainability

The validity and reliability of the FFP metric were demonstrated using a purposive sample that covered a range of medium-scale information systems. Unfortunately, the metric was never extended to include databases, an essential component of many information systems (Chapter 19).

A similar, but independently developed, metric for the size of an information system was developed by Albrecht [1979] based on *function points*. Albrecht's metric is based on the number of input items, output items, inquiries, master files, and interfaces. It also incorporates the effect of 14 *technical factors*, such as high transaction rates, performance criteria (for example, throughput or response time), and online updating; the complete set of factors is shown in Figure 15.2. Experiments to measure information system productivity rates have shown a better fit using function points than using KDSI.

Both function points and the FFP metric suffer from the same disadvantage: Information system maintenance often is inaccurately measured. When an information system is maintained, major changes to the information system can be made without changing the number of files, flows, and processes or the number of inputs, outputs, inquiries, master files, and interfaces. Lines of code is no better in this respect. To take an extreme case, it is possible to replace every line of code of an information system by a completely different line without changing the total number of lines of code.

Numerous variants of and extensions to Albrecht's function points have been proposed, including Mk II function points [Symons, 1991]. Mk II function points are widely used all over the world to estimate the size of an information system to be developed. Function points also have been extended to object-oriented information systems.

15.2.2 Techniques of Cost Estimation

Notwithstanding the difficulties with estimating size, it is essential that information system developers simply do the best they can to obtain accurate estimates of both project duration and project cost, while trying to take into account as many as possible of the factors that can affect their estimates. These include the skill levels of the personnel, the complexity of the project, the size of the project (cost increases with size, but much faster than linearly), familiarity of the development team with the domain, the hardware on which the information system is to be run, and availability of CASE tools. Another factor is the deadline effect. If a project has to be completed by a certain time, the effort in person-months is greater than if is no constraint is placed on completion time.

From the preceding list, which is by no means comprehensive, estimation clearly is a difficult problem. A number of approaches have been used, with greater or lesser success. One popular method is *expert judgment by analogy*. In this technique, a number of experts are consulted. An expert arrives at an estimate by comparing the target information system to completed information systems with which the expert was actively involved and noting the similarities and differences. For example, an expert may compare the target information system to a similar information system developed two years ago. Because the organization is familiar with the type of information system to be developed, the expert reduces development time and effort by 15 percent. However, the graphical user interface (GUI) is somewhat complex; this increases time and effort by 25 percent. Finally, the target information system has to be developed in a programming language with which most of the team members are unfamiliar, thus increasing time by 15 percent and effort by 20 percent. Combining these three figures, the expert decides that the target information system will take 25 percent more time and 30 percent more effort than the previous one. Because the previous information system took 12 months to complete and required 100 person-months, the target information system will take 15 months and consume 130 person-months.

Two other experts within the organization compare the same two information systems. One concludes that the target information system will take 13.5 months and 140 person-months. The other comes up with the figures of 16 months and 95 person-months. How can the predictions of these three experts be reconciled? One technique is the *Delphi technique:* It allows experts to arrive at a consensus without having group meetings, which can have the undesirable side effect of one persuasive member swaying the group. In this technique, the experts work independently. Each produces an estimate and a rationale for that estimate. These estimates and rationales then are distributed to all the experts, who now produce a second estimate. This process of estimation and distribution continues until the experts can agree within an accepted tolerance. No group meetings take place during the iteration process.

Valuation of real estate frequently is done on the basis of expert judgment by analogy. An appraiser will arrive at a valuation by comparing a house with similar houses that have been sold recently. Suppose that house A is to be valued, house B next door has just been sold for $205,000, and house C on the next street was sold three months ago for $218,000. The appraiser may reason as follows: House A has one more bathroom than house B, and the yard is 5,000 square feet larger. House C is approximately the same size as house A, but its roof is in poor condition. On the other hand, House C has a jacuzzi. After careful thought, the appraiser may arrive at a figure of $215,000 for house A.

In the case of information systems, expert judgment by analogy is less precise than real estate valuation. Recall that our first information system expert claimed that using an unfamiliar language would increase time by 15 percent and effort by 20 percent. Unless the expert has some validated data from which the effect of each difference can be determined (a highly unlikely possibility), errors induced by what can be described only as guesses will result in hopelessly incorrect cost estimates. In addition, unless the experts are blessed with total recall (or have kept detailed records), their recollections of completed information systems may be sufficiently inaccurate as to invalidate their predictions. Finally, experts are human and, therefore, have biases that may affect their predictions. At the same time, the results of estimation by a group of experts should reflect their collective experience; if this is broad enough, the result well may be accurate.

Another approach is to use *algorithmic cost estimation models.* In this approach, a metric, such as function points or the FFP metric, is used as input to a model for determining information system cost. The estimator computes the value of the metric; duration and cost estimates then can be computed using the model. On the surface, an algorithmic cost

COCOMO is an acronym formed from the first two letters of each word in COnstructive COst MOdel. Any connection with Kokomo, Indiana, is purely coincidental.

The *MO* in COCOMO stands for "model," so the phrase *COCOMO model* should not be used. That phrase falls into the same category as "ATM machine" and "PIN number," both of which were dreamed up by the Department of Redundant Information Department.

estimation model is superior to expert opinion, because a human expert, as was pointed out previously, is subject to biases and may overlook certain aspects of both the completed and target information systems. In contrast, an algorithmic cost estimation model is unbiased; every information system is treated the same way. The danger with such a model is that its estimates are only as good as the underlying assumptions. For example, underlying the FFP model is the assumption that every aspect of an information system is embodied in the number of files, flows, and processes. A further problem is that a significant amount of subjective judgment often is needed in deciding what values to assign to the parameters of the model.

Many algorithmic cost estimation models have been proposed. Some are based on mathematical theories as to how information systems are developed. Other models are statistically based; large numbers of projects are studied and empirical rules are deduced from the data. Hybrid models incorporate mathematical equations, statistical modeling, and expert judgment. The most important hybrid model is Boehm's COCOMO, which is described in the next subsection. (See Just in Case You Wanted to Know Box 15.1 for a discussion of the acronym COCOMO.)

15.2.3 COCOMO

Computing development time using *COCOMO* is done in two stages. First, a rough estimate of the development effort is determined. Two parameters have to be estimated: the number of lines of code in the information system to be delivered to the client and the level of difficulty of developing that information system. From these two parameters, the *nominal effort* can be computed. For example, if the information system to be developed is straightforward and estimated to be 12,000 lines of code, then COCOMO predicts that the nominal effort will be 43 person-months (but read Just in Case You Wanted to Know Box 15.2 for a comment on this value).

Next, the nominal effort must be multiplied by 15 *development effort multipliers,* such as Required software reliability and Product complexity, to yield the *estimated effort.* Guidelines are provided [Boehm, 1981] for determining the values of these multipliers for a given target information system—the multipliers can range in value from 0.70 to 1.66. For example, a network of ATMs is complex and has to be reliable. According to the COCOMO guidelines, when developing such a network of ATMs, the value of multiplier Required software reliability will be 1.15 and multiplier Product complexity will be 1.30.

The estimated effort is then used in additional formulas to determine dollar costs, development schedules, activity distributions, annual maintenance costs, and other related items. COCOMO is a complete algorithmic cost estimation model, giving the user virtually every conceivable assistance in project planning.

COCOMO has proved to be the most reliable estimation method for traditional information systems; actual values come within 20 percent of the predicted values about two-thirds of the time. The major problem with COCOMO is that its most important input is the number of lines of code in the target information system. If this estimate is incorrect, then

One reaction to the value of the effort might be, "If 43 person-months of effort are needed to produce 12,000 delivered source instructions, then on average each programmer is turning out fewer than 300 lines of code a month—I have written more than that in one night!"

A 300-line information system usually is just that: 300 lines of code. In contrast, a maintainable 12,000-line information system has to go through all the workflows of the life cycle. In other words, the total effort of 43 person-months is shared among many activities, including coding. In fact, coding on average is only about 15 percent of the total development effort.

every single prediction of the model may be incorrect. Because of the possibility that the predictions of COCOMO or any other estimation technique may be inaccurate, management must monitor all predictions throughout information system development.

15.2.4 COCOMO II

COCOMO was put forward in 1981. At that time, the only life-cycle model in use was the waterfall model. Most information system was run on mainframes. Technologies such as client-server (Chapter 18) and the object-oriented paradigm had not yet been put forward. Accordingly, COCOMO did not incorporate any of these factors. However, as newer technologies began to become accepted information system development practice, COCOMO started to become less accurate.

COCOMO II is a major revision of the 1981 COCOMO. COCOMO II can deal with a wide variety of modern techniques for developing information systems, including the object-oriented paradigm, a variety of different life-cycle models, rapid prototyping, and COTS packages. COCOMO II is both flexible and sophisticated. Unfortunately, to achieve this goal, COCOMO II also is considerably more complex than the original COCOMO. Accordingly, in order to be able to use COCOMO II, it is necessary to study Boehm et al. [2000] in detail.

COCOMO II has been calibrated using 83 projects from a variety of different domains. The model still is too new for there to be many results regarding its accuracy and, in particular, the extent to which it is an improvement over its predecessor, the original (1981) COCOMO.

15.2.5 Tracking Duration and Cost Estimates

While the information system is being developed, actual development effort constantly must be compared against predictions. For example, suppose that the estimation metric used by the information system developers predicted that the analysis workflow would last three months and require seven person-months of effort. However, four months have gone by and 10 person-months of effort have been expended, yet the analysis workflow is by no means complete. Deviations of this kind can serve as an early warning that something has gone wrong and corrective action must be taken. The problem could be that the size of the information system was seriously underestimated or the development team is not as competent as it was thought to be. Whatever the reason, there are going to be serious duration and cost overruns, and management must take appropriate action to minimize the effects.

Careful tracking of predictions must be done throughout the development process, irrespective of the techniques by which the predictions were made. Deviations could be due to metrics that are poor predictors, inefficient information system development, a combination of both, or some other reason. The important thing is to detect deviations early and to take immediate corrective action.

Now that metrics for estimating duration and cost have been discussed, the components of the project management plan are described.

15.3   Components of a Project Management Plan

A project management plan has three main components: the work to be done, the resources with which to do it, and the money to pay for it all. In this section, these three ingredients of the plan are discussed. Much of the terminology is taken from IEEE Standard 1058 [IEEE, 1998], which is discussed in greater detail in the next two sections.

Information system development requires *resources*. The major resources required are the people who will develop the information system, the hardware on which the information system is to run, and the support software such as operating systems, text editors, and version control systems (Section 11.3.3).

The use of resources of all kinds varies with time, including personnel, computer time, support software, computer hardware, office facilities, and even travel. For large projects and for almost all resources, the *Rayleigh distribution* is a good approximation of the way that resource consumption varies with time; a typical Rayleigh curve is shown in Figure 15.3. Resource consumption starts small, climbs rapidly to a peak, then decreases at a slower rate.

It therefore is insufficient in a project management plan merely to state, for example, that three senior programmers with at least five years of experience are required to construct the information system. What is needed is something like the following:

> Three senior programmers with at least five years of experience are needed, two to start three months after the project commences, the third to start six months after that. Two will be phased out when product testing commences, the third when maintenance begins.

Because resource consumption varies with time, every project management plan will be a function of time.

FIGURE 15.3

A Rayleigh Curve Showing How Resource Consumption Varies with Time

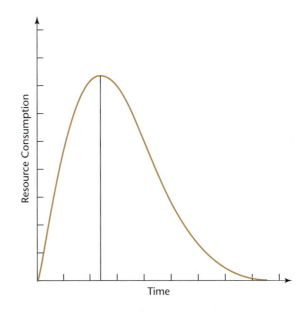

The work to be done falls into two categories. The first category is work that continues throughout the project and does not relate to any specific workflow of the information system life cycle. Such work is termed a *project function*. Examples are project management and quality assurance. The second category is work that relates to a specific workflow in the development of the information system; such work is termed an activity or a task. An *activity* is a major unit of work that has precise beginning and ending dates; consumes resources, such as computer time or person-days; and results in *work products* such as a budget, design artifacts, schedules, source code, or user's manual. An activity, in turn, comprises a set of *tasks,* a task being the smallest unit of work subject to management accountability. There are therefore three kinds of work in a project management plan: project functions carried on throughout the project, activities (major units of work), and tasks (minor units of work).

A critical aspect of the plan concerns completion of work products. The completion of a work product is termed a *milestone*. To determine whether a work product indeed has reached a milestone, it must first pass a series of *reviews* performed by fellow team members, the quality assurance group, management, or the client. A typical milestone is the completion of the design workflow after the design artifacts have passed the design review. Once a work product has been reviewed and agreed on, it becomes a *baseline* and can be changed only through formal procedures, as described in Section 11.4.

In reality, there is more to a work product than merely the information system itself. A *work package* defines not just the work product but also the staffing requirements, duration, resources, name of the responsible individual, and acceptance criteria for the work product. *Money,* of course, is a vital component of the plan. A detailed budget must be worked out and the money allocated, as a function of time, to the project functions and activities.

The issue of how to draw up a plan for information system development is addressed next.

15.4   Project Management Plan Framework

There are many ways of drawing up a project management plan. One of the best is IEEE Standard 1058 [IEEE, 1998]. The components of the plan are shown in Figure 15.4.

- The standard was drawn up by representatives of numerous major organizations involved in information system development. Input came from both industry and universities, and the members of the working group and reviewing teams had many years of experience in drawing up project management plans. The standard incorporates this experience.
- The IEEE project management plan is designed for use with all types of information systems. It does not impose a specific life-cycle model or prescribe a specific methodology. The plan essentially is a framework, the contents of which are tailored by each organization for a particular domain, development team, or technique.
- The IEEE project management plan framework supports process improvement. For example, many of the sections of the framework reflect CMM key process areas (Section 14.3.1) such as configuration management and metrics.
- The IEEE project management plan framework is ideal for the Unified Process. For instance, one section of the plan is devoted to requirements control and another to risk management, both central aspects of the Unified Process.

On the other hand, although the claim is made in IEEE Standard 1058 [IEEE, 1998] that the IEEE project management plan is applicable to software projects of all sizes, some of the sections are not relevant to small-scale software. For example, Section 7.7 of the plan framework is headed "Subcontractor Management Plan," but it is all but unheard of for subcontractors to be used in small-scale projects.

FIGURE 15.4
The IEEE Project Management Plan Framework

1. Overview
   1.1 Project Summary
      1.1.1 Purpose, Scope, and Objectives
      1.1.2 Assumptions and Constraints
      1.1.3 Project Deliverables
      1.1.4 Schedule and Budget Summary
   1.2 Evolution of the Project Management Plan
2. Reference Materials
3. Definitions and Acronyms
4. Project Organization
   4.1 External Interfaces
   4.2 Internal Structure
   4.3 Roles and Responsibilities
5. Managerial Process Plans
   5.1 Start-up Plan
      5.1.1 Estimation Plan
      5.1.2 Staffing Plan
      5.1.3 Resource Acquisition Plan
      5.1.4 Project Staff Training Plan
   5.2 Work Plan
      5.2.1 Work Activities
      5.2.2 Schedule Allocation
      5.2.3 Resource Allocation
      5.2.4 Budget Allocation
   5.3 Control Plan
      5.3.1 Requirements Control Plan
      5.3.2 Schedule Control Plan
      5.3.3 Budget Control Plan
      5.3.4 Quality Control Plan
      5.3.5 Reporting Plan
      5.3.6 Metrics Collection Plan
   5.4 Risk Management Plan
   5.5 Project Close-out Plan
6. Technical Process Plans
   6.1 Process Model
   6.2 Methods, Tools, and Techniques
   6.3 Infrastructure Plan
   6.4 Product Acceptance Plan
7. Supporting Process Plans
   7.1 Configuration Management Plan
   7.2 Testing Plan
   7.3 Documentation Plan
   7.4 Quality Assurance Plan
   7.5 Reviews and Audits Plan
   7.6 Problem Resolution Plan
   7.7 Subcontractor Management Plan
   7.8 Process Improvement Plan
8. Additional Plans

Accordingly, we now present the plan framework in two different ways. First, the full framework is described in Section 15.5. Second, a slightly abbreviated version of the framework is used in Section 15.6 for a management plan for a small-scale project, the Osbert Oglesby case study.

15.5 IEEE Project Management Plan Framework

The numbers and headings in the text of this section correspond to the entries in Figure 15.4. The terminology used has been defined in Section 15.3.

1. *Overview.*

    1.1 *Project Summary.*

    1.1.1 *Purpose, Scope, and Objectives.* A brief description is given of the purpose and scope of the information system to be delivered, as well as project objectives. Business needs are included in this subsection.

    1.1.2 *Assumptions and Constraints.* Any assumptions underlying the project are stated here, together with constraints such as the delivery date, budget, resources, and artifacts to be reused.

    1.1.3 *Project Deliverables.* All the items to be delivered to the client are listed here, together with the delivery dates.

    1.1.4 *Schedule and Budget Summary.* The overall schedule is presented here, together with the overall budget.

    1.2 *Evolution of the Project Management Plan.* No plan can be cast in concrete. The project management plan, like any other plan, requires continual updating in the light of experience and of change within both the client organization and the information system development organization. In this section the formal procedures and mechanisms for changing the plan are described, including the mechanism for placing the project management plan itself under configuration control.

2. *Reference Materials.* All documents referenced in the project management plan are listed here.

3. *Definitions and Acronyms.* This information ensures that the project management plan will be understood the same way by everyone.

4. *Project Organization.*

    4.1 *External Interfaces.* No project is constructed in a vacuum. The project members have to interact with the client organization and other members of their own organization. In addition, subcontractors may be involved in a large project. Administrative and managerial boundaries between the project and these other entities must be laid down.

    4.2 *Internal Structure.* In this section, the structure of the development organization itself is described. For example, many information system development organizations are divided into two types of groups, development groups that work on a single project and support groups that provide support functions, such as configuration management and quality assurance, on an organizationwide basis. Administrative and managerial boundaries between the project group and the support groups also must be defined clearly.

    4.3 *Roles and Responsibilities.* For each project function, such as quality assurance, and for each activity, such as product testing, the individual responsible must be identified.

5. *Managerial Process Plans.*

   5.1 *Start-up Plan.*

      5.1.1 *Estimation Plan.* The techniques used to estimate project duration and cost are listed here, as well as the way that these estimates will be tracked and, if necessary, modified while the project is in progress.

      5.1.2 *Staffing Plan.* The numbers and types of personnel required are listed, together with the durations for which they are needed.

      5.1.3 *Resource Acquisition Plan.* The way of acquiring the necessary resources, including hardware, software, service contracts, and administrative services, is given here.

      5.1.4 *Project Staff Training Plan.* All training needed for successful completion of the project is listed in this subsection.

   5.2 *Work Plan.*

      5.2.1 *Work Activities.* In this subsection, the work activities are specified, down to the task level if appropriate.

      5.2.2 *Schedule Allocation.* In general, there is interdependency among the work packages and dependency on external events. For example, the implementation workflow follows the design workflow and precedes product testing. In this subsection, the relevant dependencies are specified.

      5.2.3 *Resource Allocation.* The various resources previously listed are allocated to the appropriate project functions, activities, and tasks.

      5.2.4 *Budget Allocation.* In this subsection, the overall budget is broken down at the project function, activity, and task levels.

   5.3 *Control Plan.*

      5.3.1 *Requirements Control Plan.* As described in Part 2 of this book, while an information system is being developed, the requirements frequently change. The mechanisms used to monitor and control the changes to the requirements are given in this section.

      5.3.2 *Schedule Control Plan.* In this subsection, mechanisms for measuring progress are listed, together with a description of the actions to be taken if actual progress lags behind planned progress.

      5.3.3 *Budget Control Plan.* It is important that spending should not exceed the budgeted amount. Control mechanisms for monitoring when actual cost exceeds budgeted cost, as well as the actions to be taken should this happen, are described in this subsection.

      5.3.4 *Quality Control Plan.* The ways that quality will be measured and controlled are described in this section.

      5.3.5 *Reporting Plan.* In order to monitor the requirements, schedule, budget, and quality, reporting mechanisms need to be in place. These mechanisms are described in this subsection.

      5.3.6 *Metrics Collection Plan.* As explained in Section 14.4, it is not possible to manage the development process without measuring relevant metrics. The metrics to be collected are listed in this subsection.

   5.4 *Risk Management Plan.* Risks have to be identified, prioritized, mitigated, and tracked. All aspects of risk management are described in this section.

   5.5 *Project Close-out Plan.* The actions to be taken once the project is completed, including reassignment of staff and archiving of artifacts, are presented here.

6. *Technical Process Plans.*

   6.1 *Process Model.* In this section a detailed description is given of the life-cycle model to be used.

6.2 Methods, Tools, and Techniques. The development methodologies and programming languages to be used are described here.

6.3 Infrastructure Plan. Technical aspects of hardware and software are described in detail in this subsection. Items that should be covered include the computing systems (hardware, operating systems, network, and software) to be used for developing the information system, as well as the target computing systems on which the information system will be run and CASE tools to be employed.

6.4 Product Acceptance Plan. In order to ensure that the completed information system passes its acceptance test, acceptance criteria must be drawn up; the client must agree to the criteria in writing; and the developers must then ensure that these criteria are indeed met. The way that these three stages of the acceptance process will be carried out is described in this section.

7. *Supporting Process Plans.*

7.1 Configuration Management Plan. In this section a detailed description is given of the means by which all artifacts will be put under configuration management.

7.2 Testing Plan. Testing, like all other aspects of information system development, needs careful planning.

7.3 Documentation Plan. A description of documentation of all kinds, whether or not to be delivered to the client at the end of the project, is included in this section.

7.4 Quality Assurance Plan. All aspects of quality assurance, including testing, standards, and reviews, are encompassed by this section.

7.5 Reviews and Audits Plan. Details as to how reviews will be conducted are presented in this section.

7.6 Problem Resolution Plan. In the course of developing an information system, problems are all but certain to arise. For example, a design review may bring to light a critical fault in the analysis workflow that will require major changes to be made to almost all the artifacts already completed. In this section, the way that such problems will be handled is described.

7.7 Subcontractor Management Plan. This section is applicable when subcontractors are to supply certain work products. The approach to selecting and managing subcontractors then appears here.

7.8 Process Improvement Plan. Process improvement strategies are included in this section.

8. *Additional Plans.* For certain projects, additional components may need to appear in the plan. In terms of the IEEE framework, they appear at the end of the plan. Additional components may include security plans, safety plans, data conversion plans, installation plans, and the information system maintenance plan.

A sample project management plan appears in the next section.

15.6 Project Management Plan: Osbert Oglesby Case Study

As explained at the end of Section 15.4, several aspects of the IEEE project management plan framework are inapplicable to the development of small-scale information systems. In this section, a modified version of the framework is utilized for a project management plan for development of such a small-scale information system. Specifically, the plan is for the development of the Osbert Oglesby information system by a development organization consisting of three individuals: Pat, the owner of the company, and two systems analysts, Robin and Dale.

1. *Overview.*

   1.1 *Project Summary.*

      1.1.1 *Purpose, Scope, and Objectives.* The objective of this project is to develop an information system that will assist Osbert Oglesby, Art Dealer (OOAD), in making decisions regarding the purchase of paintings to be displayed and sold in his gallery. The information system will allow the client to buy and sell masterpieces, masterworks, and other paintings. The information system will perform the required calculations and record keeping on these paintings and produce reports listing bought paintings, sold paintings, and current fashion trends.

      1.1.2 *Assumptions and Constraints.* Constraints include the following:

         The deadline must be met.

         The budget constraint must be met.

         The information system must be reliable.

         The architecture must be open so that additional functionality may be added later.

      The information system must be user-friendly.

      1.1.3 *Project Deliverables.* The complete information system, including user manual, will be delivered 10 weeks after the project commences.

      1.1.4 *Schedule and Budget Summary.* The duration, personnel requirements, and budget of each workflow are as follows:

         Requirements workflow (one week, two team members, $3,380)

         Analysis workflow (two weeks, two team members, $6,760)

         Design workflow (two weeks, two team members, $6,760)

         Implementation workflow (three weeks, three team members, $15,210)

         Testing workflow (two weeks, three team members, $10,140)

   The total development time is 10 weeks and the total internal cost is $42,250.

   1.2 *Evolution of the Project Management Plan.* All changes in the project management plan must be agreed to by Pat before they are implemented. All changes should be documented in order to keep the project management plan correct and up to date.

2. *Reference Materials.* All artifacts will conform to the company's programming, documentation, and testing standards.

3. *Definitions and Acronyms.*

   OOAD—Osbert Oglesby, Art Dealer; Mr. Oglesby is our client.

4. *Project Organization.*

   4.1 *External Interfaces.* All the work on this project will be performed by Pat, Robin, and Dale. Pat will meet weekly with the client to report progress and discuss possible changes and modifications.

   4.2 *Internal Structure.* The development team consists of Pat (owner), Robin, and Dale (systems analysts).

   4.3 *Roles and Responsibilities.* Robin and Dale will perform the design workflow. Pat will implement the class definitions and report artifacts, Robin will construct the artifacts to handle bought paintings, and Dale will develop the artifacts that handle sold paintings. Each member is responsible for the quality of the artifacts he or she produces. Pat will oversee integration and the overall quality of the information system and will liaise with the client.

5. *Managerial Process Plans.*

    5.1 *Start-up Plan.*

        5.1.1 Estimation Plan. As previously stated, the total development time is estimated to be 10 weeks and the total internal cost will be $42,250. These figures were obtained by expert judgment by analogy, that is, by comparison with similar projects.

        5.1.2 Staffing Plan. Pat is needed for the entire 10 weeks, for the first 5 weeks in only a managerial capacity and the second 5 weeks as both manager and programmer. Robin and Dale are needed for the entire 10 weeks, for the first 5 weeks as systems analysts and designers, for the second 5 weeks as programmers and testers.

        5.1.3 Resource Acquisition Plan. All necessary hardware, software, and CASE tools for the project are already available. The information system will be delivered to Osbert Oglesby installed on a laptop that will be leased from our usual supplier.

        5.1.4 Project Staff Training Plan. No additional staff training is needed for this project.

    5.2 *Work Plan.*

        5.2.1–2 Work Activities and Schedule Allocation.

Week 1:	Met with client; determined requirements artifacts. Inspected requirements artifacts.
Weeks 2, 3:	Produced analysis artifacts; inspected analysis artifacts. Drew up specification document; client approved it. Produced project management plan; inspected project management plan.
Weeks 4, 5:	Produce design artifacts; inspect design artifacts.
Weeks 6–10:	Implementation and inspection of each module, unit testing and documentation, integration of each module, integration testing, product testing, documentation inspection.

        5.2.3 Resource Allocation. The three team members will work separately on their assigned artifacts. Pat's assigned role will be to monitor the daily progress of the other two, oversee implementation, be responsible for overall quality, and interact with the client. Team members will meet at the end of each day and discuss problems and progress. Formal meetings with the client will be held at the end of each week to report progress and determine if any changes need to be made. Pat will ensure that schedule and budget requirements are met. Risk management will also be Pat's responsibility.

        Minimizing faults and maximizing user-friendliness will be Pat's priorities. Pat has overall responsibility for all documentation and has to ensure that it is up to date.

        5.2.4 Budget Allocation. The budget for each workflow is as follows:

Requirements workflow	$ 3,380
Analysis workflow	6,760
Design workflow	6,760
Implementation workflow	15,210
Testing workflow	10,140
Total	$42,250

5.3 Control Plan. Any major changes that will affect the milestones or the budget will have to be approved by Pat and documented. There will be no outside quality assurance personnel involved. The benefits of having someone other than the individual who carried out the development task do the testing will be accomplished by each person testing another person's work products.

Pat will be responsible for ensuring that the project is completed on time and within budget. This will be accomplished through daily meetings with the team members. At each meeting, Robin and Dale will present the day's progress and problems. Pat will determine whether they are progressing as expected and whether they are following the specification document and the project management plan. Any major problems faced by the team members will immediately be reported to Pat.

5.4 Risk Management Plan. The risk factors and the tracking mechanisms are as follows:

There is no existing information system with which the new information system can be compared. Accordingly, it will not be possible to run the information system in parallel with an existing one. Therefore, the information system should be subjected to extensive testing.

The client is assumed to be inexperienced with computers. Therefore, special attention should be paid to the analysis workflow and communication with the client. The information system has to be made as user-friendly as possible.

There is always the possibility of a major design fault, so extensive testing will be performed during the design workflow. Also, each of the team members will initially test his or her own code and then test the code of another member. Pat will be responsible for integration testing and will be in charge of product testing.

The information must meet the specified storage requirements and response times. This should not be a major problem because of the small size of the information system, but it will be monitored by Pat throughout development.

There is a slim chance of hardware failure, in which case another machine will be leased. If there is a fault in the compiler, it will be replaced. These are covered in the warranties received from the hardware and compiler suppliers.

5.5 Project Close-out Plan. Not applicable here.

6. *Technical Process Plans.*

6.1 Process Model. The Unified Process will be used.

6.2 Methods, Tools, and Techniques. The workflows will be performed in accordance with the Unified Process. The product will be implemented in C++.

6.3 Infrastructure Plan. The product will be developed using ArgoUML running under Linux on a personal computer.

6.4 Product Acceptance Plan. Acceptance of the product by our client will be achieved by following the steps of the Unified Process.

7. *Supporting Process Plan.*

7.1 Configuration Management Plan. CVS will be used throughout for all artifacts.

7.2 Testing Plan. The testing workflow of the Unified Process will be performed.

7.3 Documentation Plan. Documentation will be produced as specified in the Unified Process.

7.4–5 Quality Assurance Plan and Reviews and Audits Plan. Robin and Dale will test each other's code and Pat will conduct integration testing. Extensive product testing will then be performed by all three.

7.6 Problem Resolution Plan. As stated in 5.3, any major problems faced by the team members will immediately be reported to Pat.

7.7 Subcontractor Management Plan. Not applicable here.

7.8 Process Improvement Plan. All activities will be conducted in accord with the company plan to advance from CMM level 2 to level 3 within two years.

8. *Additional Plans.* Additional Components.

Security. A password will be needed to use the information system.

Training. Training will be performed by Pat at time of delivery. Because the information system is straightforward to use, one day is sufficient for training. Pat will answer questions at no cost for the first year of use.

Information System Maintenance. Corrective maintenance will be performed by the team at no cost for a period of 12 months. A separate contract will be drawn up regarding enhancement.

15.7 Planning of Testing

One component of the project management plan frequently overlooked is test planning. Like every other activity of information system development, testing must be planned. The project management plan must include resources for testing, and the detailed schedule must explicitly indicate the testing to be done during each workflow.

Without a test plan, a project can go awry in a number of ways. For example, during product testing, the quality assurance group must check that every aspect of the specification document, as signed off by the client, has been implemented in the completed information system. A good way of assisting the quality assurance group in this task is to require that the development be traceable. That is, it must be possible to connect each statement in the specification document to a part of the design, and each part of the design must be reflected explicitly in the code. One technique for achieving this is to number each statement in the specification document and ensure that these numbers are reflected in both the design and the resulting code. However, if the test plan does not specify that this is to be done, it is highly unlikely that the design and the code will be labeled appropriately. Consequently, when the product testing finally is performed, it will be extremely difficult for the quality assurance group to determine that the information system is a complete implementation of the specification document. In fact, traceability should start with the requirements workflow; each statement in the requirements document must be connected to part of the specification document.

One powerful aspect of inspections is the detailed list of faults detected during an inspection. Suppose that a team is inspecting the analysis artifacts of an information system. As explained in Section 13.3.3, the list of faults is used in two ways. First, the fault statistics from this inspection must be compared with the accumulated averages of fault statistics from previous analysis artifact inspections. Deviations from previous norms indicate problems within the project. Second, the fault statistics from the current analysis inspection must be carried forward to the design and code inspections of the information system. After all, if there are a large number of faults of a particular type, it is possible that not all of them were detected during the inspection of the analysis artifacts, and the design and code inspections provide additional opportunities for locating any remaining faults of this type. However, unless the test plan states that details of all faults have to be carefully recorded, it is unlikely that this task will be done.

Accordingly, every test plan must specify what testing is to be performed, when it is to be performed, and how it is to be performed. Such a test plan is an essential part of Section 7.4 of the project management plan. Without it, the quality of the overall information system undoubtedly will suffer.

15.8   Training Requirements

When the subject of training is raised in discussions with clients, a common response is, "We don't need to worry about training until the information system is finished; then we can train the users." This is a somewhat unfortunate remark, implying as it does that only users require training. In fact, training also may be needed by members of the development team, starting with training in information system planning and estimating. When new information system development techniques, such as new design techniques or testing procedures, are used, training must be provided to every member of the team using the new technique.

Introduction of the object-oriented paradigm has major training consequences for an organization that, up to now, has used only the traditional paradigm. The introduction of hardware or information system tools such as workstations or a CASE environment (see Section 11.6) also requires training. Programmers may need training in the operating system of the machine to be used for information system development as well as in the implementation language. Documentation preparation training frequently is overlooked, as evidenced by the poor quality of so much documentation. Computer operators certainly require some sort of training to be able to run the new information system; they also may require additional training if new hardware is utilized.

The required training can be obtained in a number of ways. The easiest and least disruptive is in-house training, by either fellow employees or consultants. Many companies offer a variety of training courses, and colleges often offer training courses in the evenings. World Wide Web–based courses are another alternative.

Once the training needs have been determined and the training plan drawn up, the plan must be incorporated into the project management plan.

15.9   Documentation Standards

A considerable portion of the information system development effort is absorbed by documentation. It is not unusual to have to spend 150 to 200 hours on documentation for every 100 hours spent coding the system.

Standards are needed for every type of documentation. For instance, uniformity in design documentation reduces misunderstandings between team members and aids the quality assurance group. Although new employees have to be trained in the documentation standards, no further training is needed when existing employees move from project to project within the organization. From the viewpoint of information system maintenance, uniform coding standards assist maintenance programmers in understanding source code. Standardization is even more important for user manuals, because these have to be read by a wide variety of individuals, few of whom are computer experts.

As part of the planning process, standards must be established for all documentation to be produced during information system development. As we have seen, these standards are incorporated in the project management plan. Where an existing standard is to be used, the standard is listed in Section 2 of the project management plan (Reference Materials). If a standard is specially written for the development effort, then it appears in Section 6.2 (Methods, Tools, and Techniques).

Documentation is an essential aspect of the information system development effort. In a very real sense, the information system *is* the documentation, because without documentation the information system cannot be maintained. Planning the documentation effort in every detail, then ensuring that the plan is adhered to, is a critical component of successful information system production.

15.10 CASE Tools for Planning and Estimating

A number of tools are available that automate COCOMO and COCOMO II. For speed of computation when the value of a parameter is modified, several implementations of COCOMO have been written in spreadsheet languages such as Excel. For developing and updating the plan itself, a word processor is essential.

Management information tools also are useful for planning. For example, suppose that a large information system organization has 150 programmers. A scheduling tool can help planners keep track of which programmers already are assigned to specific tasks and which are available for the current project.

More general types of management information also are needed. A number of commercially available management tools can be used both to assist with the planning and estimating process and to monitor the development process as a whole. These include MacProject and Microsoft Project.

15.11 Testing the Project Management Plan

As pointed out at the beginning of this chapter, a fault in the project management plan can have serious financial implications for the developers. It is critical that the development organization neither overestimate nor underestimate the duration of the project or its cost. For this reason, the entire project management plan must be checked by the quality assurance group before estimates are given to the client. The best way to test the plan is by a plan inspection, similar to the inspection described in Section 13.3.3.

The plan inspection team must review the project management plan in detail, paying particular attention to the duration and cost estimates. To reduce risks even further, irrespective of the metrics used, the duration and cost estimates should be computed independently by a member of the quality assurance group as soon as the members of the planning team have determined their estimates.

An alphabetical list of the estimation metrics presented in this chapter appears in Figure 15.5. The section in which each is described is shown.

FIGURE 15.5

An Alphabetical List of the Estimation Methods Presented in This Chapter and the Section in Which Each Is Described

Algorithmic cost estimation models (Section 15.2.2)
COCOMO (Section 15.2.3)
COCOMO II (Section 15.2.4)
Delphi technique (Section 15.2.2)
Expert judgment by analogy (Section 15.2.2)
FFP metric (Section 15.2.1)
Function points (Section 15.2.1)
KDSI (Section 15.2.1)
LOC (Section 15.2.1)
Software science (Section 15.2.1)

Key Terms

activity, *297*
algorithmic cost estimation
    model, *293*
baseline, *297*
COCOMO, *294*
cost, *289*
Delphi technique, *293*
development effort
    multiplier, *294*
duration, *289*
efficiency, *291*
estimated effort, *294*
expert judgment by analogy, *293*

external cost, *289*
FFP metric, *291*
file, *291*
flow, *291*
function point, *292*
internal cost, *289*
KDSI, *290*
lines of code, *290*
LOC, *290*
milestone, *297*
money, *297*
nominal effort, *294*
planning, *287*

process, *291*
productivity, *291*
project function, *297*
Rayleigh distribution, *296*
resources, *296*
review, *297*
software science, *291*
task, *297*
technical factor, *292*
thousand delivered source
    instructions, *290*
work package, *297*
work product, *297*

Review Questions for Chapter 15

1. Why do we not draw up the project management plan at the beginning of the project?
2. Distinguish between internal and external cost.
3. Why is it so hard to estimate project duration and cost?
4. Give five reasons why lines of code is a poor metric for the size of an information system.
5. What is meant by expert judgment by analogy?
6. Explain the Delphi technique.
7. What is an algorithmic cost estimation model?
8. Distinguish between project functions, activities, work products, tasks, and resources.
9. What is a milestone?

Problems

15.1 Why do you think that some cynical information system organizations refer to *milestones* as *millstones?* (Hint: Look up the figurative meaning of *millstone* in a dictionary.)

15.2 What is the connection between milestones and baselines?

15.3 You are an information system engineer at Nederburg Information System Developers. A year ago, your manager announced that your next information system would comprise 7 files, 50 flows, and 86 processes.

1. Using the FFP metric, determine its size.
2. For Nederburg Information System Developers, the constant *d* in equation (15.1) has been determined to be $932. What cost estimate did the FFP metric predict?
3. The information system recently was completed at a cost of $136,500. What does this tell you about the productivity of your development team?

15.4 Why do you think that, despite its drawbacks, lines of code (LOC or KDSI) is so widely used as a metric of information system size?

15.5 You are in charge of developing the information system for an information system that uses a set of newly developed algorithms to compute the most cost-effective routes for a large trucking company. Using COCOMO, you determine that the cost of the information system will be $430,000. However, as a check, you ask a member of your team to estimate the effort using function points. She reports that the function point metric predicts a cost of $890,000, more than twice as large as your COCOMO prediction. What do you do now?

15.6 An information system maintenance plan is considered an "additional component" of the IEEE project management plan. Bearing in mind that every nontrivial information system is maintained and that the cost of maintenance, on average, is at least twice the cost of developing the information system, how can this be justified?

Term Project

15.7 Consider the Chocoholics Anonymous information system described in Appendix A. Why is it not possible to estimate the duration and cost purely on the basis of the information in Appendix A?

15.8 Draw up a project management plan for the Chocoholics Anonymous information system described in Appendix A.

References

Albrecht, A. J. "Measuring Application Development Productivity." In *Proceedings of the SHARE/GUIDE/IBM Application Development Symposium,* pp. 83–92. Monterey, CA, October 1979.

Boehm, B. W. *Software Engineering Economics.* Englewood Cliffs, NJ: Prentice Hall, 1981.

Boehm, B. W.; C. Abts; A. W. Brown; S. Chulani; B. K. Clark; E. Horowitz; R. Madachy; D. Reifer; and B. Steece. *Software Cost Estimation with COCOMO II.* Upper Saddle River, NJ: Prentice Hall, 2000.

Halstead, M. H. *Elements of Software Science.* New York: Elsevier North-Holland, 1977.

Institute of Electrical and Electronic Engineers. "IEEE Standard for Software Project Management Plans." IEEE Std. 1058-1998. New York: IEEE, 1998.

Sackman, H.; W. J. Erikson; and E. E. Grant. "Exploratory Experimental Studies Comparing Online and Offline Programming Performance." *Communications of the ACM* 11 (January 1968), pp. 3–11.

Shepperd, M., and D. C. Ince. "A Critique of Three Metrics." *Journal of Systems and Software* 26 (September 1994), pp. 197–210.

Symons, C. R. *Software Sizing and Estimating: Mk II FPA.* Chichester, UK: John Wiley & Sons, 1991.

van der Poel, K. G., and S. R. Schach. "A Software Metric for Cost Estimation and Efficiency Measurement in Data Processing System Development." *Journal of Systems and Software* 3 (September 1983), pp. 187–91.

16

Maintenance

Learning Objectives

After studying this chapter, you should be able to:

- Appreciate the importance of maintenance.
- Describe the challenges of maintenance.
- Describe the maintenance implications of the object-oriented paradigm.
- Describe the skills needed for maintenance.

Once the information system has passed its acceptance test, it is handed over to the client. The information system is installed on the client's computer and utilized for the purpose for which it was developed. Any useful information system, however, is almost certain to undergo changes after delivery, either to fix faults (corrective maintenance) or extend the functionality of the information system (enhancement).

However, as pointed out in Section 2.10, viewing maintenance solely as changes that are made to the information system after it has been delivered can lead to unexpected consequences. Instead, in this book we take the modern view of maintenance. As defined by the International Standards Organization and International Electrotechnical Commission in 1995, *maintenance* is the process that occurs when an information system artifact is modified either because of a problem or because of a need for improvement or adaptation [ISO/IEC, 1995]. In other words, in terms of the ISO/IEC definition, maintenance occurs whenever the information system is modified, regardless of whether this takes place before or after installation.

16.1 Why Maintenance Is Necessary

There are three main reasons for making changes to an information system:

- The first reason is to correct a fault, whether a requirements fault, analysis fault, design fault, coding fault, documentation fault, or any other types of fault. This is termed *corrective maintenance*.
- The second reason, *perfective maintenance,* is to improve the effectiveness of the information system. For instance, the client may wish to have additional functionality added or request that the information system be modified so that it runs faster. Improving the maintainability of an information system is another example of perfective maintenance.

- The third reason for changing an information system is *adaptive maintenance,* a change made to an information system to react to changes in the environment in which the information system operates. For example, an information system almost certainly has to be modified if it is ported to a new compiler, operating system, or hardware. With each change to the tax code, an information system that prepares tax returns has to be modified accordingly. When the U.S. Postal Service introduced nine-digit ZIP codes in 1981, information systems that had allowed for only five-digit ZIP codes had to be changed. Adaptive maintenance is not requested by a client; instead, it is externally imposed on the client.

16.2   Development and Maintenance

As previously pointed out, maintenance occurs whenever an artifact is changed. Thus, maintenance can (and does) take place over the entire life cycle of an information system. Accordingly, many information technology professionals prefer to use the term *evolution* rather than maintenance to indicate that an information system evolves over time. In fact, some view the entire information system life cycle, from beginning to end, as an evolutionary process.

This is how maintenance is viewed by the Unified Process. In fact, the word *maintenance* hardly occurs anywhere in Jacobson, Booch, and Rumbaugh [1999]. Instead, maintenance is implicitly treated merely as another increment of the information system. However, there is a basic difference between development and maintenance, a difference that will be illustrated by means of the following example.

Suppose that a woman has her portrait painted when she is 18. The oil painting depicts just her head and shoulders. Twenty years later she marries, and now wants the portrait to be modified so that it depicts both her new husband and herself. There are four difficulties that would arise if the portrait were to be changed in this way.

- The canvas is not large enough for her husband's head to be added.
- The original portrait was hung where sunlight fell on it much of the day, so the colors have faded somewhat. In addition, the brand of oil paint that was used for the original painting is no longer manufactured. For both these reasons, it will be hard to achieve consistency of color.
- The original artist has retired, so it will be hard to achieve consistency of style.
- The woman's face has aged 20 years since the original portrait was painted, so considerable work will have to be done to ensure that the modified painting is an accurate likeness.

For all these reasons, it would be laughable even to think about modifying the original portrait. Instead, a new artist will paint a new portrait of the couple from scratch.

Now consider the maintenance of an information system that originally cost $2 million to develop. There are four difficulties that have to be solved:

- Unfortunately, the disk on which the database is stored is all but full—the current disk is not large enough for more data to be added.
- The company that manufactured the original disk is no longer in business, so a larger disk will have to be bought from a different manufacturer. However, there are hardware incompatibilities between the new disk and the existing information system (Section 14.9.1), and it will cost about $100,000 to make all the changes needed to use the new disk.

- The original developers left the company some years ago, so the changes to the information system will have to be made by a team of maintainers who have never seen the information system before.
- The original information system was developed using the traditional paradigm. Nowadays we use the object-oriented paradigm (and specifically the Unified Process).

There is a clear correspondence between each portrait bullet point and the corresponding information system bullet point. The inescapable conclusion regarding the oil painting is to paint a new portrait from scratch. Does that mean that, instead of performing a $100,000 maintenance task, we should develop a totally new information system at a cost of $2 million?

The answer is that analogies should never be taken too far. Just as it is obvious that a new portrait should be painted, it is equally obvious that the existing information system should undergo maintenance at 5 percent of the cost of a new information system.

Nevertheless, there is an important lesson to be learned from this otherwise poor analogy. Whether we are dealing with portraits or information systems, it is easier to create a new version than to modify an existing version. In the case of the portrait, not only was it all but impossible to modify the existing portrait, but the cost of doing so would surely have been more than the cost of painting a new portrait from scratch. In the case of the information system, not only were the changes feasible, but the cost of doing them would be a fraction of the cost of developing a new information system from scratch. In other words, even though it is harder to make changes to existing artifacts than to construct new artifacts from scratch, economic considerations make maintenance far more preferable than redevelopment.

16.3   What Is Required of Maintainers?

During the information system life cycle, more time is spent on maintenance than on any other activity. In fact, on average at least 67 percent of the total cost of an information system can be attributed to maintenance, as shown in Figure 1.2. But many organizations, even today, assign the task of maintenance to beginners and less competent information technology professionals, leaving the "glamorous" job of development to better or more experienced professionals.

In fact, maintenance is the most difficult of all parts of the information system life cycle. A major reason is that maintenance incorporates aspects of all the other parts of the life cycle. Consider what happens when a fault report is handed to a maintainer. A fault report is filed if, in the opinion of the user, the information system is not working as specified in the user manual. There are a number of possible causes. First, nothing at all could be wrong; perhaps the user has misunderstood the user manual or is using the information system incorrectly. Alternatively, if the fault does lie in the information system, it simply might be that the user manual itself has been badly worded, and nothing is wrong with the other artifacts. Usually, however, the fault is in the code artifacts. But before making any changes, the maintainer has to determine exactly where the fault lies, using the fault report filed by the user, the source code—and often nothing else. Therefore, the maintainer needs to have far above average debugging skills, because the fault could lie anywhere within the information system. And the original cause of the fault might lie in the by now nonexistent specification or design documents, as explained in the next paragraph.

Suppose that the maintainer has located the fault and must fix it without inadvertently introducing another fault elsewhere in the information system, that is, a *regression fault*. If regression faults are to be minimized, detailed documentation for the information system as a whole and for each individual code artifact must be available. However, information technology professionals are notorious for their dislike of paperwork of all kinds, especially documentation, and it is quite common for the documentation to be incomplete, faulty, or totally missing. In these cases, the maintainer has to deduce from the source code itself, the only valid form of documentation available, all the information needed to avoid introducing a regression fault.

Having found the probable fault and tried to correct it, the maintainer now must test that the modification works correctly and no regression faults have been introduced. To check the modification itself, the maintainer must construct special test cases; checking for regression faults is done using the set of test data stored precisely for performing *regression testing* (Section 13.6). Then the test cases constructed for checking the modification must be added to the set of stored test cases to be used for future regression testing of the modified information system. In addition, if changes to the analysis or design artifacts had to be made to correct the fault, then these changes also must be tested. Expertise in testing, therefore, is an additional prerequisite for maintenance. Finally, it is essential that the maintainer document every change. The preceding discussion relates to corrective maintenance. For that task, the maintainer primarily must be a superb diagnostician to determine if there is a fault and, if so, an expert technician to fix it.

Now we turn to adaptive and perfective maintenance. To perform these, the maintainer must go through the steps of the requirements, analysis, design, and implementation workflows, taking the existing information system as the starting point. For some types of changes, additional analysis, design, and code artifacts have to be constructed. In other cases, changes to existing analysis, design, and code artifacts are needed. Thus, whereas analysis artifacts frequently are produced by analysis experts, design artifacts by design experts, and code artifacts by programming experts, the maintainer has to be an expert in all three areas. Perfective and adaptive maintenance are adversely affected by a lack of adequate documentation, just like corrective maintenance. Furthermore, the ability to design suitable test cases and write good documentation is needed for perfective and adaptive maintenance, just as for corrective maintenance. Therefore, none of the forms of maintenance is a task for a less experienced information technology professional unless a top-rank professional supervises the process.

From the preceding discussion, it is clear that maintainers have to possess almost every technical skill that an information technology professional could have. But what does he or she get in return?

- Maintenance is a thankless task in every way. Maintainers deal with dissatisfied users; if the user were happy with the information system, it would not need maintenance.
- The user's problems have frequently been caused by the individuals who developed the information system, not the maintainer.
- The information system itself may have been badly constructed, adding to the frustrations of the maintainer.
- Maintenance is looked down on by many information system developers who consider development to be a glamorous job and maintenance to be drudge work fit only for beginners or incompetents.

Maintenance can be likened to after-sales service. The information system has been delivered to the client. But now the client is dissatisfied, because either the information system does not work correctly or it does not do everything that the client currently wants, or because the circumstances for which the information system was developed have changed in some way. Unless the information system development organization also provides good maintenance service, the client will take all future information system development business elsewhere. When the client and information services division are part of the same organization, and hence inextricably tied from the viewpoint of future work, a dissatisfied client may use every means, fair or foul, to discredit the information services division. This, in turn, leads to an erosion of confidence, from both outside and inside the information services division, and to resignations and dismissals. It is important for every information system organization to keep its clients happy by providing excellent maintenance service.

So, for information system after information system, maintenance is the most challenging aspect of information technology—and frequently the most thankless.

How can this situation be changed? Managers must restrict maintenance tasks to professionals who have all the skills needed to perform maintenance. They must make it known that only top information technology professionals merit maintenance assignments in their organization and pay them accordingly. If management believes that maintenance is a challenge and that good maintenance is critical for the success of the organization, attitudes toward maintenance will slowly improve (but see Just in Case You Wanted to Know Box 16.1).

Some of the problems that maintainers face are now highlighted in a mini case study.

16.4   Temperate Fruit Committee Mini Case Study

In countries with centralized economies, the government controls the distribution and marketing of agricultural products. In one such country, temperate fruits such as peaches, apples, and pears were the responsibility of the Temperate Fruit Committee. One day, the chairman of the Temperate Fruit Committee asked a government computer consultant to computerize the operations of the Temperate Fruit Committee. The chairman informed the consultant that there are exactly seven temperate fruits: apples, apricots, cherries, nectarines, peaches, pears, and plums. The database was to be designed for those seven fruits, no more and no less. After all, that was the way that the world was, and the consultant was not to waste time and money allowing for any sort of expandability.

The information system was duly delivered to the Temperate Fruit Committee. About a year later, the chairman summoned the maintainer responsible for the information system. "What do you know about kiwi fruit?" asked the chairman. "Nothing," replied the mystified maintainer. "Well," said the chairman, "it seems that kiwi fruit is a temperate fruit that has just started to be grown in our country, and the Temperate Fruit Committee is responsible for it. Please change the information system accordingly."

The maintainer discovered that the consultant fortunately had not carried out the chairman's original instructions to the letter. The good practice of allowing for some sort of future expansion was too ingrained, and the consultant had provided a number of unused spaces in the database. By slightly rearranging certain items, the maintainer was able to incorporate kiwi fruit, the eighth temperate fruit, into the information system.

Another year went by, and the information system functioned well. Then the maintainer again was called to the chairman's office. The chairman was in a good mood. He jovially informed the maintainer that the government had reorganized the distribution and marketing of agricultural products. His committee was now responsible for all fruit produced in that country, not just temperate fruit, and so the information system now had to be modified to incorporate the 26 additional kinds of fruit on the list he handed to the maintainer. The maintainer protested, pointing out that this change would take almost as long as rewriting the information system from scratch. "Nonsense," replied the chairman. "You had no trouble adding kiwi fruit. Just do the same thing another 26 times!"

A number of important lessons are to be learned from this:

- The problem with the information system, no provision for expansion, was caused by the developer, not the maintainer. The developer made the mistake of obeying the chairman's instruction regarding future expandability of the information system, but the maintainer suffered the consequences. In fact, unless she reads this book, the consultant who developed the original information system may never realize that her information system was anything but a success. This is one of the more annoying aspects of maintenance, in that the maintainer is responsible for fixing other people's mistakes. The person who caused the problem either has other duties or has left the organization, but the maintainer now has to solve the problem.

- The client frequently does not understand that maintenance can be difficult or, in some instances, all but impossible. The problem is exacerbated when the maintainer has successfully carried out previous perfective and adaptive maintenance tasks but suddenly protests that a new assignment cannot be done, even though superficially it seems no different from what has been done before with little difficulty.

- All information system development must be carried out with an eye on future maintenance. If the consultant had designed the information system for an arbitrary number of different kinds of fruit, there would have been no difficulty in incorporating first the kiwi fruit and then the 26 other kinds of fruit.

As stated many times, maintenance is a vital part of the information system life cycle, and the one that consumes the most resources. During information system development, it is essential that the development team never forget the maintainer, who will be responsible for the information system once it has been installed.

16.5   The Management of Maintenance

Issues regarding management of maintenance are now considered.

16.5.1   Fault Reports

The first thing needed when maintaining an information system is a mechanism for changing the information system. With regard to corrective maintenance, that is, removing residual faults, if the information system appears to be functioning incorrectly, then a *fault report* should be filed by the user. This must include enough information to enable the maintainer to recreate the problem, which usually will be some sort of failure.

Ideally, every fault reported by a user should be fixed immediately. In practice, information services organizations usually are understaffed, with a backlog of work, both development and maintenance. If the fault is critical, such as if a payroll information system crashes the day before payday or overpays or underpays employees, immediate corrective action must be taken. Otherwise, each fault report must at least receive an immediate preliminary investigation.

The maintainer should first consult the fault report file. This contains all reported faults that have not yet been fixed, together with suggestions for working around them, that is, ways for the user to bypass the portion of the information system that apparently is responsible for the failure, until such time as the fault can be fixed. If the fault has been reported previously, any information in the fault report file should be given to the user. But if what the user reports appears to be a new fault, then the maintainer should study the problem and attempt to find the cause and a way to fix it. In addition, an attempt should be made to find a way to work around the problem, because it may take six or nine months before someone can be assigned to make the necessary changes to the information system. In the light of the serious shortage of information technology professionals and, in particular, information technology professionals who are good enough to perform maintenance, suggesting a way to live with the fault until it can be solved often is the only way to deal with fault reports that are not true emergencies.

The maintainer's conclusions then should be added to the fault report file, together with any supporting documentation, such as listings, designs, and manuals used to arrive at those conclusions. The manager in charge of maintenance should consult the file regularly, setting priorities for the various fixes. The file also should contain the client's requests for perfective and adaptive maintenance. The next modification made to the information system then will be the one with the highest priority.

When copies of an information system have been distributed to a variety of sites, copies of fault reports must be circulated to all users of the information system, together with an estimate of when each fault can be fixed. Then, if the same failure occurs at another site, the user can consult the relevant fault report to determine if it is possible to work around the fault and when it will be fixed. It would be preferable to fix every fault immediately and then distribute a new version of the information system to all sites, of course. Given the current worldwide shortage of good information technology professionals and the realities of information system maintenance, distributing fault reports probably is the best that can be done.

There is another reason why faults usually are not fixed immediately. It almost always is cheaper to make a number of changes, test them all, change all the documentation, and install the new version than it is to perform each change separately, test it, document it, install the new version, and then repeat the entire cycle for the next change. This is particularly true if every new version has to be installed on a significant number of computers, such as a large number of clients in a client–server network (Chapter 18), or when the information system is running at different sites. As a result, organizations prefer to accumulate noncritical maintenance tasks and then implement the changes as a group.

16.5.2 Authorizing Changes to the Information System

Once a decision has been made to perform corrective maintenance, a maintainer is assigned the task of determining the fault that caused the failure and repairing it. After the code itself has been changed, the repair must be tested, as must the information system as a whole (regression testing). Then the documentation must be updated to reflect the changes. In particular, a detailed description of what was changed, why it was changed, by whom, and when must be noted for each changed code artifact. If necessary, analysis or design artifacts also are changed, and the changes are similarly annotated. A similar set of steps is followed when performing perfective or adaptive maintenance; the only real difference is that perfective and adaptive maintenance are initiated by a change in requirements rather than by a fault report.

At this point all that would seem to be needed would be to distribute the new version to the users. But what if the maintainer has not tested the repair adequately? Before the new version of the information system is distributed and installed, it must be subjected to quality assurance performed by an independent group, that is, the members of the quality assurance group must not report to the same manager as the maintainer; it is important that quality assurance remain managerially independent (Section 13.2.3).

Reasons were given previously as to why maintenance is difficult. For those same reasons, maintenance also is fault prone. The testing of maintenance activities is difficult and time consuming, and the quality assurance group should not underestimate the implications of maintenance with regard to testing. Once the new version has been approved by the quality assurance group, it can be distributed.

Another area in which management must ensure that procedures are followed carefully is when the technique of baselines and private copies (Section 11.4) is used. Suppose a maintainer wishes to change code artifact personnelBenefits. The maintainer freezes the relevant code artifact and makes copies of all other code artifacts needed to perform the required maintenance task; often this includes all the other code artifacts in the information system. The maintainer makes the necessary changes to personnelBenefits and tests them and the new revision of personnelBenefits incorporating the changes is installed in the baseline. But, when the modified information system is delivered to the user, it immediately crashes. What went wrong is that the maintainer tested the modified version of personnelBenefits using his or her private workspace copies, that is, the copies of the other code artifacts that were in the baseline at the time that maintenance of personnelBenefits was started. In the meantime, certain other code artifacts were updated by other maintainers working on the same information system. The lesson is clear: Before installing a code artifact, it must be tested using the current baseline versions of all the other code artifacts and not the maintainer's private versions. This is a further reason for stipulating independent quality assurance—members of the quality assurance group simply have no access to maintainers' private workspaces. A third reason is that it has been estimated that the initial correction of a fault is itself incorrect some 70 percent of the time [Parnas, 1999].

16.5.3 Ensuring Maintainability

Maintenance is not a one-time effort. A well-built information system goes through a series of versions over its lifetime. As a result, it is necessary to plan for maintenance during the entire information system life cycle. For example, while performing the design workflow, for example, information hiding techniques (Section 3.6) should be employed. Documentation should be complete and correct and reflect the current version of every component artifact of the information system.

While performing maintenance, it is important not to compromise the maintainability that has been built into the information system from the very beginning. In other words, just as developers always should be conscious of the inevitable maintenance that will occur, so maintainers should always be conscious of the equally inevitable additional future maintenance. The principles established for maintainability during development are equally applicable to maintenance itself.

16.5.4 The Problem of Repeated Maintenance

One of the more frustrating difficulties of information system development is the *moving target problem* (Section 2.4). As fast as the developer constructs the information system, the client can change the requirements. Not only is this frustrating to the development team, but frequent changes can result in a poorly constructed information system. In addition, such changes add to the cost of the information system. In theory, the way to cope with this is first to perform the requirements and analysis workflows. Once the client is satisfied, the specification document is approved and the information system itself is constructed. In practice, nothing can stop the client from changing the requirements the day after the specification document has been approved. In fact, if the client is willing to pay the price, nothing can be done to prevent the requirements being changed every Monday and Thursday.

The problem is exacerbated during maintenance. The more a completed information system is changed, the more it will deviate from its original architecture, and the more difficult further changes will become. Under repeated maintenance, the documentation is likely to become even less reliable than usual, and the regression testing files may not be up to date. If still more maintenance is done, the information system as a whole may first have to be completely redeveloped.

The problem of the moving target clearly is a management problem. In theory, if management is sufficiently firm with the client and explains the problem at the beginning of the project, then the requirements can be frozen from the time the client has signed off the specification documents until the information system is delivered. Again, after each request for perfective maintenance, the requirements can be frozen for, say, three months or one year. In practice, it does not work that way. For example, if the client happens to be the president of the corporation and the development organization is the information services division of that corporation, then the president indeed can order changes every Monday and Thursday and they will be implemented. The old proverb "he who pays the piper calls the tune" unfortunately is only too relevant in this situation. Perhaps, the best that the vice president for information system development can do is to try to explain to the president the effect on the information system of repeated maintenance, and then simply have the complete information system rewritten whenever further maintenance would be hazardous to the integrity of the information system.

Trying to discourage additional maintenance by ensuring that the requested changes are implemented slowly has the effect only of the relevant personnel being replaced by others prepared to do the job faster. In short, if the person who requests repeated changes has sufficient clout, there is no solution to the problem of the moving target.

16.6 Maintenance and the Object-Oriented Paradigm

One reason put forward for using the object-oriented paradigm is that it promotes maintenance. After all, a class is an independent unit of a program. Every aspect of a well-designed information system that relates to the portion of the real world modeled by a specific class is localized to the class itself. For example, the **Bank Card Class** models every aspect of a bank card, and no aspects of a bank card are modeled by any other class. In addition, information hiding is employed to ensure that implementation details are not visible outside that class (Section 3.6). The only form of communication permitted is sending a message to an instance of that class (an object) to invoke an instance of an operation (a method).

As a consequence, the argument goes, it will be easy to maintain a class for two reasons. First, independence means that it will be easy to determine which part of an information

FIGURE 16.1
An Inheritance
Hierarchy

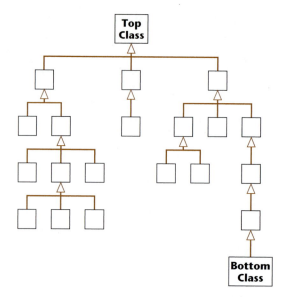

system must be changed to achieve a specific maintenance goal, be it enhancement or corrective maintenance. Second, information hiding ensures that a change made to a class will have no impact outside that class, and hence the number of regression faults is reduced greatly.

In practice, however, the situation is not quite this idyllic. In fact, there are a number of obstacles specific to the maintenance of object-oriented information systems.

One obstacle arises as a consequence of *inheritance*. Suppose new features are added to a class with no subclasses. Then, these changes have no effect on any other class. However, if a class with subclasses is changed, all its subclasses are changed in the same way.

For example, consider Figure 16.1. If a new attribute is added to class **Bottom Class,** this cannot affect any other class in any way. But if another attribute is added to class **Top Class,** then this change immediately is applied to all the classes in the diagram; the change is inherited by every class in the class hierarchy.

In other words, the strength of inheritance is that changing a class with no subclasses will not change any other class in the inheritance hierarchy. But, if a class with subclasses is changed in any way, then this change is propagated to all its subclasses. This is termed the *fragile class problem*. Thus, inheritance is a feature of object-oriented technology that can have a major positive influence on development but a negative impact on maintenance.

A second problem arises as a consequence of polymorphism and dynamic binding, concepts introduced in Section 20.3; this problem is explained in Section 20.5.

16.7   Maintenance Skills versus Development Skills

Earlier in this chapter much was said about the skills needed for maintenance. For corrective maintenance, the ability to determine the cause of a failure of a large information system was deemed essential. But this skill is not needed exclusively for maintenance of an information system—it is used throughout integration and product testing. Another vital skill is the ability to function effectively without adequate documentation. Again, the documentation rarely is complete while integration and product testing are under way. Also stressed was that skills with regard to analysis, design, implementation, and testing are essential for adaptive and perfective maintenance. These activities also are carried out during development, and each requires specialized skills if it is to be performed correctly.

In other words, the skills a maintainer needs are in no way different from those needed by information technology professionals specializing in any other aspect of information system development. The key point is that a maintainer must not be merely skilled in a broad variety of areas, but *highly* skilled in *all* those areas. Although the average information system developer can specialize in one area of information system development, such as design or testing, the information system maintainer must be a specialist in virtually every area of information system development. After all, maintenance is the same as development, only more so.

16.8   Reverse Engineering

It has been pointed out that, sometimes, the only documentation available for maintenance is the code itself. (This happens all too frequently when maintaining a *legacy information system;* that is, an information system in current use but developed some 15 or 20 years ago, if not earlier.) Under these circumstances, maintaining the information system can be extremely difficult. One way of handling this problem is to start with the code and attempt to recreate the design artifacts or even the analysis artifacts. This process is called *reverse engineering*.

CASE tools can assist with this process. One of the simplest is a pretty printer (Section 11.2), which may help display the code more clearly. Other tools construct diagrams, such as flowcharts or UML diagrams, directly from the source code; these visual aids can help in the process of design recovery.

Once the maintenance team has reconstructed the design, there are two possibilities. One alternative is to attempt to reconstruct the analysis artifacts, modify the reconstructed analysis artifacts to reflect the necessary changes, and reimplement the information system the usual way. (Within the context of reverse engineering, the usual development process that proceeds from analysis through design to implementation is called *forward engineering*. The process of reverse engineering followed by forward engineering sometimes is called *reengineering*.) In practice, reconstruction of the analysis artifacts is an extremely hard task. More frequently the reconstructed design artifacts are modified instead and the modified design then is forward engineered.

A related activity often performed during maintenance is *restructuring*. Reverse engineering takes the information system from a later workflow to an earlier workflow, for example, from implementation to design. Forward engineering takes the information system from an earlier workflow to a later workflow. Restructuring, however, takes place within one workflow. It is the process of improving the information system without changing its functionality. Pretty printing is one form of restructuring; so is converting code from traditional to object-oriented form. In general, restructuring is performed to make the code artifacts (or design artifacts or even the database) easier to maintain.

16.9   Testing during Maintenance

While an information system is being developed, many members of the development team have a broad overview of the information system as a whole. However, as a result of the rapid personnel turnover in the information services sector, it is unlikely that members of the maintenance team will have been involved in the original development. Therefore, a maintainer tends to see an information system as a set of loosely related code artifacts and generally is not aware that a change to one code artifact may seriously affect one or more other code artifacts, and hence the information system as a whole. Even if the maintainer wished to understand every aspect of the information system, the pressures to fix or to extend the information system generally are such that no time is allowed for the detailed study needed to achieve this. Furthermore, in many cases, little or no documentation is available to assist in gaining that understanding. One way of trying to minimize this difficulty is to use regression testing; that is, testing the changed information system against previous test cases to ensure that it still works correctly.

For this reason, it is vital to store all test cases, together with their expected outcomes, in machine-readable form. As a result of changes made to the information system, certain stored test cases may have to be modified. For example, if salary withholding percentages change as a consequence of tax legislation, then the correct output from a payroll information system for each test case involving withholding will change. Depending on the maintenance performed, some valid test cases will become invalid. But the computations that need to be made to correct the stored test cases are essentially the same as would have to be made to set up new test data for checking that the maintenance has been correctly performed. No additional work therefore is involved in maintaining the file of test cases and their expected outcomes.

It can be argued that regression testing is a waste of time because regression testing requires the complete information system to be retested against a host of test cases, most of which apparently have nothing to do with the code artifacts modified in the course of maintenance. The word *apparently* is critical in the previous sentence. The dangers of unwitting side effects of maintenance (that is, the introduction of regression faults) are too great for that argument to hold water; regression testing is an essential aspect of maintenance in all situations.

16.10   CASE Tools for Maintenance

It is unreasonable to expect maintainers to keep track manually of the various revision numbers and assign the next revision number each time an artifact is updated. Unless the operating system incorporates version control, a version control tool is needed. It is equally unreasonable to expect manual control of the freezing technique described in Chapter 11 or any other manual way of ensuring that revisions are updated appropriately. A configuration control tool (Section 11.4) is needed, such as PVCS or SourceSafe; CVS is an open-source configuration control tool. Even if the maintenance organization does not wish to purchase a complete configuration control tool, at the very least, a build tool (Section 11.5) must be used in conjunction with a version control tool. Another category of CASE tools virtually essential for maintenance is a fault tracking tool that keeps a record of reported faults not yet fixed. Bugzilla is an open-source fault tracking tool.

Various kinds of CASE tools can assist in reverse engineering and reengineering. Examples of commercial tools that assist by creating visual displays of the structure of the information system include Battlemap and Teamwork.

Maintenance is difficult and frustrating. The very least that management can do is to provide the maintenance team with the tools needed for efficient and effective information system maintenance.

Key Terms

adaptive maintenance, *312*
corrective maintenance, *311*
evolution, *312*
fault report, *317*
forward engineering, *321*
fragile class problem, *320*

inheritance, *320*
legacy information
   system, *321*
maintenance, *311*
moving target problem, *319*
perfective maintenance, *311*

reengineering, *321*
regression fault, *313*
regression testing, *314*
restructuring, *321*
reverse engineering, *321*

Review Questions for Chapter 16

1. What is the modern definition of maintenance?
2. Give the three main reasons for performing maintenance, and give the technical name for the corresponding type of maintenance.
3. Give four reasons why maintenance is often frustrating.
4. What are the three main lessons of the mini case study of Section 16.4?
5. Give two reasons why faults are generally not fixed immediately.
6. What is the solution to the moving target problem?
7. What is the fragile class problem?
8. What is a legacy information system?
9. Define the terms *reengineering, restructuring, forward engineering,* and *reverse engineering*.
10. Why is regression testing so important?

Problems

16.1 Why do you think that the mistake is frequently made of considering maintenance of information systems to be inferior to the development of information systems?

16.2 Consider an information system that determines whether a computer is virus free. Describe why such an information system is likely to have multiple variations of many of its code artifacts. What are the implications for maintenance? How can the resulting problems be solved?

16.3 Repeat Problem 16.2 for the automated library circulation system of Problem 5.5.

16.4 Repeat Problem 16.2 for the information system of Problem 4.9 that checks whether a bank statement is correct.

16.5 Repeat Problem 16.2 for the automated teller machine of Problem 5.6.

16.6 You are the manager in charge of maintenance in a large information system organization. What qualities do you look for when hiring new employees?

16.7 What are the implications of maintenance for a one-person information system development organization?

16.8 You have been asked to construct a computerized fault report file. What sort of data would you store in the file? What sort of queries could be answered by your tool? What sort of queries could not be answered by your tool?

References

International Organization for Standardization, International Electrotechnical Commission. "ISO/IEC 12207:1995, Information Technology—Software Life-Cycle Processes." Geneva: ISO/IEC, 1995.

Jacobson, I.; G. Booch; and J. Rumbaugh. *The Unified Software Development Process*. Reading, MA: Addison-Wesley, 1999.

Parnas, D. L. "Ten Myths about Y2K Inspections." *Communications of the ACM* 42 (May 1999), p. 128.

Pigoski, T. M. *Practical Software Maintenance: Best Practices for Managing Your Software Investment*. New York: John Wiley & Sons, 1996.

Chapter 17

User-Interface Design

Learning Objectives

After studying this chapter, you should be able to:

- Describe the key challenges in designing a user interface.
- Understand the importance of consistency in user-interface design.
- Appreciate some of the metaphors employed in user interfaces.
- Describe how the user interfaces are designed when an information system is developed using the Unified Process.

Suppose we are asked to design a screen for an information system. First we choose the background color. Green is always considered a restful color, so we decide that the background for our screen will be green. Now we have to decide on the color for the words. We want the words to "jump out" at the user, so we choose red for this purpose.

There is, however, a problem with our carefully thought out color scheme. About 7 percent of the male population is color blind (but less than 1 percent of the female population). For individuals with red–green deficiency (by far the most common type of color blindness), red and green appear to be the same color. In other words, for a sizable proportion of future users of our screen, the letters on the screen will be totally unreadable. (For more information on color blindness, see Just in Case You Wanted to Know Box 17.1.)

It appears that the design of the user interface, also known as the human–computer interface or the user–computer interface, is perhaps not quite as straightforward as we would like it to be.

17.1 Input and Output Devices

If you were to ask a computer technology professional what are the most commonly used devices for communicating with a computer, you would probably be told that until about 15 years ago, the major input device was the keyboard, but that now the mouse is extremely important. With regard to output, the usual devices are the printer and the screen. Unfortunately, this reply overlooks one of the most commonly used devices for computer input and output—the telephone.

In the Good Old Days, if I had a question regarding my bank account, I would simply call my bank and speak to a human being. Nowadays, if I call my bank, the telephone is

The first scientific analysis of color blindness (the condition medically known as monochromatism or achromatopsia) was undertaken by the great British physicist John Dalton (1766–1844), the originator of the modern atomic theory of the structure of matter. Dalton's lifelong interest in the condition was because he himself was chromatically challenged; he was red–green deficient. His scientific contribution to color vision was so great that color blindness is still frequently referred to as Daltonism.

It is said that, to her dying day, his mother believed that Dalton's condition was caused by her failing to teach him the colors when he was growing up. So, she would sit on a bench under an oak tree on the village green at Eaglesfield, Cumberland, surrounded by the younger village children. On her lap she held a large of bag of candies of different colors. She would hold up each candy in turn and, when a child identified the color of that candy correctly, he or she was given that candy to eat. Charming though this story about Dalton's mother may be, unfortunately it appears to have no basis in fact.

answered by a computer. I hear a prerecorded message like the one displayed in Figure 17.1. That is, the bank computer is communicating with me via my telephone.

I want information on my checking account, so I press 1. Now I am asked for my account number and "PIN number." I enter these numbers correctly, and I hear the list of choices shown in Figure 17.2. I want to know my account balance, but I accidentally press the 2 button. Now I hear the menu given in Figure 17.3. After hearing all three choices, I have no alternative—I simply hang up.

In this chapter, the many mistakes in the design of the banking user interface will be used to illustrate how user interfaces should be designed.

FIGURE 17.1
First Menu from Bank Computer

> Welcome to First Bank of Purgatory.
> For information on your checking account, press 1.
> For information on your savings account, press 2.
> For information on your credit card account, press 3.
> For any other information, press 4.
> To hear these choices again, press 5.

FIGURE 17.2
Second Menu from Bank Computer

> For your account balance, press 1.
> For information on a specific check, press 2.
> For information on the last 5 items credited to your account, press 3.
> For information on the last 10 items paid, press 4.
> To return to the main menu, press 5.
> To hear these choices again, press 9.

FIGURE 17.3
Third Menu from Bank Computer

> To determine the status of one check number, press 1.
> To determine the status of a range of check numbers, press 2.
> To hear these choices again, press 3.

17.2   Consistency

An important criterion in user-interface design is consistency. Compare Figures 17.1, 17.2, and 17.3; in order to have the current menu repeated, the user is told to press **5**, **9**, or **3**, respectively. This is poor design practice. It requires the listener to concentrate hard to memorize the buttons for the current set of choices, but to learn a completely different set of buttons for the next set of choices, some of which are the same as in the previous set. This type of design leads to errors, frustration, and a strong negative attitude on the part of the customer toward the business.

In the case of a printed report, the date should always appear in the same place and in the same format. It is not important whether that place is, say, the top left-hand corner or the top right-hand corner of each page. It does not matter whether the format for the date is Friday, December 03, 2004, or 12/03/04. What counts is that the user will always find the date located in the same place displayed in the same format in every report, without exception.

Many screens include items such as *buttons*. If buttons are used, they need to have the same size in all screens and to be labeled with letters in the identical font. If the buttons are colored, then they need to be colored consistently. For example, if the Help button is yellow on one screen, then it needs to be yellow on all screens.

If a user interface has a toolbar of some kind, then the toolbar always needs to be in the same place. If icons are used, for example, to label a button so that the user can return to the home page with a single click, then the icon denoting "home page" must be the same on all screens.

One of the many strengths of Macintosh applications is consistency in the user interface. The vast majority of applications developed specifically for the Macintosh can be used without studying the user manual, because the same commands have the same meaning. For example, if the user enters ⌘–D (that is, the user holds down the ⌘ or "command" key and then presses the D key), this always means *duplicate* (make a copy). This rule applies universally. It holds when working with folders, with files, or with components of a PowerPoint drawing. All a user has to do is select the item to be duplicated by moving the mouse pointer to that object and clicking on the mouse button, and then type ⌘–D. If someone were to develop a Macintosh application in which ⌘–D stood for *delete,* users would soon stop using that application. After all, who would use an application in which an item is deleted whenever the user thinks that he or she is making a copy of that item.

It is not hard to imagine the pandemonium that would reign if every keyboard had its keys arranged in a random fashion. Nevertheless, certain designers of user interfaces have thought nothing of using the same key for two totally different purposes in two different screens of the same Windows-based application. In fact, it is not enough that there be consistency within the set of screens of each individual information system used by a company. What is needed is consistency within *all* screens of *all* information systems used by that company.

17.3   Correcting Mistakes

In the banking scenario of Section 17.1, by mistake I pressed the wrong button on my telephone. There are two basic types of incorrect input that can occur. The one type of incorrect input is giving an incorrect command. The other is supplying incorrect data. An example of the latter is when the user accidentally enters a wrong digit when asked by the banking computer to enter his or her PIN. In most well-designed systems, the user would be given another opportunity to resubmit his or her PIN. After (say) three incorrect attempts, the computer may deduce that the user has no idea what the PIN for that account is and is trying to break into someone else's checking account. In other words, in a well-designed user interface, a user is given a few tries to submit data correctly. However, security considerations generally preclude an unlimited number of tries being permitted.

Consider again the banking scenario of Section 17.1. In that scenario, on hearing the menu of Figure 17.2, I pressed the wrong button. More specifically, I wanted to know my account balance, but I pressed 2—this is an example of giving an incorrect command. I then heard the menu of Figure 17.3. There was no option to Return to main menu or Return to previous menu. This is an excellent example of abysmally bad design. Instead, the designer should always consider the possibility that the user has arrived at that point as a result of issuing an incorrect command.

For example, almost every screen in a well-designed word processor or spreadsheet package has a Cancel option. If the user has arrived at that screen by mistake, the Cancel option gives him or her the opportunity to avoid giving an incorrect command. Another essential feature is the Undo command. If, on seeing the effect of a command, the user realizes that he or she gave a wrong command, the Undo command reverses the effect of the original command.

In some situations, reversing a command is hard, if not impossible. For example, when a disk is reformatted, all the data on that disk are essentially erased. Consequently, it is impossible to Undo a Reformat command. Instead, before carrying out the command, the system should ask the user if he or she really wants to Reformat the disk, explaining that the action is irreversible.

Returning to the telephone interface, the user sometimes has to make choice after choice, finally arriving at a sixth or seventh menu. If a mistake is made at this point, having to start again and repeat the torment is more than many users can tolerate. The deeper into the maze of choices the user has penetrated, the more important it becomes that the user is able to recover from an incorrect choice without having to start from scratch.

Human beings are human, and we therefore make mistakes. Every user interface must be carefully designed to take this reality into account.

17.4   Metaphors

In the description of the banking user interface, the word *menu* is used repeatedly. That word is even included in the captions to Figures 17.1, 17.2, and 17.3. Until about 25 years ago, however, the word *menu* was used almost exclusively within the context of restaurants. That is, a menu meant a list of the various choices that were open to the diner.

The word *menu* is used the same way in the user-interface context, namely, a list of choices that are open to the user. This *metaphor* has become so commonplace that the use of the word *menu* in the computer sense in Section 17.1 seems perfectly natural. (A metaphor is a figure of speech in which a word used literally in one context is used in a different context to imply the same concept in the other context. For example, the word *menu* is usually used in the context of a restaurant to refer to a card on which is printed a list of dishes from which the diner may choose. The word is used in the user-interface context to imply a list of choices, even though there is no card printed with a list of dishes in this latter context. That is, menu is used literally in the restaurant context, but metaphorically in the user-interface context.)

A wide variety of metaphors are employed in user interfaces. For example, when using a Macintosh or Windows-based system, the screen appears to be a *desktop*. There are folders, there is a trash can, there are files, as shown in Figure 17.4. However, both Macintosh

FIGURE 17.4
Desktop Metaphor

and Windows also have menus from which the user can choose an option. In addition, both operating systems make use of a third metaphor, namely, *direct manipulation,* otherwise known as *point-and-click* or *drag-and-drop*. In order to move a file from one folder to another (the desktop metaphor), the user positions the mouse pointer on the file to be moved (point), holds down the mouse button (click), moves the file to its destination (drag), and then releases the mouse button (drop). Operating systems of this kind make use of more than one metaphor at a time. The fact that most users have no problem with mixed metaphors shows that there is no reason to use just one metaphor in a user interface.

Word processors, too, make use of more than one metaphor. In some situations, a document is likened to a sheet of paper; consider menu choices such as Cut, Paste, Page Layout, and the like. In other situations, however, the word processor uses a *typesetting* metaphor, with terminology such as Font, Tab, Footnote, Header, and Print.

Another familiar metaphor is the *window* (with a lowercase "w"). A window is a portion of the screen in which a particular task is performed, the contents of a specific folder are shown, or a given Web page is displayed. The metaphor here is that we use a window in a wall to see outside. A window on the screen is not made of glass, and we certainly cannot see through it, but by referring to a particular rectangular delimited area of the screen as a window, we imply that that area of screen contains a scene of interest to us. In general, there will be a number of open windows, one of which will be the *active window*. We can Open or Close a window; both these commands are consistent with the metaphor. However, we also can Resize a window or Minimize it. Neither of these operations conforms to the metaphor. New users of windows therefore have to be instructed about these operations. Often there is more information in a window than can be displayed at one time. In this case, we use *scroll bars* on the side or bottom of the window to move to the part of the image we wish to investigate, as shown in Figure 17.5.

The *icon* is a well-known metaphor. Here a symbol of some kind stands for a folder, a document, a spreadsheet, a program, a window, or similar item. Typical icons are shown in

FIGURE 17.5 Window Metaphor, with Scroll Bars

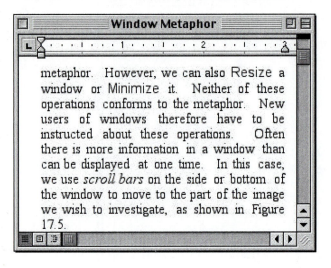

FIGURE 17.6 Radio Buttons (top) and Check Boxes (bottom)

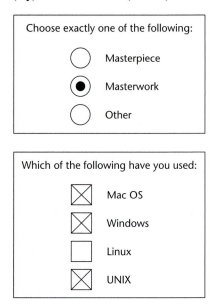

Figure 17.4. When we *double-click* on an icon, we open it. More precisely, opening a folder causes its contents to be displayed, but opening a document automatically also starts the program that manipulates that document (usually a word processor), and similarly for a spreadsheet. Thus, we have gone beyond the pre–computer age metaphor of an icon as a symbol that represents something (from the Greek word εικων, meaning a picture) to the idea that, by double-clicking on an icon, we can activate it. Of course, double-clicking is part of the point-and-click metaphor.

A graphical user interface (or GUI) utilizes a combination of many of the metaphors already mentioned, including windows, menus, point-and-click, and icons. It often also utilizes other metaphors, such as radio buttons and check boxes, as shown in Figure 17.6.

When designing a user interface for an information system, it is important that the metaphors be familiar to the users of the system. For example, a balance sheet would be an acceptable metaphor for an accounting information system designed for use exclusively by CPAs. However, if data are to be entered by clerks who have no accounting knowledge, this metaphor will inevitably lead to frequent mistakes. For example, terms such as Credit and Debit are not universally understood—and if you don't believe that, the next time you use your credit card to pay for your groceries, tell the supermarket cashier, "Please debit the total to this card," and see what happens.

17.5 Layout and Aesthetics

One of the most powerful techniques for achieving a good user interface is one of the simplest—use whitespace freely. Look at Figures 17.7 and 17.8. Both contain identical information, but Figure 17.8 is much easier to read because of the generous use of whitespace.

The rule for the use of color is simple: Use as few colors as possible, and use them consistently. Thus, if one screen has orange letters on a gray background, then all the other screens should utilize the same color scheme.

FIGURE 17.7
Hard-to-Read
Message

One of the most powerful techniques for achieving a good user interface is one of the simplest—use whitespace freely. Look at Figures 17.7 and 17.8. Both contain identical information, but Figure 17.8 is much easier to read because of the generous use of whitespace. The rule for the use of color is simple: Use as few colors as possible, and use them consistently. Thus, if one screen has orange letters on a gray background, then all the other screens should utilize the same color scheme.

FIGURE 17.8
Message of
Figure 17.7 with
Additional
Whitespace

One of the most powerful techniques for achieving a good user interface is one of the simplest—use whitespace freely. Look at Figures 17.7 and 17.8. Both contain identical information, but Figure 17.8 is much easier to read because of the generous use of whitespace.

The rule for the use of color is simple:

Use as few colors as possible, and use them consistently.

Thus, if one screen has orange letters on a gray background, then all the other screens should utilize the same color scheme.

Turning now to fonts, the same rule holds. Few things are more confusing to the eye than multiple fonts. If variation is needed, use the same font in different sizes, or use the same size font and vary the style by utilizing **boldface** or *italics*. This book uses just two different fonts, but in a variety of different sizes and styles. This gives the design a feeling of unity and consistency. In contrast, Tennessee automobile license plates between 1996 and 2000 used eight different fonts. The effect was less than pleasant.

17.6   Dynamic Interfaces

Sometimes one common user interface cannot be appropriate for all users. For example, if an information system is to be used by both information technology professionals and high-school dropouts with no previous computer experience, then it is preferable that two different sets of user interfaces be designed, each carefully tailored to the skill level of its intended users.

Even when all the users have a similar background, some users have utilized an information system more than others, and accordingly have acquired greater knowledge of the system than others who are just learning to use it. The user interface needs to take into account these varying levels of expertise in using the system. For example, instead of giving every user detailed instructions on how to use the information system, the first screen could determine whether or not the user would like introductory information. Only if the user responds that he or she wants to learn how to use the information system are such instructions given.

A more advanced version of this approach is for the information system itself to keep a record of the amount of time a given user has used the system, and to vary the quantity of instructional material on each screen accordingly. Thus, the first occasion a user logs on, he or she is automatically given directions on how to use the system. The next few times, the user may be asked if he or she would like to see this tutorial material again. After that, the information system assumes that the user has by now acquired adequate experience to navigate through the system unaided.

However, the assumption that users with some experience of the system no longer require assistance may be false, for two reasons. First, not everyone learns at the same rate.

Second, experienced users sometimes assume that they know more than they do, and they start making mistakes. What is needed is a dynamic user interface that incorporates different sets of user interfaces corresponding to varied levels of sophistication. If the information system deduces that the user would be more comfortable with a less-sophisticated user interface, perhaps because he or she is making frequent mistakes or is continually invoking help facilities, then the user automatically is shown screens more appropriate to his or her current skill level. But, as the user becomes more familiar with the information system, streamlined screens that provide less information are displayed, leading to speedier completion. This automated approach reduces user frustration and leads to increased productivity [Schach and Wood, 1986].

But irrespective of how much or how little tutorial material appears on each screen, every screen must allow the user to invoke help facilities at any time. Online help is a vital component of the user interface.

17.7 The Unified Process and the User Interface

Traditional methodologies for developing an information system have rarely incorporated techniques for designing user–computer interfaces. As a result, a number of independent approaches to user-interface design have been put forward. However, with the advent of the Unified Process, a separate technique is not needed—the design of the user interface is an integral part of the Unified Process. Of course, it should come as no surprise that the foundation for user-interface design is the use cases.

17.7.1 Requirements Workflow

A primary goal of the requirements workflow is to determine the client's requirements. The requirements are expressed in the form of use cases. Recall from Section 4.5.3 that a use case models the interaction between an information system and the environment in which the information system operates. Consider the generalized use case of Figure 17.9. The rectangle represents the **Information System** itself, whereas the stick figure models the **Actor,** an entity that is outside the information system. Consequently, the point at which the line from the **Actor** to the Activity intersects the rectangle models the user interface. Because the user interface is an integral part of every use case, the design of user interfaces is an integral part of the Unified Process.

17.7.2 Prototyping the User Interface

While performing the requirements workflow, we prototype the user interface. This is not a rapid prototype constructed to be certain that the requirements have been accurately determined, as described in Section 7.13.1—rapid prototyping is not part of the Unified Process.

FIGURE 17.9
Use Case, Showing the User Interface

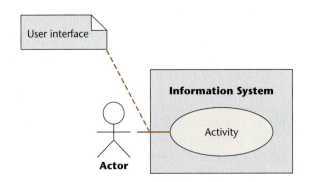

Instead, the purpose of the prototype user interface is to be sure that, when the target information system has been developed, the user is able to perform each use case effectively. Another difference is that a rapid prototype is a working model of the critical functionality of the information system, whereas the prototype user interface may be a rough sketch that depicts just the user interface (screen or report). Figures 4.17 through 4.19 depict prototype user interfaces for the Osbert Oglesby case study.

17.7.3   User-Interface Design

Designing a user interface using the Unified Process consists of five steps:

• The first task of the user-interface designer is to decide on the *elements* of the user interface [Jacobson, Booch, and Rumbaugh, 1999]. Many of these elements will be attributes of the relevant boundary class (Section 6.6); in general, each input screen, output screen, and printed report is modeled by a boundary class. Other elements will be found in the glossary (Section 4.3). In the case of the Osbert Oglesby case study, element firstNameOfArtist is an attribute of the relevant boundary class, whereas elements masterpiece and stillLife are in the glossary of Figure 4.2. The designer starts with one actor and finds all the use cases in which that actor participates. For each use case, the elements are listed. For the Osbert Oglesby case study, the use-case diagram of the requirements workflow is shown in Figure 4.8. There are three use cases: Buy a Painting, Sell a Painting, and Produce a Report. Consider, say, Buy a Painting. The description of the use case appears in Figure 4.15. The first paragraph of the description is reproduced in Figure 17.10. From this paragraph, nine elements of the user interface are immediately clear to the user-interface designer, namely, the items enumerated in the lowest nine lines of that figure. The remaining elements of the user interface can be deduced from the rest of the use-case description of Figure 4.15 (Problem 17.1).

• Second, the user-interface designer puts together a preliminary design that incorporates just the bare elements themselves. One way to do this is to put the name of each element on a Post-it note and arrange the relevant notes on a board.

• Third, the user-interface designer checks that this preliminary version of the elements of the user interface is adequate. Most screens are designed to enable a user to perform one or more actions. Accordingly, the designer has to check that the set of elements will provide all the information necessary for the user to perform those actions. Also, an outline of the help information for that screen needs to be added at this point. Finally, the designer must check that the user's responses will result in all the necessary data being supplied by the user to the information system.

FIGURE 17.10

Portion of the Description of the Use Case Buy a Painting for the Initial Requirements of the Osbert Oglesby Information System

1. Osbert inputs the details of the painting he is considering buying. These are:

   First name of artist
   Last name of artist
   Title of work
   Year of work
   Classification (masterpiece, masterwork, other)
   Height
   Width
   Medium (oil, watercolor, other)
   Subject (portrait, still-life, landscape, other)

• Fourth, the designer determines how to express those elements. Issues that need to be decided include the metaphors (Section 17.4), as well as aesthetic issues such as font, color, and layout (Section 17.5). Training and skills are needed for this; the job of user-interface designer is a specialized profession.

• Now the designer can produce the prototype user interface. Often this is done as a two-stage process. First, the user-interface designer sketches the various interfaces. A pencil sketch encourages the client and future users to suggest possible improvements. Second, once all the stakeholders are satisfied with the sketches, the designer uses a screen generator or report generator (Section 11.1) to generate the prototype user interface. In its simplest form, the resulting user interface is a printed report or a screen dump. A more sophisticated user interface is interactive. For example, the client and users can experiment with the various screens. They can input information on one screen and see the result displayed on another. An interactive prototype of this kind is clearly preferable, especially when developing COTS packages. After all, the cost of changing the user interface once the package has been widely distributed can be prohibitive.

17.7.4 Iteration

In the succeeding workflows, the various use cases are refined. The corresponding user interfaces need to be changed, too. Figure 6.3, for example, which shows the second iteration of the use-case diagram for the Osbert Oglesby case study, reflects the fact that we overlooked the use case Modify a Fashionability Coefficient. Once the missing use case has been added, the user-interface designer has to create a user interface to enable that use case. The new screen must be consistent in appearance with the earlier screens.

Look at Figure 6.20, the third iteration of the use-case diagram for the Osbert Oglesby case study. Now there are eight use cases. However, none of these are new use cases. Instead, they are refinements (iterations) of the four use cases of Figure 6.3. Similarly, the user interfaces for the eight use cases of Figure 6.20 will be iterations of the user interfaces for the four use cases of Figure 6.3.

As the Unified Process proceeds, the use cases are analyzed, designed, implemented, tested, and installed. The user interface for each of those use cases undergoes a corresponding sequence of iteration and incrementation steps.

Key Terms

active window, *329*	drag-and-drop, *329*	point-and-click, *329*
button, *327*	element, *333*	scroll bar, *329*
desktop, *328*	icon, *329*	typesetting, *329*
direct manipulation, *329*	menu, *328*	window, *329*
double-click, *330*	metaphor, *328*	

Review Questions for Chapter 17

1. Why is consistency so important in user-interface design?
2. Name six metaphors commonly utilized in user-interface design.
3. How should whitespace, color, and fonts be used when designing user interfaces?
4. What is the advantage of dynamic interfaces?
5. What are the five steps that are performed when a user-interface design is designed using the Unified Process?

Problems

17.1 Determine the elements of the user interface for the Buy a Masterwork use case of the Osbert Oglesby information system.

17.2   Determine the elements of the user interface for the **Produce a Sales Report** use case of the Osbert Oglesby information system.

17.3   Determine the elements of the user interface for the **Manage a Mortgage** use case of the MSG Foundation information system.

17.4   Determine the elements of the user interface for the **Update Annual Operating Expenses** use case of the MSG Foundation information system.

17.5   Redesign the menus of Figures 17.1 through 17.3 to reflect the principles of user-interface design expounded in this chapter.

Term Project

17.6   Determine the elements of the user interface for a use case of the Chocoholics Anonymous information system of Appendix A.

References

Schach, S. R., and P. T. Wood. "An Almost Path-Free Very High-Level Interactive Data Manipulation Language for a Microcomputer-Based Database System." *Software—Practice and Experience* 16, no. 3 (1986), pp. 243–68.

Jacobson, I.; G. Booch; and J. Rumbaugh. *The Unified Software Development Process.* Reading, MA: Addison-Wesley, 1999.

18

Introduction to Web-Based Information Systems

Learning Objectives

After studying this chapter, you should be able to:

- Describe client–server networks.
- Draw comparisons between the Web and client–server networks.
- Describe features of Web-based information systems.

There are two ways of looking at the World Wide Web (or Web, for short). The one way is to believe that the Web was brought to Planet Earth by aliens from outer space during the last decade of the twentieth century. The other way is to treat the Web as the latest in a long line of major technological breakthroughs, including client–server computing. The latter approach is followed in this chapter. To make the unavoidable history lesson a little more palatable, UML deployment diagrams have been used (Section 10.9).

18.1 Prelude to the Web

The first electronic computers were built in the 1940s. They were extremely large and unbelievably expensive. For example, the Electronic Numerical Integrator and Computer (or ENIAC, for short) weighed over 30 tons. The ENIAC consumed 140,000 watts of power. *First-generation computers* cost literally millions of preinflation dollars. Special large rooms had to be constructed, and an efficient air-conditioning system had to run continuously to remove the heat generated by the many vacuum tubes (a precursor of the transistor).

From the viewpoint of the theme of this chapter, there are two key points regarding computers built before 1960. First, they could be used by only one user at a time, as represented in Figure 18.1; a single programmer would have exclusive use of the computer for a block of

FIGURE 18.1
UML Deployment Diagram of a First-Generation Computer

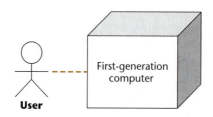

time, typically an hour. Second, they were operated in *batch mode*. The statements of a program were punched on punch cards (see Just in Case You Wanted to Know Box 18.1). The programmer would load the punch cards into the punch card reader, set a few switches, and press a button or two. The computer would read the punch cards and then run the program. The output would then be printed on a line printer (an early form of computer printer), and some data might be written to a magnetic tape. In other words, there was essentially no interaction between user and computer from the initiation of the program until its termination.

The second major precursor of the Web was *interactive timesharing*. In the early 1960s, it no longer became necessary for the user to be in the computer room to operate the computer. Instead, the computer was connected via a wire to a *dumb terminal*, that is, a keyboard and screen. A typical system could support up to 128 dumb terminals; only a few are shown in Figure 18.2. Input to the computer was performed by typing on the keyboard, and the output from the computer appeared on the screen. The system was *interactive* in that it was possible for the user to type in data whenever the program requested information. The term *timesharing* refers to the way that each user received a successive slice of computer time. For example, if there were 100 users currently active, each might receive one millisecond of computer time every tenth of a second. However, this was sufficient computer time to give every user the illusion that he or she was the only person using that computer. Most computers of this type supported not only interactive timesharing but batch mode processing as well. In other words, the slices of computer time were shared between the interactive users and one or more batch jobs, all active at the same time.

The advantage of interactive timesharing was that an extremely expensive computer could now be shared by a large number of users at the same time. The disadvantages were the cost of the computer and the fact that its operating system had to be complicated in order to be able to share out computer time among the various interactive users and the batch jobs.

Newton's Third Law of Motion states that every action has an equal and opposite reaction. So it should come as no surprise that the next breakthrough was in exactly the opposite

FIGURE 18.2
UML Deployment
Diagram of an
Interactive
Timesharing
Computer with
Six Users

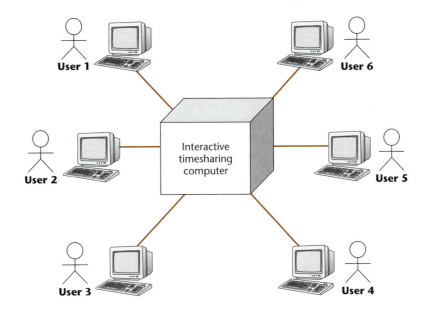

FIGURE 18.3
UML Deployment
Diagram of a
Personal Computer

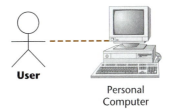

direction to timesharing. The IBM personal computer or PC (1981) was a computer used by one person at a time. It was small (but not as small as today's desktop computers) and it was cheap. Although it cost a lot more than today's far more powerful personal computers, the price was a tiny fraction of the cost of a time-sharing computer. A personal computer is shown in Figure 18.3.

The first personal computers and the first-generation computers of the 1940s were alike in two ways. Both supported only one user at a time and both were similar in computing power. One major difference between the two was that the personal computer cost more than a thousand times less than a first-generation computer and weighed more than a thousand times less than its counterpart from 35 years before.

The next breakthrough was networking; that is, connecting a set of personal computers together so that they could communicate with one another. There were a number of ways of doing this. One important configuration is the *client–server network* depicted in Figure 18.4. Here a number of personal computers, the *clients,* are connected to a central computer, the *server*. The server is a computer with a large amount of disk storage.

Figure 18.4 (which represents a client–server network) is identical to Figure 18.2 (which represents a timesharing computer) except that each dumb terminal has been replaced by a personal computer. That is, conceptually, the difference between a timesharing network

FIGURE 18.4
Client–Server
Network

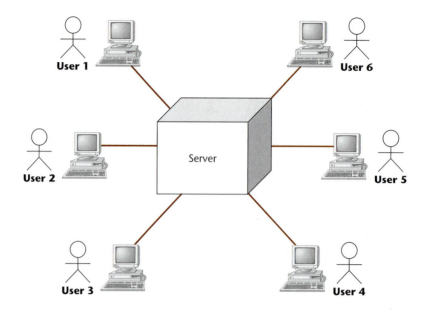

of the 1960s and a client–server network of the 1990s is that a timesharing network has only one computer, but both the server and all the clients in a client–server network are computers.

A client–server network can be used in a number of different ways, including the following two basic approaches:

- The simplest (and most wasteful) way is for the client–server network to function as a timesharing computer. In other words, the users employ their personal computers solely as communications devices, that is, as if they were dumb terminals. They utilize their keyboards to send instructions and data to the server, which then executes their programs. The results are sent back to their screens. The users make no use of the computing power of their personal computers, just the keyboard and the screen.
- The client–server network functions as a distributed computer. Users download programs from the server to their own computers and execute the programs there. The data for their programs also may be downloaded from the server, entered by the users, or both. If a computation requires a larger computer than the user has on his or her desktop, then the user will run that program on the server but, in general, the idea behind a client–server network is for as much computing as possible to be performed on each user's own computer.

A strength of a client–server network is that it promotes the sharing of both programs and data. That is, all the users can run the same programs on their own personal computers, and they can utilize data that have been stored on the server by any of the other users. However, it is not always straightforward to get one computer (a client) to communicate with another computer (the server). What is needed is *middleware,* that is, the software that promotes the interoperability of two computers. *Interoperability* is defined as the mutual cooperation of compiled code from different vendors, implemented in different languages and running on different platforms. For example, consider a nationwide network of automated teller machines (ATMs). The server is a mainframe computer running a database management system implemented by one organization; the clients, the ATMs, are running

FIGURE 18.5

A Larger
Client–Server
Network with
Different Types of
Clients and Servers

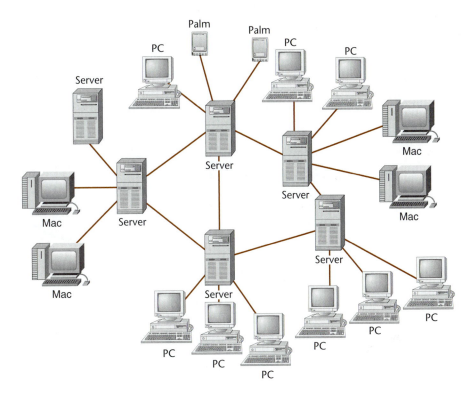

C++ code implemented by a different organization. In addition, there is communications software, and security is an essential aspect. All these components have to work together for the ATM network to function successfully.

As indicated in the previous paragraph, a client–server network does not have to be as simple as the one depicted in Figure 18.4. For example, consider Figure 18.5, which shows six servers and a number of personal computers. The personal computers and the servers can all freely communicate with one another, even though they are of different types.

Now look at Figure 18.6. This figure depicts Figure 18.5 extended to hundreds of thousands of servers and hundreds of millions of clients. As before, there are a variety of different server types and client types. The links connecting them include telephone lines, trunk lines (high-volume long distance lines), wireless links, undersea cables, and satellite links. Figure 18.6 depicts the World Wide Web.

There are major differences between information systems that run on conventional client–server networks and Web-based information systems. As is obvious from Figure 18.6, a characteristic of the Web is that it is highly heterogeneous; that is, it runs on an essentially unlimited variety of different hardware and operating systems. Portability is therefore a nonnegotiable requirement of all Web-based information systems. Fortunately, this problem has already been solved. Every computer on the Web is equipped with a Web *browser* such as Internet Explorer or Netscape Communicator. There are strict standards in place regarding the format of files that are passed over the Web. If an item conforms to these standards, then it can be handled by a Web browser. Thus, Web portability is trivial to specify, and equally trivial to achieve. For example, if a page is implemented in *HTML* (HyperText Markup Language) or in *XML* (eXtensible Markup Language, an extension of HTML), it can be read by a browser. Thus, by simply stating that the information system must conform to Web standards, portability is guaranteed.

FIGURE 18.6

The World Wide Web
The different types
of connecting lines
denote different types
of communications
links

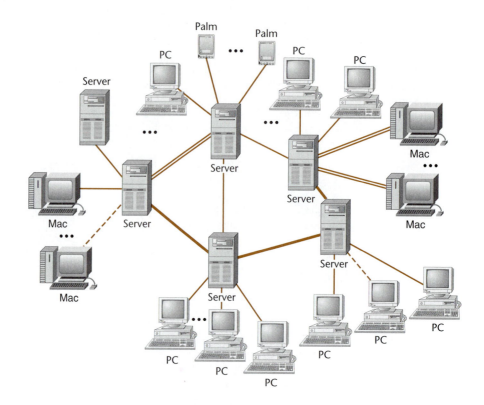

Just as with the simple client–server network of Figure 18.4, the World Wide Web (Figure 18.6) can be used in a number of different ways, including the following two basic approaches, each of which is analogous to its earlier counterpart:

- The simplest way is for the Web browser to function as a page reader. That is, Web pages are downloaded from a server to a client computer running a browser. The user uses the browser to read Web pages. For example, when purchasing an item from a website, the user browses through an online catalog. When ready to make a purchase, he or she enters data that are sent back to the server where they are checked. For example, if the user forgets to enter his or her name on the order form, the information system running on the server will detect this and send back a page pointing out the omission. When a browser is used in this fashion, the client is little more than a dumb terminal.

- The Web functions as a distributed computer. Users download programs from the server to their own computers and execute the programs there. These ported programs are called *applets*. For the sake of portability, most applets are implemented in Java— browsers almost always incorporate a Java interpreter for running applets. An applet can include software for checking data to be sent back to a server, a large video game, or software for playing music on the computer.

We now consider some security implications of the World Wide Web.

18.2   Security Issues

Consider again Cardholder Clothing Company, the e-commerce information system of Section 3.3 that allows shoppers to buy clothing over the World Wide Web using a credit card. It is standard practice for every such e-commerce system to *encrypt* credit card numbers.

That is, the number is encoded in some way. Then, if an order accidentally goes astray and appears on the screen of an individual not connected to Cardholder Clothing Company, there is no danger that that person will misuse the credit card number.

On closer examination, however, encryption of credit card numbers may not be of critical importance.

- The number of Web messages that end up in the hands of an individual other than the intended recipient is extremely small (but nonzero).

- Even if a credit card number does go astray, the unintended recipient may well be an honest person who would not dream of misusing it.

- Conversely, if crooks want to acquire credit card numbers, all they have to do is set up a genuine website that apparently sells genuine products at really good prices and encrypts all orders. Then, when orders come in, the crooks simply decrypt the credit card numbers and use the credit cards illegally.

Whereas there is nothing wrong with encryption of orders, it tends to distract attention from the real problem, which is: How are credit card numbers stored on the e-commerce company computer?

Suppose that an e-commerce company uses the highest levels of security for the transmission of credit card numbers. However, if that company then stores the credit card numbers on their computer in a way that they can be accessed by anyone in the world (see Just in Case You Wanted to Know Box 18.2), security in that company is essentially nonexistent, notwithstanding the encryption of orders while in transit. Instead, the company should store credit card numbers (and other sensitive data) in encrypted form. If there is some reason why the numbers have to be stored in unencrypted form, then they should be protected by passwords and other security mechanisms.

18.3   Analysis and Design Implications of Networks

First consider Figure 18.1, which depicts a single computer. We know how to perform the systems analysis and design for an information system implemented on this computer—it is described in Chapters 1 through 17 of this book.

Now consider Figure 18.2, an interactive timesharing computer. In what ways do we have to modify the way we perform the systems analysis and design of an information system to run on this type of computer? In fact, the only changes we need to make are to certain artifacts. For example, we need to change the requirements to state that input and output will be performed on the user's keyboard and screen, respectively. Also, the communications aspects of transferring the data to and from the computer have implications for all the workflows. As a result, issues such as security and reliability will have to handled. However, the only nontrivial implications are with regard to the detailed design and implementation artifacts.

Another issue is the user-interface implications of screen output, as opposed to the printer output of Figure 18.1. However, this topic was covered in Chapter 17, and there are no additional issues here. In short, from the viewpoint of the systems analysis and design of the target information system, there is very little extra that is needed to develop an information system for an interactive timesharing computer of the 1960s over and above what is needed for a first-generation computer of the 1940s.

Now we fast-forward to the personal computer of 1981, only to find that, from the viewpoint of systems analysis and design, there is not much difference between that personal computer and the first-generation computer of 35 years before. Yes, a personal computer

Some years ago I was reading a series of Usenet postings about a company I will call SPQR Corporation. Questions had been raised regarding the legality of the company's activities. One poster in particular, "Fred," a consultant to the company, argued vehemently that SPQR was totally above board in every way, notwithstanding extensive inquiries undertaken by attorneys general from all over the United States.

The next poster, "Joe," stated that anyone who was interested could click on the universal resource locator (URL) he gave in his posting and see Fred's credit card number. Intrigued, I clicked on the URL.

I was amazed to find a Web page containing detailed records of all SPQR customers, not just Fred's. There were over 40,000 records, each with name, address, telephone number, and credit card number and expiration date. Dishonest people worldwide could have had a field day with the information displayed on that page before it was removed about an hour later.

SPQR Corporation was shortly thereafter shut down under a barrage of cease-and-desist orders, so I have never been able to find out how the customer data became publicly available. One possibility was that SPQR had never taken any security precautions—the data had been there all the time, and Joe had simply stumbled onto the page.

Another possibility is that the customer data had been well protected by passwords. However, a disgruntled employee had realized that it was inevitable that the company would shortly be shut down by law-enforcement agencies. Fearing that he or she was about to be laid off without severance pay, the employee had taken revenge on the company by removing the password or other security protection.

A third possibility is that this was done by a senior manager, knowing that he was about to be arrested, to show SPQR customers how stupid they were to have dealt with a company like SPQR in the first place.

Whatever the real reason behind this display of the credit card data may be, the lesson is that it is unwise to give your credit card number to anyone, on the Web or elsewhere, unless you have performed due diligence regarding the trustworthiness of the recipient.

---

uses screen output, but we know how to handle that. Otherwise, the many critical differences between the two information systems are again all with regard to detailed design and implementation artifacts, not requirements and analysis artifacts, and are therefore outside the boundaries of this book.

Now we turn to Figure 18.4, the client–server network. As with Figure 18.2, the major issues are communicational in nature. Thus, other than stating certain nonfunctional requirements with regard to communications (and therefore to security and reliability), there is little that the systems analyst has to do that is different to the situation in which he or she performs systems analysis and design on the single (nonnetworked) personal computer of Figure 18.3. There are certainly many vital issues that arise when implementing an information system on a network but, as previously pointed out, they appertain to the later workflows, the workflows that are not the responsibility of systems analysts.

There are two differences between Figure 18.4 and Figure 18.5. First, the network of Figure 18.5 is much larger than the network of Figure 18.4. This is purely a networking issue—it cannot otherwise affect any other aspect of any of the artifacts. For example, a server that has to service 8 clients can be smaller and less powerful than a server for a network of 1,024 clients, but the information system running on the two networks will be identical in every other way.

Second, the network of Figure 18.4 is homogeneous, whereas the network of Figure 18.5 is heterogeneous. This has implications with regard to portability and interoperability. As pointed out at the end of the previous section, the portability issue is moot. Use of languages such as HTML and XML will ensure portability. The bad news is that interoperability can be a really hard problem to solve. The good news is that it is not *our* problem. Network specialists are hired to handle this issue, which affects detailed design and implementation artifacts. Thus, from the viewpoint of systems analysis and design, if we can handle the network of Figure 18.4, we can handle the network of Figure 18.5.

18.4   Web-Based Information Systems

The only difference between Figure 18.5 (a complex client–server network) and Figure 18.6 (the Web) is that the Web is the ultimate client–server network. All the problems of the previous section are present, and to the nth degree. For example, security on the Web has become a major nightmare. Hackers continue to break into websites with apparent ease. Viruses, worms, Trojan horses, logic bombs, and other types of noxious "hackware" abound. Solving the problem of the interoperability of two incompatible pieces of hardware running two incompatible operating systems is trivial—according to the sales literature for some middleware products. In practice, however, interoperability can be anything but trivial. All too often, the services of an experienced network consultant are needed to get two components of a network to communicate properly with one another.

However, as pointed out before, none of these problems, whether in smaller networks or larger networks, affect the subject of this book, namely, systems analysis and design using the Unified Process. In short, then, the issues arising from the development of Web-based information systems are extremely important. Some of them are remarkably hard to solve. But none of them impact the task of the systems analyst.

Key Terms

applet, *342*
batch mode, *338*
browser, *341*
client, *339*
client–server network, *339*

dumb terminal, *338*
encrypt, *342*
first-generation computer, *337*
HTML, *341*
interactive timesharing, *338*

interoperability, *340*
middleware, *340*
server, *339*
timesharing, *338*
XML, *341*

Review Questions for Chapter 18

1. What is meant by batch mode?
2. What is interactive timesharing?
3. Define the terms *client, server,* and *client–server network.*
4. What is interoperability?

Problems

18.1   What are the main similarities and differences between a first-generation computer and a personal computer?

18.2   What are the main similarities and differences between a client–server network and the World Wide Web?

18.3 From the viewpoint of systems analysis, what are the implications of the differences between a first-generation computer and a personal computer?

18.4 From the viewpoint of systems analysis, what are the implications of the differences between a client–server network and the World Wide Web?

Term Project

18.5 Suppose that the Chocoholics Anonymous information system has been implemented as stated in Appendix A. That is, the provider's terminal dials the ChocAn Data Center, and the ChocAn central computer then performs all necessary computations. Now Chocoholics Anonymous decides that the information system is to be implemented on the World Wide Web. What risks are involved, and how can they be mitigated?

19

Introduction to Database Management Systems

Learning Objectives

After studying this chapter, you should be able to:

- Describe why databases are generally superior to files with regard to data storage.
- Explain why many traditional databases are used in conjunction with object-oriented information systems.

ALVB Insurance Corporation is a large insurance company. Its information systems, all written in COBOL and developed using the traditional paradigm, collect and manipulate a wide variety of different kinds of data. For example, for each insurance policy issued by ALVB Insurance, there are policy records and premium payment records. The capital of ALVB Insurance is invested in a wide variety of different types of assets, including real estate, stocks, and bonds. For each asset type, different kinds of information are stored. For instance, when the company owns an apartment complex, there are records for each apartment (lease details, lessee details, rent payment records, repair and upkeep records), and there are expense and tax records for the apartment complex as a whole.

This tremendous quantity of data is stored in a *database*, a collection of data records organized in a way that will facilitate the storage and retrieval of the data by the company's information systems. The software that runs the database is called a *database management system*.

Realizing the many strengths of the object-oriented paradigm over the traditional paradigm, ALVB Insurance decides that all future information systems will be developed using the Unified Process. These new object-oriented information systems must access the corporation's extensive database and must therefore incorporate an object-oriented database management system.

Before describing what happens next, it is necessary to explain why databases are an integral part of most information systems.

19.1   Files and Their Problems

Stamp collecting is extremely popular in Stambury, Wyoming. Membership in the STAMbury Philatelic Society (or STAMPS, for short) has grown so large that STAMPS has bought a computer to handle the mailings of the many newsletters that the society sends to its members.

Before the computer was bought, a typewriter was used to type the name and address of each member onto an envelope. The problem with this approach is that the data are *volatile*. That is, the name and address data have to be typed afresh each time STAMPS wants a set of envelopes to be typed. This clearly is totally unacceptable.

In order to ensure that the data are *persistent,* that is, retained from run to run, a computer is used to print mailing labels. The first version of the STAMPS information system consists of two independent programs. **Program A** takes the name and address data keyed in by the operator and writes the data to a file on a *disk* (or *hard drive*). A *file* is a collection of data. Then, any time mailing labels are needed, **Program B** reads the data stored in the file and uses the data to print the mailing labels.

The UML deployment diagram of Figure 19.1 depicts the computer and its hard drive. Personal computers and workstations usually have the hard drive built into the computer casing, but mainframe computers generally have external disks. In this chapter the disk is depicted as external in order to highlight the role played by disks here.

Members resign from societies and new members join. Also, existing members can change their names and their addresses. Accordingly, **Program A** needs to be enhanced so that it can add new members to the file, delete members from the file, and change membership particulars. Changes are performed by reading the relevant record from the disk, updating it, then writing the updated record back to the disk. A program like **Program A** is sometimes referred to as a CRUD program; *CRUD* is an acronym for Create, Read, Update, and Delete, the four main operations of **Program A. Program B** is unchanged. It still reads the membership records from the disk and prints mailing labels. Figure 19.2 is a statechart for this version of the STAMPS information system. The operator has the choice to run **Program A, run Program B,** or **quit.**

Figure 19.3 shows six records in the file that contains the STAMPS name and address data. Files of this nature can easily be used to print address labels. The entire record is read. Then the **firstName** and **lastName** are extracted from the record and concatenated to form the first line to be printed on the label. The **address** portion of the record is now extracted and forms the second line to be printed.

Topical (or thematic) collecting is the collecting of stamps relating to a specific topic, such as roses, ducks, or the Statue of Liberty. Many of the members of STAMPS are particularly interested in stamps that depict chess games. Stamps showing fictional detectives are another favorite. Others collect stamps with pictures of elephants. Figure 19.4 shows the topical interests of the six members of STAMPS listed in Figure 19.3.

Topical collecting has become so popular in Stambury that STAMPS decides to send out special mailings to the members of each of the three topical groups. For example, suppose a

FIGURE 19.1
Deployment Diagram of a Computer and Its Disk

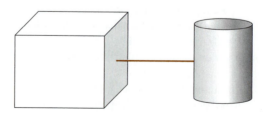

FIGURE 19.2
Statechart for
the File Version
of the STAMPS
Information System

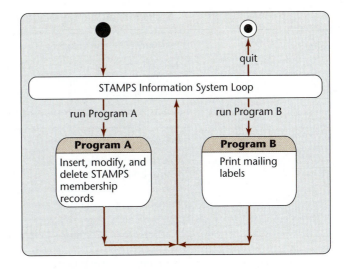

FIGURE 19.3
Six Members
of STAMPS

lastName	firstName	address
Alleyn	Ngaio	74 Marsh Meadows
Appleby	Michael	46 Innes Isle
Campion	Margery	7 Allingham Avenue
Fen	Edmund	303 Crispin Corner
Poirot	Agatha	84 Christie Close
Wimsey	Dorothy	21 Sayers Street

FIGURE 19.4
The Topical
Collecting Interests
of the Six Members
of STAMPS of
Figure 19.3

lastName	firstName	address	topicalGroup
Alleyn	Ngaio	74 Marsh Meadows	Chess, Detectives, Elephants
Appleby	Michael	46 Innes Isle	Chess, Elephants
Campion	Margery	7 Allingham Avenue	Detectives
Fen	Edmund	303 Crispin Corner	Detectives, Elephants
Poirot	Agatha	84 Christie Close	Detectives
Wimsey	Dorothy	21 Sayers Street	Elephants

notice about a forthcoming meeting of the chess topical group has to be mailed. Unfortunately, the current version of the information system cannot do this, because the file containing member records (Figure 19.3) does not contain data on topical interests. One alternative is to change **Program A** so that it creates a file like Figure 19.4, which incorporates topical information. Then **Program B** has to be changed so that it first reads the last part of each membership record, scans the topical interest(s) of the member, and then prints a label if that collector is a member of the relevant topical group.

But there is a much easier way to achieve the same thing without changing either **Program A** or **Program B**. Instead of having one large file containing data on all the members of STAMPS, three separate files are set up, one for each topical group. This is shown in Figure 19.5. This solves the problem. In order to send a mailing to just the collectors of stamps depicting chess games, only the first file in Figure 19.5 is run with **Program B**, yielding a set of labels for just those members of STAMPS who collect chess stamps. It seems that the problem is solved.

In fact, the problems are only just beginning.

FIGURE 19.5

Separate Files for
Each Topical Group
of STAMPS

Collectors of Stamps Depicting Chess Games

lastName	firstName	address
Alleyn	Ngaio	74 Marsh Meadows
Appleby	Michael	46 Innes Isle

Collectors of Stamps Depicting Fictional Detectives

lastName	firstName	address
Alleyn	Ngaio	74 Marsh Meadows
Campion	Margery	7 Allingham Avenue
Fen	Edmund	303 Crispin Corner
Poirot	Agatha	84 Christie Close

Collectors of Stamps Depicting Elephants

lastName	firstName	address
Alleyn	Ngaio	74 Marsh Meadows
Appleby	Michael	46 Innes Isle
Fen	Edmund	303 Crispin Corner
Wimsey	Dorothy	21 Sayers Street

Problem 1   Whenever a mailing has to go to one of the three topical groups, the information system works fine. But if a mailing has to go to all the members of STAMPS, then there is duplication or triplication. In order to be sure that a label is printed for every member, all three separate files need to be processed. But this means that two labels are printed for individuals like Michael Appleby who are members of two groups, and three labels are printed for Ngaio Alleyn, who is a member of all three topical groups. (In traditional database theory, this is called *redundant information*.)

Problem 2   Ngaio Alleyn moves to a new house. In order to be sure that all her notices are correctly addressed, all three files have to be changed. (In traditional database theory, this is called an *update anomaly*.)

Problem 3   Dorothy Wimsey is no longer interested in collecting stamps depicting elephants, so she resigns from that topical group. Her name is deleted from the third file in Figure 19.5. Because Dorothy now is not a member of any of the three topical groups, her membership details do not appear in any of the three files, so she receives none of the notices of STAMPS. (In traditional database theory, this is called a *deletion anomaly*.)

In this section a set of problems have been highlighted by describing the woes of a small philatelic society. These problems pale into insignificance when we are dealing with huge sets of records, like those of ALVB Insurance. Correspondingly, in the next section a solution for STAMPS is described that is equally applicable to vast data sets.

19.2   Tables

Figure 19.6 depicts the membership list of STAMPS of Figure 19.3 with one addition—each member now has a membership number. Figure 19.7 depicts the membership of the three topical groups but, instead of incorporating the names and addresses of the members, now only the membership number is included. Superficially it might seem that there is no

FIGURE 19.6

The Six Members
of STAMPS of
Figure 19.3 Showing
Their Membership
Numbers

membershipNumber	lastName	firstName	address
145	Alleyn	Ngaio	74 Marsh Meadows
177	Appleby	Michael	46 Innes Isle
214	Campion	Margery	7 Allingham Avenue
216	Fen	Edmund	303 Crispin Corner
639	Poirot	Agatha	84 Christie Close
880	Wimsey	Dorothy	21 Sayers Street

FIGURE 19.7

Tables for Each
Topical Group
of STAMPS

Collectors of Stamps Depicting Chess Games

membershipNumber
145
177

Collectors of Stamps Depicting Fictional Detectives

membershipNumber
145
214
216
639

Collectors of Stamps Depicting Elephants

membershipNumber
145
177
216
880

difference between this situation and the previous one. But the small change has simultaneously solved all three problems of the previous section.

Problem 1 When a mailing has to go to all the members of STAMPS, then Program B prints a (unique) label for every member listed in Figure 19.6. Each member appears exactly once in that table, so the problem of duplication (or triplication) cannot occur. Program B has to be changed so that it can handle the membership numbers, but this is easy to do.

Problem 2 When Ngaio Alleyn moves to a new house, only the one entry in Figure 19.6 has to be changed. Names and addresses now appear in only one place, namely, the table of Figure 19.6, so a change of name or of address is straightforward and can be handled by Program A, suitably modified to handle membership numbers as well as the other items previously stored in the file.

Problem 3 If Dorothy Wimsey decides that she is no longer interested in collecting stamps depicting elephants and resigns from that group, her membership number (880) is deleted from the third table in Figure 19.7. But her membership details remain in the table of Figure 19.6, so she continues to receive all the notices of STAMPS that are sent to every member.

FIGURE 19.8

Extended Tables for Each Topical Group of STAMPS

Collectors of Stamps Depicting Chess Games

membershipNumber	yearInWhichTheCollectorJoinedThisTopicalGroup
145	1997
177	1985

Collectors of Stamps Depicting Fictional Detectives

membershipNumber	doesTheCollectorHaveTheCompleteSetOfTwelve1972 NicaraguanStampsDepictingFictionalDetectives?
145	Yes
214	No
216	Yes
639	Yes

Collectors of Stamps Depicting Elephants

membershipNumber	numberOfElephantStampsInTheCollection
145	123
177	112
216	75
880	90

Finally, it is still possible to print mailing labels for just the members of one topical group. For example, suppose labels have to be printed for members of the chess topical group. The top table in Figure 19.7 is submitted to Program B. Program B has to be modified to read each membership number in turn and then look up the corresponding name and address data in Figure 19.6. The first number in the top table is 145. From the table in Figure 19.6, Program B determines that this is the membership number of Ngaio Alleyn, so it prints an address label for her. The next number in the table is 177, so a label is printed for Michael Appleby. The change to Program B is relatively easy to make. STAMPS now has an information system that has all the capabilities that the society needs. In fact, the information system can even be extended to incorporate additional information, as shown in Figure 19.8.

19.3   Traditional Database Systems

Although there are different types of traditional databases, the overwhelming majority of traditional database management systems are relational. In a *relational database,* the data are stored in tables, like Figure 19.6 together with Figure 19.8. In this database, the *primary key* is membershipNumber in Figure 19.6. This key is also used to label records in other tables, for example, in the three tables of Figure 19.8, so that they can be associated with the primary records. When used in this way, membershipNumber is termed a *foreign key.*

There is a major difference between an information system that makes use of a database management system and the STAMPS information system. In the case of the STAMPS information system, the software (Program A and Program B) is explicitly written to manage the data. In the case of an information system that makes use of a database management

FIGURE 19.9
Database Instruction
Embedded in
COBOL Code

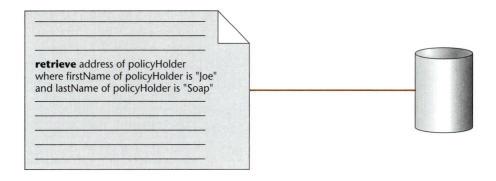

FIGURE 19.10
Representation of the
Execution of the
Database Instruction

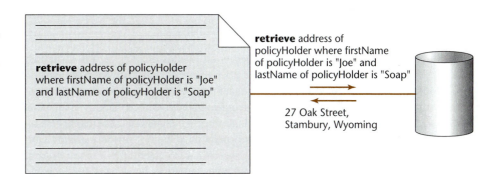

system, the writing of data to the disk and the retrieval of data from the disk are handled by the database management system. Examples of such relational database management systems include DB2, Oracle, Informix, and Sybase on mainframe computers and Microsoft Access on personal computers.

The way that an information system interfaces with a database management system is usually by embedding database instructions within the source code. All of the information systems of ALVB Insurance, the large insurance company, are written in COBOL. Database instructions are then embedded inside the COBOL source code, as shown in the deployment diagram of Figure 19.9. (Source code is usually represented as a note in UML.)

Suppose we want to know the address of policyholder Joe Soap. This can be achieved with the database instruction

> **retrieve** address of policyHolder
> where firstName of policyHolder is "Joe"
> and lastName of policyHolder is "Soap"

For this approach to work, the COBOL code first has to pass through a precompiler to convert the instructions to the database management system into COBOL. The resulting all-COBOL program is then compiled, linked, and run in the usual way. Then, when the database instruction is executed, the database management system searches the database for the policy-holder record for Joe Soap and returns his address to the COBOL program. This is represented in Figure 19.10.

Database instructions of this kind can be embedded within a wide variety of traditional programming languages, including C and COBOL. Typical database instructions include **insert, delete,** and **update.** As with **retrieve,** the program has to supply the information that the database management system needs to identify the record to be **insert**ed, **delete**d, or **update**d. Suppose that the program instructs the database management system to **insert** a record for a new policy holder, Jane Jones, with policy number 123–456–789. Suppose further that the primary key is policyNumber and that the table of policy holders is sorted by policyNumber. Then, all that the programmer needs to do is embed an **insert** command into the COBOL code and ensure that the name and number of the new policy holder are keyed in by the operator and passed to the database instruction. The database management system then ensures that the new record is inserted into the correct place in the correct table. In other words, the database management system manages the database itself; the programmer is responsible for writing code that invokes the database management system and provides it with the data it needs.

19.4   Object-Oriented Database Systems

As explained at the beginning of this chapter, ALVB Insurance wants to use the object-oriented paradigm for all its new information systems, and this means using an object-oriented database management system, too. However, there are two reasons why ALVB Insurance will not be using an object-oriented database management system for some time.

The first reason is that object-oriented database management systems are still too complex for use by most information technology services groups. Until recently, object-oriented database management systems were essentially a research topic. At the time of writing, object-oriented database management systems are slowly starting to become commercially available. Unfortunately, like most first-generation software products, these object-oriented database management systems are not as easy to use as their traditional counterparts. In fact, most of them require an extensive background in object-oriented database theory.

The second reason is far more important. ALVB Insurance has invested hundreds of millions (if not billions) of dollars in its traditional (relational) database and the traditional information systems that interact with the database. If the database were to be converted into an object-oriented database, then the many existing traditional information systems would not be able to access the new database. They would have to be totally rewritten, at enormous cost.

One "solution" would be to have two databases, one traditional and the other object-oriented. However, this would be ridiculous. After all, a major reason for using a database is to have just one copy of each record so that if, for example, the address of a policy holder changes, this change needs to be made in only one place. Having two databases will mean that there will be two copies of everything. Worse, in order to keep the two databases consistent, there will have to be two versions of every new information system, one traditional to update the traditional database and one object-oriented to update the object-oriented database!

There is no alternative for ALVB Insurance—the company has to continue using its traditional database. Does this mean that information systems developed using the object-oriented paradigm cannot use databases, one of the most powerful tools of information technology? Not at all. What happens is that a hybrid system is developed, with the object-oriented information system interfacing with a traditional database management system. Instead of embedding database management system instructions in source code written in a traditional language such as COBOL or C, the same (or similar) instructions are embedded in C++ or Java code. The database management system now has two tasks. First, as before, it has to manage the database. Second, when writing data to the database, it has to extract the data from an object, convert the data into a record, and write the record to the traditional database. Similarly, after retrieving a record from the traditional database, it has to insert the record into an object. In other words, the database management system also has to perform conversions from traditional to object-oriented systems, and vice versa.

19.5   Database Design and the Unified Process

It is easy to use a database management system—as shown in Section 19.3, all that needs to be done is to insert commands to the database management system into the source code. On the other hand, the *design* of a database requires specialized skills, including detailed knowledge of the theory of databases. For this reason, Information Systems curricula almost invariably include at least one course on databases. It therefore should come as no surprise that the Unified Process does not explicitly include database design.

19.6   The Future of Object-Oriented Database Management Systems

It seems likely that object-oriented database management systems will eventually become as easy to use as traditional database management systems. Nevertheless, if the ALVB Insurance Corporation is anything to go by, object-oriented database management systems would never be used because of the investment in existing traditional database management systems.

This is only partly true. Certainly, when a company has a huge investment in its traditional database management system and information systems, it will still be ruinously expensive for such a company to convert both database and information systems to the object-oriented paradigm. Instead, new information systems will be written using the object-oriented paradigm, but will interface with the traditional database, as explained in Section 19.4. However, when a new company starts up, it will use the object-oriented paradigm for both its information systems and its database management system.

Thus, legacy systems (Section 16.8) are the biggest obstacle to the widespread utilization of object-oriented database management systems, just as they are to object-oriented information systems in general. However, the object-oriented paradigm is the paradigm of choice today for the development of new information systems, and this will lead to the adoption of object-oriented database systems in the future.

Key Terms

CRUD, *348*	disk, *348*	primary key, *352*
database, *347*	file, *348*	redundant information, *350*
database management system, *347*	foreign key, *352*	relational database, *352*
deletion anomaly, *350*	hard drive, *348*	update anomaly, *350*
	persistent, *348*	volatile, *348*

Review Questions for Chapter 19

1. What is a database?
2. What is a database management system?
3. Distinguish between a file and a database.
4. Distinguish between a primary key and a foreign key.

Problems   19.1   Explain how a traditional database management system is used with a traditional information system.

19.2   Explain how a traditional database management system can be used with an object-oriented information system.

19.3   What are the major obstacles to the widespread adoption of object-oriented database management systems?

19.4   What problems that arise when files are used can be obviated by the use of a traditional database?

19.5   If you were hired to advise STAMPS regarding their existing traditional database management system, would you advise that organization to use an object-oriented database instead? Explain your answer.

Term Project

19.6   Could the Chocoholics Anonymous information system of Appendix A be implemented using an object-oriented database system? Explain your answer.

20

Technical Topics

Learning Objectives

After studying this chapter, you should be able to:

- Distinguish between source code and compiled code.
- Explain what compilers and linkers do.
- Describe the key issues in the theory of modularity.
- Describe polymorphism and dynamic binding.

This chapter describes a variety of more technical issues, including compilers and linkers, modularity, and polymorphism and dynamic binding.

20.1 Source Code and Compiled Code

Programmers do not write all parts of a program. Instead, every computer comes with numerous *run-time routines* that a programmer can invoke. For example, if a programmer wants an information system to print a report, he or she does not have to write the code that checks that the printer is on, that there is paper in the in-tray, and so on. Instead, all that is needed is for the programmer to include a statement such as print or write (the precise term depends on the programming language used). Then, at *run time* (when the program is executed), the relevant run-time routines handle all aspects of the printing. These include the necessary checks before printing, transferring the data to be printed from the computer itself to the printer, and so on.

A program exists in three forms. First, there is the *source code,* that is, the statements written by the programmer. The source code is written in a language such as COBOL, C, C++, or Java. The problem is that a computer can understand only one language, namely, the stream of 0s and 1s (*binary*) known as *machine code*. Thus, the source code needs to be transformed into machine code before a computer can execute it. As shown in Figure 20.1, this transformation is performed in two stages. First, the source code written by the programmer is *compiled* (translated) into what is usually termed object code. The term *object code* has nothing whatsoever to do with the object-oriented paradigm. Accordingly, in this book we refer to object code as *compiled code*. Then, the compiled code is combined with the run-time routines it needs to form an *executable load image* as shown in Figure 20.1.

FIGURE 20.1

Compilation of
Source Code into
Compiled Code,
Which Is Linked
Together with
Run-Time Routines
to Make an
Executable
Load Image

FIGURE 20.2

Compilation of One
Source Code Module,
Followed by Linkage
of All 100 Compiled
Code Modules with
the Run-Time
Routines to Make
an Executable
Load Image

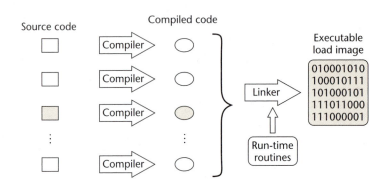

The first information systems were small; anything over a thousand lines of code was considered unusual. But as information systems grew larger, it became apparent that monolithic information systems are inefficient. Consider an information system consisting of one large block of 5,000 lines of code. If even a single statement has to be changed, the entire 5,000-line information system has to be compiled all over again, as in Figure 20.1. Compilation of one large information system is a slow process, one that has to be repeated each time the code is changed.

However, when that same information system is constructed as 100 smaller code artifacts (or *modules*), each consisting of 50 lines of code, then only 50 lines of code have to be recompiled each time a module is changed. Of course, each time the code is changed it is necessary to *link* the 100 compiled modules together with the run-time routines to form an executable load image. However, recompiling one module and then linking the newly recompiled module together with the 99 unchanged compiled code modules and the run-time routines takes considerably less time than recompiling and relinking 5,000 lines of code. This situation is shown in Figure 20.2, which depicts the recompilation of one of the 100 modules followed by the linking of all 100 compiled code modules into an equivalent executable load image.

It is clear that a large information system has to be decomposed into modules. The question is: How is this decomposition to be performed?

20.2   Modularity

To appreciate the issues involved, consider again Cardholder Clothing Company, the e-commerce company of Section 3.3 that currently allows the user to order clothes over the World Wide Web and charge the purchase to a Mastercard or Visa credit card. Now suppose that Cardholder Clothing Company management have just signed an agreement with American Express, Inc., so that customers can now also charge their purchases to an

American Express card, in addition to the two existing credit cards. If the part of the information system that deals with credit cards is spread over a large number of different modules, then the maintenance programmer will have to look at the entire information system to determine which modules are involved. He or she then has to study each of those modules in depth to determine whether that module has to be changed and, if so, in what way. Finally, when all the changes have been made, the modules that were modified have to be tested, and the documentation for those modules has to be changed to reflect the modifications that have been made.

In contrast, suppose that only one module handles all the credit card aspects of the Cardholder Clothing Company information system. In this case, the programmer has to understand just that one module, modify it, test it, and document it. Not only will this be much quicker than examining every module, it is likely to be a less error-prone approach, whereas if the credit card functionality is spread over the entire information system, there is a good chance that the programmer will overlook a part of the information system that needs to be changed.

Thus, an important criterion for dividing an information system into modules is to ensure that functionality coincides with module boundaries. When the maintenance programmer wants to modify the information system so that it can accept American Express cards, he or she need look at only the module that handles credit cards. Then, the programmer can make the necessary changes to that module so that the information system also can handle American Express cards in exactly the same way that it currently handles Visa and Mastercard.

What is described in this section is *cohesion*. A module has high cohesion if the methods (implementations of the operations) of that module are strongly related to one another and weakly related to the methods of the other modules. Cohesion is a fundamental principle of traditional design. The traditional paradigm can be summarized as follows:

- Determine the client's needs (requirements phase).
- Draw up the specifications (analysis phase).
- Design the information system as a set of modules with high cohesion (design phase).
- Code the modules (implementation phase).

As previously stated, the traditional paradigm was extremely successful with the smaller information systems that were the norm when the traditional paradigm first became popular in the late 1970s. The reason for these successes was that the traditional paradigm was the first systematic approach to information system development—almost any method is superior to no method at all.

Now consider the design criterion of maximizing the cohesion of a module. There are two aspects to a module: the data of the module and the operations performed on the data by the methods of that module. Cohesion relates solely to operations; it ignores data. The weakness of the traditional paradigm is that it concentrates on the operations and essentially ignores the data. This weakness has been described in this section within the context of traditional design, but similar observations can be made about traditional systems analysis and, indeed, almost all the other techniques of the traditional paradigm. In contrast, what is needed is a paradigm that gives equal weight to data and operations—the object-oriented paradigm.

The concept of cohesion was first put forward in 1976 within the context of the theory of composite/structured design [Stevens, Myers, and Constantine, 1976]. Various levels of cohesion were enumerated. The best was functional cohesion; a module has functional cohesion when it performs only one operation. The concept of functional cohesion is typical of the traditional paradigm, because it is concerned with operations and ignores data.

FIGURE 20.3
UML Representation
of Credit Card Class

Credit Card Class
cardNumber nameOfCardholder expirationDate
validateTransaction ( ) chargeTransactionToCard ( ) creditPaymentToCard ( ) printMonthlyStatement ( )

FIGURE 20.4
(a) Multiple instances
of both attributes and
methods; (b) single
instance of methods,
multiple instances of
attributes

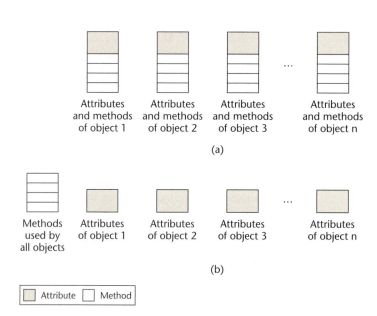

Attributes and methods of object 1   Attributes and methods of object 2   Attributes and methods of object 3   ...   Attributes and methods of object n

(a)

Methods used by all objects   Attributes of object 1   Attributes of object 2   Attributes of object 3   ...   Attributes of object n

(b)

▨ Attribute   ☐ Method

The second best form of cohesion was informational cohesion. A module has informational cohesion when it performs a number of related operations, all on the same data. Figure 3.8 (reproduced here as Figure 20.3) depicts a module of informational cohesion that deals with credit cards. It has three data items (attributes): cardNumber, nameOfCardholder and expirationDate. There are four operations (methods) performed on the data: validateTransaction, chargeTransactionToCard, creditPaymentToCard, and printMonthlyStatement. Figure 20.3, as the caption shows, is a class. That is, a class is a module with informational cohesion (now considered superior to functional cohesion).

The run-time implementation of classes (or, more precisely, of objects) has an interesting feature. Suppose that we develop an information system for the credit card company that uses the object of Figure 20.3. Suppose further that our information system is powerful enough to process 1,000 credit card transactions simultaneously. For each such transaction, we will need an object that is an instance of the class depicted in Figure 20.3. That is, for each transaction there will be one instance of cardNumber, nameOfCardholder and expirationDate, and one instance of the code for validateTransaction, chargeTransactionToCard, creditPaymentToCard, and printMonthlyStatement. This is shown in Figure 20.4(a).

This makes no sense at all. We obviously need to have one instance of the attributes of the object for each transaction—that is, one instance of cardNumber, nameOfCardholder, and expirationDate—but we certainly do not need multiple instances of the operations performed on the data. All that is needed is a single instance of each code module

Are classes as important as objects? In reality, classes are far more important than objects. Object-oriented analysis should really be called class-oriented analysis, because specifications use classes, not objects. Similarly, object-oriented design should be called class-oriented design; the output of the design workflow is a document that again uses classes, not objects. Furthermore, the object-oriented paradigm should be called the class-oriented paradigm, because objects enter into it only in the implementation workflow. But even in the implementation workflow, classes are central. If you look at Java or C++ code, you will see the word **class** wherever a class is needed, but there is no word **object**. It is an accident of history that objects were put forward before classes, and that the resulting paradigm is therefore said to be "object oriented" rather than "class oriented." We cannot change history, so in this book the standard terminology is used, namely, *object-oriented paradigm, object-oriented analysis, object-oriented design,* and *object-oriented programming language.* This is done to avoid confusion, despite the fact that the standard terminology is incorrect, and that we should replace the adjectival phrase *object-oriented* by *class-oriented* in each case.

that can be used by every data instance. After all, the attributes portion of each object is small; all that is needed is space to store a 16-digit number and two amounts. But the methods portion is likely to be thousands of lines of code in length, and redundant multiple copies of this code will soon overflow the memory of our computer, bringing the machine to a halt.

Instead, what we want is shown in Figure 20.4(b). Now there is an instance of the attributes for each credit card transaction, plus just a single instance of the code that can perform the necessary operations on all those data instances. What do we have to do to achieve this?

The answer is: nothing. When an object-oriented programming language such as C++ or Java is used, the declaration of a class within the information system has two effects. First, when the information system is run, just one copy of all the methods declared within that class is created. Second, whenever the information system requires a new object (for instance, when a new credit card transaction is processed in our credit card company information system), just the data portion of the object is generated. In other words, an object-oriented programming language behaves exactly as in Figure 20.4(b).

For yet another insight into classes, read Just in Case You Wanted to Know Box 20.1.

20.3 Polymorphism and Dynamic Binding

Carbon occurs in nature in different forms, including hard diamonds and soft graphite (from which pencil "lead" is made). In chemistry and geology, the phenomenon of the same substance (carbon in this instance) occurring in different forms is called *polymorphism,* from two Greek words meaning "many shapes." The term *polymorphism* is also used in object-oriented information systems to describe a similar phenomenon.

Consider again Figure 3.10 (reproduced here for convenience as Figure 20.5), which shows superclass **Bank Card Class** with subclasses **Credit Card Class** and **Debit Card Class.** Statements are printed each month in which there is activity on a credit card account or a debit card account. In a traditional information system, there have to be two different functions (methods), the one called print_monthly_statement_for_credit_card and the other print_monthly_statement_for_debit_card, as shown in Figure 20.6 (the

FIGURE 20.5
Credit Card Class
and Debit Card
Class Are Subclasses
of Bank Card Class

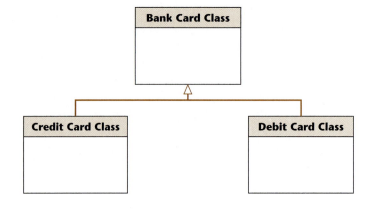

FIGURE 20.6
Traditional
Implementation of
Bank Cards

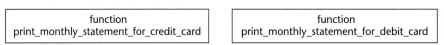

FIGURE 20.7
Object-Oriented
Implementation
of Bank Cards
Reflecting
Polymorphism and
Dynamic Binding

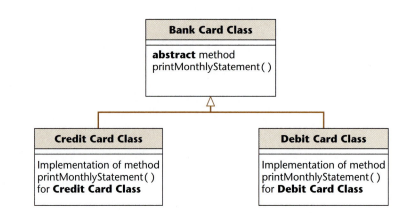

underscore in the function names is explained in Just in Case You Wanted to Know Box 3.1). Then, while the information system is running, each card in turn is examined. If it is a credit card, then the monthly statement is printed by function print_monthly_statement_for_credit_card, but if it is a debit card, then the statement is printed by print_monthly_statement_for_debit_card.

In contrast, when an object-oriented information system is developed, the situation is much simpler and is handled automatically. Refer to Figure 20.7. In **Bank Card Class** (the superclass) we declare an **abstract** (or **virtual**) method, printMonthlyStatement. Then, in each of the subclasses, we implement a method for printing that type of monthly statement. In more detail, the **abstract** (or **virtual**) method in **Bank Card Class** is called printMonthlyStatement. The implementations in each of the two subclasses also are called printMonthlyStatement. That is, there are three methods called printMonthlyStatement, namely, the **abstract** (or **virtual**) method and the two implementations, one for each of the two card types. Then, when the monthly statements are being printed by the information system, the system automatically detects whether a specific card is a credit card or a debit card and invokes the appropriate version of the implementation of printMonthlyStatement.

In Figure 20.7 there are two different implementations of method printMonthlyStatement. That is, there are multiple "shapes" of that method, which is why the term *polymorphism* is used to describe this aspect of an object-oriented information system. Furthermore, the decision as to which of the two implementations to use to print a given monthly statement is made by the information system at the time that the relevant statement is about to be printed. That is, the relevant version of printMonthlyStatement is "bound" to the credit card or debit card while the information system is running. *Dynamic binding* is the technical term for the automatic "binding" of a method to an object while the information system is running ("dynamic").

The use of polymorphism and dynamic binding makes it easier to develop an object-oriented information system than a traditional one. After all, there is no need to write code to test whether an object is (say) a credit card or a debit card and then invoking the appropriate function to print the monthly statement. Instead, with an object-oriented information system, at run time the decision is made automatically by the information system; the compiler for the object-oriented programming language in which the information system is implemented generates the necessary instructions.

20.4   Example of Polymorphism and Dynamic Binding

As stated in Section 8.4, there are three factors that are used while performing the design workflow in deciding to which class to allocate a method. Two of the factors, responsibility-driven design and inheritance, were described in that section. A third factor is polymorphism and dynamic binding.

To see how this is done, we return to the MSG Foundation case study. Consider Figures 7.43 and 7.46, which respectively include message 3: Print list of mortgages and message 3: Print list of investments. We therefore need method printAsset to be able to print either an investment or a mortgage.

In the case of the traditional paradigm, we would need to have two different functions, namely

print_investment

print_mortgage

There would thus be a separate function for each asset type. The information system would first have to determine the type of the asset, and then invoke the appropriate function.

With the object-oriented paradigm, however, we can utilize polymorphism. We need to have two different versions of the same method, both named printAsset. At run time (dynamic binding), the object-oriented system automatically determines the class of the object and invokes the appropriate version of the method printAsset; we do not need to write code to test the class of the object and then invoke the correct method.

At first sight, it would seem that the way to do this is to use the same approach that we used in Section 8.4.2 for methods setAssetNumber and getAssetNumber. That is, the two classes that use method printAsset, namely, **Investment Class** and **Mortgage Class,** are both subclasses of **Asset Class.** Accordingly, perhaps we should allocate method printAsset to class **Asset Class,** as shown in Figure 20.8.

Unfortunately, this does not work. The problem is that we have used inheritance instead of polymorphism. That is, method printAsset in class **Asset Class** is inherited, *unchanged,* by the two subclasses. In other words, in Figure 20.8 we have one version of printAsset that is used by both subclasses. This cannot work, because the attributes of an investment are different from those of a mortgage, so one print method will not do. Instead, what we need

FIGURE 20.8
Wrong Allocation of
Method **printAsset**

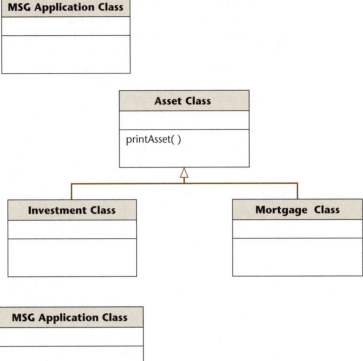

FIGURE 20.9
Correct Allocation of
Method **printAsset**

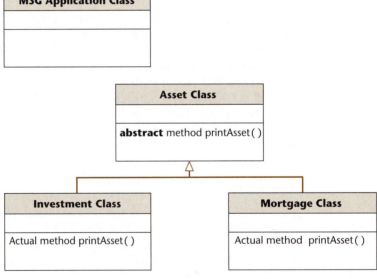

are two different versions, both called printAsset, and we want our object-oriented run-time system to apply the appropriate one, automatically.

The correct way of doing this is shown in Figure 20.9. The first difference between Figure 20.8 and Figure 20.9 is that, in Figure 20.9, method printAsset in class **Asset Class** has been declared to be **abstract** (or **virtual**). This is a directive to the compiler that **Asset Class** does not have its own implementation of method printAsset. Instead, whenever method printAsset is invoked, the object-oriented run-time system must first determine the class of the object that is invoking method printAsset. There are two possibilities: The object can be an instance of class **Investment Class** or an instance of class **Mortgage Class.** Then, the run-time system must go to the appropriate class and execute the implementation of method printAsset that is found there.

This is shown in Figure 20.9. As reflected in that diagram, there are two different actual implementations of method printAsset: the implementation in **Investment Class** and the implementation in **Mortgage Class.** Depending on the class of the object (**Investment Class** or **Mortgage Class**), the appropriate implementation is invoked.

In summary, the sole impact on the superclass (in this case **Asset Class**) is that an **abstract** (**virtual**) statement is inserted there; there is no implementation in the superclass. Then, in both of the subclasses (in this case, **Investment Class** and **Mortgage Class**), there is a subclass-specific implementation of the method. Because there are multiple implementations of the method (in this case, two implementations of method printAsset), the method is polymorphic (literally, "many shapes"). At run time, the object-oriented system determines the class membership of the object in question, and then invokes the appropriate version of the implementation of the method. There is no need to write the code to implement this.

20.5 Maintenance Implications of Polymorphism and Dynamic Binding

Consider again Figure 20.9. It shows an implementation of a base class named **Asset Class,** together with two subclasses, **Investment Class** and **Mortgage Class.** In the implementation of base class **Asset Class,** a dummy (**abstract** or **virtual**) method printAsset is declared. Then, a specific implementation of the method appears in each of the two subclasses; each method is given the identical name, printAsset, as shown in Figure 20.9. Now suppose that the information system fails and the run-time system prints a message stating that the cause of the failure is "method printAsset." In general, there is no way for the maintainer to tell which of the two versions of method printAsset (the version in subclass **Investment Class** or the version in subclass **Mortgage Class**) was responsible.

The strength of polymorphism and dynamic binding is that we do not have to specify which version of printAsset is to be invoked at run time; it is handled automatically by the object-oriented run-time system. We can have two methods with the same name, and potential ambiguity is automatically resolved. Conversely, however, the fact that there are two methods with the same name means that, when something goes wrong and the run-time system prints a message stating the name of the method that is responsible, we cannot tell which of the two identically named methods is the cause of the problem. Polymorphism and dynamic binding indeed are extremely powerful aspects of object-oriented technology that promote the development of an object-oriented information system. However, they can have a deleterious impact on maintenance.

Key Terms

binary, *357*
cohesion, *359*
compiled code, *357*
compiler, *357*
dynamic binding, *363*

executable load image, *357*
linker, *358*
machine code, *357*
module, *358*
polymorphism, *361*

run time, *357*
run-time routines, *357*
source code, *357*

Review Questions for Chapter 20

1. Distinguish between source code, compiled code, and an executable load image.
2. What is a module?
3. What is the advantage of modularity?
4. What is meant by the cohesion of a module?

5. Define what is meant by polymorphism (in the computer context).

6. Define what is meant by dynamic binding.

7. Give a strength of polymorphism and dynamic binding.

8. Give a weakness of polymorphism and dynamic binding.

Problems

20.1 The object-oriented paradigm should be called the class-oriented paradigm. Why has the name not been changed?

20.2 What do we have to do to ensure that, when multiple objects are involved, there is only one copy of each of their methods in memory?

20.3 What happens if we use polymorphism without dynamic binding?

20.4 What happens if we use dynamic binding without polymorphism?

Reference

Stevens, W. P.; G. J. Myers; and L. L. Constantine. "Structured Design." *IBM Systems Journal* 13, no. 2 (1974), pp. 115–39.

Term Project: Chocoholics Anonymous

Chocoholics Anonymous (ChocAn) is an organization dedicated to helping people addicted to chocolate in all its glorious forms. Members pay a monthly fee to ChocAn. For this fee they are entitled to unlimited consultations and treatments with health-care professionals, namely, dietitians, internists, and exercise experts. Every member is given a plastic card embossed with the member's name and a nine-digit member number, and incorporating a magnetic strip on which that information is encoded. Each health-care professional (*provider*) who provides services to ChocAn members has a specially designed ChocAn computer terminal, similar to credit card devices in shops. Both providers and members have name, number, address, city, state, and ZIP code attributes. In order to receive health-care services from ChocAn, the member hands his or her card to the provider, who slides the card though the card reader on the terminal. The terminal then dials the ChocAn Data Center, and the ChocAn central computer verifies the member number. If the number is valid, the word Validated appears on the one-line display. If the number is not valid, the reason is displayed, such as Invalid number or Member suspended; the latter message indicates that dues are owed (that is, the member has not paid dues for at least a month) and member status has been set to suspended.

In order to bill ChocAn after a health-care service has been provided to the member, the provider again passes the card through the card reader or keys in the member number. When the word Validated appears, the provider keys in the date the service was provided in the format MM–DD–YYYY. The date of service is needed because hardware or other difficulties may have prevented the provider from billing ChocAn immediately after providing the service. Finally, the provider uses the Provider Directory to look up the appropriate six-digit service code corresponding to the service provided. For example, 598470 is the code for a session with a dietitian, while 883948 is the code for an aerobics exercise session. The provider then keys in the service code. To check that the service code has been correctly looked up and keyed in, the information system then displays the name of the service corresponding to the code (up to 14 characters) and asks the provider to verify that this is indeed the service that was provided. If the provider has entered a nonexistent code, an error message is printed. The provider also can enter any additional comments about the service provided, if needed.

The information system now writes a record to disk that includes the following fields:

Current date and time (MM–DD–YYYY HH:MM:SS).

Date service was provided (MM–DD–YYYY).

Provider name (25 characters).

Provider number (9 digits, previously entered by the provider).

Provider type (internist, dietitian, exercise specialist).

Member name (25 characters).

Member number (9 digits).

Service code (6 digits).

Service name (20 characters).

Description of service provided (40 characters).

Comments (100 characters) (optional).

The information system next looks up the fee to be paid for that service and displays it on the provider's terminal. For verification purposes, the provider has a form on which to write the current date and time, the date the service was provided, name of member and member number, service code, and fee to be paid. At the end of the week, the provider totals the fees to verify the amount to be paid to that provider by ChocAn for that week.

At midnight on Friday, the main accounting procedure is run. It reads the week's file of services provided and prints a number of reports. Each report also can be run individually at the request of a ChocAn manager at any time during the week.

Each member who has consulted a ChocAn provider during that week receives a list of services provided to that member, sorted in order of service date. The report includes

Member name (25 characters).

Member number (9 digits).

Member street address (25 characters).

Member city (14 characters).

Member state (2 letters).

Member ZIP code (5 digits).

For each service provided, the report includes a line stating

Date of service (MM–DD–YYYY).

Provider name (25 characters).

Service name (20 characters).

Each provider who has billed ChocAn during that week receives a report containing the list of services he or she provided to ChocAn members. To simplify the task of verification, the report contains the same information as is entered on the provider's form, in the order that the data were received by the computer. At the end of the report is a summary including the number of consultations with members and the total fee for that week. That is, the fields of the report include

Provider name (25 characters).

Provider number (9 digits).

Provider street address (25 characters).

Provider city (14 characters).

Provider state (2 letters).

Provider ZIP code (5 digits).

For each service provided, the report includes a line stating

Date of service (MM–DD–YYYY).

Date and time data were received by the computer (MM–DD–YYYY HH:MM:SS).

Member name (25 characters).

Member number (9 digits).

Service code (6 digits).

Fee to be paid (up to $999.99).

Total number of consultations with members (3 digits).

Total fee for week (up to $99,999.99).

A record consisting of electronic funds transfer (EFT) data is then written to a magnetic tape; banking computers will later ensure that each provider's bank account is credited with the appropriate amount.

A summary report is given to the manager for accounts payable. The report lists every provider to be paid that week, the number of consultations each had, and his or her total fee for that week. Finally, the total number of providers who provided services, the total number of consultations, and the overall fee total are printed.

During the day, the information system is run in interactive mode to allow operators to add new members to ChocAn, to modify members who have resigned or suspend those whose dues are in arrears, and to update member records. Similarly, provider records are added and updated.

Your organization has been awarded the contract to write only the data processing software for this system; another organization will be responsible for the communications software, for designing the ChocAn provider's terminal, and for implementing the EFT component. The contract states that at the acceptance test, the data from a provider's terminal must be simulated by keyboard input and data to be transmitted to a provider's terminal display must appear on the screen. A manager's terminal must be simulated by the same keyboard and screen. Each member report must be sent to its own file. The name of the file should begin with the member name, followed by the date of the report. The provider reports should be handled the same way. As for the EFT data, all that is required is that a file be set up containing provider name and number and the amount to be transferred.

Object-Oriented Design: Osbert Oglesby Case Study

This appendix contains the final iteration of the class diagram for the Osbert Oglesby case study. The overall class diagram is followed by UML diagrams for the 17 component classes, in alphabetical order. These UML diagrams show the attributes and the methods. As explained in Section 10.2, the UML visibility prefixes are – for **private,** + for **public,** and # for **protected.**

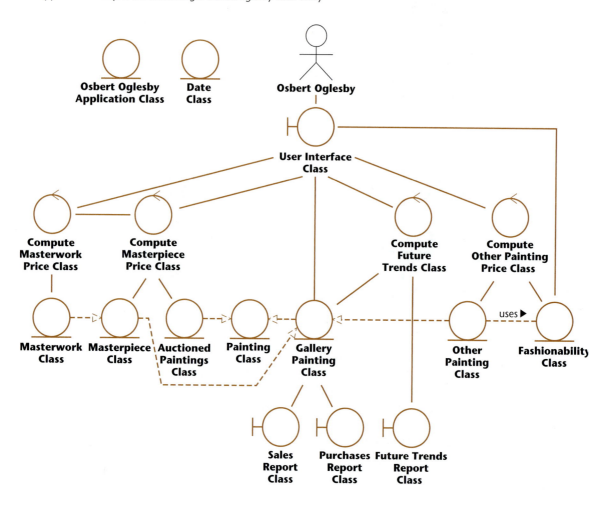

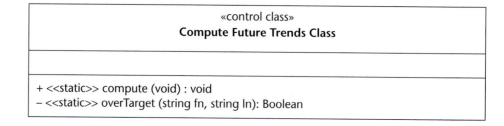

«entity class»
Auctioned Paintings Class
auctionPrice : float # auctionDate : Date
+ getAuctionDate ( ) : Date + setAuctionDate (d : Date) : void + getAuctionPrice ( ) : float + setAuctionPrice (p : float) : void + readAuctionData (fileName : ifstream&) : void

«control class»
Compute Future Trends Class
+ <<static>> compute (void) : void – <<static>> overTarget (string fn, string ln): Boolean

«control class»
Compute Masterpiece Price Class
+ <<static>> getAlgorithmPrice (masterpiece : GalleryPainting) : float

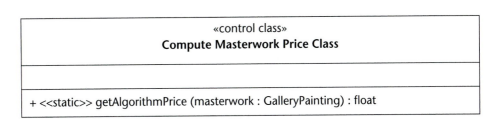

«control class»
Compute Masterwork Price Class
+ <<static>> getAlgorithmPrice (masterwork : GalleryPainting) : float

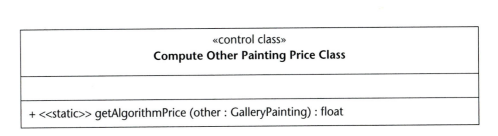

«control class»
Compute Other Painting Price Class
+ <<static>> getAlgorithmPrice (other : GalleryPainting) : float

«entity class»
Date Class
– year : int – month : int – day : int
+ Date ( ) + getYear ( ) : int + getMonth ( ) : int + getDay ( ) : int + setYear (y : int) : void + setMonth (m : int) : void + setDay (d : int) : void + parseDate (dateStr : string) : Boolean + compare (aDate : Date) : int + subtractOneYear ( ) : void – validDate ( ) : Boolean + <<friend>> operator << (o : std::ostream&, d : const Date&) : std::ostream&

«entity class»
Fashionability Class
coefficient : float # firstName : string # lastName : string
+ getFirstName ( ) : string + setFirstName (n : string) : void + getLastName ( ) : string + setLastName (n : string) : void + getCoefficient ( ) : float + setCoefficient (c : float) : void + getDescription ( ) : void + addNewFash ( ) : void + readFash (fileName : ifstream&) : void + writeFash (fileName : ofstream&) : void

«entity class»
Future Trends Report Class
+ «static» printReport (string tempFn, string tempLn) : void

«entity class»
Gallery Painting Class
algPrice : float # purchasePrice : float # targetPrice : float # sellPrice : float # classification : string # purchaseDate : Date # saleDate : Date # sellerName : string # buyerName : string # sellerAddr : string # buyerAddr : string
+ getClassification ( ) : string + setClassification (c : string) : void + getPurchaseDate ( ) : Date + setPurchaseDate (d : Date) : void + getSaleDate ( ) : Date + setSaleDate (d : Date) : void + getSellerName ( ) : string + setSellerName (n : string) : void

```
+ getBuyerName ( ) : string
+ setBuyerName (n : string) : void
+ getSellerAddr ( ) : string
+ setSellerAddr (a : string) : void
+ getBuyerAddr ( ) : string
+ setBuyerAddr (a : string) : void
+ getAlgPrice ( ) : float
+ setAlgPrice (p : float) : void
+ getPurchasePrice ( ) : float
+ setPurchasePrice (p : float) : void
+ getTargetPrice ( ) : float
+ setTargetPrice (p : float) : void
+ getSellPrice ( ) : float
+ setSellPrice (p : float) : void
+ getGalleryInformation ( : void) : void
+ addNewPainting ( : void) : void
+ buy ( : void) : void
+ readBought (fileName : ifstream&) : void
+ writeBought (fileName : ofstream&) : void
+ addNewSale ( : void) : void
+ sell ( : void) : void
+ readSold (fileName : ifstream&) : void
+ writeSold (fileName : ofstream&) : void
```

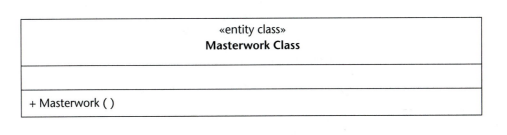

| «entity class» |
| **Masterwork Class** |
| |
| + Masterwork ( ) |

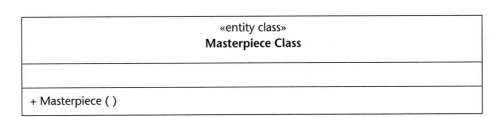

| «entity class» |
| **Masterpiece Class** |
| |
| + Masterpiece ( ) |

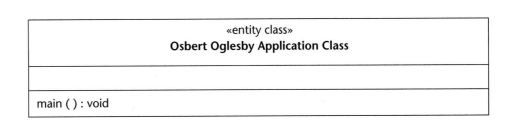

| «entity class» |
| **Osbert Oglesby Application Class** |
| |
| main ( ) : void |

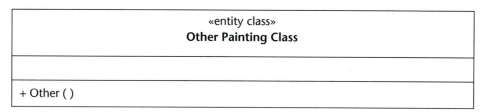

| «entity class» |
| **Other Painting Class** |
| |
| + Other ( ) |

| «entity class» |
| **Painting Class** |
| # height : float
width : float
firstName : string
lastName : string
title : string
paintingDate : Date
saleDate : Date
medium : string
subject : string |
| + getFirstName ( ) : string
+ setFirstName (fn : string) : void
+ getLastName ( ) : string
+ setLastName (ln : string) : void
+ getTitle ( ) : string
+ setTitle (t : string) : void
+ getPaintDate ( ) : Date
+ setSaleDate (t : string) : Date
+ getSaleDate (d : Date) : void
+ getMedium ( ) : string
+ setMedium (m : string) : void
+ getSubject ( ) : string
+ setSubject (s : string) : void
+ getHeight ( ) : float
+ setHeight (h : float) : void
+ getWidth ( ) : float
+ setWidth (w : float) : void
+ getDescription ( ) : void |

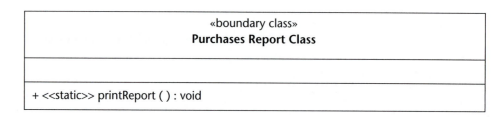

| «boundary class» |
| **Purchases Report Class** |
| |
| + <<static>> printReport ( ) : void |

| «boundary class» |
| **Sales Report Class** |
| |
| + <<static>> printReport ( ) : void |

| «entity class» |
| **User Interface Class** |
| |
| + <<static>> clearScreen ( ) : void
+ <<static>> pressEnter ( ) : void
+ <<static>> displayMainMenu ( ) : void
+ <<static>> displayReportMenu ( ) : void
+ <<static>> displayBuyPaintingMenu ( ) : void
+ <<static>> addArtist (fn : string, ln : string) : void
+ <<static>> compareStr (str1 : string, str2 : string) : int
− <<static>> removeQ (str : string&) : void |

Appendix  C

Object-Oriented Design: MSG Foundation Case Study

This appendix contains the final version of the class diagram for the MSG Foundation case study. The overall class diagram is followed by UML diagrams for the 10 component classes, in alphabetical order. These UML diagrams show the attributes and the methods. As explained in Section 10.2, the UML visibility prefixes are – for **private,** + for **public,** and # for **protected.**

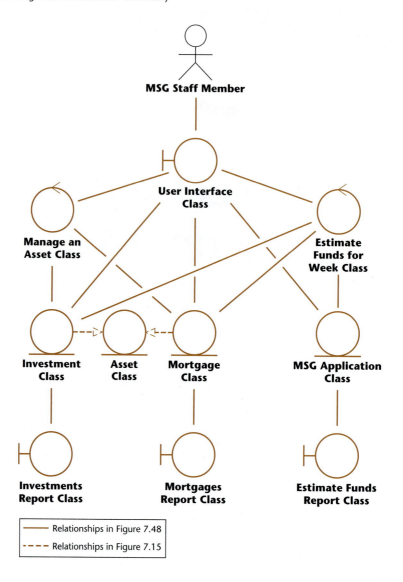

MSG Staff Member

User Interface Class

Manage an Asset Class

Estimate Funds for Week Class

Investment Class

Asset Class

Mortgage Class

MSG Application Class

Investments Report Class

Mortgages Report Class

Estimate Funds Report Class

——— Relationships in Figure 7.48
- - - Relationships in Figure 7.15

«entity class»
Asset Class
assetNumber : string
+ getAssetNumber ( ) : string + setAssetNumber (a : string) : void + **abstract** read (fileName : RandomAccessFile) : void + **abstract** obtainNewData ( ) : void + **abstract** performDeletion ( ) : void + **abstract** write (fileName : RandomAccessFile) : void + **abstract** save ( ) : void + **abstract** print ( ) : void + **abstract** find (s : string) : Boolean + delete ( ) : void + add ( ) : void

«control class»
Estimate Funds for Week Class
+ <<static>> compute ( ) : void

«boundary class»
Estimate Funds Report Class
+ <<static>> printReport ( ) : void

«entity class»
Investment Class

– investmentName : string
– expectedAnnualReturn : float
– expectedAnnualReturnUpdated : string

+ getInvestmentName ( ) : string
+ setInvestmentName (n : string) : void
+ getExpectedAnnualReturn ( ) : float
+ setExpectedAnnualReturn (r : float) : void
+ getExpectedAnnualReturnUpdated ( ) : string
+ setExpectedAnnualReturnUpdated (d : string) : void
+ totalWeeklyReturnOnInvestment ( ) : float
+ find (findInvestmentID : string) : Boolean
+ read (fileName : RandomAccessFile) : void
+ write (fileName : RandomAccessFile) : void
+ save ( ) : void
+ print ( ) : void
+ printAll ( ) : void
+ obtainNewData ( ) : void
+ performDeletion ( ) : void
+ readInvestmentData ( ) : void
+ updateInvestmentName ( ) : void
+ updateExpectedReturn ( ) : void

«boundary class»
Investments Report Class
+ <<static>> printReport ( ) : void

| «control class» |
| **Manage an Asset Class** |
| |
| + <<static>> manageInvestment ( ) : void |
| + <<static>> manageMortgage ( ) : void |

| «entity class» |
| **Mortgage Class** |
| – mortgageeName : string |
| – price : float |
| – dateMortgageIssued : string |
| – currentWeeklyIncome : float |
| – weeklyIncomeUpdated : string |
| – annualPropertyTax : float |
| – annualInsurancePremium : float |
| – mortgageBalance : float |
| + <<static final>> INTEREST_RATE : float |
| + <<static final>> MAX_PER_OF_INCOME : float |
| + <<static final>> NUMBER_OF_MORTGAGE_PAYMENTS : int |
| + <<static final>> WEEKS_IN_YEAR : float |
| + getMortgageeName ( ) : string |
| + setMortgageeName (n : string) : void |
| + getPrice ( ) : float |
| + setPrice (p : float) : void |
| + getDateMortgageIssued ( ) : string |
| + setDateMortgageIssued (w : string) : void |
| + getCurrentWeeklyIncome ( ) : float |
| + setCurrentWeeklyIncome (i : float) : void |
| + getWeeklyIncomeUpdated ( ) : string |
| + setWeeklyIncomeUpdated (w : string) : void |
| + getAnnualPropertyTax ( ) : float |
| + setAnnualPropertyTax (t : float) : void |
| + getAnnualInsurancePremium ( ) : float |
| + setAnnualInsurancePremium (p : float) : void |
| + getMortgageBalance ( ) : float |
| + setMortgageBalance (m : float) : void |
| + totalWeeklyNetPayments ( ) : float |
| + find (findMortgageID : string) : Boolean |
| + read (fileName : RandomAccessFile) : void |
| + write (fileName : RandomAcessFile) : void |
| + obtainNewData ( ) : void |
| + performDeletion ( ) : void |
| + print ( ) : void |
| + <<static>> printAll ( ) : void |
| + save ( ) : void |
| + readMortgageData ( ) : void |
| + updateBalance ( ) : void |
| + updateDate ( ) : void |
| + updateInsurancePremium ( ) : void |

```
+ updateMortgageeName ( ) : void
+ updatePrice ( ) : void
+ updatePropertyTax ( ) : void
+ updateWeeklyIncome ( ) : void
```

«boundary class»
Mortgages Report Class

+ <<static>> printReport ( ) : void

«entity class»
MSG Application Class

– <<static>> estimatedAnnualOperatingExpenses : float
– <<static>> estimatedFundsForWeek : float

– <<static>> getAnnualOperatingExpenses ( ) : float
– <<static>> setAnnualOperatingExpenses (e : float) : void
+ <<static>> getEstimatedFundsForWeek ( ) : float
+ <<static>> setEstimatedFundsForWeek (e : float) : void
+ <<static>> initializeApplication ( ) : void
+ <<static>> updateAnnualOperatingExpenses ( ) : void
+ <<static>> main ( )

«boundary class»
User Interface Class

+ <<static>> clearScreen ( ) : void
+ <<static>> pressEnter ( ) : void
+ <<static>> displayMainMenu ( ) : void
+ <<static>> displayInvestmentMenu ( ) : void
+ <<static>> displayMortgageMenu ( ) : void
+ <<static>> displayReportMenu ( ) : void
+ <<static>> getChar ( ) : char
+ <<static>> getString ( ) : string
+ <<static>> getInt ( ) : int

Appendix **D**

C++ Implementation: Osbert Oglesby Case Study

A complete C++ implementation of the Osbert Oglesby case study can be found at http://www.mhhe.com/schach/.

Appendix **E**

Java Implementation: MSG Foundation Case Study

A complete Java implementation of the Osbert Oglesby case study can be found at http://www.mhhe.com/schach/.

Index